The Phenomenological Movement

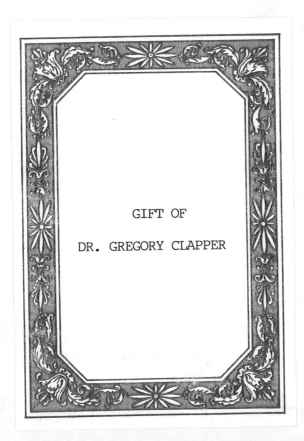

PHAENOMENOLOGICA

COLLECTION FONDÉE PAR H.L. VAN BREDA ET PUBLIÉE SOUS LE
PATRONAGE DES CENTRES D'ARCHIVES-HUSSERL

5

HERBERT SPIEGELBERG

The Phenomenological Movement

A HISTORICAL INTRODUCTION

SECOND EDITION

Fifth impression

Comité de rédaction de la collection:
Président: S. IJsseling (Leuven);
Membres: M. Farber (Buffalo), E. Fink † (Freiburg i. Br.),
L. Landgrebe (Köln), W. Marx (Freiburg i. Br.),
J. N. Mohanty (New York), P. Ricoeur (Paris), E. Ströker (Köln),
J. Taminiaux (Louvain), K. H. Volkmann-Schluck (Köln);
Secrétaire: J. Taminiaux

HERBERT SPIEGELBERG

The Phenomenological Movement

A HISTORICAL INTRODUCTION

SECOND EDITION
Fifth impression

VOLUME ONE

MARTINUS NIJHOFF / THE HAGUE / 1978

ISBN 90 247 2084 2
90 247 2085 0 (vol. I)

PRINTED IN THE NETHERLANDS

TABLE OF CONTENTS
VOLUME ONE

List of Illustrations [XIX]

Preface [XXI]

Preface to the Second Edition [XXXIII]

Introduction

1. The Phenomenological Movement Defined   1
2. Pseudo-Phenomenologies   7
   A. Extra-Philosophical Phenomenologies   8
   B. Philosophical Phenomenologies   11
3. Preview   20

Part One | The Preparatory Phase

I. FRANZ BRENTANO (1838–1917): FORERUNNER OF THE PHENOMENOLOGICAL MOVEMENT

1. Brentano's Place in the History of Phenomenology   27
2. Brentano's Purpose: A Scientific Reformation of Philosophy   28
3. A New Psychology as the Foundation for Scientific Philosophy   33
4. A New Type of Empiricism   35
5. Descriptive Psychology versus Genetic Psychology   36
6. A New Type of Experience: Inner Perception versus Introspection   38
7. "Intentionality": The Basic Psychological Phenomenon   39
8. A "Natural" Classification of Psychical Acts   42
9. A Fundamental Law of Psychical Phenomena   43

10. The Awareness of Time   44

11. An Analogue of Self-Evidence as the Basis for Ethical Knowledge   44

12. Brentano's Fight Against "Fictitious Entities"   47

13. How Far Was Brentano a Representative of "Psychologism"?   49

Selective Bibliography   50

II. CARL STUMPF (1848–1936): FOUNDER OF EXPERIMENTAL PHENOMENOLOGY

1. Stumpf's Place in the History of Phenomenology   53
2. The Role of Phenomenology in Stumpf's Work   55
3. General Characteristics of Stumpf's Phenomenology   58
   a. The Subject Matter of Phenomenology Consists of Primary and Secondary Phenomena   59
   b. Phenomenology Constitutes a Neutral Science or Pre-Science (*Vorwissenschaft*)   59
   c. Phenomenology is the First of the Neutral Pre-Sciences   60
   d. Phenomenology is not an Independent Discipline for Specialists, but Rather the First Layer in the Study of Every Established Science   60
   e. Phenomenology, while a Descriptive Science, has to be Studied by all Suitable Methods, Including the Experimental One   61

4. Some Concrete Phenomenological Contributions   62
   a. The Distinction Between Dependent and Independent Parts and the Experience of Substance and Attribute   62
   b. The Experience of Causal Nexus   62
   c. The Experience of "Feel-Sensations" (*Gefühlsempfindungen*)   63
   d. The Discovery of Structural Laws among Empirical Materials not based upon Induction   63
   e. The Discovery of the *Sachverhalt*   64

5. The Relationship of Stumpf's and Husserl's Phenomenologies   65

Excursus: Stumpf's Phenomenology and William James's Psychology   66

Selective Bibliography   69

Part Two | The German Phase of the Movement

III. THE PURE PHENOMENOLOGY OF EDMUND HUSSERL
(1859–1938)

A. *Introductory*   73

B. *Constants in Husserl's Conception of Philosophy*   75

  1. The Ideal of Rigorous Science   76

  2. Philosophic Radicalism   82

  3. The Ethos of Radical Autonomy   94

  4. The Wonder of All Wonders: Subjectivity   87

  5. Husserl's Personality and His Philosophy   88

C. *Variables in the Development of Husserl's Philosophy*   91

  1. The Pre-Phenomenological Period   91
      a. The Critique of Psychologism   93
      b. The Conception of a Pure Logic   95
         Excursus: Meinong's *Gegenstandstheorie* and Husserl's Logic   98

  2. The Beginnings of Phenomenology as the Subjective
      Correlate of Pure Logic   101
      a. Husserl's Semantics   104
      b. Husserl's Doctrine of Universals (Essences)   105
      c. The Intentionality of Consciousness   107
         Excursus: William James's Significance for Husserl's Pheno-
                   menology   111
      d. Phenomenological Intuiting (*Anschauung* and *Wesensschau*) 117

  3. Phenomenology Becomes "First Philosophy"   118
      Excursus: Wilhelm Dilthey and Edmund Husserl   122

  4. The Birth of the Phenomenological Movement and the
      Beginnings of Transcendental Phenomenology   124
      a. Self-Givenness – Phenomenology and Positivism   128
      b. Phenomenology of Perception and Self-Evidence   131
      c. The Phenomenological Reduction   133
         Excursus: Santayana's Ultimate Scepticism Compared With
                   Husserl's Phenomenological Reduction   138
      d. The Phenomenological Residue: Ego Cogito Cogitata Mea   140
         (1) The Phenomenological Ego   140
         (2) The Cogitations   141
         (3) The Cogitata   142
      e. Phenomenological Idealism   142

Excursus: Husserl and Josiah Royce   144
f. Phenomenological Constitution and the Consciousness of
   Time   146
g. Phenomenology and Psychology   149

5. The Final Radicalization of Transcendental Phenomenology   152
   a. Intersubjectivity and Transcendental Monadology   157
   b. The Idea of the Life-World (*Lebenswelt*)   159

D. *In Place of an Appraisal*   163

Selective Bibliography   163

IV. THE OLDER PHENOMENOLOGICAL MOVEMENT

A. *The Phenomenological Circles*   168

1. The Göttingen Circle   169

2. The Munich Circle   171
   Note: Phenomenology and Conversion   172

B. *Alexander Pfänder (1870–1941): From Phenomenological Psychology to Phenomenological Philosophy*   173

1. Pfänder's Place in the Phenomenological Movement   173

2. The Place of Phenomenology in Pfänder's Philosophy   175

3. Pfänder's Conception of Phenomenology   178
   a. Phenomenological Psychology   179
   b. Phenomenological Philosophy   180

4. Examples of Pfänder's Phenomenology   185
   a. The Phenomenology of Directed Sentiments (*Gesinnungen*)   186
   b. The Phenomenology of Basic and Empirical Essences   188
   c. The Phenomenology of the Perception of Oughtness   189

5. Concluding Remarks   191
   Selected Bibliography

6. Pfänder's Following   192

C. *Adolf Reinach (1883–1917): The Phenomenology of
   Essences*   195

1. Reinach's Place in the Phenomenological Movement   195
2. Reinach's Conception of Phenomenology   197
3. Illustrations of Reinach's Phenomenology   201

a. Reinach's Theory of Social Acts   202
b. Essential Laws Concerning Legal Entities   203
Selective Bibliography   205

D. *Moritz Geiger (1880–1937): From Phenomenological*
   Esthetics toward Metaphysics   206

1. Geiger's Conception of Phenomenology   208

2. Illustrations of Geiger's Phenomenological Analyses   212
   a. The Phenomenology of Esthetic Enjoyment   213
   b. The Phenomenology of Existential Depth   214
   c. The Phenomenology of the Unconscious   216
   Selective Bibliography   218

E. *Other Members of the Göttingen and Munich Circles*   218

1. Wilhelm Schapp (1884–1965)   219

2. Kurt Stavenhagen (1885–1951)   219
   Selective Bibliography

3. Hedwig Conrad-Martius (1888–1966)   220
   Selective Bibliography

4. Dietrich von Hildebrand (1889–1966)   222
   Selective Bibliography

5. Jean Hering (1890–1966)   223
   Selective Bibliography

6. Edith Stein (1891–1942)   223
   Selective Bibliography

7. Fritz Kaufmann (1891–1958) see XIII

8. Alexandre Koyré (1892–1964)   225
   Selective Bibliography

9. Roman Ingarden (1893–   )   225
   Selective Bibliography

V. THE PHENOMENOLOGY OF ESSENCES: MAX SCHELER
                     (1874–1928)

1. Max Scheler's Place in the Phenomenological Movement   228

2. Scheler's Basic Concerns   231

3. Phenomenology in the Development of Scheler's
   Philosophy   235

4. Scheler's Conception of Phenomenology   239
  a. The Doctrine of the "Phenomenologic Controversy" (*phäno-
    menologischer Streit*)   242
  b. The Idols of Self-Knowledge   243
  c. The Phenomenon of Resistance as the Criterion of Reality 244
  d. Scheler's Phenomenological Reduction   245

5. Scheler's Phenomenology in Action   251
  a. Value and Oughtness   251
    (1) The Intuitive A Priori   251
    (2) Non-Formal ("Material") Values   253
    (3) Value, Ideal Oughtness, and Moral Oughtness   256
  b. The Phenomenology of Cognitive Emotion   256
  c. Ethical Absolutism and Relativity   258
    (1) Variations in the Valuations or Acts of Value-Experien-
      ces   258
    (2) Relativity of Ethics   258
    (3) Relativity of Types of Actions   259
    (4) Relativity of the Practical Morality   259
    (5) Relativity of Customs   259
  d. The Phenomenology of Sympathy   259
  e. Knowledge of Other Minds   261
  f. Phenomenology of Religion   262

6. Toward an Appraisal of Scheler as a Phenomenologist   265

7. Scheler's Following   267

Selective Bibliography   268

VI. MARTIN HEIDEGGER (1889–   )
AS A PHENOMENOLOGIST

1. On Understanding Heidegger   271

2. Heidegger's Place in the History of Phenomenology   275

3. Heidegger's Basic Theme: The Quest for Being and
  Time   283

4. The Development of Heidegger's Thought of Being   291
  a. Preparatory Period   292
  b. The Phenomenological Period   297
  c. Under the Sign of Hölderlin   309

5. Heidegger's Conception of Phenomenology   318
  a. Hermeneutic Phenomenology   318
  b. Hermeneutics in Action   326
    (1) Ipseity (*Jemeinigkeit*) and "Existence"   326
    (2) Being-in-the-World   328

(3) The Impersonal ("People")   329
(4) Moods and "Facticity"   330
(5) Anxiety and Nothingness   331
(6) Concern (*Sorge*) as the Fundamental Structure of
    Human Being   333
(7) Death   333
(8) Temporality   334
(9) Historicity   337
c. Phenomenology in Heidegger's Philosophy since *Sein und
   Zeit*   339

6. Toward an Appraisal of Heidegger's Phenomenology   346
   a. To What Extent is Heidegger a Phenomenologist?   347
   b. Strengths and Weaknesses of Heidegger's Phenomenology   349

7. Heidegger's Following and Phenomenology   353

Selective Bibliography   354

VII. PHENOMENOLOGY IN THE CRITICAL ONTOLOGY OF
     NICOLAI HARTMANN (1882–1950)

1. Hartmann's Relation to the Phenomenological Movement   358

2. Hartmann's Philosophical Objective: Critical Ontology   360
3. The Role of Phenomenology in Hartmann's Philosophical Development   367

4. Nicolai Hartmann's Version of Phenomenology   374

5. Illustrations of Hartmann's Phenomenology   379
   a. "Metaphysics" of Knowledge   379
   b. The Givenness of Reality   382
   c. The Discovery of Value and the Narrowness of the Value
      Consciousness   384
   d. Activated Ideals (*Aktuales Seinsollen*)   385

6. Toward an Appraisal of Hartmann's Phenomenology   386

7. Hartmann's Following and Phenomenology   388

Selective Bibliography   389

VOLUME TWO

Part Three | The French Phase of the Movement

Introductory [395]

VIII. THE BEGINNINGS OF FRENCH PHENOMENOLOGY

1. The Soil   398
2. A Brief Outline of the Receptive Phase   401
3. Phenomenology and Existentialism   408
4. Phenomenology and Hegelianism   413
5. Phenomenological Existentialism and Literature   415
6. Phenomenological Existentialism and Marxism   418

IX. GABRIEL MARCEL (1889–   ) AS A PHENOMENOLOGIST

1. Marcel's Relations to the Phenomenological Movement   421
2. Marcel's Concern   425
3. The Development of Marcel's Philosophy   428
4. Marcel's Conception of Phenomenology   434
5. Marcel's Phenomenology in Action   438
6. The Phenomenology of Having   440
7. Concluding Observations   442
Selective Bibliography   443

X. THE PHENOMENOLOGY OF JEAN-PAUL SARTRE
(1905–   )

1. On Understanding Sartre   445
2. Sartre's Place in the Phenomenological Movement.   449

3. Sartre's Central Theme: Freedom versus Being   455

4. The Role of Phenomenology in the Development of
   Sartre's Thought   459
   a. Sartre's Pre-Phenomenological Period   459
   b. Phenomenological Psychology   462
   c. Phenomenological Ontology   467
   d. Phenomenological Existentialism   473

5. Sartre's Conception of Phenomenology   476
   a. The Common Ground   477
   b. Distinguishing Characteristics   479

   (1) The Elimination of the Transcendental Ego and Its
       Final Significance: Phenomenology of Human
       Existence   479
   (2) Pre-Reflective Consciousness. Reflection and Pheno-
       menology   482
   (3) The Negative Character of Consciousness   484
   (4) Freedom   485
   (5) Anguish   486
   (6) Bad Faith   487
   (7) Intentionality and Transphenomenality   488
   (8) Facticity and "Engagement"   490
   (9) Transcendence   491
   (10) Phenomenological Method and Existential Psycho-
        analysis   492

6. Sartre's Phenomenology in Action   497
   a. Imagination   498
   b. The Magic of the Emotions   500
   c. Absence and Nothingness   503
   d. The Gaze (Regard)   505
   e. The Body   507

7. Toward an Appraisal of Sartre's Phenomenology   509

8. Sartre's Following   511

Selective Bibliography   513

XI. THE PHENOMENOLOGICAL PHILOSOPHY OF
MAURICE MERLEAU-PONTY (1908–1961)

1. Merleau-Ponty's Position in the Phenomenological
   Movement   516

2. Guiding Themes in the Philosophy of Merleau-Ponty   524

3. The Development of Merleau-Ponty's Phenomenology   528

4. Merleau-Ponty's Conception of Phenomenology   531

5. Some Key Chapters from Merleau-Ponty's Phenomenology   540
   a. The Structure of Behavior and the Phenomenology of *Gestalt*   540
   b. Perception   544
   c. The New *Cogito:* Being-Within-the-World (*Être-au-Monde*)   549
   d. Subjectivity and Temporality   552
   e. Conditioned Freedom   553
   f. The Social World: Speech and Language   556

6. Toward an Appraisal of Merleau-Ponty's Phenomenology   557

7. Merleau-Ponty's Following   561

Selective Bibliography   562

XII. CURRENT DEVELOPMENTS IN FRENCH PHENOMENOLOGY

A. *Paul Ricoeur (1913–)*   563

1. Ricoeur's Place in the Phenomenological Movement   564

2. Ricoeur's Guiding Interests   568

3. Ricoeur's Development   569

4. Ricoeur's Conception of Phenomenology   572

5. The Phenomenology of the Will   575

6. Concluding Observations   579

Selective Bibliography   578

B. *The Phenomenology of Esthetic Experience: Mikel Dufrenne (1910–)*   579

C. *The Phenomenology of Value: Raymond Polin (1910–)*   585

D. *Some Affiliated Thinkers*   590

   1. Raymond Aron (1905–)   590

   2. Maurice Nédoncelle (1905–)   591

   3. Pierre Thévenaz (1913–1955)   591

   4. Henry Duméry (1920–)   591

Part Four / Phenomenology at Midcentury
XIII. THE WIDER SCENE

A. *The Scene Outside France*   595

1. Germany: Eclipse and New Stirrings   596
2. Belgium: Louvain, the New Center   603
3. The Netherlands: Extensions   605
4. Switzerland: A New Phenomenological Anthropology   607
5. Italy: Scatterings   608
6. Eastern Europe: First Response, Blackout, and
    Remnants   609
7. Spain: Ortega's Part and Its Significance   611
8. The Ibero-American World: Double Wave   619
9. Oriental Countries: Sprinklings   622
10. Great Britain: Low Ebb   623
11. United States: Spurts and New Outlets   626

B. *The Outlook*   640

C. *Desiderata*   644

1. General Needs   644
2. Anglo-American Needs   647

Part Five / Principles and Appraisals
XIV. THE ESSENTIALS OF THE PHENOMENOLOGICAL METHOD

A. *Phenomenology and Phenomenological Method*   655

B· *The Phenomenological Method as a Protest against
    Reductionism*   656

C. *The Steps of the Phenomenological Method*   658

1. Investigating Particular Phenomena   659
    a. Phenomenological Intuiting   659
       Excursus: Does Phenomenology Explore only Subjective
         Phenomena?   666
    b. Phenomenological Analyzing   669
    c. Phenomenological Describing   672

2. Investigating General Essences (Eidetic Intuiting)   676

3. Apprehending Essential Relationships   680

4. Watching Modes of Appearing   684

5. Exploring the Constitution of Phenomena in Consciousness   688

6. Suspending Belief in Existence   690

7. Interpreting Concealed Meanings   694

D. *In Conclusion*   698

Chart I: Survey of the Development of Phenomenology in Germany   702

Chart II: Survey of the Development of Phenomenology in France   706

Index of Subjects, Combined with a Selective Glossary of Phenomenological Terms   709

Index of Names   729

Supplement   737

Index of Names to the Supplement   764

LIST OF ILLUSTRATIONS

Facing page

1. From FRANZ BRENTANO's manuscripts for his Vienna
   lectures 1888/89. Photo by his son Dr. John C. M.
   Brentano, Highland Park, Illinois. – The entry in brackets is by Oskar Kraus   27
2. Bust of young BRENTANO by Kaspar Zumbusch in the
   possession of Dr. Brentano, who also kindly supplied
   the photo   28
3. Photo of a lost oil portrait of FRANZ BRENTANO by
   Rudolf Stumpf, son of Carl Stumpf. Copyright Erna
   Stumpf, Göttingen   49
4. CARL STUMPF. Drawing by Rudolf Stumpf   53
5. EDMUND HUSSERL (1905). Photo Peter Matzen; Göt-
   tingen. Copy supplied by Dr. Theodor Conrad, Starn-
   berg   73
6. Two consecutive pages from the Brentano-Husserl
   correspondence in the Brentano Archives. Photo
   supplied by Dr. John C. M. Brentano   88/89
7. Publisher's announcement of Husserl's yearbook. Original in the Brentano Archives. Photo supplied by Dr.
   John C. M. Brentano   124
8. Announcement of Husserl's Lectures at the University
   of London. Original in the Husserl Archives, Louvain   155
9. EDMUND HUSSERL (1931). Drawing by Rudolf Stumpf.
   Copyright Erna Stumpf, Göttingen   163
10. Philosophische Gesellschaft, Göttingen (1912). Photo
    supplied by Dr. Theodor Conrad   170

11. ALEXANDER PFÄNDER (1940). Photo by Gerhard Isselmann, Teisendorf   173

12. JOHANNES DAUBERT (about 1905). Photo supplied by Mrs. Daubert, Mainburg   173

13. ADOLF REINACH (about 1912). Photo supplied by Jean Hering   173

14. MORITZ GEIGER (about 1930). Photo supplied by Mrs. Elisabeth Geiger, Göttingen   173

15. MAX SCHELER. Photo supplied by Dr. Theodor Conrad   228

16. MARTIN HEIDEGGER (about 1930). Photo by Luise M. Engler   308

17. NICOLAI HARTMANN (about 1945). Photo from Heimsoeth, Heinz und Heiss, Roberts, eds., *Nicolai Hartmann. Der Denker und sein Werk*   358

18. GABRIEL MARCEL. Universal Photo 3.308, supplied by the Ambassade de France à Bruxelles   421

19. JEAN-PAUL SARTRE. Photo by Roger Parry, supplied by the Ambassade de France à Bruxelles   445

20. MAURICE MERLEAU-PONTY. Photo from Pages de France n° 10.393, supplied by the Ambassade de France à Bruxelles   516

PREFACE

The present attempt to introduce the general philosophical reader to the Phenomenological Movement by way of its history has itself a history which is pertinent to its objective. It may suitably be opened by the following excerpts from a review which Herbert W. Schneider of Columbia University, the Head of the Division for International Cultural Cooperation, Department of Cultural Activities of Unesco from 1953 to 56, wrote in 1950 from France:

The influence of Husserl has revolutionized continental philosophies, not because his philosophy has become dominant, but because any philosophy now seeks to accommodate itself to, and express itself in, phenomenological method. It is the *sine qua non* of critical respectability. In America, on the contrary, phenomenology is in its infancy. The average American student of philosophy, when he picks up a recent volume of philosophy published on the continent of Europe, must first learn the "tricks" of the phenomenological trade and then translate as best he can the real import of what is said into the kind of analysis with which he is familiar. ...... No doubt, American education will gradually take account of the spread of phenomenological method and terminology, but until it does, American readers of European philosophy have a severe handicap; and this applies not only to existentialism but to almost all current philosophical literature.[1]

These sentences clearly implied a challenge, if not a mandate, to all those who by background and interpretive ability were in a position to meet it. At the time I read it, I personally saw no chance of attacking this task, much as I hoped that someone in closer contact with the main current of phenomenology and with better facilities than I had at the time would tackle it.

[1] "Philosophic Thought in France and the United States" in *Philosophy and Phenomenological Research* XI (1951), 380.

This chance and the sense of an obligation to try my hand at the task came to me two years later as a result of a semester as visiting professor at the University of Michigan, where I had offered a seminar on the development of phenomenology and existentialism. At the end of this seminar Paul Henle suggested to me very persuasively that I prepare an introduction to the Phenomenological Movement for American readers. This suggestion coincided with an invitation from the National Council on Religion in Higher Education to act as a consultant on phenomenology during its "Week of Work" in 1952. So I finally yielded to the temptation, although I still felt dubious in view of the scope and difficulty of the task and of my own limitations.

I owe it to the reader to be frank about these limitations and about the kind of bias which he may expect from me. During my university studies in Germany I had spent one semester at Freiburg in 1924–25, during which I was able to take part in one of Edmund Husserl's advanced seminars.[1] But I received my main phenomenological training at Munich under Alexander Pfänder. At least as far as my point of departure is concerned, I am therefore more closely associated with the so-called Older Phenomenological Movement than with the Freiburg phenomenologists. In later years, until I left the Continent in 1937, I made at least some efforts to widen this perspective. But I must leave it to others to decide whether this peculiar background has slanted my account in the direction of a "reactionary" deviation of phenomenology or whether it gives me the advantage of being more of a neutral outsider. I certainly cannot claim the objectivity of an impartial historian. Very often it seemed to me that I was more of a witness, though too often only an indirect witness, with the primary obligation of preserving certain facts as to which I believe I have more authentic information than is usually available, and of counteracting the many legends which have already overgrown the historical reality.

My first attempt to tackle the job, undertaken immediately after my return from Ann Arbor, was anything but an unqualified success. Nevertheless, it made Paul Henle again take

---

[1] I have given a partial account of this semester in the centennial volume *Edmund Husserl, 1859–1959* (*Phaenomenologica* 4), pp. 57–59.

the initiative, this time by interesting the Division of Humanities
of the Rockefeller Foundation in my enterprise as part of its
program in promoting intercultural understanding. This led to a
first grant to Lawrence College, which made it possible for me to
take a year's leave of absence. The grant included a travel
aliowance, which gave me a chance, after an absence of sixteen
years, to return to Europe for three crowded months, during
which I was not only able to collect an unexpected amount of
material and information about the pre-war period, but also to
become acquainted with the new developments, especially in
France. It was this first acquaintance with the second flowering
of phenomenology which made me realize – too late – the full
magnitude of my assignment. Fortunately, the officers of the
Rockefeller Foundation took an understanding view of my
predicament and after a year's interval enabled me to take
another half-leave in 1955–56. To the Rockefeller Foundation
and particularly to Mr. Chadbourne Gilpatric belongs the major
credit for having made this book possible.

It would be hopeless for me to try to list the names of all those
who have supported the present enterprise by suggestion,
encouragement, intercession, information, permissions, criticisms,
and in other ways. A task which really calls for cooperative
effort lays its single attacker under all the more heavy debt to
those whose services he has to enlist. The abridged story of the
book mentions the share of those who had a decisive influence
on the birth, the growth, and the survival of this book. Only by
way of example do I want to acknowledge some further major
debts:

to Maurice Mandelbaum for his careful reading of and comments
on the first complete version of the text;

to the Husserl Archives in Louvain, and particularly to its
dynamic director H. L. Van Breda o.f.m., for permission to use
its invaluable collection and to utilize it in the present book;

to his assistant Rudolf Boehm for repeated investigations and
critical comments;

to Nathan M. Pusey and Douglas M. Knight, past and present
Presidents of Lawrence College, whose sympathetic interest and
readiness to release me from academic duties were essential to
the growth of the book;

to Hastings A. Brubaker, the Librarian of Lawrence College, who helped me particularly with the problem of snowballing interlibrary loans;

to my long-suffering main typist, Mrs. Ruth Lesselyong at the Faculty Office;

and last, but nearly most, to the unbelievable Bayard Quincy Morgan of Stanford University for his unfailing assistance, particularly his stylistic criticism, which has often led to a sharpening of the thought behind the expression, and for his unparalleled help with the proofreading; in the latter task Fred Kersten also took a valued share.

No book of this scope could materialize without the sharing of trials, tribulations, and financial sacrifices by one's family. Adding to this a constant moral support, listening as a living touchstone to untested ideas, censoring of early drafts, and non-directive counselling by the clinical psychologist, my wife Eldora Haskell Spiegelberg, gives a faint idea of what the present enterprise owes to her – and to our daughters Gwen and Lynne, whose impatient inquiries "When is Daddy going to finish his book?" were no small incentive for getting on with the job.

ॐ

My immediate assignment, as I conceived of it, was to prepare an introduction to phenomenology primarily for the benefit of American readers. It should help them gain at least a sympathetic understanding of a philosophical movement which, for better or worse, has become one of the most influential currents of thought in the world outside the Anglo-American and this side of the Soviet orbit. Even a convinced missionary, carrying his own message to the more benighted parts of the world, has at least to be familiar with the superstitions of the unredeemed. Besides, there are alarming signs that Anglo-American philosophy has not been too effective in making converts in the critical areas of the struggle for philosophic allegiance. Somehow it fails to meet the needs of a fear- and doubt-ridden western world. My first and major concern, then, was to put into the hands of the Anglo-American philosophic public a guide as faithful and concise as possible toward the understanding of one aspect of this territory.

Yet, large though such an assignment turns out to be, I confess I would derive little satisfaction from merely supplying a tool for cultural strategy. I believe that phenomenology, properly presented, and submitted without the exaggerated fanfare which has done it severe harm in a climate more sober and more critical than the European Continent, has a definite mission at the present juncture in Anglo-American philosophy. I submit that some of its analyses may help in removing certain obstacles which block the way of a genuine empiricism. By these I mean specifically a narrow positivism and a dogmatic behaviorism, which are largely responsible for a sense of philosophic frustration and barrenness both inside and outside the Anglo-American orbit, in philosophical as well as in non-philosophical circles. There are obvious differences between the situation on the Continent which phenomenology encountered at the beginning of the century and the present situation in the Anglo-American world. But this does not prevent some of its answers from being pertinent even at a different time and place. Suggesting this does not imply that phenomenology is the panacea for all of today's philosophical ills; nor is it a substitute for the considerable virtues of non-phenomenological, especially analytic philosophy.

I am of course well aware of the fact that this is not the first attempt at such an introduction; and it is to be hoped that it will not be the last one. It seems to me proper to pay tribute here to at least some of my predecessors, notably to Dorion Cairns, Marvin Farber, and Alfred Schuetz.[1] Had I not been given to understand by the friends who encouraged me to undertake the

---

[1] See, for instance:

Dorion Cairns, "Phenomenology," Ch. 28 in Ferm, Virgilius, ed., *A History of Philosophical Systems* (New York, Philosophical Library, 1950), pp. 353–364.

Marvin Farber, "Phenomenology," in Runes, Dagobert, ed., *Twentieth Century Philosophy: Living Schools of Thought* (New York, Philosophical Library, 1943), pp. 343–370.

Alfred Schuetz, "Some Leading Concepts of Phenomenology" in *Social Research* XII (1945), 77 ff.

Quentin Lauer's *The Triumph of Subjectivity. An Introduction to Transcendental Phenomenology* (New York, Fordham University Press, 1958) is according to its very subtitle an account restricted to Husserl; it gives only inadequate and often misleading information about his predecessors and successors.

present larger work that their pioneer efforts had not yet filled the need, I would have preferred, instead of entering this field, trying to do more phenomenology rather than to write about it. But while I would admit that the needs of some readers will be met better by the briefer studies of my predecessors, I felt it my duty to make an independent effort to offer a service which is so badly needed. This duty seemed incumbent especially on one who has had such a unique opportunity as I have enjoyed to collect and present the evidence.

In contrast to what has previously been done, my own undertaking is both more ambitious and more modest. For its aim is (1) to give a conspectus of the whole range of the Phenomenological Movement, not only of Husserl's part in it; (2) to help understand the background and the reasons for the phenomenological "teachings" in terms related to today's Anglo-American philosophizing; (3) to take account of, and wherever possible to clarify or answer, the more significant misunderstandings and criticisms of phenomenology. At the same time I would like to point out that I am far from identifying myself with all the doctrines which I shall have to present, not only in view of the fact that a good many of them flatly contradict each other. In fact, I intend to state frankly where I consider the present output of phenomenology unsatisfactory.

On the other hand I do not propose to give systematic accounts of the complete views of the thinkers presented. Instead, I want to focus on such guiding themes in their thought as can open to the Anglo-American reader the most direct access to the core of the phenomenological method, and to stimulate him to go on from there on his own. To this extent and in this sense the material offered will even be slanted. I had to simplify and at times to oversimplify perhaps to the point of unfairness and possible offense to the victims. While any selective and critical account cannot avoid this fault, I should at least wish to disclaim any conscious bias.

⁊ꙮ

Next, I owe the reader an explanation of the way in which I shall introduce him to this elusive philosophy. Specifically, I must explain why the present introduction takes the form of a history of the Phenomenological Movement.

Among the many misconceptions which this book is meant to rectify is the idea that there is such a thing as a system or school called "phenomenology" with a solid body of teachings which would permit one to give a precise answer to the question "What is phenomenology?" The question is more than legitimate. But it cannot be answered, since, for better or worse, the underlying assumption of a unified philosophy subscribed to by all so-called phenomenologists is an illusion. Besides, "phenomenologists" are much too individualistic in their habits to form an organized "school." It would go too far to say that there are as many phenomenologies as there are phenomenologists. But it is certainly true that, on closer inspection, the varieties exceed the common features. In fact, the thought of the founder of the Phenomenological Movement changed so much, and to the very end, that it cannot be presented adequately except by showing how it developed. The same holds true of later phenomenologists like Heidegger and Sartre; thus far the presentation and interpretation seems to me to suffer from a neglect of the developmental aspect of their philosophies.

Under these circumstances the most appropriate introduction to phenomenology would seem to follow the course of its actual growth. Any attempt to determine a common core within its varieties had better be postponed to the end of this account. Even then the identification of such a core will not be easy. It poses the problem of how to extricate the essential structure of phenomenology from its empirical expressions. For not all these empirical expressions are equally adequate manifestations of the underlying idea. Phenomenology itself is given through various appearances. In fact, there is room for something like a phenomenology of phenomenology. But leaving aside such unsettling considerations, we may as well admit that this situation will be a source of disappointment to all those with little time and with the understandable desire for a capsule formula. All I can do is to refer them to the chapter on "The Essentials of the Phenomenological Method," which attempts to organize the variety of phenomenologies into a systematic pattern. But such an organization can be no substitute for the examination of the concrete phenomena which alone can support any final interpretation.

There are, however, also more immediate reasons which make me believe that the chief need, especially for Anglo-American readers, is that of a plain and frank account of the origins, the growth, and the ramifications of a movement whose variety is more characteristic than its connecting unity. The Phenomenological Movement is more than Husserl's phenomenology. While it is true that Husserl is the founder and remains the central figure of the Movement, he is also its most radical representative, and that not only in the sense that he tried to go to the roots, but that he kept digging deeper and deeper, often undermining his own earlier results; he was always the most extreme member of his Movement and hence became increasingly the loneliest of them all. But if one wants to know about the Phenomenological Movement in its full breadth, one has to include the thought of those thinkers who are often mentioned as Husserl's "followers" or "pupils," but rarely if ever described by their own views and especially their more or less "heretical" deviations from Husserl's position. Very little of this variety is accessible thus far in English. Thus the most crying need seems to me that of providing an easier access not only to Husserl's own development but to the development of the movement as a whole. Only on the basis of such a fuller picture of its main thinkers does it make sense to reflect on possible common denominators. For it can by no means be taken for granted that the common name of phenomenology, whether claimed from the inside or imposed from the outside, and in the latter case whether accepted or rejected, is the expression of a common substance.

The attempt to write such an historical introduction must not be confused with the writing of a definitive history of the Phenomenological Movement as such. Quite apart from the limitation of the assignment, which I hope has kept me from being carried away by the fascination of the subject, the time for such a formidable enterprise is not yet at hand.[1] Not only is phenome-

[1] Among the pioneer studies in the history of phenomenology I shall mention only the book by Franz Josef Brecht, *Bewusstsein und Existenz. Wesen und Wege der Phänomenologie* (Bremen, Johs. Storm Verlag, 1948), an interpretation of the development from Brentano through Husserl and Scheler to Heidegger focusing on the problem of the intentionality of consciousness, which Brecht considers solved

nology itself still history in the making; even its historiography is still in the formative stage.

It is however true, as I have come to realize more and more, that there is more than a local need for historical research into the history of the Phenomenological Movement as a whole. There is particular need for continued collecting and securing of the invaluable source material that still exists in the memories and letters of the eye witnesses of the beginnings of phenomenology, an enterprise which the Husserl Archives in Louvain have initiated so magnificently. I have made a special effort to salvage as much as possible of such information, though I do not always utilize it in the present account.

The absence of a comprehensive history of the Phenomenological Movement even in Europe has made it necessary to delve into parts of the story which I believe are generally unknown. In fact, a considerable part of the story seems to me unknown even to the protagonists of recent phenomenology. This is particularly the case with the French perspective of earlier German phenomenology, which usually overestimates the coherence of the Phenomenological Movement, for instance in the relationship between Husserl, Scheler, and Heidegger. Also, too much of the best early German phenomenology published in Husserl's yearbook has so far remained practically unknown and hence ineffective. In such cases the lack of information and the very misconceptions of the actual events have themselves been factors, and at times productive factors, in the history of phenomenology. But even if legends are part of history itself, this is no reason to let them completely overgrow the facts, as far as these can still be ascertained. I am under no illusion that these legends can still be banished. But the facts should at least be made available to those who are interested not only in the appearances of phenomenology but in phenomenology itself.

I confess that, in approaching and in facing the task of selecting

by Heidegger's concept of *Dasein*. An even more authentic but briefer analysis of this development can be found in Ludwig Landgrebe's article, "Husserls Phänomenologie und die Motive zu ihrer Umbildung" (*Revue internationale de philosophie* II (1939), republished in *Phänomenologie und Metaphysik* (Bremen, Schröder, 1949), pp. 56–100). – Julius Kraft's *Von Husserl zu Heidegger* (2nd edition, Frankfurt, Verlag Öffentliches Leben, 1957) is according to its very subtitle a "critique of phenomenological philosophy" given from the standpoint of an anti-intuitionist rationalist, which presents the historical evidence only so far as it supports his negative conclusions.   [1]

the facts and putting them together, I have often felt a peculiar thrill in seeing a landscape which probably has never been surveyed in such scope before. But I have also become uneasy at the responsibility of laying down patterns for future visitors of the scene. I felt particularly uneasy about the thinkers omitted from the story, even more than about those included. I therefore want to make it plain that my selections lay no claim to finality. In many cases they are determined by considerations of suitability for effective presentation. In this sense and to this extent the present history has been influenced by pragmatic considerations – pragmatic in the interest of optimum intelligibility. But even within the restricted scope of this plan completeness was out of the question. Nearly every one of the thinkers mentioned might easily and profitably have been made the subject of a monograph. But such completeness would have interfered with clarity and continuity. The compromise I have been striving for is (1) to describe in each case the general framework for the phenomenological work of the thinkers I include; (2) to indicate by way of a bird's-eye view the scope of their phenomenological studies; (3) to present, at least in one special case for each, an example of their best efforts, particularly when these efforts are little known but worth knowing about; and (4) to add enough criticism to indicate where work that has sailed under the banner of phenomenology is, to say the least, open to suspicion and should not be considered as representative of phenomenology as a whole.

Thus, as far as history is concerned, this book can be at best another step in the direction of the recovery of the phenomenological past. Too many of the relevant facts are not yet accessible, if they ever will be. This is true not only of texts, but particularly of correspondence. A good deal of this belongs to the merely human side of the story, which often cannot, and even should not, be told. Even though the subsequent story contains more biographical information about the main thinkers than the previous, more idea-focused accounts, it avoids as far as possible the merely personal angle, the mere anecdote, and the *chronique scandaleuse*. Some of it may be relevant to an understanding of the more puzzling protagonists of our story. But it is irrelevant to the story itself.

The present account of the development of the Phenomenological Movement will include only phenomenological philosophy. The original plan was to add a survey of the influence of phenomenology upon non-philosophical studies, such as psychology, psychopathology, and even psychiatry, upon mathematics, the natural sciences, the social sciences, and the humanities, and, last but not least, on the study of religion. The omission is all the more serious since in countries such as the United States the impact of phenomenology is perhaps more pronounced and fruitful in these outlying fields than in philosophy proper. All the same it should be pointed out from the very start that, as far as the Phenomenological Movement as a whole is concerned, the present story remains incomplete. As long as the names of Hermann Weyl, Karl Jaspers (as psychopathologist), Ludwig Binswanger, Erwin Straus, and Eugène Minkowski do not figure at all in such an account, or do so only incidentally, important parts of the picture are missing. To add them would, however, not only have delayed the completion of the central story, it would also have swelled the bulk of the present manuscript intolerably. At the moment all I can do is to openly admit this shortcoming and to express the hope that someone, if not I myself, will be able to fill the gap.[1]

Finally, something should be said about the proper use of this work. I am well aware of the fact that few if any of the potential readers will be prepared to read a book of this size from cover to cover. In fact what most of them will be looking for is a compact little introduction to what phenomenology is all about and what its main results are. I am sorry that, given the vastness of the actual subject matter and my own limited powers of condensation, I am unable to oblige. All I can suggest to those with moderate curiosity and in an often legitimate hurry is that they turn from the introduction to the last chapter, sampling as much as they can on the way. One of my concerns was to write the individual chapters about the different phases and figures of the movement in such a manner that they can be consulted separately, even though they do not yield the reader

---

[1] For a good but by no means comprehensive beginning of the history of phenomenological psychology see Stephan Strasser, "Phenomenological Trends in European Psychology" in *Philosophy and Phenomenological Research* XVIII (1957), 18–34.

all they should without the preceding and subsequent chapters. No chapter is meant to be dispensable, nor is any of them meant to be completely dependent on its predecessor. Such in fact is the connection among the main figures of the Phenomenological Movement. They belong together, but they do not lean upon one another.

A word should be added about the bibliographical aids that follow each chapter. Again they are addressed primarily to the Anglo-American reader. Not even in the listing of the original works of the phenomenologists described have I aimed at completeness. But I tried not only to identify all the translations but also to appraise them summarily on the basis of samples I had taken – in view of the crucial role of such translations a badly needed but obviously delicate undertaking. As far as the secondary literature is concerned I mention only the most important works not written in English, adding brief characterizations. However, I did attempt an almost complete listing of the English-speaking literature, often going beyond the published bibliographies.

The indexes, particularly the subject index, which tries to incorporate a first glossary of the main phenomenological terms, may speak for themselves; so should the chronological charts.

This may also be the place to mention three abbreviations which will be found throughout the text:

JPPF for *Jahrbuch für Philosophie und phänomenologische Forschung* (Halle, Niemeyer, 1913–1930);

PPR for *Philosophy and Phenomenological Research*. A Quarterly Journal. (University of Buffalo, 1941 ff.);

PA for Van Breda, H. L., ed., *Problèmes actuels de la phénoménologie* (Paris, Desclée de Brouwer, 1951).

❧

The ultimate criterion for the success of this introduction will be whether it can entice the reader further, either to the original sources of this account, or, better, to the ultimate source for all phenomenological research, the "things themselves."

Appleton, Wisconsin, U.S.A.
August 1959

H. Sp.

PREFACE TO THE SECOND EDITION

The new edition of this book is a revision only in a restricted sense: The bulk of the text consists of a photomechanic reproduction of the first edition, in which only such minor errors as the birth year of Maurice Merleau-Ponty have been corrected. The real changes have been relegated to a supplement which is appended without being incorporated into the original text; only numbers in the margin of the new edition indicate the passages to which the supplement refers. While the primary reason for this arrangement is merely technical, there seem to me some special virtues in this necessity: users of the first edition have a right to know where I misled them, and they will even have a chance to acquire the supplement separately. Also, some of the changes are of such a character that I would like to draw special attention to them.

The supplement includes two types of changes: amendments and additions. As to the amendments, such as the one on Sartre's German studies (p. 462f.), I am fully aware that even they cannot always establish "the truth" of the matter, even as far as the bare facts are concerned; in the cases of Scheler and Heidegger I have pointed this out explicitly. But I hope I have at least approximated the irrecoverable past better than before. The additions concern either the history of phenomenology up to 1958, when I completed my original manuscript, or the period since then. In preparing these additions I have not changed my criteria of historical selection but only applied them to facts previously unknown to me. In particular, I have made no attempt to bring an accelerating runaway story up-to-date. I have concentrated on such recent developments as seem to me significant for the future and for a better understanding of the past and present by Anglo-American readers. Even my attempt to keep up the bibliographies and the listing of translations may not be complete. This had better be done by periodic reports and particularly by a critical review of translations, for which the need is as urgent as ever, now that more and more ambitious translations are being published.

I would also like to acknowledge immediately some limitations of this revision. Perhaps the most serious one is my failure to rewrite the chapter on Maurice Merleau-Ponty in the light of the irreparable loss which French phenomenology in particular has suffered by his most untimely death. My only excuse is that a full historical treatment should await the collection and examination of all his unpublished papers. I would offer the opposite excuse for my continuing delay in giving a fuller presentation and discussion of the work of Roman Ingarden. New and important publications of his have appeared, and interest in his work has grown considerably in the United States, especially after his visit here. But his most important work is still incomplete and is, like so many of his other works, still inaccessible to non-Polish readers. At this time I can do no more than repeat and reinforce my earlier recommendations in addition to pointing out some of his new publications. Furthermore, I should like to express my particular dissatisfaction with my previous account of the phenomenological situation in post-war Germany. The close-up of a year spent in Munich under a Fulbright grant on a different assignment has shown me the difficulty of getting a fair perspective of the new growth following the forest-fire of the Nazi period. But I still fail to see any convincing evidence of a renaissance of first-hand phenomenologizing.

Of the special opportunity which a new edition gives to an author to review his reviewers I intend to take merely limited advantage. I am certainly indebted to all those who have taken this book seriously, at times too seriously. For my warnings against expecting from it the definitive history of phenomenology have not always been heeded. This book can be at best the pacemaker of such a history, if it can ever be written. I was too far away in space and too close in time to the subject of my story to enjoy the desirable optimum perspective. The American perspective not only hides many sides of the phenomenon of phenomenology but presents others only in lateral profile.

To compare the spectrum of reviews, from the near-total rejection by Marvin Farber to the most surprising commendations by British reviewers, is in any case a puzzling experience which may make a narcissistic author doubt the identity of his brainchild. Most of what I would have to say about Farber's review article on "The Phenomenological Tendency" in the *Journal of Philosophy* (LIX, 1962, 429–39) I have put in a special reply in the same journal (LX, 1963, 584–88), to which I may refer the interested reader. But I would like to use this opportunity to express my relief at the fact that Hans-Georg Gadamer, who gave this book an unexpected priority in his comprehensive review of recent phenomenological literature in the *Philosophische Rundschau* (XI, 1963, 1–12) and generously acknowledged its informational value, has authorized me in a personal letter to state that he no longer upholds his strictures against my frame of interpretation (*Deutungshorizont*), at least as far as my presentation of the motto *"Zu den Sachen"* and the phenomenological reduction are concerned; I am looking forward to his announced rectification in the near future. I would also like to acknowledge the concrete aids I received in Eric Weil's encouraging review in *Critique* (185, 1962, 906–9). Otherwise I can do little more than acknowledge the generous comments of my main critics.[1]

Finally, I would like to mention the prospect that the hope I expressed in the Preface of the first edition for a closing of what seemed to me the most serious gap in my account, the absence of an adequate picture of the contribution of phenomenology to

---

[1] They are, in the order in which they have come to my attention: W. Mays (*Philosophical Books*), V. C. Chappell (*Ethics*), Thomas Langan (*Modern Schoolman*), Gustav E. Mueller (*Books Abroad*), R. B. MacLeod (*Contemporary Psychology*), Richard Schmitt (*Review of Metaphysics*), Jean Hering (*Revue d'histoire et de philosophie religieuse*), V. J. McGill (*Philosophy and Phenomenological Research*), Charles Taylor (*Mind*), Wilbur Long (*Personalist*), James V. McGlynn (*New Scholasticism*), Richard M. Zaner (*Social Research*), Pietro Chiodi (*Rivista di Filosofia*), Quentin Lauer (*Erasmus*), Maurize Natanson (*Journal of the History of Philosophy*), Samuel L. Hart (*Philosophical Review*).

psychology, psychopathology, and psychiatry, can be fulfilled. My Fulbright year in Germany, which enabled me to collect the main materials, and a generous grant from the National Institute of Mental Health should enable me to undertake this task in the near future.

Washington University
St. Louis, Mo.   H. Sp.
December 1963

In the present impression of the Second Edition I have corrected merely minor errors, but added references to more recent bibliographies. I am particularly indebted to Dr. Eberhard Avé-Lallemant in Munich for several corrections.

July 1968   H. Sp.

1. The Phenomenological Movement Defined

The first decision any historiographer has to make is where to begin his story. Unless he wants this decision to be completely arbitrary, he should also be prepared to justify it by a clear conception of the unifying theme for his account. Unfortunately, this demand cannot be satisfied so easily in the case of the history of phenomenology. The difficulties of stating point-blank what phenomenology is are almost notorious.[1] Even after it had established itself as a movement conscious of its own identity, it kept reinterpreting its own meaning to an extent that makes it impossible to rely on a standard definition for the purpose of historical inclusion or exclusion.

In fact, the very term "movement," applied to phenomenology, requires some explanation and justification. It is by no means common among the "insiders." But even less so is the expression "school," a label which has been imposed on phenomenologists only from the outside and is certainly not at all called for in view of the actual structure of the group.[2] Actually the word

[1] Among recent characteristic expressions of this situation see Maurice Merleau-Ponty, *Phénoménologie de la perception* (Gallimard, 1945), Avant-Propos; Pierre Thévenaz, "Qu'est-ce que la phénoménologie"? (*Revue de théologie et de philosophie.* Lausanne, 1952, pp. 9–30, 126–140, 294–316); Paul Ricoeur, "Sur la **Phénoménologie**" (*Esprit*, XXI (1953), pp. 821–839).

[2] Thus neither "movement" nor "school" are terms which seem to occur anywhere in Edmund Husserl's published writings. Informally, however, as in an important letter to Stanton Coit of September 18, 1927, he spoke of a "movement" (*Bewegung*) headed by himself. There is also the interesting fact that Husserl censored the draft of a prospectus of phenomenological publications submitted to him by his publisher, Max Niemeyer, which was to be headed by the title "Works of Edmund Husserl and of his School;" for he crossed out the words "and of his School" (*und seiner Schule*) and replaced them by the phrase "and of the circle of phenomenological researchers" (*und des phänomenologischen Forscherkreises*).

used first by the German insiders in the earlier days was that of "Kreis" (circle), with several sub-circles within the larger circle, a word much more appropriate for the loose and informal association of the members of a group lacking any school-like organization in an academic sense.

In what sense, then, does such a vague term as "movement," which is much more appropriate on the political, the social, or the artistic scene, apply to a philosophy like phenomenology? The following seem to me the main supports for the metaphor: (1) Phenomenology is a moving, in contrast to a stationary, philosophy with a dynamic momentum, whose development is determined by its intrinsic principles as well as by the "things," the structure of the territory which it encounters. (2) Like a stream it comprises several parallel currents, which are related but by no means homogeneous, and may move at different speeds. (3) They have a common point of departure, but need not have a definite and predictable joint destination; it is compatible with the character of a movement that its components branch out in different directions.

In fact this is very much what happened in the case of the Phenomenological Movement, whose original ingredients, as we shall see, came from very different sources, and, even at the time of the first phenomenological platform (1913), were never completely co-ordinated. Husserl's own course within the movement may well be compared with a spiral converging upon an inner center, in this case the phenomena of the subjective sphere. Yet at several turns of this spiral some of his followers were flung off at a tangent, as it were, following up lines suggested by Husserl himself during an earlier phase, while he himself had already changed his course. Thus today the pattern of the phenomenological movement seems to resemble that of an unfolding plant more than that of a river. This does not mean that the separate destinations of the various currents of the movement are contradictory, and hence that they cancel each other out. They rather represent the pursuit of definite and essential assignments of the movement in the total pattern of the phenomenological task: the descriptive investigation of the phenomena, both objective and subjective, in their fullest breadth and depth.

But the main problem arises in connection with the interpretation of the adjective "phenomenological." It begins with
the denotation of the term "phenomenology." Were it not older
than the Phenomenological Movement proper, the question of
delimitation would be much simpler and less urgent. But the
fact is that until about 1910 the word was practically everyone's
for the asking. Even now, the only protection for the at times
all too fashionable term is its ponderousness and tongue-twisting
ugliness. But even this repellent has not been sufficient to make
it foolproof against misuse, in accordance with C. S. Peirce's
terminological injunctions,[1] which worked well enough in his
own case when in 1904 he replaced "phenomenology" by such
neologisms as "phaneroscopy" or "phenoscopy."[2]

Thus, our major problem is to decide where to draw the line
between phenomenologists and non-phenomenologists. It would
be easy enough to make such a decision by arbitrary definition.
But this is exactly the kind of definition which phenomenology
wants to avoid. For its definitions are to be based on an intuitive
grasp of the essential affinities of the things which our definitions
try to embrace. In fact I would like to use this very occasion to
demonstrate the way in which a phenomenological definition,
based on the structure of the phenomena, can be built. The reader
who lacks the time and patience to wait for the decision, however,
is invited to skip the following pages.

In trying to define any movement of thought, be it phenomenology, positivism, or psychoanalysis, the first task is to decide
the range of phenomena to be covered, i.e., to stake out the
definiendum. The following criteria could be used:

α. the one-sided option of a self-declared member of such a movement;
β. the recognition by others, such as (a) the founder of the movement,
(b) a representative group of insiders, and (c) a similar group of outsiders;
γ. the historian's decision based on certain objective criteria in the
thought of the thinker in question, (a solution particularly easy to apply
where the label is posthumous, as is the case with most "isms" before the
18th century);
δ. any combination of the three preceding criteria.

But here are some of the complications which these criteria
would encounter in the case of the Phenomenological Movement:

[1] *Collected Papers*, edited by Charles Hartshorne and Paul Weiss, 5.413.
[2] See "Husserl's and Peirce's Phenomenologies" in *PPR* XVII (1957), 197 f.

1. In basing the decision on the one-sided option of self-declared phenomenologists we would have to consider that phenomenology has shared the
fate of a good many names, first fashionable and then old-fashioned: It
has been invoked excessively by the faddists and shunned prudishly by
the overscrupulous, independent-minded self-thinkers. The claim of such
[1]   self-styled phenomenologists as Traugott K. Oesterreich (*Phänomenologie
des Ich*) need not be honored at its face value, nor need the modest disclaimers of a Karl Jaspers. This situation has become intensified as a
result of Husserl's radicalization of phenomenology. By now, even
members of the original Göttingen circle declare that they are no longer
sure whether or not they "belong." Besides, there are chiefly personal
reasons for the abandonment of the label, as in the case of Heidegger.
Finally, many would-be phenomenologists reject labels on principle
(Gabriel Marcel) or adopt them only for limited parts of their philosophy
(Ernst Cassirer, Nicolai Hartmann, and Wolfgang Koehler).
2. Recognition by others could provide us theoretically with as specific
a criterion as the founder's say–so (β, a), since there is no doubt that the
fountainhead and leader of the Phenomenological Movement proper was
Edmund Husserl, even though there were supplementary and independent sources for it. But for one thing, Husserl's death and the absence
of anything like an apostolic succession have made this criterion un-
workable. Besides, even during Husserl's lifetime there were such per-
plexing cases as his accolade to Karl Jaspers, who first demurred and
later reneged emphatically[1]; or the case of the anthropologist, Lucien
Lévy-Bruehl, to whom, as late as 1935, Husserl paid the extraordinary
compliment of having anticipated his latest program, apparently to the
utter astonishment of the one so complimented.[2] On the other hand,
Husserl's express repudiation of such protagonists as Max Scheler,
Martin Heidegger, and Nicolai Hartmann and of many others by
implication, has reduced the range of phenomenology practically to the
solitary founder himself and his private assistants, Ludwig Landgrebe
and Eugen Fink. What further diminishes the usefulness of this criterion
is that Husserl, partly because of his impaired vision, could read only
very selectively during his later years and did not even keep up with the
literature that appeared under the flag of phenomenology.
3. Consulting exclusively either the insiders (βb), or the outsiders (βc),
of phenomenology would presuppose some form of organization. But,
more or less definite rumors notwithstanding, the Movement, even during
its German phase, never went beyond the formation of circles whose
periphery was anything but a line and which had better be described as
condensations. The only more definite and stable nucleus could be sought
among the co-editors of the eleven volumes of the *Jahrbuch für Philosophie
und phänomenologische Forschung* between 1913 and 1930. The recent
so-called *International Phenomenological Society* amounts to little more
than a list of subscribers to the journal *Philosophy and Phenomenological
Research*. And so far there is even less organization among the French
phenomenologists. Thus a poll among insiders or outsiders exclusively
would be impracticable. Nevertheless, the judgment of the innermost
circle of Husserl's early collaborators on the *Jahrbuch*, if available, would

---

[1] *Rechenschaft and Ausblick* (München, Piper, 1951), p. 327 f.
[2] Oral communication from Aron Gurwitsch.

constitute a fair presumption for or against the phenomenological claims of a possible pretender.

What are the chances for an outside historian to find an objective criterion that would enable him to divide up the controversial area? Actually the task of discovering a criterion that is not completely arbitrary threatens to involve us in a vicious circle. We might try to discover it by studying a group of phenomena for their most essential characteristics. But how can we even select such a group without knowing their characteristics from the very start? While this is not the place for a discussion of the general problem involved, it may at least be suggested that, even without prior definition and grouping, the phenomena show certain structures, articulations, affinities, and incompatibilities which indicate the proper place for the cutting knife, as in any anatomical dissection.

The question therefore arises whether as amorphous and complex a field of phenomena as that of the Phenomenological Movement contains enough articulation for such a meaningful dissection. I believe it does, and I shall attempt to make this clear to the reader from the very account of the thinkers to be included. In the final chapter I shall then attempt to make explicit the characteristics which correspond to this articulation of the field and which will allow us to formulate objective criteria for "membership" in the Phenomenological Movement.

For the immediate purposes of a first selection I shall adopt a mixed criterion, partly subjective and partly objective. It will be based chiefly on what came to be the closest approach to a phenomenological platform ever formulated, i.e., the statement sent out by the publisher and later printed at the head of the *Jahrbuch für Philosophie und phänomenologische Forschung*, "edited by Edmund Husserl in conjunction with Moritz Geiger, Alexander Pfänder, Adolf Reinach, and Max Scheler," who were joined or replaced later by Martin Heidegger and Oskar Becker. This statement contained the following key sentences:

It is not a system that the editors share. What unites them is the common conviction that it is only by a return to the primary sources of direct intuition and to insights into essential structures derived from them (*die originären Quellen der Anschauung und die aus ihr zu schöpfenden Wesenseinsichten*) that we shall be able to put to use the great traditions of philosophy with their concepts and problems; only thus shall we be in a position to clarify such concepts intuitively, to restate the problems on an intuitive basis, and thus, eventually, to solve them, at least in principle.[1]

On this basis I shall use the following criteria for drawing the line around the Phenomenological Movement in the full sense:

[1] The style of this statement and personal information received from Alexander Pfänder in the thirties make me believe that this text was drafted by Edmund Husserl himself. No correspondence relative to this document has been found.

α. Explicit or implicit adoption by the would-be phenomenologist of the two methods mentioned above, i.e., (a) direct intuition (in a sense still to be clarified) as the source and final test of all knowledge, to be incorporated as faithfully as possible in descriptions; (b) insight into essential structures as a genuine possibility and a need of philosophical knowledge.

β. Conscious adherence, however qualified, to the Movement as such in full awareness of these methodical principles. Short of such an expression, a thinker may well be considered as "really" belonging to the Movement, but it would be unfair to read him into it as an actual member.

The adoption of such rather liberal criteria for inclusion in the Phenomenological Movement in the full sense does not prevent the recognition of a wider fringe around it which cannot and must not be ignored in view of the more or less lively interaction between adjacent and parallel thinkers and movements. Besides, it must be remembered that such precursors of Husserl as Franz Brentano and Carl Stumpf, who, as we shall see, may very well qualify for some if not for all of the objective criteria above, could hardly have been expected to join a movement started by one of their students. All the more will it be important not to overlook them completely, quite apart from their historical role as teachers and supporters of Husserl. Consideration of these marginal figures will provide us with a conception of

α. *phenomenology in the widest sense* which would include those who fulfill the objective criteria stated above without identifying themselves subjectively with the Phenomenological Movement. Next, we distinguish

β. *phenomenology in the broad sense*, as described by the "platform" of 1913;

γ. *phenomenology in the strict sense*, which, in addition to cultivating intuitive experience (without limitation to sensationalistic sources) and to the intuitive study of essences, pays special attention to appearances, i.e., to the essential ways in which objects of whatever nature appear subjectively in experience;

δ. *phenomenology in the strictest sense* (as gradually developed by Husserl), i.e., a phenomenology in sense γ. which also utilizes a special operation, termed "phenomenological reduction," and, on the basis of this operation, pays special attention to the way in which the appearances of an object are constituted in and by consciousness.[1]

2. Pseudo-Phenomenologies

Our willingness to consider and to give due credit to developments not strictly belonging to the Phenomenological Movement must not lead to an indiscriminate inclusion of everybody and everything that is even remotely related to it. Thus the mere occurrrence of the word "phenomenology" in a given text constitutes no sufficient reason for admission. Recent developments in France have led to the unquestioned belief that Hegel's phenomenology forms part and parcel, if not the main root, of current phenomenology. It will therefore be of particular importance to examine and to eliminate certain equivocations which have arisen from the checkered history of the very term "phenomenology."

That this term existed long before Husserl adopted and assimilated it seems at times not to be sufficiently realized, at least not among philosophers. This fact in itself provides a measure

---

[1] Paul Ricoeur (*Esprit* XXI, 821) tries to solve the problem of delimiting the Phenomenological Movement by the following statement (my translation):

Fundamentally, phenomenology is born as soon as we treat the manner of appearing of things as a separate problem (*problème autonome*) by "bracketing" the question of existence, either temporarily or permanently.

Such a formula, interpreted literally, would keep out the Husserl of the *Logische Untersuchungen*, who had not yet introduced "bracketing" in his publications until the *Ideen* of 1913. Actually, this is hardly Ricoeur's intent, since he himself wants to house under the roof of his definition the Kantian as well as the Hegelian phenomenologies, none of which practice the bracketing operation, certainly not explicitly. What he seems to mean, then, is that a phenomenology "worthy of its name" will pay special attention to the way of appearing of "things, ideas, values, and persons," very much in the strict sense stated under γ.

While this would give us much wider scope, and would actually include most epistemologists beginning with Plato, it might easily remain too narrow for some of the members of the early phenomenological circles in Göttingen and Munich, such as Reinach, Pfänder, and Scheler, not to mention Heidegger, who were much more intent on *what* appears than on *how* it appears. Nevertheless, what they did present could perhaps not have been obtained without explicit attention to the manner of its appearing. Thus, while what they offer may not be phenomenology in the strict sense γ, it represents definitely phenomenologically founded philosophy. Hence Ricoeur's demarcation line serves the very useful purpose of blocking out the area for phenomenology in the two stricter senses. But it would be unwise to define the Phenomenological Movement as a whole in this way, thereby eliminating the larger movement from which the narrower has emerged and for which it still provides the matrix.

of the degree to which Husserl gave the old term a richer and more dynamic philosophical meaning than any of his predecessors. But this must not make us overlook the fact that it has a much longer history, although, as we shall see, a rather disjointed one. Actually, the term seems to have been invented several times independently. After all, the formation of a compound like "phenomenology" was almost inevitable, once "phenomena" seemed worth studying at all, and once "-ologies" had become the fashion. In fact, the conception of a "logos" of the "phaino-mena" is quite Platonic and can be traced more or less explicitly to Plato's attempt to salvage (σώζειν) the appearances from the world of Heraclitean flux by relating them to the world of the logos, i.e., of the changeless Forms.

The main purpose of this section will be to explore, in addition to listing, these "non-phenomenological" uses of the term "phenomenology," and to determine how far they are based on mere coincidences or on deeper affinities with each other and with phenomenology proper. To this end we shall divide these uses into two groups, a philosophical and an extra-philosophical one.

A. EXTRA-PHILOSOPHICAL PHENOMENOLOGIES

In modern usage the word "phenomenon" is no longer limited to philosophers. It has become naturalized particularly among scientists, for instance in the form in which it can be found in Newton's writings.[1] Thus it is the natural sciences which lend themselves primarily to the establishment of special phenome-nologies.

α. The priority for the use of the term in a scientific context would seem to go to Immanuel Kant, at least according to mere date of publication. For it was in his *Metaphysische Anfangsgründe der Naturwissenschaft* of 1786 that he applied it to the last of his four branches of the science of matter, dealing with "motion or rest only in relation to their appearance to us." This phenomenology was thus concerned specifically with the

---

[1] Goethe, although he never uses the term "phenomenology," has often been presented as a proto-phenomenologist, chiefly on the basis of his anti-Newtonian doctrine of the phenomena of color (see, e.g., Hedwig Conrad-Martius and Ludwig Binswanger). Certain parallels between his approach and Husserl's phenomenology, and perhaps even more that of others, are unmistakable (see Fritz Heinemann, "Goethe's Phenomenological Method" in *Philosophy* IX (1934), 67–81). Never-theless Goethe's primary concern was not philosophy, but merely a natural science of the color phenomena different from Newton's.

basic problem of relativity or absoluteness of motion, as it appeared at the time. While thus restricted to a problem in physics, this phenomenology had nevertheless a place in the embracing framework of Kant's philosophical system. As a matter of fact, Kant's choice of a term which seems to have remained exclusively his own appears to be very much a result of his passion for symmetrical compartmentalization. In the particular context the term "phenomenology," released from a more philosophical use which will be mentioned below, proved to be a handy label.   [1]

β. A less specialized use can be found two years later in the third edition of the *Encyclopaedia Britannica* of 1788, in the article "Philosophy" by J. Robison, where however philosophy, being defined as "the study of the phenomena of the universe with a view to discover the general laws which indicate the powers or natural substances, to explain subordinate phenomena and to improve art," practically coincides with our present use of the term science. Phenomenology is here characterized as that part of philosophy which merely describes, arranges, and relates the phenomena after the manner of the usual systems of astronomy or of Newton's optics, and which represents merely "philosophical history."

A similar and even more influential use of the term can be found in Sir William Whewell's *Philosophy of the Inductive Sciences* (1847), where *phenomenology* occurs in the context of the "palaetiological sciences" (i.e., sciences which deal with more ancient conditions of things), as that branch of these studies which is to be followed by *aetiology* and *theory*. Among such phenomenologies Whewell mentions particularly phenomenological uranology, phenomenological geography of plants and animals, and even a phenomenological glossology. Among their tasks he stresses classification, "which requires genius and good fortune" for the discovery of natural classes.[1]

γ. One use of the term "phenomenology" which now strikes us as rather surprising occurs in the scientific writings of Ernst Mach, the philosophical positivist. In an address of 1894, for instance, he postulated a "general physical phenomenology" (*umfassende physikalische Phänomenologie*) to comprise all the areas of physics, with the assignment to form the most abstract concepts of physical research, starting from mere descriptions and proceeding by way of comparisons among the phenomena in the various branches of physics.[2]

One year later, in an address on "The Contrast between Mechanical and Phenomenological Physics," Mach characterized Newton's and his own "phenomenological approach" as an "attempt" to purge physics of superfluous unessential additions and to "remove all metaphysical elements"; in other words, phenomenological physics represented to him the fulfillment of the program of economy of thought in the spirit of Occam's razor. Likewise the physicist Ludwig Boltzmann, himself an opponent of this type of physics, distinguished between (1) a *mathematical phenomenology* after the manner of Heinrich Hertz, as the more extreme edition, where the physicist simply jots down equations without deriving

---

[1] *Op. cit.*, Book X, p. 645.
[2] "Über das Prinzip der Vergleichung in der Physik," republished in *Populärwissenschaftliche Vorlesungen* (1896). Husserl was familiar with this use, to the extent of reviewing this particular address in his "Bericht über deutsche Schriften zur Logik aus dem Jahre 1894" in *Archiv für systematische Philosophie* III (1897), 243 ff.: he even did so in terms of unqualified approval.

them, in order to compare them subsequently with the phenomena, (2) a *general phenomenology* after the manner of Ernst Mach which describes a fact like electricity simply as the sum of the experiences we have had and expect to have in the future, and (3) an *energetic phenomenology* which tries to identify what is common to all the phenomena of mechanics, etc.[1]

Albert Einstein, who on occasion uses the term, also wants to move beyond a merely phenomenological physics and even claims that "the greatest achievement of Newton's mechanics lies in the fact that its consistent application has led beyond ... phenomenological representation, particularly in the field of heat phenomena."[2] A. d'Abro takes a similar position when he contrasts the "phenomenological theories," which confine themselves to "macroscopic" observables, with "microsopic theories," which postulate "hidden occurrences."[3]

Somewhat differently Max Planck in "The Meaning and Limits of Exact Science" (1947) contrasts the "phenomenological world" as the "scientific world picture gained by experience" with "the real world" in the absolute metaphysical sense of the world "real."[4]

Henry Margenau, in a stimulating article "Phenomenology and Physics" in *PPR* V (1945), 269–280, seems to be aware of the difference between what he calls "phenomenalistic" physics and philosophical phenomenology. But he ascribes to the latter, at least at the start, rather misleadingly the "claim to thoroughgoing explanation" rather than to description, which is not mentioned in this context.

All these uses are of course related to the merely descriptive as opposed to the explanatory conception of physics in G. R. Kirchhoff's school of theoretical physics, for which mechanics was nothing but the attempt to describe the motions occurring in nature as completely and simply as possible without explaining them. Phenomenology in this sense is part and parcel of positivism.

8. Another adoption of the term "phenomenology" for non-philosophical purposes – unrelated especially in the beginning to philosophical usage – occurs in the study of religion. Thus the Dutch founder of the comparative history of religion, P. D. Chantepie de la Saussaye, began the first edition of his classic *Lehrbuch der Religionsgeschichte* of 1887 with a "phenomenological part," designed to "order the main groups of religious phenomena without explaining them by doctrinaire reduction in such a way that the most important aspects and viewpoints emerged from the material itself." Standing halfway between the philosophy of religion and the history of religion, yet without coinciding with the psychology of religion, it dealt with such topics as the objects, the kinds, and the places and times of worship, with saints, religious groups, and sacred documents in general. This religious study has spread vastly, to be sure not always under the term "phenomenology."[5] More recently, Gerardus Van der Leeuw's

---

[1] *Populäre Schriften* (Leipzig, 1905), p. 219.

[2] "Physics and Reality," *Journal of the Franklin Institute*, vol. 221, March 1936; reprinted in *Ideas and Opinions* (New York, Crown Publishers, 1954), pp. 302 ff.

[3] *The Decline of Mechanism in Modern Physics* (New York, Van Nostrand, 1939), pp. 90 f.

[4] *Scientific Autobiography and Other Papers* (New York, Philosophical Library, 1949), p. 101 ff.

[5] See, for instance the Groningen dissertation on *"Phänomenologie der Religion"* by Eva Hirschmann (1940), who distinguishes as many as twelve such phenomenologies of religion.

"phenomenology" of religion [1] shows an attempt to link up an impressive array of the main types of religious phenomena with philosophical phenomenology, though only in a special postcript, called "Epilegomena." To be sure, this attempt has very much the character of an afterthought. Actually, for Van der Leeuw it is Heidegger rather than Husserl who is the main representative of phenomenology. Nevertheless, from here on the older enterprise merges with the wider current of the Phenomenological Movement in philosophy. But it would be unfair to overlook the independent origins of the phenomenology which has arisen from the comparative study of religion. Yet it would be just as misleading to confuse a mere typology of religious institutions with a phenomenology in the philosophical sense, which concentrates on the religious acts and contents in religious experience and explores their essential structures and relationships.   [1]

B. PHILOSOPHICAL PHENOMENOLOGIES

α. The first documented use of the term "phenomenology" as such occurs in the *Neues Organon oder Gedanken über die Erforschung und Bezeichnung des Wahren und der Unterscheidung von Irrtum und Schein* (1764) by Johann Heinrich Lambert, one of the more independent, epistemologically oriented followers of Christian Wolff. For him, phenomenology is the theory of illusion (*Schein*) and of its varieties, forming in this role the concluding fourth part of a study of the means for finding the truth. Interesting though this theory is even for later phenomenology, it is obvious that it has nothing to do with an intuitive method for achieving insights into essential structures.

β. It would seem that it was Lambert's inspiration which was to some extent responsible for the temporary philosophical use of the term in the preparatory stages of Kant's *Critique of Pure Reason*, the work which at one time he even contemplated dedicating to Lambert (Academy Edition XVIII, 64). For it was in a letter of September 2, 1770 to Lambert that Kant first mentioned the need of a "negative science (phaenomenologia generalis)," to precede metaphysics as a propaedeutic discipline, with the assignment to determine the validity and the limits of the principles of sensory knowledge. In the famous letter to Marcus Herz of February 21, 1772, announcing his projected work on the limits of sensibility and of reason, he stated that the first theoretical part was to consist of two parts: (1) general phenome-

[1] *Phänomenologie der Religion* (Tübingen, 1933): English translation under the title *Religion in Essence and Manifestation*. A Study in Phenomenology (New York, Macmillan, 1938).

nology ("*die Phänomenologie überhaupt*") and (2) metaphysics, "according to its nature and its method." Thus Kant's first phenomenology was clearly nothing but what he called "Critique of Pure Reason" in a later paragraph of the same letter, and hence by no means a study of mere illusions, as in Lambert. But there is no clear indication that he considered it also as a study of phenomena in contrast to things in themselves (*noumena*), as one might suspect. Nevertheless, such a critique of human knowledge has by itself little if any affinity with today's full-fledged phenomenology. To be sure, it must not be overlooked that the later Husserl found himself increasingly in sympathy and agreement precisely with Kant's *Critique of Pure Reason*, apparently without being aware of the fact that there was even a terminological bridge for his latter-day rapprochement to Kant's critical philosophy. There is certainly much in the *Critique of Pure Reason* that lends itself to interpretation by Husserl's late phenomenology. It is another question how valid this interpretation can be.

γ. Hegel's *Phenomenology of the Spirit* represents a much more acute, intriguing, and debatable case. For one thing, Hegel certainly succeeded in elevating phenomenology to the rank of a full philosophical discipline which made a lasting impression. Besides, while the German Phenomenological Movement never considered Hegel as a phenomenologist in the full sense, the present French phenomenologists seem to take his inclusion in the phenomenological movement for granted (see Chapter VIII).

Johannes Hoffmeister has now traced the lineage for Hegel's use of the term "Phänomenologie," beginning with Lambert.[1] Fichte's *Wissenschaftslehre* of 1804 represented a particularly important phase in this transformation. Here phenomenology received the assignment of deriving the world of appearances (in the Kantian sense) from consciousness as the primary fact and source of all other facts. However, even for Hegel the term remained fluid enough to cover two conceptions of rather different scope: (1) the *Phenomenology of the Spirit* of 1807, being Part I of his "*System der Wissenschaft*," which was never com-

[1] *Phänomenologie des Geistes* (Hamburg, Meiner, 1952). Editor's Preface, pp. VII–XVII.

pleted, and (2) the phenomenology of the subjective spirit, which formed a rather subordinate intermediate link in the system of the *Encyclopedia of the Philosophical Sciences* of 1817 between his "anthropology" and his "psychology." In its original and more important role, as the first part of Hegel's system, phenomenology presented the drama of the genesis of "Science" (*das Werden der Wissenschaft*), showing first the mere sensuous consciousness and then, rising with dialectical necessity, the various forms of self-consciousness up to that form of absolute knowledge which Hegel interpreted as philosophy. As he put it, phenomenology is the Golgotha (*Schädelstätte*) of the Absolute Spirit, a museum, as it were, which preserves the records of his painful ascent to self-understanding. In this developmental morphology of the Spirit the phenomena under investigation were neither illusions nor mere appearances, but stages of knowledge, beginning with our pre-scientific natural or naive consciousness, leading up the "ladder" to the "ether" of philosophy. "Phenomenon" was therefore here simply whatever made its appearance on the scene, as it were, but not an appearance of something other than itself.[1]

How far has such a phenomenology any connection with the phenomenology of our day? Husserl himself apparently never answered this question and does not seem to have studied Hegel more than casually and in the manner of his teacher Brentano[2], who saw in Hegel a case of "extreme degeneration of human thought." To be sure, later on Husserl revised this appraisal to the extent that, along with his heightened regard for Kant, he also usually included "the post-Kantian German Idealists" among the significant, though immature, contributors to a phenomenological philosophy. But only once in his last work does he mention Hegel or his phenomenology explicitly in such a context (*Husserliana* VI, 204 f.). The absence of any reference to [1] this precedent may well serve as a measure of Hegel's eclipse in the Germany of the time.

This poses the question of how far the French phenomenologists are right in annexing the Hegelian phenomenology as a precursor,

---

[1] *Phänomenologie des Geistes*, pp. 26, 66 f.
[2] For such traces see *Husserliana* VII, 312, note 2 (1924). – For Brentano consult Oskar Kraus, *Franz Brentano*, pp. 18, 158 ff.

if not as the initiator, of phenomenology proper. At least this much can be said in favor of such an attempt, however unhistorical it may be: Hegel's emphasis on the priority of consciousness or subjectivity as the starting point of the philosophical system, and also his beginning from naive consciousness however Hegelianized, is at least in line with Husserl's later approach. So is his insistence on philosophy as a science rather than as a romantic super-poetry. But this must not make us overlook certain other features which fit in poorly with the initial and fundamental aspirations of a phenomenological philosophy: (1) Phenomenology, as Part I of Hegel's initial system (disregarding here the much more incidental role it plays in his later, fully developed system), was not based on a specific method, but constituted merely a morphology of consciousness discovered without the application of a new phenomenological method. Specifically, there is no mention of any suspension of belief after the manner of Husserl's "reduction." (2) There is no explicit reference to anything like an intuitive method, even though Hegel wants his phenomenology to start from concrete experience. But there is considerable emphasis on the "effort" of the "concept," as opposed to the Romantic "intellectual intuition" of Schelling. (3) There is no particular interest in insight into essential structures over and above what is implied in the use of the general dialectical method. Besides, it is exactly this dialectical method with its dubious claim to logical self-evidence that is phenomenologically questionable.

One feature in Hegel's phenomenology that might seem to put it much closer to Husserl's is that it also deals with phenomena or "appearances" (*Erscheinungen*), or, more specifically, with the appearances of the Spirit, i.e., its manifestations in which it appears "for itself." But at this point we have to be on our guard against a fundamental and rather fateful equivocation of the word "appearance": Hegel's appearances of the spirit constitute stages in the development or history of consciousness; in this sense he is concerned with an ontological problem, and the appearances are nothing but progressive realizations of the ideal of "scientific consciousness." By contrast, Husserl's problem is epistemological. His "appearances" are the slanted views ("*Abschattungen*") through which an identical thing makes its appearance, as it occurs particularly in perception; as long as these appearances do not replace the thing that appears *through* them, as they do under phenomenalism, these appearances differ fundamentally from the Hegelian appearances, which are not transparent toward something appearing through them.[1] Hence the Hegelian "appearance" is primarily an expression of a developing entity in reality, namely "science," and definitely not the way in which an object is given through its appearances.

δ. Another case of an early relatively independent phenomenology is that of Eduard von Hartmann. Apparently the term appears for the first time in the seventh edition (1875) of his central work, the "Philosophy of the Unconscions" (*Philosophie des Unbewussten*), as the title of its first part (*Phänomenologie des Unbewussten*) in contrast to the *Metaphysik des Unbewussten*, which forms its second part. He used it even more conspicuously three years later (1878) in the first edition of his "Phenomenology of the Moral Consciousness," (*Phänomenologie des sittlichen Bewusstseins*), where it stands for "an inventory as complete as possible of the empirically given territory of moral consciousness, together with a critical elucidation of these internal data and of their mutual relations, and with speculative development of the principles holding them together."

Besides, Hartmann looked upon his *Philosophy of Religion* (1882) as a phenomenology of religious consciousness. (Preface to the 10th edition of the *Philosophy of the Unconscious*.) Also in his *Aesthetics* (1886) at least the second systematic part was meant to be a "phenomenology of the esthetic consciousness." However, Hartmann met with so little understanding of his conception of phenomenology that at the request of his publisher he decided to leave off the objectionable word from the title of the second edition, "since there are people who can be scared by a title which gives them trouble even in pronouncing it" (p. 6). Yet he wanted it restored in the final third edition.

It is highly probable that Hartmann's fondness for the term "phenomenology" in his ethics, philosophy of religion, and esthetics was a reflexion of his admiration for precisely these

---

1 Thus Hegel protests against the distinction between an "empty appearance" of science and science itself. Science itself is *Erscheinung*, "though not yet fully carried out and spread out in its truth." (ed. Hoffmeister, p. 66).

parts of Hegel's philosophy. But even then, e.g., in the preface to the second edition of the *Phänomenologie des moralischen Bewusstseins*, he was anxious to point out that this phenomenology "differs from Hegelian dialectics externally, by spurning the forced Hegelian trichotomies, and internally, by its empirically inductive character and by the abhorrence of contradiction and of the higher truth or reason allegedly contained in it" (p. 19).

In order to determine the real meaning of Hartmann's conception one would have to examine more closely the content of his phenomenological works. Thus the ethics offers primarily a study of the pseudo-moral consciousness, followed by that of the genuine moral consciousness, according to motives, goals, and foundations. This however is not meant to be merely a historical or psychological study. Rather does Hartmann want to describe typical forms of moral consciousness in its evolution, using historical phenomena merely as illustrations. Thus far, one might therefore think very well of a simplified version of Hegel's phenomenology of consciousness. But there are additional features. For one thing, Hartmann thinks of his phenomenological studies as inductive support for his metaphysics. Besides, at times Hartmann presents the phenomenological investigation of his phenomena as one which is not affected by their possible illusory character, a feature which may well presage the neutrality toward claims of validity in later phenomenology (Preface to the 11th ed. of the *Philosophie des Unbewussten*, p. XXIII). But this alone is not sufficient to consider Hartmann's morphology of consciousness as more than an isolated landmark on the way from Hegel to Husserl.[1]

ε. The first independent philosophical use of the term "phenomenology" by an English-speaking philosopher occurs in Sir William Hamilton's *Lectures on Metaphysics*, given from 1836 on, but not published until after his death in 1858. Here, in Lecture VII, phenomenology appears in the form of a *Phenomenology of Mind*: "It is commonly called *Psychology* or the *Inductive Philosophy of Mind*: we might call it *Phenomenal Psychology*." It has to answer the question: "What are the facts or phaenomena to be observed?" and is contrasted with the "*Nomology*

---

[1] See also "*Religionsphilosophie*" in *Ausgewählte Werke* V, p. VI on the phenomenological attitude (*Haltung*) and VI, p. III ff.

of Mind," which is expected to discover "not contingent appearances but the *necessary* and universal facts," and with a *"Metaphysics proper*," which draws "inferences of unknown being from its known manifestations," also called *ontology* or *inferential psychology*. The classes of phenomena to be studied by this phenomenology are the following three: (1) phenomena of our cognitive faculties, (2) phenomena of our feelings, and (3) phenomena of our conative powers.

Hamilton gives no indications as to the source of his terminological innovation. It may well be the result of the adoption of the extra-philosophical usage exemplified especially by the Newtonian physical sciences and reinterpreted around the same time by Sir William Whewell, rather than a reminiscence from Hamilton's reading of Hegel, which was anyhow relatively slight and unsympathetic.[1]

As to the significance of this usage – which apparently remained restricted to Hamilton himself – it is obvious that in his sense phenomenology coincided with the merely descriptive and classificatory phase of empirical psychology, which has since become a purely scientific concern. It hardly needs pointing out that, even if he had undertaken this task in more detailed fashion than he did, it would not yet have amounted to a phenomenology in the sense of the Phenomenological Movement.

A similar but probably unrelated use of the term "phenomenology" occurs with the Herbartian founder of *Völkerpsychologie*, Moritz Lazarus. Actually he distinguishes between *phenomenology*, as the descriptive representation (*darstellende Schilderung*) of the factual parts of mental life, and *psychology*, as the dissecting explanation (*zergliedernde Erklärung*) of its "elements," causes, and conditions. But the whole distinction is restricted to one sentence in an inconsequential footnote of his three volumes of essays on *Das Leben der Seele* (II (1885), 346).

ζ. The last example of a philosophical phenomenology independent of the Phenomenological Movement, and at the same time its first instance on the American Continent,[2] is the

[1] It should also be noted that, judging from a quotation in his *Discussions on Philosophy and Literature* (New York, 1853, p. 636), Hamilton was familiar with Lambert's *Neues Organon*, from which he even quoted passages on "Phaenomenologie."

[2] John Dewey's brief article "Phenomenology" in Baldwin's *Dictionary of Philosophy and Psychology* of 1902 mentions only the phenomenologies of Hegel, Eduard von Hartmann, and Kant.

phenomenology of Charles Sanders Peirce, the initiator of the original pragmatism. To be sure, he used the term "phenomenology" only during the brief but significant period between 1902 and 1904 and replaced it later almost completely by such neologisms as "phaneroscopy," "ideoscopy," and "phenoscopy." This phenomenology grew out of Peirce's sustained effort to develop a system of categories corresponding to the main classes of phenomena that make up our world. The point of departure for this enterprise was Kant's list of categories. But later Peirce discovered that his new system had led him surprisingly close to that of Hegel, whom, as he stated repeatedly, he had despised in his early days. When in his *Minute Logic* of 1902 he first made use of the term "phenomenology" he was well aware of Hegel's precedent. To be sure, he denied having been influenced in his ideas by Hegel. But he did believe that a system of categories very much like his own occurred in Hegel's *Phänomenologie* – mistakenly, since it was not the *Phenomenology of the Spirit*, but the *Encyclopedia of the Philosophical Sciences*, which contained such a system. Nevertheless, Peirce remained aware of these differences, and it was the increasing awareness of these differences which determined him, scrupulous as he was in his terminology, to abandon his claim. It is, however, most unlikely that the thought of Husserl entered into these considerations, although by 1906 Peirce was familiar enough with him to call him "the distinguished Husserl." [1]

All the same, there are remarkable parallels between Peirce's phenomenology and that of the Phenomenological Movement. There is Peirce's impressive plea for unprejudiced direct inspection free from theorizing interpretations (*Collected Papers* 5.42) and for elimination of physiological and related speculations (1.287). There is, furthermore, Peirce's stress on the fact that phenomena are not restricted to mere empirical facts, but that they include everything that can be conceivably experienced and may even occur in wild dreams. And, finally, there is Peirce's insistence on the distinction between essence and existence and his censure of Hegel for its neglect (5.37).

Thus Peirce's phenomenology, at least according to its pro-

---

[1] See my article on "Husserl's and Peirce's Phenomenologies" in *PPR* XVII (1957), 164–185.

fessed program, may well fulfill the objective specifications of the first phenomenological platform, i.e., of phenomenology in the broad sense β. Nevertheless, it must not be overlooked that Peirce's attempt to classify the phenomena or "phanerons" according to firstness, secondness, and thirdness reveals an interest in ontological systematization which is unparalleled among phenomenologists. Also Peirce displays little if any interest in reflection upon subjective phenomena and particularly upon the way in which his categories are given in experience. This disinterest in the subjective aspects finds expression also in his intransigent rejection of psychology in philosophy, which outdoes even Husserl, whom Peirce actually reproached for having relapsed into psychologism in the second volume of his *Logische Untersuchungen*. (4.7).

Phenomenology, not unlike other philosophical movements such as pragmatism, has also been a "new name for old ways of thought" (William James). But like them it has reorganized and focussed this thought to such an extent and in such a manner that a new form of philosophy with a gestalt of its own has emerged, giving new life and new momentum to some of its forerunners. Thus, while it certainly would be senseless to claim Peirce as an advocate of Husserlian phenomenology before its rise, it remains true that there is considerable congeniality between Peirce and phenomenology in the broad sense, particularly those more objectivistic or ontologistic strands of it which will stress the "turn to the object" as its major features.   [1]

This concludes our survey of conceivable claimants to priority over Husserl and the Phenomenological Movement, as far as such claims could be based on prior use of the *term* "phenomenology." It would be a very different and practically interminable undertaking if we tried, without regard to the label, to extend this examination to all those possible pretenders who, under different flags, have anticipated the whole or parts of the phenomenological method in their actual procedure. But, apart from the endlessness of such an assignment, there is little need for it in view of the fact that actual claims are not frequently advanced, except by over-zealous disciples of Husserl's predecessors. There will be sufficient occasion in the following chapters to point out

such priorities, coincidences, and actual influences. But it would
exceed the framework of this study to show in detail how much
phenomenology was already realized in the preceding 2400 years
of the history of philosophy, either by way of annexation or by
assimilation on the part of the historian.[1]

3. Preview

Little purpose would be served in a book of this type by an
introductory summary of its contents. But it might be advisable
to offer some explanation for the outlay of the subsequent story.

Less than any other philosophy did phenomenology enter the
scene out of nowhere. There was not even anything premeditated
and spectacular about the way in which it grew slowly in the
mind of its founder. Hence an attempt at a full understanding
of its rise and its early impact would seem to call for a particularly
thorough study of its nineteenth century background, especially
as it presented itself in the minds of the founding fathers of
phenomenology. Yet after a few false starts I decided to abandon
the hopeless attempt to reconstruct in a brief sketch their
perspective on this "still darkest of all centuries of the modern
age" (Heidegger). Suffice it to refer the reader to the picture
available in the earlier and more traditional accounts of the
second half of the century, and to its major features: (1) the
decline and fall of speculative philosophy in the grand Hegelian
manner; (2) the accelerated progress of the natural sciences as
well as of the historical sciences (*Geisteswissenschaften*), which led
to the growth of a peculiar relativistic historicism; (3) the very
temporary and limited success of the attempts at building new
speculative syntheses on the new scientific foundations as
exemplified by the semi-speculative philosophies of Hermann
Lotze, Eduard von Hartmann, Wilhelm Wundt, and Herbert
Spencer; (4) the more powerful attempts of natural science itself
to take over the task in the form of a sweeping materialism and
monism; (5) the equally brusque and successful attempt of positivism in its continental and British versions to dispose of the
remnants of speculative thought and to replace it by a merely
"scientific" study of the "phenomena," the given, stripped to

---

[1] See, for instance, Michael Landmann, "Socrates as a Precursor of Phenomenology" in *PPR* II (1941), 15–42.

the "immediate" sense data of positivism; (6) the related effort to convert philosophy into a branch of psychology, an effort that led to the development of what was later labelled as "psychologism"; and finally (7) the more and more frequent attempts to recover safe ground by reviving and revising abandoned phases of European thought, such as Neo-Kantianism, and, in very different quarters, Neo-Thomism. From this picture, however, the names of thinkers would have to be omitted who since then have begun to dominate the scene because of their impact today, notably Kierkegaard, Marx, and also largely Nietzsche, who in his own time seemed to be merely a troublesome amateur on the outskirts of serious philosophy. The resulting pattern would thus be that of a philosophy in a lingering crisis of reorientation, still threatened in its very existence from the outside, having lost most of its earlier prestige, uncertain of its mission, either on the point of capitulating to the sciences, struggling to keep up with them, or seeking safe ground by retrenchment or a return to deserted earlier positions. This was the situation which the new phenomenology had to meet and which it did meet so effectively.

The present account will begin immediately with the preparatory phase of phenomenology (Part I). From this period we shall single out the figures of Husserl's teacher, Franz Brentano, and of his oldest student, Carl Stumpf, less because they, too, occasionally made use of the term "phenomenology," than because some of their ideas anticipated and to some extent influenced Husserl. However, whatever phenomenological motifs can be discovered at this stage, they do not yet result in a phenomenological philosophy in the sense of the later movement, from which both Brentano and Stumpf stayed demonstratively aloof.

During its first and major period, prior to the Second World War, phenomenology remained by and large a German affair. As such it constitutes the topic of Part II. Its main phase was the slow formation and transformation of the idea of phenomenology resulting from the quest for a philosophy as rigorous science in the mind of its recognized founder, Edmund Husserl. But this incontestable fact must not make us forget that during the early years of the century a group of younger German phi-

losophers, students of Theodor Lipps in Munich, were moving
in a similar direction. From their contacts with Husserl and
from a certain amount of interaction sprang the Phenomenological Movement in its Göttingen form. It must also be realized
that from the very start phenomenology as a movement fanned
out in several directions. The members of the older Munich
group were already fully established thinkers when they made
contact with Husserl. Thus they more or less continued in their
own way after the first happy encounter and saw no reason to
follow Husserl on his course toward a more and more subjectivistic and idealistic radicalization of phenomenology. Max Scheler's
case stands out as that of another independent thinker whose
way crossed that of both Husserl and the Munich group: to him
phenomenology meant chiefly an approach to his own much more
ambitious objectives. The same is true of Nicolai Hartmann,
a much more systematic and critical convert to phenomenology.
But the most spectacular case was that of Martin Heidegger,
who, espousing phenomenology in a rather early phase of his
development, nearly carried it away with him toward his
"ontology" or "Thought of Being," which had little if any
resemblance to Husserl's pronounced transcendentalism. As a
matter of fact, Heidegger's whole relationship to phenomenology
calls for a careful reappraisal, all the more since his subsequent
loss of interest in the label nearly spelled the at least temporary
end of phenomenology in Germany. To be sure, the formal
termination of German phenomenology was chiefly the work of
more powerful political forces. It still remains to be seen whether,
now that Nazism has disappeared, phenomenology will recapture
some of its former role in German philosophy.

However, there can be no question that during the thirties
the center of gravity of the Phenomenological Movement shifted
to the west. In fact, at that time it entered a peculiarly French
phase, which forms the theme of Part III. After first absorbing
some of the German tradition, French phenomenology developed
an amazing creative vigor. It owes some of its distinctive form
to its peculiar interpretations and, at times, misinterpretations
of Scheler, Heidegger, and Husserl (in that order) by Gabriel
Marcel, Sartre, and Merleau-Ponty. Their unique fusion of
phenomenology and existentialism has humanized and socialized

phenomenology to an extent and in a manner which sets it apart from Husserl's transcendental subjectivism, from Heidegger's anti-subjectivistic "thought of being," and from Scheler's cosmic perspectives.

While French phenomenology has held a decided lead in the period between 1935 and the present, its spread to and its status in other parts of the world deserves at least passing notice, as attempted in Part IV. The picture revealed by this survey is, however, far from uniform. It ranges all the way from total assimilation, as in the Ibero-American countries, to indifference and downright rejection, as in England. But these differences in the reception of phenomenology are less important than the fact that thus far no major original works comparable to those in France have emerged from these areas. – Based upon these finds and those of the earlier parts I shall risk a concluding diagnosis and prognosis of phenomenology in midcentury, combined with certain suggestions and recommendations.

Against the background of this panorama, I have finally, in Part V, tried to formulate the essentials of the phenomenological enterprise. This attempt is critical as well as analytical, in some respects even reconstructive. But here I cannot claim to speak for anyone but myself. This admission should serve as a warning both to those who expect this book to present nothing but a statement of impersonal doctrine, and to those who might suspect me of setting myself up as an authority which I want to disclaim emphatically.

PART ONE

THE PREPARATORY PHASE

Descriptive Psychologie
oder
beschreibende Phänomenologie
1888/89.

1. First page of Franz Brentano's lecture notes
on "Descriptive Psychology or Describing Phenomenology"

I

FRANZ BRENTANO (1838–1917): FORERUNNER
OF THE PHENOMENOLOGICAL MOVEMENT

1. Brentano's Place in the History of Phenomenology

How far is it legitimate to begin the history of the Phenomenological Movement with Franz Brentano? Certainly Brentano
himself did not claim to be a phenomenologist, although he lived
long enough to see the Phenomenological Movement spread even
beyond Husserl. In fact, as far as he followed Husserl's development at all, his reaction, in spite of his persistent friendship and
good will, was one of growing bewilderment and dismay.[1]

Nevertheless, the term "phenomenology" does occur in Brentano's unpublished writings, for instance, as the alternative title
of his notes for the course on Descriptive Psychology which he
gave at the University of Vienna in 1888–1889. But apparently
this was only during a transitional phase of his philosophical
development.[2] Thus Brentano's inclusion in the history of phe-

[1] According to his own statements in his unpublished correspondence, especially
with Oskar Kraus and Anton Marty, Brentano never read any of Husserl's mature
and especially his phenomenological publications, partly because after 1902 his eye-
sight no longer allowed him any first-hand study. Husserl himself, in an important
correspondence between 1904 and 1906, which deserves publication, and again on
the occasion of his visit with Brentano in Florence in 1907, tried hard to interpret
his independent development to the revered master, but, as he himself felt, with
little success. See his "Erinnerungen an Franz Brentano" in Oskar Kraus, *Franz Brentano* (München, Beck, 1919), p. 165 f., and Brentano's account of his visit in a letter
to Hugo Bergmann of March 27, 1907 published in *PPR* VII (1946), 93.

[2] The original of the highly interesting notes for the course on "Deskriptive Psychologie oder beschreibende Phänomenologie" (Ps 77) is now among the posthumous
papers in the possession of Dr. John C. M. Brentano, who kindly permitted me to
inspect them. (Husserl's studies under Brentano (1884–1886) preceded this text by
more than two years.) According to Oskar Kraus (Introduction to Franz Brentano's
Psychologie vom empirischen Standpunkt. Leipzig, Felix Meiner, 1924, p. XVII),
Brentano had announced this course the year before simply as *"Deskriptive Psychologie,"* (Ps 76) a title which, judging from Brentano's own Introduction to *Vom Ur-*

nomenology must be justified by deeper reasons. These could be found in Husserl's repeated and unstinted acknowledgments of his decisive debt to Brentano. But so did he acknowledge his debt to William James, as we shall see later. Also, Husserl never tried to pin the label of phenomenology on the man whom he called "my one and only teacher in philosophy." Thus the main reason for crediting Brentano with having prepared the ground for phenomenology must be sought in specific elements of his philosophy which have influenced and even permeated the full-fledged phenomenology of Husserl and his successors.

Obviously, this does not require or justify a full account of Brentano's philosophy, much as it deserves it for its own sake.[1] Instead, what I propose to do is first to give an idea of Brentano's basic philosophical objectives and then to show how those features of his philosophy are a result of this primary and pervading concern.

2. Brentano's Purpose: A Scientific Reformation of Philosophy

What even Brentano's more independent students described as the most impressive fact about his personality and about his teaching was his almost messianic sense of a mission.[2] What exactly was this mission, as he conceived of it? He never undertook to state it programmatically. Nevertheless, occasional statements and his actions make it plain that he considered it

---

sprung sittlicher Erkenntnis (1889), he even planned to use for a new book. Two years later (1890–91) the same course is announced under the title "Psychognosie." (El 74) Hence it would seem that the term "Phänomenologie" in the title of the 1888–89 notes, which, as far as I could establish, is not resumed and discussed in the lectures themselves, reflects Brentano's dissatisfaction with the first title and his efforts to replace it by a better one. In any event, since Brentano's psychology was conceived from the very start as a study of psychological phenomena, the choice of such a term was obvious enough without any need to credit it, for instance, to Sir William Hamilton, with whose writings, incidentally, Brentano was fully familiar; witness his *Psychologie vom empirischen Standpunkt*. The fact that Brentano also spoke of physical phenomena would of course have been against the choice of the term as the title for a new psychology. This would have been different with a term like *"phänomenale Psychologie,"* which does occur in places as early as 1874. See, e.g., *Psychologie vom empirischen Standpunkt* (ed. O. Kraus), p. 105.

[1] This has been done, at least for Brentano's last but also least influential phase, in Alfred Kastil's posthumous monograph, *Die Philosophie Franz Brentanos* (Francke, Bern, 1951), unfortunately without sufficient references to the sources of this account.

[2] Carl Stumpf, "Erinnerungen an Franz Brentano" in Oskar Kraus, *Franz Brentano*, pp. 90, 116; also Edmund Husserl, "Erinnerungen an Franz Brentano," *op. cit.*, p 154.

2. Franz Brentano at about twenty

his task to bring about a "universal revolution, or better, a fundamental reformation of philosophy" in the service of mankind.[1] This reformation had both a negative and a positive side. On the negative side it involved for Brentano himself a radical emancipation from the merely traditional beliefs of his personal background and his age. Positively it meant a new sustained effort to restore a philosophy which, as a result of preoccupation with practical concerns, of scepticism, and of dogmatic mysticism had undergone decline after decline from the dignity of a conscientious attempt to achieve theoretical knowledge. Its ultimate objective, however, was to remain "wisdom," a wisdom which, as Brentano confidently believed, would yield a proof of the divine source of all being. But such a renewed philosophy in the spirit of its ascending phases, as it prevailed among the Greeks until Aristotle, in the age of Thomas Aquinas and in modern philosophy from Bacon to Leibniz, would have to eschew all aspirations to grandiose speculative constructions.

Brentano was ready to pay the price for such a reformation, even in the form of personal suffering and professional disappointments – and these he certainly had to undergo. His most painful and most fateful emancipation was that from his native religious faith. Born of a well-to-do Catholic family, which in spite of its Italian name had been established in Southern Germany for centuries, Franz Brentano reflected the religious seriousness of the Romantic period to the extent that for eight years he tried to combine the career of a philosopher with the life of a priest. Yet even in the theses he presented at his inauguration as a lecturer ("*Habilitation*") at the University of Würzburg, he proclaimed the complete independence of philosophy from theology. However, the occasion which first shook the pattern of his life and faith to the foundations was the struggle that preceded the proclamation of the dogma of papal infallibility. No mean theologian himself, Brentano prepared a special brief against it, which Bishop Ketteler, one of the leaders of the unsuccessful opposition to the dogma, presented to the assembled German Bishops in Fulda.[2] The defeat in this struggle against

---

[1] See, e.g., *Über die Zukunft der Philosophie* (Leipzig, Meiner, 1929), p. 12.
[2] For this episode see Alfred Kastil's Introduction to Franz Brentano, *Die Lehre*

extreme ecclesiastical authoritarianism neither made Brentano capitulate, after the fashion of his ecclesiastical sponsors, nor join the secession of the Old Catholics under the leadership of Ignaz Döllinger. Henceforth he worked out his religious problem by himself, trying to remove the contradictions between "so-called supernatural revelation" and reason, and rejecting such dogmas as the trinity, the incarnation, and eternal punishment. Some of his posthumous works, in fact his most voluminous one, "*Vom Dasein Gottes*," contain the systematic development of a philosophical religion, for which, however, he did not proselytize. Much of it resembles the views of the eighteenth century Deists, although Brentano continued to believe in direct divine providence. Yet he was not a rationalist either. One of the finest expressions of his general attitude can be found in a letter to his pupil and friend, Carl Stumpf, which contained the following sentences:

To me a man who does not contemplate hardly seems to be living, and a philosopher who does not cultivate and practice contemplation is not worthy of his name: he is not a philosopher but a scientific craftsman and among the philistines the most philistine.[1]

Brentano's separation from the Church, including as it did his one-sided resignation from the priesthood, cost him at once his philosophical career in Würzburg, where he had taught for seven years with brilliant success. In 1874 he was appointed to a full professorship at the University of Vienna, but he had to resign again when, after six years, he decided to marry. Continuing for fifteen more years as a mere unsalaried lecturer ("*Privatdozent*"), he counted among his numerous productive students of this period such men as Alexius Meinong and Edmund Husserl. Finally, in 1895, when the Austrian authorities refused him the permanent appointment which he had reason to expect, he retired from teaching completely, spending the rest of his life as a private scholar in Italy and Switzerland, while some of his students made spectacular careers in the academic world. Two of these, who have become of considerable importance for the

Jesu und ihre bleibende Bedeutung (Leipzig, Meiner, 1922), p. IX. – Brentano's brief has now been published by Ludwig Lembert in *Archiv für mittelrheinische Kirchengeschichte VII* (1955), 295–334.

[1] Carl Stumpf, "Erinnerungen an Franz Brentano" in Oskar Kraus, *Franz Brentano*, p. 93.

Phenomenological Movement, shared not only Brentano's denominational background, but followed him also in his religious secession: Carl Stumpf, who, inspired by his example, had even entered a seminary for the priesthood, and Anton Marty, who had actually taken orders. It was thus clearly more than a coincidence that the new philosophical movement was matched by a rejection of dogmatic authority in religion, a rejection which was preceded by a serious examination of its credentials and by a sincere attempt to experience the life demanded by faith.[1]

One more emancipation deserves mention as a sign of Brentano's moral independence. Coming from a politically liberal German family, whose most outspoken and best-known member was his younger brother, the economist Lujo Brentano, Franz had never been a German nationalist. But unlike other success-drugged liberals he never became reconciled to the unification of Germany by Prussian force, nor did he overlook in the "Realpolitik" of Bismarck's Reich the danger to the freedom and integrity of the individual and the seeds for international disaster.[2] He opposed the philosophy of "might is right" and was even a decided pacifist.[3] In fact, he felt increasingly as a citizen of the world, to whom national citizenship meant very little. But of even greater importance here is the complete absence of philosophic and scientific nationalism from Brentano's philosophizing. It accounts in part for his interest – still rather unfashionable in Germany at that time – in such thinkers as Auguste Comte, John Stuart Mill, and Herbert Spencer. It seems characteristic both for the time and for Brentano that he found it necessary to include in the preface of his *Psychologie* of 1874 the following paragraph:

There can be no such thing as a peculiarly national psychology – were it even a German one – as little as there is a peculiarly German truth. This is why I have taken account in my work of the eminent achievements of the modern English philosophers no less than of those of the Germans.

Yet in the present context Brentano's most important emancipation remains that of his philosophizing. While at the time of his initial studies the primacy of Neo-Thomism was not yet fully

---

[1] One of the strongest expressions of this anti-authoritarianism occurs in an open letter in which in 1901 Brentano supported Theodor Mommsen in his struggle for freedom from presuppositions in science (*voraussetzungslose Forschung*) and specifically against endowed denominational chairs in State universities. It contained the following sentences: "As we see it, the one who sins against truthfulness is not he who speaks and teaches as a believer, but rather he who tries to market under the label of pure science propositions to which he is committed by his creed. ... However great our respect for positive religious thinking may be, it is a fact that it lacks self-evidence. Neither is it immediate insight nor is it knowledge stringently deduced therefrom." *Die vier Phasen der Philosophie* (Leipzig, Meiner, 1926), p. 138 f.

[2] See, for instance, his *Last Wishes for Austria* and his letter to Herbert Spencer in 1872, quoted in Alfred Kastil, *op. cit.*, pp. 12 f.

[3] *Vom Ursprung sittlicher Erkenntnis*. Second edition (Leipzig, Meiner, 1921), p. 10; see also Appendix V: *Epikur und der Krieg* (pp. 87–91).

established among Catholic philosophers, it is obvious that the scholastic tradition was his major point of departure. It was, in fact, Aristotle who became the focus of his philosophical studies, and while he considered the Aristotelian system as ultimately untenable, he nevertheless devoted to it all the energies of his considerable historical scholarship, beginning with his important doctoral thesis *Von der mannigfachen Bedeutung des Seienden nach Aristoteles* (On the Multiple Meaning of "What is" according to Aristotle). As to Thomas Aquinas and the Scholastics in general, with whose writings he was of course as familiar as one could expect during the early days of Neo-Scholasticism, he criticized them much more freely than he did Aristotle in his *Psychologie*. However, his main opposition was directed against the German Idealists beginning with Kant, who, except for a certain esthetic merit, represented for him nothing but the declining phase of one of the great periods of philosophy, in which Bacon, Descartes, Locke, and Leibniz were the peaks. This repudiation was based on considerable familiarity with Kant and Schelling, while his direct acquaintance with Hegel seems questionable.

This determined emancipation from the philosophic tradition of the time made him also look for support among contemporary thinkers. He found some of it in science-minded German philosophers like Lotze, but even more in foreign thinkers like the French positivists and the British empiricists. In fact, Brentano engaged John Stuart Mill in a considerable correspondence – the Brentano Archives contain eleven unpublished letters – while preparing his *Psychologie vom empirischen Standpunkt.* Especially from the letter quoted by Brentano in this work and from the subsequent invitation to Mill's retreat in Avignon it appears that Mill was impressed by Brentano's originality. Mill's sudden death prevented a personal meeting which might well have become memorable for Brentano's development. However when soon afterwards he visited England, he made there the direct acquaintance of such independent spirits as Herbert Spencer and Henry Newman (later Cardinal), and of such religious non-conformists as the evolutionist St. George Jackson Mivart and the critical Bible scholar William Robertson Smith.

If these events show the negative side of Brentano's reformatory spirit, what was the goal of his reconstructive efforts?

At least in one respect Brentano shared the ambitions of the positivists from his very start as an independent philosopher. In his fourth habilitation thesis of 1866 he had proclaimed that "the true method of philosophy is none other than that of natural science." Similarly, in his inaugural lecture in Vienna "On the Reasons for Despondency in Philosophy" and in his later lecture on "The Future of Philosophy" he not only tried to refute the arguments of the critics of philosophy, but recommended again imitating the method of the concrete natural sciences. By the same token Brentano resisted the temptation to build a system of his own rather than to make solid contributions to the investigation of limited topics.

On the other hand, unlike the positivists, Brentano was by no means ready to abandon the goal of a metaphysics pursued in the scientific and critical spirit of Aristotle. "However philosophy may have misjudged its limits: there remains for it an area of questions whose answer need not be abandoned and, in the interest of mankind, cannot be abandoned." [1]

3. A New Psychology as the Foundation for Scientific Philosophy

Where, then, can philosophy hope to find a basis for such a scientific renewal? Certainly not in an uncritical return to Aristotle, which Brentano had never intended; for according to Carl Stumpf's account of Brentano's Würzburg years, even his first course on metaphysics revealed his disagreement with "the Philosopher" in such basic matters as the list of categories and in the distinction of matter and form. In lecturing on the founder of positivism, August Comte, on whose philosophy he even published a "first article," [2] he explored sympathetically the

[1] Über die Zukunft der Philosophie (Leipzig, Felix Meiner, 1929), p. 98. When soberly examined, the reasons generally given for the hopelessness of the metaphysical enterprise seemed to him inconclusive, once it was realized that the "mysticism" and "dogmatism" of the German Idealists was nothing but a travesty of genuine metaphysics. Now the time seemed ripe for a slow reconstruction based on the adoption of the best methods and results of the science of the day. The case for such a reconstruction was to Brentano all the more urgent. For he believed that in his days only philosophy could fill mankind's needs for convincing answers to metaphysical, moral, and religious questions, answers which in Brentano's opinion the churches were no longer able to supply.

[2] "Auguste Comte und die positive Philosophie" in Chilianeum. Blätter für katholische Wissenschaft, Kunst und Leben. Neue Folge, II (1869), 16–37, re-

chances of the positivistic renewal, asserting that in spite of
Comte's atheism "perhaps no other philosopher of recent time
deserved our attention as much as Comte." Nevertheless, he did
not follow Conte in his wholesale condemnation of metaphysics.
Even less could he accept his repudiation of psychology. In fact,
the discussion of the problem of immortality in his lectures
involved him for the first time in an extensive treatment of
psychological questions.[1] This, in combination with his intensive
study of John Stuart Mill, must have confirmed his conclusion
that psychology was to be the proper lever for the necessary
reform of philosophy and for the restoration of a scientific
metaphysics, a belief which finds vivid expression both in his
inaugural Vienna lecture and in the Preface to his *Psychology*
(1874).

Thus far Brentano seemed to be slated for an uncritical
adoption of the nineteenth century psychologies of a James,
Mill, Fechner, Wundt, or Lotze, and the stage set for a classical
demonstration of *"psychologism."* What changed this prospect
was Brentano's realization that none of these psychologies could
fill his specifications. What they seemed to lack was the indispensable preliminary clarification of their fundamental concepts.
It was this basically philosophic task which absorbed Brentano
in his psychological studies, much as he utilized in them the
beginnings of a scientific psychology as far as it existed at the
time. In fact, what he hoped for from his own approach was that
it would make this psychology truly scientific and replace the
many rivalling psychologies of his day by *one* psychology. Only
after the development of such a psychology would it be possible
to approach the final metaphysical questions such as the relation
between mind and body and the chances of immortality, which
remained Brentano's ultimate concern, although he never published anything on these subjects and none of his pertinent manuscripts have been printed.[2]

Hence, most of Brentano's actual psychological work may

printed in *Die vier Phasen der Philosophie* (Leipzig, Meiner, 1926), p. 99 ff. – No
further articles appeared.

[1] Carl Stumpf, "Erinnerungen an Franz Brentano" in Oskar Kraus, *Franz
Brentano*, p. 106.

[2] For a synthetic reconstruction of his views of the "spirituality and immortality
of the soul" by Alfred Kastil, see *Religion und Philosophie* (Bern, Francke, 1954),
p p. 185 ff.

fittingly be described as philosophical prolegomena to an empirical psychology. It is typical of Brentano's conscientious and almost over-scrupulous way of treatment that he never let himself be rushed into premature conclusions. Nor did he publish-more than the first part of his psychology, covering not more than two of the six books which he had been planning. All he did later (in 1911) was to republish some of its chapters in an enlarged edition. But he also left a vast number of manuscripts, some of which have been published posthumously.

4. A New Type of Empiricism

There can be no doubt that when Brentano published the first volume of his *Psychologie vom empirischen Standpunkt*, he followed closely the tradition of modern empiricism. It begins with the following momentous sentences:

> The title I gave to my book characterizes its subject-matter and its method. My standpoint in psychology is empirical: Experience alone is my teacher. But I share with others the conviction that a certain ideal intuition (*"ideale Anschauung"*) can well be combined with such a standpoint.

While the acceptance of the empirical source of knowledge is unequivocal, one might well wonder about the additional source of knowledge indicated by the phrase *"ideale Anschauung."* The *Psychologie* itself gives no explicit clarification nor does any other of Brentano's published writings. Not even his expositors seem to have tried to clarify it. However, a reading of the book in the light of this phrase makes it plain enough that Brentano's accounts of psychological phenomena were based largely on a consideration of idealized types rather than on detailed observation and compilation of concrete cases with all their complexities. In other words, "ideal intuition" was not only a selective experience but also largely one stylized for its typical or essential features.

There are even indications that in the subsequent elaboration of his own thought, Brentano did not altogether reject non-empirical sources of knowledge. While he always repudiated a priori knowledge after the manner of Kant's synthetic a priori (to Brentano a completely gratuitous prejudice), he did admit more and more the occurrence and importance of insights other than those gained by mere induction from experience. It is significant that this happens chiefly in his ethical writings, specifically in a note added to his lecture *Vom Ursprung sittlicher Erkenntnis* (1891) which refers to insights about the goodness or badness of love and hatred respectively as achieved "at one stroke and without any induction." [1] Nevertheless, Brentano wants this type of knowledge to be interpreted as a special kind of experience capable of revealing necessities and impossibilities in the relationships between empirical phenomena such as love and hatred, much as these themselves are given by experience in the primary sense. It is apparent that Brentano was moving toward the recognition of a new type of experience not allowed for in traditional empiricism and foreshadowing a new and widened epistemology.

5. Descriptive Psychology versus Genetic Psychology

The contents of Brentano's "empirical psychology" might well surprise the empirical psychologist in today's sense. For, at least in the published parts, little if any space is devoted to the presentation and discussion of the concrete findings of psychology up to his time, although Brentano showed and presupposed familiarity with them and studied some of the basic questions they raise. Thus the Weber-Fechner laws are examined critically, while the laws of association never occur. In fact, it was only gradually and after the publication of his first volume that Brentano himself fully realized the newness of his own approach. According to Oskar Kraus, this realization even accounts for the abandonment of the projected later volumes. He tried to develop the new approach in his still unpublished Vienna lectures (on "Descriptive Psychology" or "Psychognostics"). The new psychology was to comprise two major divisions: descriptive psychology and genetic psychology. Of these, descriptive psychology was to be the basic part. For according to Brentano any causal study of psychological phenomena was hopeless before the psychologist had sufficiently clarified and described what it

---

[1] *Vom Ursprung sittlicher Erkenntnis.* Second Edition (Leipzig, Meiner, 1921), p. 61 and other passages quoted there. See also his Vienna Lectures on Logic (1874–1895), now published in *Die Lehre vom richtigen Urteil* (Bern, Francke Verlag, 1956), pp. 162 ff., where he criticizes explicitly Mill's rejection of a priori knowledge.

was that he wanted to explain. While at the time such a descriptive psychology, and in fact its very name, was apparently a complete innovation, Brentano believed that he had precedents for his distinction in the subdivisions of several other sciences, notably in descriptive anatomy and physiology, or, even more explicitly, in the descriptive part of geology, at one time called "geognosy," and its causally oriented counterpart, once called "geogony." ("Petrography" and "petrogenesis" are more limited terms, still in current use.) Thus he even coined the name *"Psychognosie"* for the study of the descriptive part of psychology, to which he devoted his major efforts in the field.

How far does the parallel between descriptive psychology and the so-called descriptive sciences really apply? Only a close comparison of the two enterprises in action can tell the full story. Yet it would seem that enterprises such as descriptive anatomy, while much more intricate in their concrete assignments, had their jobs already laid out for them as far as subject-matter and major subdivisions were concerned, with the main articulations of the phenomena clearly indicated. This was certainly not the case with the descriptive psychologist, faced with the problem of how to confine and how to divide his sprawling, elusive, and amorphous territory. In fact, it was precisely this problem of identifying clearly the subject-matter and the basic divisions of the phenomena, rather than their detailed description, which became Brentano's preoccupation in descriptive psychology. Clearly, before any such descriptions can make scientific sense to us, we have to know the basic articulation of the field and the chief categories that we can use for its description. For instance, are sensations, feelings, judgments separate phenomena of equal rank? Here the prerequisites of any protocol description seem to be either missing or highly controversial. It thus appears that what descriptive psychology demands at the very outset, as a basis for any description and classification, is a peculiar intuitive examination of the phenomena for their primary properties, for their "natural affinities," and for their diversities. Thus description, as it occurs in Brentano's case, is based primarily on careful intuitive consideration of the structural properties of the phenomena as to general features and specific characteristics. This is certainly a very different thing from the mere routine description of the butterfly collector or the cataloguer, who has his field and his descriptive categories all cut out for him.

Still another fact about this new descriptive psychology should be noted: Brentano asserts its logical priority over, and relative independence of, genetic psychology, and consequently of the natural sciences like physics and physiology, which he himself had previously heralded as the entering wedge and bright hope of a scientific future for psychology. This is the beginning of a reversal in the relative position of these sciences, under which a "pure" psychology, i.e., a psychology free from non-psychological admixtures, will try to supply its own basis and indirectly one of the bases for sciences like psychophysics and physiological psychology, which thus far seemed to take precedence. Psychology no longer takes its cue from the other natural sciences; it establishes itself as an autonomous enterprise, if not as a separate one.

6. A New Type of Experience: Inner Perception versus Introspection

How can such an autonomous descriptive psychology hope to succeed? Would this not mean relapsing into the type of introspection which ever since Comte's attack has been, if not completely discredited, at least under grave suspicion?

Brentano's answer to this apprehension consisted in pointing out the difference between two types of awareness of psychological phenomena, related though they were. As far as purposive self-observation or introspection was concerned, he shared the common distrust of its reliability. He did however not admit any such defect in inner perception, the immediate awareness of our own psychological phenomena, of our joys or desires, our sadness or rage. To this awareness, restricted, to be sure, to the immediate present, Brentano even ascribed infallible self-evidence. However, such inner perception was possible only "in the margin" (*nebenbei*), while our main attention was turned toward external objects in a perception which he considered to be always fallible. Consequently, it still remained impossible to lay hold of the content of this self-evident inner perception as explicitly as a psychological science would require. Brentano's way out of this dilemma was his claim that it was always possible to observe the immediate trace of an inner perception while it was still within the range of immediate memory. This solution admittedly introduced a first source of possible error. But Brentano believed that it offered enough of a basis for an empirical science of psychology, and that it did so even in the case of those strong emotions which could not be directly observed when experienced. Nevertheless, Brentano's solution leaves us with the paradox of a self-evidence whose range, restricted as it is to the experiencer's immediate present, would seem to be infinitesimally small, and which, as far as accessibility to the psychologist through the mediation of memory is concerned, is certainly no longer illusion-proof. While thus the distinction leaves self-evidence intact for prescientific experience, it denies it to the psychological scientist. His only comfort would be that he shares his plight with all other scientists.

7. "Intentionality": The Basic Psychological Phenomenon

Brentano's first concern in psychology was to find a characteristic which separates psychological from non-psychological or "physical" phenomena.[1] It was in connection with this attempt that he first developed his celebrated doctrine of intentionality as the decisive constituent of psychological phenomena.

The sentence in which he introduces the term "intentionality" is of such crucial importance that I shall render it here in literal translation:

Every psychical phenomenon is characterized by what the Scholastics of the Middle Ages called the intentional (or sometimes the mental) inexistence of an object, and what we should like to call, although not quite unambiguously, the reference (*Beziehung*) to a content, the directedess (*Richtung*) toward an object (which in this context is not to be understood as something real) or the immanent-object-quality (*immanente Gegenständlichkeit*). Each contains something as its object, though not each in the same manner. In the representation (*Vorstellung*) something is represented, in the judgment something is acknowledged or rejected, in

[1] Brentano's use of the term "phenomenon" has neither "phenomenological" nor "phenomenalist" implications; nor is it related to the Kantian distinction between "phenomenon" and "noumenon." He uses it exactly in the same sense as did the scientists of the time and as his philosophical neighbors, Auguste Comte and John Stuart Mill. In so doing he wants to avoid specifically any premature commitment to the metaphysical assumptions of a "psychology with a soul," after the manner of Aristotle or Descartes. To be sure, there are indications of a much more critical and advanced concept of "Phänomen" at the beginning of Brentano's lectures on "*Deskriptive Psychologie oder beschreibende Phänomenologie*" of 1888–1889.

desiring it is desired, etc. This intentional inexistence is peculiar alone
to psychical phenomena. No physical phenomenon shows anything like
it. And thus we can define psychical phenomena by saying that they are
such phenomena as contain objects in themselves by way of intention
(*intentional*).[1]

Actually, this first characterization of the psychological
phenomenon makes use of two phrases: "intentional inexistence"
and "reference to a content." It is the first of these phrases
which has attracted most attention, and it has even given rise
to the view, supported by both anti-scholastics and neo-scholastic
critics, that this whole doctrine was nothing but a loan from
medieval philosophy. While a quick reading of the passage may
seem to confirm this view, it is nevertheless misleading. "Intentional inexistence," which literally implies the existence of
an "intentio" inside the intending being, as if imbedded in it,
is indeed a Thomistic conception. But it is precisely this
conception which Brentano himself did not share, or which in
any case he abandoned, to the extent of finally even dropping
the very term "intentionality." [2]

Thus, the second characterization of the psychic phenomenon, "reference to an object," is the more important and the
only permanent one for Brentano; it is also the one listed ex-

---

[1] *Psychologie vom empirischen Standpunkt* I, Buch II, Kapitel I § 5 (pp. 125 f.)

[2] Brentano's originality is revealed by a comparison of his usage with that of
Thomas Aquinas. For the term "intentio," as used in scholastic philosophy, signifies
the peculiar image or likeness formed in the soul in the process of acquiring knowledge,
thus representing, as it were, a kind of distillate from the world outside. This "intentio'
is linked up with the so-called species theory of human knowledge, which goes back
to Aristotle's theory of perception as the reception of the form of an object without
its matter. Thomas Aquinas distinguishes actually an *intentio sensibilis*, an *intentio
intelligibilis*, and at times even an *intentio intellecta*. In a similar vein, the much-used
scholastic terms *prima* and *secunda intentio* refer to concrete objects and to logical
categories, respectively. Never is there any suggestion of a reference to an object
as the distinguishing characteristic of these "intentions."

Comparing this conception of intention with Brentano's, one notices first that
Brentano never uses the term "intention" in isolation but only in combinations like
"intentional inexistence" or "intentional relation," phrases which have no standing
among the genuine Scholastics. Nor does he ever mention formal images of the
scholastic type. It is true that wherever he uses the adjective "intentional" he still
betrays traces of the scholastic doctrine about the immanence of the object known
within the soul. But it was this very doctrine of the mental inexistence of the object
of knowledge in the soul which Brentano came to reject during what Brentano
scholars call the crisis of immanence ("*Immanenzkrise*") of 1905. Subsequently, as
far as I can make out, even the term "intentional" disappears from Brentano's
psychological vocabulary; see *Psychologie*, II, 133, Oskar Kraus' Introduction to
III, p. XLIV, and Brentano's own disapproval of his former usage, though for different reasons, in II, 8, second footnote.

clusively in the Table of Contents, beginning with the first edition. What is more: as far as I can make out, this characterization is completely original with Brentano, except for whatever credit he himself generously extends to Aristotle for its "first germs" in a rather minor passage of the *Metaphysics* (1021 a 29). It was certainly none of Brentano's doing that this new wholly unscholastic conception came to sail under the old flag of "intentionality." [1] Reference to an object is thus the decisive and indispensable feature of anything that we consider psychical:

No hearing without something heard, no believing without something believed, no hoping without something hoped, no striving without something striven for, no joy without something we feel joyous about, etc.

Physical phenomena are characterized, by contrast, as lacking such references. It also becomes clear at this point that Brentano's psychological phenomena are always acts, taking this term in a very broad sense which comprises experiences of undergoing as well as of doing, states of consciousness as well as merely transitory processes.

Here, then, Brentano for the first time uncovered a structure which was to become one of the basic patterns for all phenomenological analysis. True, the positivists and even the later William James and more recently Bertrand Russell have tried to get rid of this phenomenon. But on closer examination their major counterarguments turn out to hinge on the alleged superfluousness of this phenomenon in the economy of science and on the possibility of describing the situations involved in terms of various kinds of behavior. But in view of such careful analyses as those of Roderick M. Chisholm [2] it seems more than doubtful that these attempts to dispense with intentionality have been successful. However, superfluous or not, what mattered to Brentano was: What is the verdict of our uncensored experience, however uneconomical?

One obvious and frequent objection to Brentano's use of the

---

[1] For a more detailed and documented account of the terms "intention" and "intentionality," see my article "Der Begriff der Intentionalität in der Scholastik, bei Brentano und bei Husserl" in *Philosophische Hefte*, ed. by Maximilian Beck, V (1936), 72–91.

[2] *Perceiving: A Philosophical Study* (Ithaca, 1957), pp. 168 ff.

concept "intentionality," as a distinguishing characteristic for psychical phenomena, is that it is too narrow. For there are plenty of psychical phenomena – for instance, moods – which have no referents such as perception and desire have. Brentano's anticipating answer to this objection is significant, if only as a sample of the way in which he interprets phenomena which do not fit directly into his pattern. It consists in the distinction between a primary and a secondary object or referent. The primary object is the one outside to which the psychological phenomenon refers; the secondary one is the psychical phenomenon itself. This double reference makes it possible for him to maintain that, while there may be no primary referent to certain psychical phenomena, there always has to be a secondary one; otherwise the phenomenon would not even be conscious. This raises of course the question how far reflexive consciousness is essential to all the phenomena which psychology rightfully covers. Brentano's somewhat sweeping answer is that unconscious psychological phenomena are self-contradictory, hence fictitious.

8. A "Natural" Classification of Psychical Acts

Acts referring to objects are thus the proper study of psychology. Brentano's next question is: What are the basic types of these acts? Perhaps the most significant and lasting of Brentano's findings in his own eyes was the division of the psychological phenomena into three basic classes: "representations" (*Vorstellungen*), judgments (*Urteile*), and what, short of a better name, he called acts of love and hatred (*Lieben und Hassen*), which were to include desires and feelings, a class which in English might best be labelled as "emotive acts." Not that Brentano claimed any originality for this division: as usual he extended generous credit for it to others, in this case especially to Descartes and, for the distinction between representations and judgments, to John Stuart Mill. All the same, Brentano's emphasis on the element of acceptance and rejection in judgment was an original discovery which exerted considerable influence. But just as important to Brentano himself, though less convincing, especially at first sight, was the unification of the emotional and volitional phenomena of feeling and desire under the one heading of "love."

What in this context is possibly even more significant than these distinctions themselves is the way in which Brentano tried to derive them. Since all psychological acts are characterized mainly by their references to objects, it is in the different ways or "qualities" of these references that the main distinction of these classes must be found. Such differences are discovered in immediate experience or, more specifically, in inner perception. But what is the basis for the fundamental classes among these many types of reference and, more specifically, for the rather unusual way of separating representations and judgments on the one hand and for crowding together feeling and desire on the other? Here Brentano refers us once more to a peculiar type of experience. In passing from mere representation to the asserting and denying judgment we encounter a sharp break in the series of phenomena, whereas in going from feeling to willing we find a continuous series of transitions without sharp demarcation lines. It is thus a characteristic experience of continuity or of discontinuity in the serial survey of the phenomena which provides the main basis for a "natural" classification. This fact promises to free classification from the semblance of complete arbitrariness by anchoring it in the essential structures of the phenomena themselves.

9. A Fundamental Law of Psychical Phenomena

At first sight one might suspect that the three fundamental classes of psychical phenomena are all of equal rank. This, however, is by no means Brentano's view. Instead, "representations" constitute the primary phenomena: they provide the indispensable foundation for the phenomena of judgment and love respectively and even form part of them. Brentano's reason for their primacy is their relative simplicity, independence, and omnipresence in all psychological phenomena. As to their relative independence, Brentano points out that while a being without judgment and love, equipped merely with representations, is conceivable, the converse does not hold. Thus a characteristic form of experiment in imagination assists us in tracing these relationships. Hence the law that every psychological phenomenon is either a representation or based upon a representation is not founded on mere induction; yet it presupposes experiential acquaintance with the phenomena. Nor does it seem to be simply true by the definition of a psychical phenomenon. Thus it forms the first of those essential structural relationships of which we are going to hear much more, once we enter the field of phenomenology proper.

10. The Awareness of Time

There is nothing new about the philosophical puzzle of time. But it has assumed fresh poignancy in the philosophizing of the phenomenologists. The fountainhead for this renewed and intensified interest was again in Brentano's thinking.

According to Oskar Kraus no other problem, with the exception of the problem of Deity, took so much of Brentano's attention and effort. The peculiar angle of his attack came from his interest in the question of how time is given in our experience. Specifically, what is the difference in the way we experience present time from the ways in which past and future times appear? Brentano's most important and clearest answer, consistent with his theory of intentional reference, was that the difference lies in the way in which we refer to a phenomenon when we *represent* it, not when we *judge* it. Hence it is our representations which are characterized by temporal modes. Also, while present time is given us directly, past and future times appear to us only indirectly by way of our present representations of ourselves as experiencing the past or as experiencing the future event. Ultimately this led Brentano close to asserting that non-present events are nothing real by themselves but always dependent upon present events. Whatever the merits of Brentano's probings, the approach to the problem of time from the perspective of present givenness proved to be uncommonly provocative and fertile for such students of his as Anton Marty, and especially for Edmund Husserl, who was to use them as the point of departure for his momentous lectures on the inner consciousness of time.

11. An Analogue of Self-Evidence as the Basis for Ethical Knowledge

One area in which Brentano's ideas influenced the Phenomenological Movement without Husserl's mediation is ethics.

But even in Husserl's case it deserves mention that the only lectures of Brentano which Edmund Husserl ever attended were those on practical philosophy, which have now been published.[1] During Brentano's lifetime only one little work of his on ethics appeared, his enlarged Vienna lecture of 1889, entitled *Vom Ursprung sittlicher Erkenntnis*. It is however thus far the only one of his writings which has been published in English translation. In this form it earned the enthusiastic praise of no less a critic than G. E. Moore, who recommended it in 1903 as "a far better discussion of the most fundamental principles of ethics than any others with which I am acquainted" – this in spite of the fact that by implication he found even Brentano guilty of the notorious naturalistic fallacy.[2]

Seemingly this little work was nothing but the result of a special occasion, though it was an occasion which is worth remembering. For it contains Brentano's reply to an earlier lecture given by the foremost German jurisprudent of the time, Rudolf von Jhering, before a lawyer's club in Vienna. In this lecture "On the Genesis (*Entstehung*) of the Feeling of Right and Wrong" Jhering had propounded the typical historical and sociological relativism of nineteenth century students of law, which ridiculed all ideas of a natural law and a justice independent of human enactment, and which interpreted all law as well as all beliefs about right and wrong as merely results of social forces; a relativism which in its implications sanctioned the "might is right" philosophy behind an increasingly cynical power politics. Thus Brentano's answer to Jhering constituted a challenge to the relativistic spirit of the age in general and to its legal philosophy in particular. This did not mean that Brentano denied the historical facts of the genesis of our ideas and feelings of right and wrong. But there remained a question different from that of historical genesis, that of the "sanction" or valid ground of our beliefs, or, as Brentano finally put it, that of the basis (*Ursprung*) of our moral knowledge. That there is knowledge of what is right and wrong by nature is what Brentano made bold to assert. But he did so no longer on mere dogmatic grounds or for the

---

[1] *Grundlegung und Aufbau der Ethik*, edited by Franziska Mayer-Hillebrand (Bern, Francke, 1952).

[2] *International Journal of Ethics* XIV (1904), 115–23. See also *Principia Ethica* (1903) Preface, p. X f.

reasons offered by the neo-scholastic philosophers, the only ones who were still upholding natural law against the concentric attacks of the historical school, the utilitarians, the positivists, and the evolutionists. Nor did Brentano defend any innate ideas of right and wrong, which he, as much as everyone else, consider-ed discredited by the British empiricists. The foundation for his belief in objective standards of right and wrong had to be scien-tific, and he tried to establish it in his new psychology.

The starting point for this psychological deduction of ethical objectivity was Brentano's classification of psychical phenomena. Among these, the theoretical judgment and the emotive acts showed a striking parallelism, not only in being founded on representations, but also in being either positive or negative. Moreover, he found a definite experience of self-evidence attached to certain judgments when they were characterized as, and known to be, true. Now Brentano claimed that even the emotive acts of "love" and "hate" showed similar characteristics. Just as valid thinking according to logical norms presented itself with a character of natural superiority (*natürlicher Vorzug*), so emotive acts, specifically the ones described in ethical norms, presented themselves as right or wrong with an "analogue" of theoretical self-evidence. This "analogue" of the right emotion, just like the genuine self-evidence of the true judgment, was experienced as something very different from the blind preference charac-teristic of mere prejudice. The merely instinctive force of the latter contrasted sharply with the convincingness (*einleuchten*) of genuine self-evidence.

Everyone experiences the difference between the one and the other kind of judging; here, as anywhere else, the final elucidation can consist only in pointing to this experience, just as in the case of any other concept.[1]

These were the differences of which empiricists like David Hume had not been sufficiently aware. To love insight and to hate error were not merely matters of personal taste; these acts were characterized as right with a "self-evidence" comparable to that attached to our belief in the law of contradiction. Similarly, relative degrees of goodness and badness were given in acts of preferring the better to the worse which announced their correct-

---

[1] *Vom Ursprung sittlicher Erkenntnis*, § 26.

ness by the accompanying "self-evidence." However, Brentano admitted that differences in degree of goodness could not be measured with the same scientific accuracy.

The significance of Brentano's attempt to demonstrate that the emotions, hitherto considered as hopelessly subjective and irrational, contain a distinctive character claiming objectivity hardly needs underscoring, even if the experience of this analogue of theoretical self-evidence does not of itself establish its validity, as little as does uncritical self-evidence in the theoretical field.

It should be noted that Brentano's ethical theory does not by any means assert the existence of absolute and eternal values to which our loving or hating responds and which make them right or wrong. All Brentano claims is that certain emotive acts have the peculiar characters of rightness or wrongness attached to them. The experience of "self-evidence," illuminating, as it were, our love as right, is the source of our ethical knowledge and of our assigning rightness and wrongness to certain actions and circumstances in the world. Hence Brentano does not say that our right love is the answer to values in the referents of our emotive acts. One may wonder whether this attempt to base ethics on peculiar features within the emotive acts does not ultimately deprive them of that very convincingness which he had wanted to vindicate for them. For it would seem that according to this theory self-evidence and its emotive analogue simply attach to certain acts like an ultimate brute fact without any further intelligible reason. One would have no insight into the ground why a particular act of love should be characterized as right rather than as wrong except for the ultimate fact that our act of love displays the sign of self-evidence. Why it should display this sign rather than its opposite remains as unintelligible as why a particular wave length should be associated with the color sensation of greenness rather than of redness.

12. Brentano's Fight Against "Fictitious Entities"

At this point it becomes necessary to mention a trend in Brentano's thought which might almost be called anti-phenomenological. It became, in fact, more pronounced in the years after 1901, at the very time when most of his students moved beyond the master by acknowledging a much wider range of phenomena.

Brentano's philosophical universe was fundamentally a simple one, and he wanted to keep it simple. It consisted of physical and psychical phenomena plus whatever his philosophical theology would allow him to add by way of a Divine Being. So Brentano abhorred increasingly any attempt to "multiply entities" in the manner in which this had happened in medieval scholasticism and again in recent speculative philosophy. This made him object strenuously to the recognition of independent status for such non-psychological phenomena or "irrealia" as contents of thought, states of affairs, relations, universals, ideals, values, and norms. All that he could acknowledge was the existence of "res," i.e., of real things and of real thinkers. Universals, being and non-being, possibility and necessity could exist only as thought by such real thinkers. A systematic criticism of language had thus to reinterpret terms which seemingly asserted the independent existence of such entities after the manner of syncategorematic expressions such as conjunctions or particles, which make sense only in combination with names, in the present case with names describing the thinkers of these entities. Otherwise, referents of expressions, ordinary or philosophical, that did not point to physical or psychical objects were to be considered as mere "entia rationis" or fictitious entities. This "reism" was mitigated only by the fact that Brentano, in his determined opposition to nominalism, asserted that all thought about the real could be expressed only in universals and that in fact our experience shows us only what is universal – a doctrine shared to a considerable extent by Bertrand Russell.

It is not easy to determine Brentano's reasons for this retrenchment, which is so peculiar to his later years. It may well be that some of the conclusions of his more original students like Stumpf, Meinong, and Husserl made him increasingly reluctant to admit new and complicating phenomena. Meinong's *Gegenstandstheorie* and Husserl's phenomenology in particular – apparently he saw no difference between the two – appeared to him as utterly fantastic, if not downright traitorous to his own scientific intentions. This refusal to go beyond physical and psychical phenomena, combined with the reinterpretative efforts to find substitutes for "fictitious entities," marks the limit of Brentano's

3. Franz Brentano at about seventy

empiricism and, as seen from the standpoint of later phenomenologists, of his phenomenological approach. But it does not
detract from his fundamental contributions to the development
of a phenomenological philosophy. These might be summed up
once more under the following headings:

α. the widening of traditional empiricism by admitting
experiences hitherto overlooked or neglected, including even
some non-inductive insights into the essential structures and
relationships of empirical material;

β. the development of a new descriptive psychology;

γ. the discovery of intentional reference;

δ. the description of an analogue of self-evidence in ethics.

13. How Far Was Brentano a Representative of "Psychologism"?

It was certainly not without reason that, although according
to all available information Husserl himself had never charged
Brentano with "psychologism," the impression that he had done
so spread immediately after the appearance of the first volume
of Husserl's *Logische Untersuchungen*, in which the name of
Brentano was missing almost too conspicuously. Certainly
Brentano himself was very sensitive to this impression, even
though Husserl in private conversation and by letter tried his
utmost to undo it.

In one sense – the strict sense of the term used by Husserl in
his book – the charge would certainly not hold: Brentano never
attempted to derive logical from psychological laws, thus converting them into merely probable inductive generalizations
with the ensuing sceptical and relativistic consequences.[1]
On the contrary, Brentano had made it amply clear that he
considered logic to be beyond the range of legitimate scepticism,
and that to him the case for certain and reliable knowledge was
fully established.

But there is another sense of the term "psychologism" in

---

[1] It is, however, true that in his lectures on Logic, given between 1874 and 1895
and now published by Franziska Mayer-Hillebrand under the title *Die Lehre vom
richtigen Urteil* (Bern, Francke, 1956), Brentano stated repeatedly that logic, as the
theory of correct judgment, borrows some of its propositions from psychology (p. 4),
that it even presupposes the results of psychology (p. 7), and that it depends chiefly
upon this science (p. 15); in other words, psychology is a necessary, though presumably not the sufficient, foundation of logic.

which the matter is not so clear: namely, the view that what is not physical must be psychical, and consequently that psychology must be the basic science for all but the physical sciences. This view can indeed be traced in and illustrated from a considerable number of Brentano's writings. Thus in his inaugural Vienna lecture of 1874 he had given psychology in its relation to the social sciences and "all the other branches of philosophy" a role parallel to that of mathematics and dynamics in their relation to the natural sciences. In fact, when Brentano finally rejected all non-physical and non-psychical contents of thinking as mere fictitious entities, it became inevitable to assign to all "non-real" things, including logical laws, a merely psychological status.

But even if, to Brentano, psychology is thus the basic science for a scientific philosophy, we must bear in mind what we have found out about the transformations of this psychology in his new pattern of thought. For his is no longer a psychology based on, and waiting for, physics and physiology, but a pure psychology based on independent sources. It is no longer an associationist psychology but one based on the "intentional" or reference structures of the psychological phenomena and acknowledging characters like self-evidence among the psychic acts. And it is a psychology not restricted to mere induction, but one which allows for a new type of experience giving access to immediate structural insights. Thus, while eventually Brentano remains a believer in psychology as the necessary if not the sufficient foundation of philosophy, it is at least a psychology liberated from the physicalism and physiologism of the preceding period, which had given rise to the sceptical psychologism that was to become the target of Husserl's counterattack.

SELECTIVE BIBLIOGRAPHY

Major Works

Psychologie vom empirischen Standpunkt (1874); incomplete second edition with supplements under the title *Klassifikation der psychischen Phänomene* (1911). The posthumous edition in 3 volumes by Oskar Kraus (1924, 1925, 1928) contains further additions and editorial introductions and notes.

Translations: Spanish (1935), French (1944), English (by D. B. Terrell) in preparation, parts of which are to appear in Chisholm, Roderick, ed., *Realism and the Background of Phenomenology* (Chicago, Free Press).
Vom Ursprung sittlicher Erkenntnis (1889)
  Translations: English, under the title *The Origin of the Knowledge of Right and Wrong* (1902), by Cecil Hague – adequate, but not beyond improvement.

Major Posthumous Publications

Versuch über die Erkenntnis (Kastil) (1925)
Vom Dasein Gottes (Kastil) (1929)
Wahrheit und Evidenz (Kraus) (1930)
Grundlegung und Aufbau der Ethik (Mayer-Hillebrand) (1952)
Religion und Philosophie (Mayer-Hillebrand) (1954)
Die Lehre vom richtigen Urteil (Mayer-Hillebrand) (1956)   [2]

Monographs in French and German

GILSON, LUCIE, *Méthode et métaphysique selon F. Brentano*. Paris, Vrin, 1955
——, *La psychologie descriptive selon F. Brentano*. Paris, Vrin, 1955
  Both very competent and helpful studies.
KASTIL, ALFRED, *Die Philosophie Franz Brentanos*. München, Lehnen, 1951
  Published after the death of the author by Franziska Mayer-Hillebrand; attempts a systematic presentation of Brentano's last views; no indexes.
KRAUS, OSKAR, *Franz Brentano*. München, Beck, 1919
  Includes contributions by Carl Stumpf and Edmund Husserl and a complete list of Brentano's publications during his lifetime.

Studies in English

BERGMANN, HUGO, "Brentano's Theory of Induction," *PPR* V (1945), 281–92
BRIGHTMAN, E. S., "The Finite Self," in Barrett, Clifford, ed., *Contemporary Idealism in America*. New York, Macmillan, 1932
  Sections IV and V of this article (pp. 183–192) present B.'s view of the self as an example of a non-idealist but congenial position.
EATON, HOWARD, *The Austrian Philosophy of Value*. Norman, University of Oklahoma Press, 1929
  The first three chapters discuss aspects of Brentano's philosophy relevant to value theory; the chapter on his empirical psychology omits "intentionality."
KUBÁT, DAVID, "Franz Brentano's Axiology. A Revised Conception," *Review of Metaphysics* XII (1958), 133–41
TERRELL, DAILEY BURNHAM, "Intentionality and Metaphysics in the Philosophy of Franz Brentano." Paper read at the annual meeting of the American Philosophical Association, Western Division, in Madison, 1959.

TERRELL, DAILEY BURNHAM, "Franz Brentano's Axiology Some Corrections to Mr. Kubáts Paper," *Review of Metaphysics* XII (1959), [1] 639–48

Ph. D. Theses

BEAR, HARRY, *The Theoretical Ethics of the Brentano School*. A Psycho-epistemological Approach. Columbia University, 1955

ESTALL, HENRY M., *Studies in the Philosophy and Psychology of Franz Brentano*. Cornell University, 1938

TERRELL, DAILEY BURNHAM, *Ethics, Language, and Ontology*. A Study of the Implications of F. Brentano's *Sprachkritik* for Ethical Theory. University of Michigan, 1956

WURZBERGER, WALTER S., *Brentano's Theory of A priori Judgments*. Harvard University, 1951

Most Comprehensive Recent Bibliography

[2] GILSON, LUCIE, *Méthode et métaphysique selon F. Brentano*, pp. 16–23

4. Carl Stumpf (1922)

CARL STUMPF (1848–1936): FOUNDER OF
EXPERIMENTAL PHENOMENOLOGY

1. Stumpf's Place in the History of Phenomenology

The name of Carl Stumpf figures rarely, if ever, in historical accounts of phenomenology. And it is true that by no stretch of definition could Stumpf be turned into a full-fledged phenomenologist. Stumpf himself made this amply clear in his (posthumous) epistemology, where he devoted eleven pages to a severe criticism especially of Husserl's phenomenology. Nevertheless, there is no other philosopher or psychologist of comparable stature and position who has been so important for the spread of phenomenology in the broader sense and for putting the phenomenological approach to scientific use. Hence his significance may actually be greater than that of the Phenomenological Movement in the stricter sense, although those who transmit his impulses may not be aware of them.

At least in one respect the case for including Stumpf in the story of the Phenomenological Movement is stronger than for including Brentano: Stumpf used the term "phenomenology" prominently and permanently to designate a field of studies for which he claimed an important place in the pattern of scientific research. And he did so at a time when Husserl's phenomenology was already in the making, and in clear awareness of this fact.[1]

[1] It is true that, on merely terminological grounds, Husserl has priority over Stumpf. For apparently it was not until 1905, in the Treatise *"Zur Einteilung der Wissenschaften"* (*Abhandlungen der Preussischen Akademie der Wissenschaften*, Berlin 1906), that Stumpf adopted the term, hence four years after the appearance of the second volume of Husserl's *Logische Untersuchungen*, where for the first time Husserl had made extended and specific use of it. What is more, Stumpf, in justifying

There are considerable biographical reasons for putting Stumpf between Husserl and Brentano and, moreover, in close proximity to Husserl. By ten years Husserl's senior, he was the first outstanding student of Brentano to achieve an impressive success for Brentano's way of philosophizing. Thus his spectacular university career took him from the appointment as Brentano's successor in Würzburg at the age of 25, via Prague, Halle, and Munich to Berlin at age 46. It was during the five years in Halle between 1884 and 1888 that he was joined by Husserl, who came to him from Vienna with Brentano's recommendation, first as a graduate student and then as a colleague. The lasting connection between the two Brentano pupils found its most telling expression twelve years after Stumpf's departure from Halle, when Husserl dedicated his first major phenomenological work, the *Logische Untersuchungen*, "to Carl Stumpf, in admiration and friendship."

However, the decisive reason for giving Stumpf as prominent a place as I do here is the role he played in introducing phenomenological methods into psychology and transmitting them to some of its most active researchers. In particular, Stumpf's approach permeated the work of the gestaltists (chiefly through Wolfgang Köhler, Max Wertheimer, and Kurt Koffka), the Group Dynamics movement (through Kurt Lewin), and, indirectly, the new "phenomenological psychology" of Donald Snygg and Arthur W. Combs. In the history of phenomenology Stumpf must be put at the parting of the roads where the wider Phenomenological Movement branched off from the main philosophical current, at a time, to be sure, when Husserl's own conception of phenomenology had not yet fully crystallized. This did not prevent later contacts and cross-fertilization between these branches, although on the whole the interaction

his terminological choice, refers to Husserl's antecedent usage and defends his own as more appropriate. However, as will appear soon, the same does not hold true for the thing named by the term. Here Stumpf could claim priority. The truth about the terminological matter would seem to be that in 1905 Stumpf was still taking advantage of the situation described in my Introduction, where the fairly obvious term was everybody's for the asking, as it had been C. S. Peirce's during the two preceding years (between 1902 and 1904). At that time even Husserl was still far from having developed and formulated a clear conception of his new method, and he certainly did not claim any monopoly of the word. It was not until around 1910 that it became identified with Husserl's new philosophical approach and with the movement which it began to inspire.

seems to have been regrettably weak. Nevertheless, Stumpf's work became the point of departure for a freer and more influential phenomenological movement which also paved the way for a more sympathetic interest in the philosophical and more radical movement initiated by Husserl.

2. The Role of Phenomenology in Stumpf's Work

More than once Stumpf testified that the decisive experience of his academic life was his attendance at the public disputation in Würzburg at which Franz Brentano, then about to begin his teaching at the university, was defending the thesis that the future of philosophy depended on the adoption of the methods of natural science. It was chiefly the idea of a philosophical renaissance after the "dark age" of philosophical speculation which impressed the young Catholic law student, Stumpf.[1] When he gave his inaugural address before the Berlin Academy 28 years later he derived his own work from the

urgent desire to examine questions of fundamental importance, beginning with the concrete materials from specific fields of phenomena, and keeping in intimate touch with the specialized sciences, as opposed to the talk back and forth in half-understood and incompletely defined generalities by which philosophical speculation is so prone to proceed.

Stumpf had therefore no ambition to create a final philosophical system, much as he remained aware of the place of the problems he investigated in the total context of philosophy. But it was significant for him as well as for the whole period that he used as a motto for the autobiographical survey of his work the following passage from his colleague in Berlin, Wilhelm Dilthey:

We spurn construction, love investigation, and react sceptically against the machinery of a system. ... We are content if, at the end of a long life, we have driven multiple shafts of scientific research which lead into the depth of things; we are content to die on the road.

---

[1] Stumpf, who, following Brentano's religious example, attended a seminary for the priesthood for one year, was able to withdraw without creating a scandal and without leaving the Church formally until very much later and for relatively minor reasons. However, his later religious development led Stumpf far beyond Brentano, whose theism was too optimistic for him. He finally adopted a type of Spinozistic pantheism, which rejected Brentano's efforts at a satisfactory theodicy as futile. See his letter to William James in R. B. Perry, *The Thought and Character of William James*, II, 342 ff., 741 ff.

Stumpf considered himself a decided empiricist at least as much as Brentano did. Locke and Leibniz, rather than Kant and Hegel, were his philosophical models. But Hume was not: what he objected to in Hume's version of empiricism was insufficient caution in observing and describing: it had made him overlook phenomena such as the nexus between impressions precisely in the notorious cases of substantial unity and causal dependency. Also, in contrast to Brentano and to positivists like his erstwhile colleague at Prague, Ernst Mach, Stumpf felt no hesitation in recognizing entities other than "things." In fact, the empiricist Stumpf even talked freely of a priori knowledge, which to him, however, did not mean knowledge purged of all experience. On the contrary, this knowledge was to be derived from an analysis of empirical material, not from that of concepts. In analysing this material he tried to discover the structural connections between its elements. However, in order to discover these connections we have to carry out experiments in imagination. But even the experiment in reality proves helpful, if not indispensable, to Stumpf, who was himself one of the pioneers of experimental psychology.[1] But he denied emphatically that this procedure meant anything like induction after the fashion of John Stuart Mill. Instead, he referred to a fundamental capacity of our consciousness to grasp the general in the particular and the necessary in the contingent, something for which the old expression "intuitive knowledge" would be acceptable if it were not loaded with so many misleading associations. Specifically, Stumpf wanted to keep out the idea of a merely passive staring at the phenomena. What he wanted was active exploration by a whole set of mental operations.

Stumpf's life work incorporates the impressive results of this approach. Actually it has left its mark on what is commonly called psychology even more strongly than on philosophy. However, this very division did not make much sense in Stumpf's own eyes. Stumpf opposed "psychologism," a term which he had used even before Husserl and by which he understood the reduction of all philosophical and specifically of all epistemological issues to psychological ones. But he opposed at the same time and much more specifically the anti-psychologistic position of

[1] *Erkenntnislehre*, I, 160.

the Neo-Kantians, who in the name of Critical Philosophy (*Kritizismus*) wanted to remove *all* psychological foundations from philosophy.[1] For Stumpf there could be no watertight compartments, not between the sciences and even less so between philosophy and the sciences: "The prescription of blinkers fails wherever empirical connections are involved, and where deductive insights are impossible." [2] Actually, Stumpf's largest and most influential works, notably his books on the psychological origin of the idea of space (1873) and his two volumes on the psychology of sound (1883 and 1890), sailed at the time under the flag of psychology and contained "descriptive" as well as "genetic" investigations (in Brentano's terms). Nevertheless, in retrospect Stumpf characterized these books, like most of his "psychological" work, as mere phenomenological preparations for psychology.[3]

What was the reason for this surprising reinterpretation? Perhaps the best way to understand this development would be to consider Brentano's concept of the physical phenomenon, the counterpart of his psychical phenomenon, which was the center of Brentano's scientific interest. As to physical phenomena, Brentano had denied them all real existence other than that conferred upon them by being thought about (i.e., "merely intentional existence") on the familiar ground that they contradicted themselves. Primary examples of such physical phenomena are color, sound, and heat. But implicitly Brentano included among them also all the objects of the natural or physical sciences – indeed a rather startling implication in view of his unlimited admiration for the natural sciences as the model even for psychology and philosophy.

Even Brentano had engaged a good deal in the descriptive study of these phenomena, largely under the heading of "psychology of sensation" (*Sinnespsychologie*), with little concern for the fact that according to his own definition of psychological phenomena he was really trespassing on the field of the physical

---

[1] "Psychologie und Erkenntnistheorie" in *Abhandlungen der I. Classe der k. Bayerischen Akademie der Wissenschaften* XIX (1891), pp. 467–508.

[2] "Zur Einteilung der Wissenschaften," p. 34.

[3] "Selbstdarstellung" in Raymund Schmidt, ed., *Die Philosophie der Gegenwart* (Leipzig, Meiner, 1924), p. 40, translated in C. Murchison, ed., *A History of Psychology in Autobiography* (Worcester, Mass., Clark University Press), I (1930), p. 425.

sciences. Apparently it was this fact which led Stumpf increasingly to the realization that there were really two types of physical phenomena: those dealt with traditionally by the psychologists in studies on sensation, and those investigated by the physical sciences proper, such as atoms, molecules, vibrations, and similar items. In other words, Stumpf, like the early explorers, came to see that the continent which he had been investigating was really not the alleged East India of Brentano's psychology but the America of phenomenology, now identified as a continent in its own right.

As early as his *"Tonpsychologie"* of 1883 he had felt the incongruousness of the very term "psychology of sound" and defended this "daring abbreviation" only on the basis of German usage. However, his ultimate objective had always been the study of the psychological effects of sounds by way of experiences or functions in the perceiver. Actually, it was this interest which had lured the unusually musical Stumpf into this vast and fascinating area. After having been detained more or less indefinitely in what he later considered as a mere advanced post (*"Aussenwerk"*) of psychology he came to appreciate the independent significance of these studies. But it was apparently not until the beginning of the new century that he concluded that this was really not psychology at all, but an independent enterprise. Thus, when he finally outlined his system of the sciences in his Academy treatise of 1905, he adopted the term "phenomenology" for the study of the first group of "physical" phenomena distinguished above, leaving the second group to the traditional natural sciences. Phenomenology was thus to take care of what in Brentano's system of the sciences had remained a no man's land between the physical sciences and psychology, while in his actual research he had been confining it unjustifiably to the domain of psychology.

3. General Characteristics of Stumpf's Phenomenology

Having thus mapped out a field for a new science of which he had been giving demonstrations all along, Stumpf now proceeded to describe its nature more explicitly. In what follows I shall attempt to point out the main characteristics of Stumpf's phenomenology in a few programmatic sentences.

a. The subject matter of phenomenology consists of primary and secondary phenomena – By phenomena (*Erscheinungen*) in general Stumpf understands the objective correlates of Brentano's psychical phenomena or acts, or, as he is now going to call them, "psychical functions" (*psychische Funktionen*), in which case the word "function" has, however, no teleological connotation, as it has in the functional psychology of John Dewey, with whose beginnings Stumpf was familiar. In contrast to Brentano, he does not deny reality to these phenomena but emphasizes that as contents they are as real as are the functions. Whether or not they can also exist independently of these functions Stumpf does not want to decide in advance. While he sees no logical contradiction in such an existence, he does not subscribe blindly to the naive realism of our uncriticized beliefs. The decision as to this point has to be left to the physical sciences. – By "primary phenomena" Stumpf understands those contents of our immediate experience which are given to our senses (*Sinneserscheinungen*), by "secondary phenomena" he means the images of these as they occur in memory.

Stumpf's phenomena do not include those contents which are not given to but formed by the mind, such as aggregates (*Inbegriffe*), concepts (*Begriffe*), contents of judgments or states of affairs (*Sachverhalte*) and values (*Werte*), which Stumpf calls "*Gebilde*" (constructs) and assigns to another new discipline, called "*Eidologie.*" Nor does phenomenology include relations as they occur among the phenomena and the *Gebilde*, which he assigns to a third study, called "*Verhältnislehre*" (doctrine of relations).

b. Phenomenology constitutes a neutral science or pre-science ('Vorwissenschaft') – By calling phenomenology a pre-science, Stumpf does not mean to deny it scientific rank. On the contrary, he considers it to be an indispensable foundation of the sciences, both the natural sciences and what in the German tradition he calls "Geisteswissenschaften," i.e., actually the social sciences and the humanities. With relation to this division phenomenology constitutes a neutral science, which supplies the building materials, as it were, for both of them. Its task is the analysis and description of the immediately given contents of our acts or functions, the study of their relationships and of their structural laws preparatory to the study of their causal dependencies on factors other than the phenomena, which is reserved for the sciences proper.

Stumpf credits his erstwhile colleague at the University of Prague, the brilliant physiologist Ewald Hering, with the first clear realization of the need for such a pre-science. Actually Hering himself, in his first communications on the sense of light, especially the most important one of 1874, and even in his final posthumous book *Die Lehre vom Lichtsinn* (1920), never used the term "phenomenology"; nor did he postulate a separate discipline to deal with the phenomena of the optical sense. But it is true that as the first requirement of a scientific study of color he stressed, in opposition to Helmholtz, the need of a conscientious analysis and systematic arrangement of the phenomena regardless of their causal conditions and based exclusively upon the properties of the colors themselves. It was this approach that led to such results as the doctrine of the four basic achromatic simple colors, the "natural system of colors," the discovery of lustre and voluminousness in color, and the distinction between color and brightness.

c. PHENOMENOLOGY IS THE FIRST OF THE NEUTRAL PRE-SCIENCES – After the previous characterization of the three neutral pre-sciences, phenomenology, eidology, and the theory of relations, little if anything will be needed to show that phenomenology is the basic one among them. No constructs can be built without the material supplied by the phenomena, and relations presuppose them directly or indirectly as the relata among which they occur.

d. PHENOMENOLOGY IS NOT AN INDEPENDENT DISCI-PLINE FOR SPECIALISTS, BUT RATHER THE FIRST LAYER IN THE STUDY OF EVERY ESTABLISHED SCIENCE – Stumpf never believed in dissecting the world at the price of destroying connections. Nor did he believe in specialization to the degree of having specialists working in splendid but sometimes rather poverty-stricken isolation. Nor did he want to found a school which set itself off as an orthodox sect against other groups of researchers. Specifically, he did not want phenomenologists with special academic chairs to cultivate his new pre-sciences by themselves. What he did want was to subordinate his new division to the traditional ones and to farm out the new job of phenomenology among physicists, physiologists (of the Hering type), and psychologists. Thus phenomenology was to be simply the basic stage of scientific research, to be treated in the first part of each scientific textbook, and followed by causal research investigating the dependence of these phenomena on factors other than the phenomena.

e. PHENOMENOLOGY, WHILE A DESCRIPTIVE SCIENCE, HAS TO BE STUDIED BY ALL SUITABLE METHODS, IN-CLUDING THE EXPERIMENTAL ONE – The idea of an experimental phenomenology may come as a shock to those who are used to the sublime purism of phenomenology in the philosophical sense. In order to understand what is involved, one has to look a little more closely at what Stumpf himself did in a field like the phenomenology of sound. Studying, for instance, the fundamental properties of simple tones (i.e., those corresponding to vibrations of the sine type) he paid special attention not only to pitch, intensity, and quality but also to the experimentally varied conditions under which these phenomenal properties appeared; likewise, in studying the fundamental musical phenomenon of consonance, he investigated painstakingly under what conditions it was or was not possible to hear the phenomenal partial tones in consonance (or rather "out of it" – the German term is *"heraushören"*) by attention or habitual practice.

While much of this experimental work included study of the physical stimuli and even new methods to control them (such as the destruction of overtones by interference tubes) the purpose of this collateral work was always to allow for the precise selection and presentation of the phenomena. Such control facilitated not only the observation and description but also the variation of the phenomena. Besides, it allowed reliable communication among phenomenological researchers.

Surely, such an experimental phenomenology is not a matter to be accepted uncritically. On the other hand the chance of experimental work in phenomenology has given the phenomenological approach new applications and has yielded substantial results for scientific psychology.

4. Some Concrete Phenomenological Contributions

There would be no dearth of illustrations for Stumpf's type of phenomenology, since he himself characterized his most monumental work, the psychology of sound, as mere phenomenology.[1] In the present context it seems more appropriate to select such specific insights as have proved of particular importance for the development of the Phenomenological Movement, some of them even in Husserl's work.

a. The distinction between dependent and independent parts and the experience of substance and attribute – In examining the relations between such characteristics as spatial extension and color and as pitch and timbre, Stumpf came to distinguish between what he at first called *psychological parts* and later *dependent parts* or *attributes*, i.e., parts which could not be separated, not even in imagination, and *physical* or *independent* parts, which could, such as spatial segments. This separableness or inseparableness appeared to him as something structural, not based on a merely psychological ability or disability of our personal imagining, and thus in his sense as knowable a priori.

With regard to the stalemated problem of substance and attribute this distinction seemed to allow for a new empirical account. While attributes were experienceable as dependent parts, substance was to be interpreted as the whole of such parts in close fusion, and, as such, fully given in experience.

b. The experience of causal nexus – In contrast to Hume, Stumpf claimed that experience, pursued to its full depth, revealed causal linkage among certain phenomena. A

---

[1] For a concise summary of his findings, see his autobiography (*op. cit.*, pp. 40–45; English version in Murchison, ed., *op. cit.*, pp. 425–430).

particularly clear case of such an experience he found in the relation between our attention and its effects on the course and shape of our ideas.

c. THE EXPERIENCE OF "FEEL-SENSATIONS" ('GE-FÜHLSEMPFINDUNGEN') – In the area of the emotions Stumpf advocated, on purely phenomenological grounds, yet only after a careful consideration of alternative theories, the recognition of a new type of sensations which he called *Gefühlsempfindungen*, i.e., of sensations similar in content to feelings. His main point was that elemental feelings such as merely physical pains and pleasures, feelings of bodily well-being and of pleasantness and unpleasantness were, according to their descriptive charac-teristics, very much like simple sensations of color and sound, which had always been recognized as sensations. True, these sensations were strongly tinged by the "function" that responded to them. But they were nevertheless to be sharply distinguished from these functions themselves.

It belongs in the same context that Stumpf opposed the well-known theory which sailed chiefly under the name of his friend William James, according to which body sensations were the basic factors and the true motives of emotions. To Stumpf this was in direct conflict with the immediately given phenomena as we experience them.

d. THE DISCOVERY OF STRUCTURAL LAWS AMONG EMPIRICAL MATERIALS NOT BASED UPON INDUCTION – It was Stumpf who first supplied some of the prize exhibits of what later came to be called phenomenological *"Wesensschau"* or intuition of (material) essences: that color could not be with-out extension, while extension (or better: the extended) was quite conceivable, and even experienced, without color, for instance in the touch experience of a blind mathematician like Saunderson. Among the structural laws in the realm of sounds were some like the one that the line of phenomenal pitches could be extended at both ends indefinitely, being, in con-trast to the phenomenal colors, one-dimensional, and further-more that each conceivable new sound would have a place on this line of pitches. These connections were supposedly necessary and their opposite impossible, not because of the weakness of our imagination, but because of the structure of the phenomena when fully grasped.

e. THE DISCOVERY OF THE 'SACHVERHALT' – In the field of logic Stumpf was the first to face up to the necessity of going beyond Brentano's rigid disjunction between physical and psychical phenomena by acknowledging that there were peculiar entities not falling into either class. Such were the specific "contents" to which our judging acts referred, often called *Urteilsinhalte*, expressed, for instance, in the clause "that there are atoms," which our subsequent acts either acknowledged or rejected. They might well be dependent on these acts, as in fact Stumpf, in assigning them to the "constructs" of his "eidology," seems to have thought. But they were nevertheless distinct from the acts. His name for them, which has prevailed in subsequent phenomenological literature and has spread even beyond, was *"Sachverhalte"* (states of affairs), though Meinong preferred a more technical term, *"Objektiv."* Needless to say, these contents were among the first innovations of Brentano's students of which their master sharply disapproved as "fictitious entities."

What were the lasting contributions of Stumpf to the Phenomenological Movement as a whole? In summary we might put them in the following terms:

α. the identification and painstaking exploration of a field of phenomena not covered by the physical or the psychological sciences in Brentano's sense, as the proper object for a new science under the name of phenomenology;

β. the realization of the importance of a systematic study of this area of neutral phenomena as being the matrix for all the sciences;

γ. the demonstration that this area could be studied with all the rigor of scientific, and even of experimental, techniques;

δ. the discovery of structural laws within the concrete

phenomena of a character fundamentally different from, and more valid than, merely probable inductive generalizations.

5. The Relationship of Stumpf's and Husserl's Phenomenologies

Although a final comparison between Stumpf's and Husserl's phenomenologies would not be possible until we have a full picture of Husserl's thought, some observations on their mutual relations may be meaningful even at this stage.

To begin with, how did they themselves interpret their relationship? Husserl first took official cognizance of Stumpf's phenomenology in 1913 in a note attached to one of the central chapters of his *Ideen zu einer reinen Phänomenologie und phänomenologischen Philosophie*. At that time he had already developed his own version of phenomenology considerably beyond the stage which Stumpf knew in 1905, the year when he adopted the label for his pre-science of phenomena (*Erscheinungen*). To Husserl Stumpf's use of the term had a "completely different meaning," which gave rise to frequent confusions of their ideas. Stumpf's phenomenology was in any case much more limited in scope, α. by the exclusion of "functions" or acts, which had been the chief subject of Husserl's phenomenological studies at the time of the *Logische Untersuchungen*; β. by the restriction to the mere raw materials (the *"hyle,"* as Husserl came to call it) of our full intentional acts; γ. by not having passed through the purging stage of "phenomenological reduction," commonly called "bracketing"; short of this refinement Stumpf's phenomena remained on the level of a mere phenomenological psychology, a level which Husserl could acknowledge as a preparatory phase for his pure phenomenology, but which could claim nothing of the dignity of that fundamental science toward which he was striving.

As seen from Stumpf's side, Husserl's phenomenology had a different character at the time when Stumpf himself adopted the term (1905) from the one it had when he finally looked back at Husserl's full-fledged conception. At the first stage, when even Husserl had not yet dropped the designation "descriptive psychology" for what he was doing, the replacement of Brentano's label by "phenomenology" seemed to Stumpf an unnecessary and misleading innovation; *unnecessary*, because, in order to avoid the dangers of "psychologism" which lurk in a genetic psychology, there was no need to conceal their common subject matter (i.e., acts or functions) by the use of the term "phenomenology," *misleading*, because the term "phenomenology" seemed to Stumpf much more suited as the name for his own badly needed study of *Erscheinungen*. On the other hand, this did not prevent Stumpf from giving ample recognition to Husserl's actual work in the field, particularly in the two Berlin Academy treatises in which he advocated his own new conception.

This appraisal of Husserl changed after the latter's phenomenology had blossomed out under the new light of the phenomenological reduction. But it was only in his posthumous *Erkenntnislehre* (1939) that Stumpf returned to the field for a more extended discussion. While this discussion is fresh and highly revealing both as to Stumpf's own thought and as to his perspective on Husserl's work and on the whole Phenomenological Movement, one cannot but feel that Stumpf, in pointing out some of its weaknesses and pitfalls, had not kept fully abreast of developments and, specifically, had failed to realize the full meaning and purpose of Husserl's new procedures. Here is one of the melancholy cases where fellow-workers in the phenomenological field have drifted apart and misunderstood each other, partly as a result of lack of contact and exchange of ideas.

Nevertheless, there remains enough common ground and affinity among the two types of phenomenology to keep them connected. Both wanted to start from an unbiased description of the immediate phenomena. Both undertook to find more than merely empirical generalizations and to study the essential structures in and between these phenomena. Both recognized the world of logical structures as something apart from mere psychological acts. Considering merely these points, Stumpf satisfies more than amply the criteria we have been using in defining the Phenomenological Movement in the wider sense.

Excursus: Stumpf's Phenomenology and William James's Psychology

On October 30, 1882, a young and then unknown assistant professor of philosophy from Harvard, William James, called unintroduced on an even younger professor of philosophy in Prague, Carl Stumpf. During the following three days they spent about twelve hours in conversation and liked each other so much that William James, in an elated letter to his wife about his visit to Prague (which also included briefer interviews with the positivistic physicist Ernst Mach and the "phenomenological" physiologist Ewald Hering), announced that he would engage Stumpf in a regular correspondence; [1] it was to last intermittently until James's death.[2] To Stumpf this friendship meant so much that later he devoted to James an independent little book based in part on his personal recollections.[3]

These facts by themselves are generally known and do not warrant particular emphasis. But what is not yet realized is that the brief encounter in Prague was one of the more momentous events in the pre-history of phenomenology. In order to understand this, one must take account of more specific evidence concerning the influences that passed from the one to the other.

There is no reason to suspect Stumpf's praise of James's *Principles of Psychology* as "the best of all psychologies." As late as 1927 he paid tribute to its lasting effects in words like the following:

In English speaking countries no thorough investigation of psychical life in its peculiar nature even remotely equal in penetration and scope has been carried out since Locke. The entire edifice of English Associationistic Psychology, so admirable in itself, was thus shaken to its foundation and a correctly drawn outline of the psychical life mapped out.

There is little doubt that Stumpf saw in this psychology the best realization thus far of the program of a descriptive psychology. It was presumably in this sense that he was to recommend it to Husserl when he met with him in Halle, with results which we will be able to trace in the next chapter. To be sure, Stumpf, like most of James's European friends, had little sympathy with his increasing involvement in pragmatism. Nor did his "radical empiricism" find sympathetic reception from Stumpf. James's monistic attempt to reduce the variety of the universe to the one element "pure experience" resembled and in fact owed too

---

[1] See James's letter to Mrs. James in *The Letters of William James*, edited by his son Henry James. (Boston, Little, Brown and Company, 1926), I, 211–213.

[2] See Ralph Barton Perry, *The Thought and Character of William James*, II, Chapter LXII.

[3] *William James nach seinen Briefen* (Berlin, Pan Verlag, 1927).

much to the positivism of Stumpf's colleague of Prague days, Ernst Mach, which he considered "impossible and unfruitful." But this did not put an end to Stumpf's admiration and friendship for James, the descriptive psychologist.

James expressed a similar esteem for the "good and sharpnosed Stumpf," whom he called his "favorite experimental psychologist" (R. B. Perry). In the *Principles* (II, 282) he even said: "Stumpf seems to me the most philosophical and profound of all these writers (i.e., the theorists of space perception, like Hering) and I owe him much." At least during his "dualistic" period, in which he distinguished between object and subject (*Principles* I, 220), James was in full agreement with Stumpf's differentiation between phenomena and functions. He also liked Stumpf's nativistic account of space perception. Besides, it seems not unlikely that Stumpf's influence led to James's lively interest and study of Brentano's *Psychologie,* which left a number of traces in the text of the *Principles.*[1]

Finally, there is evidence that precisely Stumpf's phenomenology made a considerable impression on James. It can be found in connection with Stumpf's attempt in 1907 to awaken James's interest in the distinction between phenomena and functions, as Stumpf had developed it in the two Academy treatises of 1906, which contained the first explicit statement of his conception of phenomenology. Apparently this attempt elicited more than the usual response on James's part. For in his last letter to Stumpf, written presumably shortly before his death, James included the following sentence:

The thing of yours that has most interested me of late is the *Erscheinungen und psychische Funktionen,* wherein you differ from things that I have printed in a way to make me take notice and revise.[2]

---

[1] Among the six references to the *Psychologie,* including two extended excerpts in translation, all more or less approving, the outstanding one occurs in the classic chapter IX on "The Stream of Thought," where James pays Brentano's chapter on the unity of consciousness (Book II, Chapter IV) the remarkable compliment of "being as good as anything with which I am acquainted" (I, 240), and again one for the "admirable chapter" (Book II, Chapter VII) where Brentano had worked out the distinction between conception and belief (or "judgment," in Brentano's terms) (II, 286). There is also nearly conclusive evidence for the fact that it was due to Brentano's reference in the *Psychologie* that James knew of the scholastic doctrine of "intentional inexistence" of the objects of knowledge, to which he alludes in his address on "The Tigers in India" (1895), republished in *The Meaning of Truth* (New York, Longmans, Green and Company, 1909), pp. 43–50.

[2] R. B. Perry, *op. cit.,* II, 204.

It seems not altogether impossible that such a revision would have led James to an assimilation of a phenomenology of the Stumpfian variety, even though C. S. Peirce had failed to persuade him of the importance of his version of it in 1904.[1]

SELECTIVE BIBLIOGRAPHY

Major Works

Tonpsychologie (1883, 1890) 2 vols
  Translation: Selection from vol. II in Rand, Benjamin, ed., *Modern Classical Psychologists*. Boston, Houghton Mifflin, 1912, pp. 619–623
Erscheinungen und psychische Funktionen (1906). *Abhandlungen der Berliner Akademie*, 1907
Zur Einteilung der Wissenschaften (1906). *Ibid.*, 1907
Selbstdarstellung (in Schmidt, Raymund, ed., *Die Philosophie der Gegenwart*, V (1924), 205–265
  Translation in Murchison, Carl, ed., *History of Psychology in Autobiography*. I (1930), 389–441
Erkenntnislehre. 2 vols. Edited by Felix Stumpf. Leipzig, Johann Ambrosius Barth, 1939 f.

Studies in English

BORING, EDWIN G., *A History of Experimental Psychology*, New York, Century, 1929, pp. 351–361
LEWIN, KURT, "Carl Stumpf," in *Psychological Review* XLIV (1937), 189–194

For a fuller bibliography *see*

(1) *Selbstdarstellung* (German version)
(2) Ziegenfuss, Werner, *Philosophen-Lexikon*. Article "Stumpf, Carl," II, 660

---

[1] R. B. Perry, *op. cit.*, II, 431. On Peirce's attempt to make James a phenomenologist see my article "Husserl's and Peirce's Phenomenologies" in *PPR* XVII (1957), 167 ff.

PART TWO

THE GERMAN PHASE OF THE MOVEMENT

5. Edmund Husserl (1905)

III

THE PURE PHENOMENOLOGY OF EDMUND HUSSERL
(1859–1938)

> I attempt to guide, not to instruct, but merely to show
> and to describe what I see. All I claim is the right to
> speak according to my best lights – primarily to myself
> and correspondingly to others – as one who has lived
> through a philosophical existence in all its seriousness.
> *Die Krisis der europäischen Wissenschaften und die*
> *transzendentale Phänomenologie* (1936) (*Husserliana*
> VI, 17)

A. INTRODUCTORY

Phenomenology is not confined to Edmund Husserl's philosophy. That it comprises more is one of the main points I want to establish in this book. But it would not even be correct to say that all of Edmund Husserl's own philosophy is phenomenology. For it was not until Husserl had nearly reached the age of forty that his philosophical thinking matured into his conception of phenomenology. Nevertheless it remains true that the central figure in the development of the Phenomenological Movement was, and still is, Edmund Husserl. Hence a discussion of his phenomenology will have to be the center of this history of the Movement.

The fact that Husserl's thinking underwent many important shifts, even after he had reached the conception of phenomenology, raises the question how far it is possible to present his philosophy as a systematic whole, all the more since its final stage embodies by no means its most complete form. Certainly its earlier phases are much more accessible to the Anglo-American reader and far from exhausted in their significance. Now, the present account obviously does not and cannot claim to cover the whole ground of Husserl's systematic thought. Under these circumstances I propose to attempt a combination of a historical and an analytical approach. The frame will be a rough picture of Husserl's philosophical development. Into this frame I shall insert at the proper places more detailed accounts of Husserl's most important doctrines, in such a way that not only the motivation for the genesis of phenomenology but also for Husserl's continuing development becomes as understandable as the available material can make it.

Various periodizations of Husserl's philosophical development have been suggested, the most noteworthy being the one by his best authorized assistant in Freiburg, Eugen Fink, who orients these periods around the three main geographical stations of Edmund Husserl's academic career. This career began at the University of Halle, where he was a *Privatdozent* from 1887 to 1901, continued in Göttingen for fifteen years (1901–1916), and ended in Freiburg im Breisgau, where Husserl held a full professorship until his retirement in 1929, and where he died in 1938 at the age of 79. But it seems more appropriate to describe these periods as stages in his conceptions of phenomenology. I shall therefore divide Husserl's philosophical career into (1) the pre-phenomenological period, which lasts through the better part of his Halle years and corresponds to the ideas formulated in the first volume of his *Logische Untersuchungen*; (2) the period of phenomenology as a limited epistemological enterprise, which corresponds to the second volume of the *Logische Untersuchungen* and includes the first years in Göttingen; (3) that of pure phenomenology as the universal foundation of philosophy and science, which takes shape around 1906 and soon leads not only to the formulation of a new transcendentalism but of a characteristic phenomenological idealism, whose increasing radicalization is the main theme of Husserl's period in Freiburg.

This whole development could also be indicated by the analogy of a spiral. The pre-phenomenological period begins with an attempt to interpret mathematics by a psychology beginning with the subject; its partial failure takes him to the formulation of an objectivist program of a pure logic free from psychology. The early phases of phenomenology involve equal emphasis on both the subjective and objective aspects of experience in their essential correlation. The development of pure phenomenology leads again to a preponderance of the subjective as the source of all objectivities, only that the subjective is now conceived as on a higher, "transcendental" level above empirical psychology. The rather unusual course of this curvilinear development may at the same time account for the alternate attraction and repulsion that Husserl's philosophy exerted on so many congenial minds whose development followed a more rectilinear path.

But before presenting the leading ideas from each of these periods I shall attempt to point out some of the motifs which remain the same throughout the whole course of Husserl's philosophical development. Their persistence may even help to explain some of the changes which his thought underwent.

A passing word may be in order concerning certain difficulties which confront Husserl's reader and which test particularly the translator of his later works. For Husserl's style with all its powerful insistence is anything but simple and straightforward. Even more taxing, however, is his tendency to attach uniquely modified meanings to traditional terms and even to stretch them far beyond their accepted range without introducing clarifying re-definitions. This procedure sets in with the very term "phenomenology" itself and affects such crucial terms as "constitution," "function," and even purely German terms like *"Leistung."* At times this gives Husserl's final conclusions a rather puzzling ambiguity. In such cases all that can be done is to point out the difficulty frankly and to interpret such expressions in the light of the context, i.e., primarily the context of the phenomena to which they point, however ambiguously. The uniqueness of these phenomena is at the same time the ultimate explanation and the partial justification for the puzzling formulations which Husserl employs.[1]

B. CONSTANTS IN HUSSERL'S CONCEPTION OF PHILOSOPHY

At no stage of his career does Husserl present us with a philosophical system. Certainly he never aspired to develop his philosophy into a speculative synthesis. But this does not mean that he abandoned the goal of systematic philosophy in the sense of a philosophy which works patiently and painstakingly at the solution of limited though fundamental problems. If Husserl's work could be compared with that of the traditional philosophies at all, it would have to be called a system in reverse: rather than building upwards, Husserl digs deeper and deeper, trying at the same time to lay ever firmer foundations for established insights. The writer will never forget the ascetic

---

[1] For an additional aid see the *Guide for Translating Husserl* by Dorion Cairns, announced for *Phaenomenologica*.

enthusiasm of Husserl's exhortation at a student reception in 1924 "not to consider oneself too good for foundation work." This conception of the task of philosophy also accounts for the characteristic mixture of pride and humility with which Husserl referred to his final ambition as that of being a "true beginner." [1]

But not only is Husserl's philosophy no constructive system, in which the main problems of traditional philosophy are taken up in due order. His was a philosophy which remained constantly in the making. This does not exclude the persistence of certain constants throughout all these changes. They consist of dymanic ideas, which may also explain Husserl's shifts from one phase to another. I shall describe the most important among them under the following headings: 1. the ideal of rigorous science; 2. the urge to go down to the sources (philosophical radicalism); 3. the ethos of radical autonomy; 4. the "wonder of all wonders": subjectivity.

1. The Ideal of Rigorous Science

Much of Husserl's impact upon his students and upon his contemporaries is due to the feeling he conveyed of complete commitment to his cause. Like Brentano he had the sense of a mission, which he himself finally expressed in terms of the new existential philosophy, much as he otherwise rejected it. Some of these expressions are not free from pathos. But through them speaks an ethos which has the ring of burning sincerity. Deducting from his pronouncements whatever one may ascribe to the Germanic atmosphere of professorial oratory, one cannot escape the impression of a single-minded devotion to a cause with which Husserl identified himself more and more.

However, Husserl's conception of his philosophic mission differed not a little from that of his revered teacher Brentano. Not problems of metaphysics, and particularly not of theological metaphysics, were the attraction to philosophy for Edmund Husserl, the young mathematician and physicist. Certain defects in the foundations of his major study, mathematics, first caught

[1] Nachwort zu *Ideen*; see *Husserliana* V, 161. – In this connection belongs the story told by Husserl himself in 1929 about the pocket knife which he had received as a child. Considering that the blade was not sharp enough he ground it again and again until it became smaller and smaller and finally disappeared. Emmanuel Levinas, the witness, adds that Husserl told this story in a depressed vein (*Husserliana* I, p. XXIX).

his attention and dominated his early philosophic interests; young Bertrand Russell had the same experience some ten years later, after reading J. S. Mill. What Husserl craved in mathematics, as everywhere else, was scientific rigor. This consuming concern determined his final choice of a philosophic teacher as well as of his own career. As he himself expressed it:

It was from (Brentano's) lectures that I took the conviction which gave me the courage to choose philosophy as the vocation of my life, the conviction namely that philosophy too was a field of serious work, that it too could be treated in the spirit of strictest science, and hence that it had to be treated so.[1]

However, from the very start the conception of scientific method had a rather different meaning for Husserl than for Brentano. First of all, for Husserl scientific rigor was primarily the rigor of the deductive sciences familiar to the mathematician, rather than that of the inductive natural sciences, an ideal which Brentano had taken over largely from Auguste Comte and John Stuart Mill. Nevertheless, it was precisely doubts as to the foundations of mathematics, and particularly of arithmetic, which had sent Husserl back to logic and to philosophy for possible support. At first Brentano's new "empirical" psychology seemed to offer hope for the necessary new foundations. But soon it turned out that even this science could not satisfy the rigor of Husserl's demands, and that only a new and more fundamental science could: phenomenology.

Rumors and misunderstandings to the contrary notwithstanding,[2] Husserl's commitment to the ideal of a rigorous science never wavered, however outdated it appeared in an atmosphere of growing hostility to science, especially in Germany. It only assumed different forms and emphasis in the midst of a rapidly changing intellectual climate. But this commitment must not be confused with the uncritical worship of "science" so common among naturalistic philosophers.

In order to understand fully Husserl's attitude toward science,

---

[1] "Erinnerungen an Franz Brentano" in Oskar Kraus, *Franz Brentano*, p. 154.

[2] See e.g., Maurice Merleau-Ponty in *Les Philosophes célèbres* (Paris, Mazenot, 1956), pp. 17, 427; also Alphonse de Waelhens in "Husserl et la phénoménologie" *Critique* VII (1951), 1054. In the few places where in 1935 Husserl seems to be saying that philosophy as a rigorous science is a dream now ended (for instance, in *Husserliana* VI, 508) the context makes it plain that he was speaking in bitter irony about the times, not about himself.

[1]

it is important to take account of a development which has not struck the American consciousness as forcibly as it has the European: the so-called "crisis of science." The New World, especially as regards the spectators and cheerleaders of science,[1] still displays a naive faith in science as the panacea for all the ills and problems of our time, apparently unaware of the fact that this faith is no longer shared by many of the front-line scientists, who have to grapple with the mounting perplexities and moral problems posed by their astonishing findings.

Now the picture looks very different from the European perspective. There is of course plenty of panic-mongering behind the hue and cry about the crisis and sometimes even about the collapse of modern science, and some of it betrays the malicious satisfaction of mere obscurantism. But there is also a keen realization that no amount of boasting about the practical triumphs of the sciences can conceal the fact that science has run into theoretical puzzles which defy all conventional so-lutions, beginning with those posed by the theory of relativity and by the new quantum theory. It almost seems that enlarged control over nature is bought at the price of diminished intelligibility. There is thus no longer any good reason for accepting the word of science as the final answer to all conceivable questions. Even among the British scientist-philosophers, who are not easily given to crisis hysteria, we find the voice of Whitehead telling us that science has reached a "turning point":

The stable foundations of physics have broken up. . . . The old foundations of scientific thought are becoming unintelligible. Time, space, matter, material, ether, electricity, mechanism, organism, configuration, structure, pattern, function, all require reinterpretation. What is the sense of talking about a mechanical explanation when you do not know what you mean by mechanics? . . . If science is not to degenerate into a medley of ad hoc hypotheses, it must become philosophical and must enter upon a thorough criticism of its own foundations.[2]

There is, in fact, a striking likeness in the diagnosis of this scientific crisis in the nearly simultaneous but independent work of Husserl and Whitehead, although there is no evidence for mutual or one-sided influence: Whitehead, in *The Concept of*

---

[1] Even the criticism of Husserl by his most active American interpreter, Marvin Farber, often reflects this attitude.

[2] *Science and the Modern World* (New York, Macmillan, 1926), p. 24 f.

Nature (1920) and again in *Science and the Modern World* (1926), found the source of both the grandeurs and miseries of modern science in the "bifurcation" which it introduced between a merely objective and a merely mentalistic or private branch of nature. Similarly Husserl, in his last work on *Die Krisis der europäischen Wissenschaften und die transzendentale Phänomenologie* (1936), blamed the contemporary crisis on the split between Galilean objectivism and Cartesian subjectivism. This does not mean that Whitehead and Husserl also agreed on the therapy. But there is enough in Whitehead's appeal to a return to the realism of immediate "prehension" as the matrix of all scientific abstractions to make a comparison with some of Husserl's last and particularly fertile ideas appropriate.

Nevertheless, there is reason to deny emphatically that Husserl considered the recent crisis as beyond the control of a reformed science and even as depriving science of its model meaning for philosophy. And, like Whitehead, Husserl was hopeful that philosophy, after a phenomenological reorganization, would be in a position to assist even the objective scientist in the clarification and critique of his unclarified fundamental concepts and assumptions.[1]

Husserl's critique of modern science included, however, two more serious strictures which called for radical readjustments: (1) the degeneration of science into an unphilosophical study of mere facts, as exemplified by positivistic science, which Husserl held responsible for the fact that science had lost its significance for man's life as a whole, and for his life purposes in particular; (2) its "naturalism," which had rendered science incapable of coping with the problems of absolute truth and validity.

As to the first stricture, it is to be noted that Husserl is not concerned with the technical usefulness of science, which is obvious enough, but with its chances of making life itself more significant. For a full appraisal of his real concern one must know of the great debate in the Germany of the early twenties raised by Max Weber's lecture on "Science as a Vocation," in which he had stated bluntly that science was constitutionally unfit to settle questions of value and hence questions of meaning for

---

[1] *Cartesianische Meditationen* (*Husserliana* I) p. 180.

personal existence.[1] All it could do was to supply us with factual and technical data for decisions which were essentially extra-scientific.

Actually, in the days of his essay on "Philosophie als strenge Wissenschaft" (1910) Husserl himself took a stand very similar to Weber's, though for rather different reasons: At that time, a philosophy aiming at *Weltanschauung* seemed to Husserl incompatible with the objectives of philosophy as a rigorous science. So, in the interests of both, he had advocated complete separation of the two enterprises; scientific philosophy, requiring a long and laborious approach toward a goal in the indefinite future, *Weltanschauung* demanding definite and immediate decisions here and now.

But this whole situation changed for Husserl after the First World War, as it did in a different climate for Bertrand Russell.[2] During the War itself Husserl, who lost a brilliant son in action, had refrained deliberately from taking an active part by writing or speaking for the war effort. But in the aftermath he found it impossible to stay aloof from the questions of the day. Now the incapacity and unwillingness of science to face problems of value and meaning because of its confinement to mere positive facts seemed to him to be at the very root of the crisis of science and of mankind itself. In contrast to the science of the Renaissance, which had been part of a comprehensive philosophical scheme, a positivist science of mere facts appeared as a truncated science endangering man, and in fact endangering itself, by a "decapitation." Science itself was crying out for a philosophy that would restore its contact with the deeper concerns of man. To Husserl, it was obviously his phenomenology which was to fill this need. But this did not imply that Husserl intended to side with the fashionable revolt against science. On the contrary, he meant to aid it, not to abolish it, both by strengthening it internally and by backing it up in its role as an aid to the realization of man's fundamental purpose in life.

Husserl's second stricture against contemporary science, its lapse into "naturalism," must be understood in the light of a

[1] "Wissenschaft als Beruf." Translated by H. G. Gerth and C. Wright Mills in *Essays in Sociology* (New York, Oxford University Press, 1946), pp. 129 ff.
[2] Introduction to *Selected Papers* (New York, *Modern Library*), p. XI.

meaning of this ambiguous term which differs considerably from what it stands for in present American philosophy. Specifically, when Husserl opposed naturalism he did not mean to plead for supernaturalism. And obviously he did not identify naturalism with the scientific approach. Actually he assigned to the term a meaning of his own, particularly in his programmatic essay on "Philosophy as a Rigorous Science," namely that of the view which sees the whole of the world as either physical or psychical, hence to be explored merely by the natural sciences, including psychology. It thus leaves no room, for instance, for ideal entities such as meanings or laws as such. To a naturalism which thus identifies norms with natural facts, or derives the first from the second in the manner of the notorious naturalistic fallacy, Husserl is indeed uncompromisingly opposed. But protesting against such a narrow conception of the range of science as defined by the objects of the traditional natural sciences does not imply a repudiation of natural science. It only calls for its supplementation in areas where the standard methods of the inductive sciences do not apply.

What, then, is the meaning of the rigor which Husserl wants his science of philosophy to achieve? Actually he never discusses the sense of this omnipresent term explicitly. But it is now obvious that the quest for rigor does not consist in a mere copying of the methods of the "exact sciences." Their unquestionable progress must not be minimized. But there are flaws in their foundations, in their methodology, and in their interpretation of their results, particularly in the case of the crucial science of psychology. Thus the meaning of Husserl's standard of rigor can be derived only from a closer examination of his conception of science, which can be found, for instance, at the end of the first volume of his *Logische Untersuchungen*. Here science stands for a system of knowledge connected by reasons in such a manner that each step is built upon its predecessor in a necessary sequence. Such a rigorous connection requires ultimate clarity in basic insights and a systematic order in building further propositions upon them. This is the rigor which philosophy would have to achieve to become truly scientific.

In 1906, during a crisis of his inner and outer career, Husserl wrote the following sentences in his diary:

I have been through enough torments (*Qualen*) from lack of clarity and from doubt that wavers back and forth. ... Only one need absorbs me: I must win clarity, else I cannot live; I cannot bear life unless I can believe that I shall achieve it.[1]

2. *Philosophic Radicalism*

Husserl's passion for ultimate scientific rigor leads in its logical prolongation to another motif, which he stated explicitly only in his later writings, particularly after World War I: his philosophical radicalism. More and more Husserl came to see the distinguishing feature of philosophy, in comparison with other rigorous sciences, in its radical nature. Radicalism, however, in this context did not stand for any extremist fanaticism, so alien to Husserl's scholarly pattern of life, but for a going to the "roots" or the "beginnings" of all knowledge, i.e., to its ultimate foundations. In fact, Husserl would have liked to call philosophy "archeology," had this term still been available to philosophers. It was this spirit of radicalism which had led the rigorous-minded mathematician Husserl to philosophy, and which was to guide him in his search for a philosophy more rigorous and more radical than those which he had encountered on his way. The same spirit was responsible for the continuing radicalization of his own philosophy and prevented its final consolidation at any given stage.

But where were these roots or beginnings of knowledge to be found? Husserl's first and most obvious answer was: in the "things," the *Sachen*, the phenomena in the customary sense, to which all our concepts ultimately referred. This was the period of his celebrated "turn to the object" (*Wende zum Gegenstand*). Yet increasingly, in the process of digging down to the roots of these phenomena by means of his new phenomenological analysis, and of trying to give a full and ruthlessly honest account of his beliefs, Husserl came to the conviction that these roots lay deeper, namely in the consciousness of the knowing subject to whom these phenomena appeared, i.e., in something which he later came to call "transcendental subjectivity." Thus the "turn to the object" was supplemented by a "turn to the subject" by way of a new kind of reflection which left his erstwhile followers on the road to the "object" far behind.

---

[1] "Persönliche Aufzeichnungen" ed. by Walter Biemel. *PPR* XVI (1956), 297.

One of the most debated expressions of Husserl's radicalism was his aspiration to supply by his phenomenology a philosophy "free from presuppositions" (*voraussetzungslos*). It is easy to exaggerate and even to ridicule such a program. It should be realized that it had a very special significance in the Germany of his day, where it had come to the fore in connection with a political controversy over the legitimacy of establishing and reserving special chairs in state universities for Catholic professors only. That phenomenology and, for that matter, philosophy would not accept any restrictions by denominational ties was obvious enough a demand.

Sometimes *Voraussetzungslosigkeit* has been misinterpreted in the sense of a pretense of total rejection of any beliefs whatsoever, and of a program to start the philosophic enterprise from absolute zero, even without language and logic. While a full clarification of this issue would presuppose and deserve considerable discussion for its own sake,[1] it will suffice here to point out that in Husserl's case the phrase "freedom from presuppositions" stands for the attempt to eliminate merely presuppositions that have not been thoroughly examined, or, at least in principle, been presented for such examination. It is thus not freedom from all presuppositions, but merely freedom from unclarified, unverified, and unverifiable presuppositions that is involved.

Husserl's relentless effort to achieve radical clarification and justification of all claims to knowledge has earned him the dubious reputation of being an extreme rationalist. And it is true that, to the end and amidst the triumphs of rampant irrationalisms, he maintained his faith in the mission and power of human reason, as he interpreted it, to examine our beliefs, to defend them if valid, and to reject and replace them, if found invalid.[2] But it is a far cry from this conception of rationalism in the spirit of responsible and self-critical accounting to the much narrower rationalisms which provide the favorite targets and caricatures of so much contemporary anti-ration-

---

[1] Marvin Farber in his essay "The Ideal of a Presuppositionless Philosophy" in *Philosophical Essays in Memory of Edmund Husserl* (Cambridge, Harvard University Press, 1948), pp. 44–64, has made a valuable start in this direction.

[2] See especially his last lecture on "Die Krisis des europäischen Menschentums und die Philosophie," given before the "Wiener Kulturbund" in 1935 (*Husserliana* VI, 314–348, particularly pp. 336 ff.).

alism. Husserl's "ratio" did not mean the anti-emotional intellect (*Verstand*), but understanding insight and comprehensive wisdom, or, in a wider sense, "*Vernunft*" in the sense of Kant. Nor did it mean anti-empiricism: Husserl himself opposed as absurd what he called the old rationalism of the eighteenth century, which substituted for the world of our immediate life-experience mathematical constructions in the style of physics (physicalistic or objectivistic rationalism). But even more strenuously did he combat that lazy irrationalism which was threatening a return to barbarism. In a remarkable letter of March 11, 1935, to Lucien Lévy-Bruehl, the French investigator of primitive mentality, Husserl characterized his own enterprise as

a method by which I want to establish, against mysticism and irrationalism, a kind of super-rationalism (*Überrationalismus*) which transcends the old rationalism as inadequate and yet vindicates its inmost objectives.

3. The Ethos of Radical Autonomy

One might well wonder whether there is not an even deeper reason for Husserl's strange passion for rigor and radicalism. I shall leave it to the biographers and psychoanalysts to speculate on specific roots in Husserl's personality. But he himself mentions with increasing vigor an ethical motive which deserves explicit statement and emphasis: man's responsibility for himself and for his culture, which can be satisfied only by a science and a philosophy giving the fullest possible account of all our claims and beliefs.[1]

This responsibility as Husserl conceived of it is primarily a responsibility of each one for himself. With this sense of responsibility as an inescapable duty Husserl combined the Kantian pride of man as being a law unto himself and being responsible only to himself. The ethos of this responsibility requires that man know about himself and about his situation as far as that is in his power. This involves his responsibility for developing science as his best chance for securing such knowledge. It also implies his responsibility for a philosophy as his only chance to secure ultimate foundations for this scientific enterprise.

[1] See, for instance, Husserl's letter of 1934 to the President of the Eighth International Congress of Philosophy in Prague (*Actes*, p. XLI–XLV):

Philosophy is the expressive tool (*Organ*) of a new type of historical existence of mankind, namely existence based on the spirit of autonomy. The genuine shape of autonomy is that of scientific responsibility to oneself. The prime shape of cultural products coming from such a spirit is the sciences, which in turn are dependent members of the one full and complete science, philosophy.

However, this responsibility for science and philosophy was not merely a personal affair. More and more, as the social conditions around the scientific and philosophic enterprise became unfavorable and finally catastrophic, Husserl saw and stressed the social and cultural responsibility of this enterprise for and to mankind. In fact, he referred to the philosophers as agents (*Funktionäre*) of mankind: By examining the foundations of our threatened civilization, they are to prepare the groundwork for a reconstructed humanity. In his more sanguine moods, Husserl described this mission of philosophy in the spirit of Socrates and Plato[1] as that of an ethical "renewal."[2]

John Dewey in his *The Quest for Certainty* sees in the philosophies of the Platonic tradition, with their search for absolutely certain and immutable knowledge, an attempt to escape from the perils and uncertainties of practical action. That Husserl's philosophizing is an expression of this craving for absolute or "apodictic" certainty cannot be denied. But in his case this quest was anything but the result of escapism. For one thing, Husserl admitted plainly and increasingly the limitations and hazards of such a quest. Yet the main and best reason for Husserl's objective was his ethos of moral autonomy. It made him renounce all territory that he had not thoroughly examined himself and seek for foundations which were not based upon mere tradition and habit. In fact, eventually Husserl preferred the uncertainty of the "mere beginner" to the false security of a Platonism whose metaphysics he had never accepted.

But was this ethos of autonomy really as radical as Husserl claimed? How far, for instance, is it reflected in Husserl's attitude toward theology and religion? This question is all the more in order since it has been asserted recently – and that on the basis of reports from witnesses of Husserl's last days – that Husserl had something like a deathbed conversion.[3] This is not the place to appraise the questionable evidence from a period which should anyway be excluded from an evaluation of Husserl's

---

[1] "Die Idee einer philosophischen Kultur" in !*Japanisch-Deutsche Zeitschrift für Wissenschaft und Technik*, I (1923), 45–51.

[2] "Erneuerung: Ihr Problem und ihre Methode." *Kaizo*, 1922, pp. 84–92.

[3] John M. Oesterreicher, *Walls Are Crumbling* (New York, Devin-Adair, 1952), pp. 95 ff. For an evaluation of this evidence see Andrew H. Osborn in *Library Journal*, LXXVIII (1953), 2209.

philosophy. Besides, it must not be forgotten that Husserl, while born into the Jewish religion, had become a Protestant in his twenties, largely as a result of his study of the New Testament. While outward religious practice never entered his life any more than it did that of most academic scholars of the time, his mind remained open for the religious phenomenon as for any other genuine experience.

Beyond that, considerable and more valid evidence for Husserl's religious attitude can be derived from his more confidential notes and correspondence. Thus, it would be hard to explain away the religious and even theistic phraseology which occurs in the above mentioned diary entry of 1906. Recent publications from the Louvain papers[1] together with letters, especially to some of his Catholic correspondents,[2] allow us to give the following indications of his incipient theology:

α. Husserl expected that his phenomenology, and particularly its teleological interpretation of consciousness, would in time become helpful in aiding theological insight. But as for himself, Husserl merely remarked half-wistfully: "Wish I were that far."

β. Husserl repudiated uncompromisingly and repeatedly any kind of theological dogma.

γ. Husserl disclaimed theism in the usual sense. To be sure, there are in his *Ideen zu einer reinen Phänomenologie* references to the idea of an epistemological God as a perfect knower. But Husserl never claimed any theological significance for this deliberate fiction. Beyond that, the idea of God seems to have entered his later thinking only in the shape of a final goal of the constitutive functions of consciousness. Apparently he did not make up his mind about the question whether or not such a Deity was a personal being. And it almost looks as if, as the goal of human consciousness, Deity is still very much in the making, i.e.,
[1] God is merely a becoming God.

But these theological rudiments are no clear guide to his personal religious convictions, especially if we interpret religion in the sense of dependence and reliance upon a power not our-

---

[1] See Alwin Diemer, *Edmund Husserl*, esp. pp. 375 ff.
[2] Letter to Father Erich Przywara S.J. (July 15, 1933), to Father Daniel Feuling (March 30, 1933), and to the leading Humanist of the Ethical Culture Society,
[2] Stanton Coit (September 18, 1927).

selves. Here, it seems, there were at least two trends side by side in Husserl's personal attitude: On the one hand a trend toward absolute philosophical autonomy and responsibility, which expressed itself, among other things, in his disapproval of catholicizing tendencies among his own students:

Unfortunately there is a great movement toward conversion – a sign of inner distress. A true philosopher cannot be other than free: the essential nature of philosophy is the most radical autonomy.[1]

But on the other hand, especially in extreme situations, Husserl expressed a touching faith in divine aid which would support him if only he himself tried his utmost. It was in such moods that he spoke about his vocation and even about his mission under God's will to find new ways for philosophy and science.

4. The Wonder of All Wonders: Subjectivity

Phenomenology in general may be characterized as a philosophy which has learned to wonder again and to respect wonders for what they are in themselves, where others see only trivialities or occasions to employ the cleaning brush. But not all these wonders are of equal importance. To Husserl in particular there was one wonder which exceeded them all, "the wonder of all wonders," as he called it: "the pure ego and pure consciousness." [2] The wonder about this phenomenon seems to have been the focal and fundamental experience of Husserl's philosophical existence, and it became so increasingly, as his phenomenology developed. The central mystery was to Husserl not Being as such, but the fact that there is such a thing in this world as a being that is aware of its own being and of other beings. This fascination accounts for Husserl's growing emphasis on the subjective aspect of phenomenology and for its shift from the "object" to the subjectivity of the existing ego:

Whether we like it or not, whether (for whatever prejudices) it may sound monstrous or not, this (the "I am") is the fundamental fact (*Urtatsache*) to which I have to stand up, which, as a philosopher, I must never blink for a moment. For philosophical children this may be the dark corner haunted by the specters of solipsism or even of psychologism and

---

[1] Letter to Roman Ingarden of November 25, 1921.
[2] See especially *Ideen* III (*Husserliana* V, 75) and the beginning of the London Lectures of 1922 ("The wonder of all wonders is the pure ego and pure subjectivity.").

relativism. The true philosopher, instead of running away from them, will prefer to illuminate the dark corner.[1]

At the same time Husserl expected that from this corner he would be able to unravel the problems of philosophy. This led him, in the *Cartesian Meditations*, to the climactic resumption of Augustine's exhortation: "Don't go abroad. Truth dwells inside man."

5. *Husserl's Personality and His Philosophy*

Nothing would seem more incongruous for our understanding of a philosopher like Husserl than to divert interest from his cause to a consideration of its proponent. And it is actually not this philosophy itself but rather its fate and the fate of the Phenomenological Movement which require at least a glance at the "subject" at the root of this philosophy.

Any attempt at a more than chronological portrait of a personality as complex as Husserl's would be premature before all the relevant materials have been collected and made available to a psychological historian equally immune to indiscriminate idol-making and idol-breaking. Husserl was human in more than one sense of the term, but he was also a human with a unique devotion to a task much bigger than himself, one far beyond the range of the average individual.

What I intend to offer here is merely a partial explanation for some of the paradoxes in the history of the Phenomenological Movement. One of these is the fact that a philosophy so determined to make itself scientific and to encourage cooperative and progressive enterprise as in the other sciences failed in this attempt almost from the very start; that, in fact, the founder of this new movement found himself toward the end of his career in an almost tragic isolation, which he himself, with a kind of wry humor, compared with that of a solipsist, and which he finally tried to interpret as a necessity and a virtue.[2]

We shall see later how far solipsism remained a permanent threat to Husserl's final philosophy. But apart from this aspect, the problem had also a very personal meaning for Husserl. His

---

[1] *Formale und transzendentale Logik*, p. 209 f. – See also *Krisis* (*Husserliana* VI) 82.
[2] See the letter of 1934 to the Prague Congress mentioned in the footnote on page 84, p. XLIV.

6. From the Correspondence between Franz Brentano and Edmund Husserl.
Transcript on back page.

Transcript of the end of Franz Brentano's letter to Edmund Husserl of October 7, 1904

Dass Sie in vielen Beziehungen sich frei von der einst empfangenen Lehre zu entfernen scheinen, kränkt mich, wie Sie ja wohl auch nicht zweifelten, in keiner Weise. Selbst immer noch am Alten ändernd und hoffentlich besserend, habe ich meinen Schülern nur Aufmunterung dazu gegeben. Und wer könnte sich mehr über einen Fortschritt des einstigen Schülers freuen als der einstige Lehrer. Und nun noch freundschaftliches Lebewohl! Hochachtungsvoll

Franz Brentano

Transcript of the beginning of Edmund Husserl's answering letter to Franz Brentano

Göttingen, den 11. u. 15. Okt. 1904
Wöhlerstr. 11

Mein hochverehrter Lehrer!

Ein Brief von Ihrer Hand – welch grosse und unverhoffte Freude! Von Herzen beglückt es mich zu hören, dass Sie meiner noch, und in so grosser Güte gedenken. Ich selbst habe es nicht vergessen, wie sehr ich Ihnen zu danken verpflichtet bin, wie tief Sie durch Ihre Vorlesungen und Schriften auf meine philosophische Entwicklung eingewirkt und wie viele Stunden edelster Erhebung Sie mir dereinst durch Heranziehung zum persönlichen Verkehr vergönnt haben. Nun ist es freilich anders gekommen, als ich es damals für möglich hielt. Ich begann als Jünger Ihrer Philosophie (soweit Sie sie damals ausgebildet hatten) und konnte, als ich zur Selbständigkeit herangereift war, bei ihr nicht stehen bleiben. Das ward mir nicht leicht. Von Natur ist wo(h)l kein Bedürfnis bei mir stärker ausgeprägt als zu verehren, mich denen, die ich verehre in Liebe anzuschliessen und mit Eifer für sie einzutreten. Aber zwiespältig wie meine (Natur leider ist, lebt in mir auch ein unbändiger kritischer Sinn, der unbekümmert um die Neigungen meines Gemütes kühl zergliedert und das ihm als unhaltbar Erscheinende rücksichtslos verwirft.)

thinking was fundamentally a monologue, even when he confronted merely an intimate group. At times he tried to break through the ring of his own ideas. Thus he assigned to his private assistant Eugen Fink the role to act as his opponent, comparable to the "devil's advocate" in the proceedings for the canonization of a saint.[1] But ultimately even in such attempts to "philosophize together" (*symphilosophein*) he always remained his only partner.

Yet, even more than most other philosophers, he longed for a following, and he was always, and perhaps increasingly, anxious to show his basic agreement with the great traditions. This strange ambivalence has perhaps never been described more poignantly than in one of his letters to his teacher Brentano:

Probably no other urge in my constitution is more developed than that to revere, to follow those whom I love reverently, and to take their side with eagerness. But as my nature unfortunately has two sides, there is also in me an indomitable critical sense which, unconcerned about my emotional inclinations, analyzes coolly and rejects ruthlessly what appears to it untenable. Thus bound by sentiment, free by intellect, I pursue my course with scant happiness. Always inclined to acknowledge the superiority of others and to let them lead me upward, again and again I find myself compelled to part company with them and to seek my own way. Instead of continuing to build on the foundations laid by others as I would so gladly do, I have to build, in despair of the strength of their work, new foundations of my own: a troublesome, wearisome, and besides, a grovelling job. How I would like to live on the heights. For this is what all my thinking craves for. But shall I ever work my way upwards, if only for a little, so that I can gain something of a free distant view? I am now 45 years old and I am still a miserable beginner. What can I hope for? I do not read much and only works by original thinkers (whose number is few and far between) and whatever new things I find there are for me always a challenge to revise my own positions.[2]

In a subsequent letter he vigorously asserted his philosophical autonomy against Brentano's intimation that his work revealed the eagerness of an academic careerist:

Certainly I have not been an ambitious *Privatdozent* eagerly looking out for the public and for the government. Such a one will publish both much and frequently. He will let himself be influenced in his problems and methods by the fashion of the day, and he will in so doing lean as far as possible on the influential and famous ones (Wundt, Sigwart, Erdmann,

[1] Personal communication.

[2] Letter of October 15, 1904. I am deeply indebted to Dr. J. C. M. Brentano, the son of Franz Brentano, for giving me access to the correspondence between his father and Edmund Husserl.

etc.) and take special heed not to contradict them radically. I have done the exact opposite of all this, and hence it is not astonishing that for fully 14 years I have remained *"Privatdozent"* and have come even here (to Göttingen) only as *"Extraordinarius"* and against the wish of the faculty. For nine years I have published practically nothing, and I have made enemies of almost all the influential people. The latter by the fact that I have chosen my problems myself and have gone my own ways: furthermore, in my criticisms I have not allowed any other considerations to enter than those of the subject matter (die *"Sache"*). Incidentally, I have acted this way not in order to be virtuous, but from a compelling necessity. The things themselves gained such power over me that I could not do otherwise – in spite of the burning desire for a modest position which could give me outward independence and the chance of a wider personal influence. Those were hard times for myself and for my family, and re- membering what I had to bear, I do not like to be lumped with those climbers who have never lived for causes (die *Sachen*), let alone suffered for them, and hence can claim for themselves all the outward success and honor.[1]

The intensity of this drive for independence in Husserl's own development and of his manner of expressing it may well explain both why he temporarily attracted and eventually repelled other thinkers. To be sure, even such repulsion did not always express rejection of their ideas. It was in a sense Husserl's own example which set the model for further emancipation from his own over- powering influence. Besides, it was easier to discuss Husserl's ideas with him over the printed page than when confronted by his own irresistible monologue, his piercing glance riveted on his audience or on some point far off in space. For in discussion he would use questions and suggestions of others merely as stimulants to set the wheels of his own thought in ceaseless motion. So it was that even in the early days of Husserl's teaching there was relatively little fruitful discussion in his presence.

One more such paradox seems to call for comment: There is in Husserl's philosophizing, and partly even in its printed ex- pression, a striking disproportion between programmatic an- nouncements of epochal discoveries to be made within the "infinite horizons" opened up by his new methods, and the long- deferred and never complete fulfilment of such promises; there is also the agonizing story of manuscripts withheld and withdrawn, leading to the phantastic accumulation of 45,000 pages, written in shorthand, and now preserved in the Husserl Archives in

[1] Letter of January 1, 1905.

Louvain. This disproportion is matched by alternate expressions of exuberant pride over his new achievements and of near-despair and self-abasement in view of the small actual progress made thus far. In fact, we know now that several times during his life-time, e.g., in 1905 and in the early twenties, Husserl went through periods of acute dejection. These may not have exceeded variations within the normal range. Nevertheless, there was in Husserl's personality a characteristic ambivalence between feelings of elated superiority and ecstatic productivity on the one hand, and crushing feelings of inferiority and paralyzing discouragement on the other. [1]

I shall refrain from speculating on the roots of this ambivalence. It would be easy enough to account for it on the basis of Husserl's impossibly high aspirations, which grew along with his achievements, and of the inevitable realization that in no single lifetime could he hope to fulfill them himself. Besides, it was inevitable that he came to realize how hard it was for him to find collaborators independent enough to live up to his own demand of autonomy and yet faithful enough to follow him through all the twists and turns of his philosophic development. Somewhere along the line they were bound to be thrown off on a tangent. And yet to the very end Husserl clung to the firm hope of having at last found the true disciple, able and willing to continue his work. The sometimes grotesque mistakes of his judgment as to his potential heirs must be seen in the light of his blinding absorption in his task and his sense of responsibility for it.

Some of the paradoxes and failures of Husserl's philosophy can be understood by taking account of his personality in its strengths and in its weaknesses. Nevertheless, our main plea remains that his philosophy and its development be understood in the light of its internal logic and of the cause (the "*Sachen*") to which he felt so thoroughly committed.

C. *VARIABLES IN THE DEVELOPMENT OF HUSSERL'S PHILOSOPHY*

1. The Pre-Phenomenological Period

A first item in Husserl's biography to be considered is his initial training as a mathematician under Karl Weierstrass, the famous theorist of the functions of complex variables, and under

Leopold Kronecker, noted, among other things, for his revealing aphorism: "God made the integers, everything else is man-made." In fact, Husserl's studies in this field and in science at the Universities of Leipzig, Berlin, and Vienna (1876–81) took him as far as the Ph. D. with a thesis on the calculus of variations. Subsequently, he even held a brief assistantship under Weierstrass. Then, from 1884 to 1886, when Husserl had returned to Vienna for some more studying, he went to hear Franz Brentano, the controversial ex-priest, now no longer even a professor. Apparently his motivation was partly curiosity, partly the advice of his friend and fellow-Bohemian Thomas G. Masaryk, later President of Czechoslovakia. Up to that time Husserl's interest in philosophy had been rather desultory, and even the great Wilhelm Wundt in Leipzig had failed to make an impression upon him. Brentano soon aroused his interest in his new scientific psychology and philosophy. Yet Husserl's own questions were still only in the area of mathematics, in particular in the theory of arithmetic, which figured little in Brentano's philosophizing. Thus, when Husserl had finally decided to take up a university career in philosophy in Halle under Brentano's older pupil Carl Stumpf, he wrote a "habilitation" thesis on the concept of number with the subtitle "Psychological Analyses." His subsequent first book of 1891, volume I of his never completed *Philosophie der Arithmetik*, which he dedicated to Franz Brentano, was described as "psychological and logical studies." The objective of these studies in the philosophy of mathematics was to derive the fundamental concepts of mathematics from certain psychological acts, which were traced with remarkable detail.[1] The tools for this attempt were taken chiefly from John Stuart Mill. Husserl had studied his *System of Logic* intensively, and he always retained a high regard for Mill, even when he made him the favorite target of his later criticisms. In fact, the British empiricists from Locke to Hume were Husserl's introductory readings in philosophy and remained of basic importance to him all through his later development. Often he gave them credit for having developed a first though inadequate type of phenome-

---

[1] For a valuable account of the main ideas in this volume see Marvin Farber, *The Foundation of Phenomenology*, Chapter II. Their validity in themselves is not affected by the fact that Husserl reinterpreted their significance.

nology. He even kept recommending them to his students, as I know from personal experience, as one of the best approaches to phenomenology.

During the next four years Husserl's ideas underwent a radical shift. This led to the complete abandonment of his plan to derive arithmetic from psychology. One factor, but not the only one, in this reorientation was his exchange with Gottlob Frege. It is certainly true that Frege had contended long before Husserl that logic and psychology were fundamentally different studies; and he had done so with particular force in his review of the [1] *Philosophie der Arithmetik*. In any event, by 1895 Husserl began to present in his lectures his celebrated critique of psychologism, which, as published in 1900 in the first volume of his *Logische Untersuchungen*, the *Prolegomena zu einer reinen Logik*, immediately stirred up considerable interest and excitement among logicians and psychologists.[1]

a. THE CRITIQUE OF PSYCHOLOGISM – What was this psychologism? The term is actually older than Husserl's use of it. He himself gives credit for it to Stumpf, who had used it as early as 1891 (see above p. 56) and who mentions in turn as its source another philosopher at the University of Halle, the renowned Hegelian historian Johann Eduard Erdmann, a fact which almost suggests a local tradition.[2] Nevertheless, compared with Stumpf's wider use, Husserl's, oriented as it was at the time toward problems of logic, is more specific. While he claimed that the term was meant merely as a descriptive, not as a derogatory label, he defined it as the view that "the theoretical foundation for the construction of logic ..., is supplied

---

[1] Much to Husserl's disappointment, the *Logische Untersuchungen* were never reviewed in the Anglo-American magazines of the time. However, Bertrand Russsell, in his survey of "Philosophy in the Twentieth Century," published first in *The Dial* in 1924, referred to it as "a monumental work"; also, in a spontaneous letter to Husserl of April 19, 1920, now in the Husserl Archives at Louvain, he mentioned the fact that he had the second edition with him in prison during his term for pacifist activities in 1917.

[2] There is, however, also an American predecessor: Orestes Brownson (1803–1876), the Catholic Transcendentalist, used it in his essay on "Ontologism and Psychologism" as early as 1874 (*Works* II, 468–486). According to him "pure, unmitigated psychologism asserts the subject as its own object, or at least as furnishing its object, from its own resources, independently of the real order of objective truth." Needless to say, he rejects it as an error "even more dangerous" than ontologism.

by psychology, and specifically by the psychology of knowledge";
to put it more pointedly, psychologism, for Husserl, stood for
the view that psychology was both the necessary and the
sufficient foundation of logic. John Stuart Mill's characterization
of logic in his *Examination of Sir William Hamilton's Philosophy*
provided the chief illustration for psychologism, while the
German psychologist and philosopher Theodor Lipps, the
originator of the empathy theory, was its main domestic example. It must not be overlooked, however, that later on even
Husserl used the term with a wider meaning. Thus in his *Formale
und transzendentale Logik* (1929) he extended it to any attempt
to "psychologize," i.e., to convert into psychological experiences
objects of whatever type. Obviously this wider type of psychologism has applications beyond logic, e.g., in such fields as ethics,
aesthetics, theology, sociology, etc.

In building up his case against logical psychologism, to which
he gives a remarkably full and fair hearing, Husserl first tries
to show the absurdity of its consequences and then to attack
the prejudices on which it is based. Among these consequences
Husserl first considers the relevance of any psychological laws
for the validity of logical principles. Mill and Spencer had tried
to interpret the law of contradiction as a psychological law,
based on our actual thinking. To Mill it was "one of our earliest
and most familiar generalizations from experience," based on
the observation "that belief and disbelief are two different
mental states excluding one another." [1] But granting the
factual premise (which may well be doubted psychologically),
does this justify more than a probable inference for the future
of our own thinking? And what does it prove about the propositional law itself that a statement cannot be both true and
false?

Another consequence is that psychologism logically implies
sceptical relativism. For as soon as we make logical laws depend
on psychological characteristics of human thinkers, we make them
also relative to these thinkers and consequently make man in
all his instability the measure of everything. And to Husserl
relativism is a self-defeating position: It denies the possibility of

---

[1] *System of Logic.* Book II, Ch. VII, 5.

all knowledge while asserting its own truth. In fact it even destroys the very meaning of truth and falsehood.

Then Husserl attacked the "psychologistic prejudices" directly, notably the following:

α. Rules for psychological phenomena like thinking must be derived from psychology;

β. The subject-matter of logic is nothing but psychological phenomena;

γ. Logic, which appeals to the criterion of self-evident certainty, deals with a special type of feeling, which, like any other feeling, is the proper study of psychology.

In answer to α. Husserl points out that any truth, not only truths about our psychological make-up, could be relevant for rules of thinking. Psychological laws enter only where such rules are technical instructions adjusted particularly to human nature.

Prejudice β. he meets by stating that just as mathematics does not deal with our operations of counting but with numbers (as Frege had already shown, and as Husserl now conceded), its "sister study, logic" is not concerned with the operations in which we form concepts, judgments, and inferences. Instead it investigates the products of these operations, i.e., such "ideal" entities as concept, proposition, conclusion, etc.

To γ. he replies: It is a mistake to think that logic deals with feelings of self-evidence qua feelings. At best, logic is interested in a statement of the conditions under which the phenomenon of self-evidence may arise.

Thus the refutation of the prejudices of psychologism involves at the same time a first survey, analysis, and description of the logical realm in its irreducible structure. For Husserl's *Prolegomena* were not meant to be only destructive. He had started out with showing the need of a theoretical science of logic for logic as a practical discipline for thinking. Now, after rejecting the aid of psychology, he proceeded to outline the idea of a pure logic purged of psychological admixtures.

b. THE CONCEPTION OF A PURE LOGIC – Husserl himself freely admitted that this was anything but a new idea. He mentions Kant, Herbart, Lotze, and Leibniz among its proponents and reserves special credit for the nearly forgotten

Bernhard Bolzano, "one of the greatest logicians of all times." [1]

But Husserl's own blueprint shows several original features, among which I shall mention merely what one might call the two-level structure of pure logic. The first level is that of the propositions or "truths" studied by the logic of statements (*"apophantics"*) as composed of meanings and their various combinations. The second level consists of the "things" to which these statements refer, i.e., of the states of affairs (*Sachverhalte*) which they assert, the relations, complexes, and other configurations which they can enter and which are to be investigated by what Husserl calls a *formal ontology*.

Actually, this two-level pattern incorporates two one-level conceptions of pure logic, formulated most impressively by Bolzano and by Meinong respectively. Bolzano had organized his pure logic on the propositional level around representational ideas, propositions, and truths (*Vorstellung an sich, Satz an sich, Wahrheit an sich*). Meinong knew only of the "state of affairs," which he had named *"Objectiv,"* and of other categories of formal ontology. Husserl's conception incorporated both these levels, that of the propositions, which are valid or invalid, and that of the states of affairs, which do or do not "subsist," as Bertrand Russell rendered Meinong's term. ("To be the case" might be a less hypostatizing equivalent of the rather harmless German word *"bestehen"*.)

However, the development of this pure logic in Husserl's own published writings is rather sketchy, although the mathematician Husserl continued to show interest in its mathematical formalization. He even seems to have taken notice of Bertrand

---

[1] This does not prevent Husserl from remaining critical of Bolzano's general philosophical position and of what he considered his naive Platonism. Thus, as early as March 27, 1905, he protested in a letter to Brentano:

I must add that all mystic-metaphysical exploitation of "Ideas," ideal possibilities, etc., is completely foreign to me. Even Bolzano does not make his "Vorstellungen an sich" and "Sätze an sich" real. These conceptions of Bolzano and the fact that in the first two volumes of his *Wissenschaftslehre* there are valuable logical accounts which are independent of empirical psychology have had a strong influence on me, as has Lotze's reinterpretation of the Platonic doctrine of Ideas. Nevertheless, I cannot call Bolzano a "teacher" or "leader" with regard to what I have given in the *Logische Untersuchungen*. What I offer are fragments of a theory of knowledge and of a phenomenology of knowledge. Both are foreign to Bolzano. He was an eminently mathematical and logical brain, but the most subtle conceptual analyses and formal logical theories go together in him with an almost naive epistemology. There is not a trace in him of the idea of a phenomenological elucidation of knowledge, (nor is there in Lotze).

An even fuller evaluation of Bolzano's work can be found in Husserl's draft for a "Vorrede" for the second edition of the *"Logische Untersuchungen"* in *Tijdschrift voor Philosophie* I (1939), 128–130.

Russell's work, but remained sceptical toward the value of a merely symbolic logic and of logical calculus, in which he took no active share. His *Formale und transzendentale Logik* (1929) contains some important additions to the conception of pure logic. Among them is that of a third level of logic, likewise of ideal structure, namely, that of speech, which consists of the identical sentences that express our propositional meanings: ideal, since, even when uttered at different times and places and by different speakers, they remain identically the same sentences.[1]

How far can this picture be related to the teachings of recent semiotics, especially to the distinctions between syntactics and semantics? As far as syntactics is concerned, it seems worth pointing out that Husserl himself developed the idea of a theory of syntactic forms and even of an a priori grammar for all possible languages.[2] On the other hand, it must not be overlooked that he applied the term syntax both to propositions and to sentences, and that he assigned priority to the theory of the syntactical forms of the propositions from which the forms of the sentences were to be derived. For semantics, understood as a study of the relationships between the signs and the designata, Husserl did not set aside any separate study; yet his later phenomenology of meanings includes the theoretical insights from which rules concerning legitimate and illegitimate meanings could be derived. Husserl was primarily concerned in pure logic as a study of the designata of our symbols, both as propositional meanings and as ontological objects meant through them, prior to studying their relationship to the stratum of linguistic expressions. Such study may then lead to the formulation of semiotic laws and rules.

Husserl's major interest, once he had established the possibility of a pure logic, turned immediately to different problems. He left its more systematic development to works like Alexander Pfänder's *Logik* (1921), which investigated the logic of concepts, of propositions, and of inferences, and to studies undertaken by some of his students based on this work, which dealt with the

---

[1] For a fuller development of this conception, see Dorion Cairns, "The Ideality of Verbal Expression" in *PPR* I (1941), 453–462.

[2] *Logische Untersuchungen* II, 1, IV; *Formale und transzendentale Logik*, § 1 f. and Beilage I.

logic of questions, of assumptions, and of laws and commands. Roman Ingarden, one of Husserl's Polish students, gave a particularly impressive application of this type of analysis to the literary work of art, in which he explored separately and in considerable detail its three main layers, the acoustic, that of the meanings, and that of the objects meant, without neglecting additional aspects and the total structure of the work.[1]

Excursus: Meinong's "Gegenstandstheorie" and Husserl's Logic

At this point a brief discussion of the relation between Husserl's phenomenology and the "Gegenstandstheorie" of Alexius Meinong seems in order, especially since Meinong's philosophy received a much earlier and more successful hearing in the Anglo-American world than either Husserl's or, for that matter, Brentano's. As early as 1904 Bertrand Russell devoted three sympathetic articles to it in Mind. G. E. Moore, C. D. Broad, and other leaders of the new British realists shared this interest. In the States Wilbur M. Urban was his chief American spokesman, who is now followed by Roderick M. Chisholm. It was not until the following decade that Husserl's philosophizing began to arouse interest.[2]

The mutual relationship between Husserl and Meinong provides a story of parallel developments combined with unhappy rivalry, where one might have hoped for a generous exchange of ideas. Even with full access to the relevant data one may doubt whether it is worth while to determine who preceded whom in the advocacy of the new ideas. The sad fact remains that, after initial friendly acknowledgments of agreements and even an occasional exchange of letters, the relations between Meinong and Husserl became more and more strained by the time the more successful Meinong had come out with his full-fledged Gegenstandstheorie (1902). Husserl saw in it and in the very name an

---

[1] Alexander Pfänder's Logik appeared in JPPF IV (1921). So did, in JPPF X (1928), Ernst Heller's Zur Logik der Annahme. Friedrich Löw's "Logik der Frage" came out in Archiv für die gesamte Psychologie LXVI (1928), 357–436. Roman Ingarden's Das literarische Kunstwerk was published by Max Niemeyer (Halle, 1931) and reviewed in Mind XLI (1932), 97 ff. by P. Leon. The author's Gesetz und Sittengesetz, published by Max Niehans Verlag (Zurich, 1935), was reviewed by H. B. Acton in Mind XLVII (1938), 264 f.

[2] See J. N. Findlay, "The Influence of Meinong in Anglo-American Countries" in Meinong Gedenkschrift (Graz, Steierische Verlagsanstalt, 1952), pp. 9–20.

unacknowledged loan from the "general theory of objects" (*allgemeine Gegenstandstheorie*) which he had advocated in at least two of the sections of his *Logische Untersuchungen* of 1901, and an inferior form at that. Meinong in turn, who, without using the name *Gegenstandstheorie*, had carried out studies in the area designated by it for at least a decade before, resented this implication so much that from then on he completely stopped referring to Husserl's work. But even in his admirable autobiographical abstract of his own work Meinong stated that he felt himself closer to phenomenology than to any other contemporary philosophical movement.[1]

What makes Meinong's philosophizing relevant to a history of the Phenomenological Movement is the fact that from 1874 to 78 Meinong was one of Brentano's students, who, like Carl Stumpf, his senior by 5 years, and Husserl, his junior by 6 years, had gone beyond his master very much in the same direction as they had. Among the three, Meinong was the one who kept least in touch with Brentano, although he lived and taught geographically closest to him, even after he had moved on from Vienna to the University of Graz. Yet in Brentano's eyes there was practically no difference between Meinong's and Husserl's deviations.

In the present context the only pertinent doctrine of Meinong is his theory of objects (*Gegenstandstheorie*), in which he tried to include a number of items which the existing sciences had left "homeless" (*heimatlos*), as he put it.[2] Among them he counted not only qualities given merely to our senses, but also such things as "negative objects." In fact, Meinong even acknowledged "impossible objects" like round squares as legitimate denizens of this world, since they could be referred to in true or false statements. His final system of these objects comprised four main groups: (1) theoretical objects, (2) objectlike entities (*Objektive*), (3) objects of appraisal (*Dignitative*), and (4) objects of desire (*Desiderative*). Among these it was the "*Objektiv*" which aroused most interest. Meinong interpreted it as a peculiar

---

[1] *Selbstdarstellung* in Schmidt, Raymund, ed., *Philosophie der Gegenwart*, Vol. I (1921), p. 55 f. – Husserl, in his diary notes of 1906, expressed the relationship in the following terms: "We are like two travellers in the same dark continent. Of course we often see the same thing and describe it, but often differently, in accordance with our different masses of apperception." (*PPR* XVI (1956), 296).

[2] For a fuller account see J. N. Findlay, *Meinong's Theory of Objects* (Oxford, Oxford University Press, 1933).

complex entity which was asserted in a judgment or assumed in an assumption; its most appropriate expression was the noun clause of a statement like "it is true (false) *that there are atoms.*" Meinong also distinguished between several kinds of these *"Objektive."* He did not claim for them the kind of reality which can be found in full-bodied concrete objects. But since they were more than nothing, he used the current German verb *"bestehen"* as the most appropriate name for this type of secondary existence, without describing it in greater detail. Obviously, the *"Objektiv"* in this sense was very much the same thing that Stumpf had called *"Sachverhalt."* Yet Meinong felt that the latter term was inadequate, since it would apply only to the factual *Objektiv*, not to a neutral one. But like Stumpf Meinong did not recognize any intermediate layer of meanings between acts and states of affairs, as Husserl did.

Among other features in Meinong's philosophy which make it congenial to phenomenology are its liberalized attitude toward new phenomena; its interest in phenomena without reality status; the development of Brentano's empiricism in the direction of an empirically founded apriorism; and finally, its emancipation from an admitted initial psychologism. Nevertheless, there remain considerable differences in approach and content even from Husserl's early phenomenology. There is in Meinong a decided preference for ontological questions, and little if any interest in the questions of how such entities are given. Specifically, Meinong shows no interest in the key phenomenon of intentionality, which remained the main link between Brentano and Husserl. As far as Meinong's philosophizing parallels phenomenological thinking, it would come closest to the object-centered phenomenology of the older Göttingen Circle.

The relation between Meinong's *Gegenstandstheorie* and Husserl's phenomenology may be summed up in the following manner:

α. For both, the Brentano of the Vienna years had been the point of departure, and both had moved beyond him in the direction of a liberalized admission of phenomena other than physical and psychical.

β. They both had discovered the need of developing a

systematic study of types of objects thus far neglected in ontology.

γ. Both emphasized the importance of disregarding questions of existence in the study of these objects.

On the other hand, Meinong, in his much more objectivistic approach, had no particular interest in the analysis of consciousness and in the ways of appearance of an object, which became the dominating concern of Husserl's phenomenology.

2. The Beginnings of Phenomenology as the Subjective Correlate of Pure Logic

After the appearance of the first volume of the *Logische Untersuchungen*, for most of his readers Husserl was a realistic objectivist, and his emphasis on ideal laws even seemed to predispose him for full-fledged Platonism. It came therefore as something of a shock to those who had expected a systematic development of the idea of a pure logic when the second volume, appearing in 1901 under the title "Investigations concerning the Phenomenology and Theory of Knowledge," presented six loosely connected studies, of which at most the first four ("Expression and Meaning," "The Ideal Unity of the Species and the New Theories of Abstraction," "Concerning the Doctrine of Whole and Part," and "The Difference Between Dependent and Independent Meanings and the Idea of a Pure Grammar") could be considered preparatory for a systematic pure logic. The two remaining and largest studies dealt, however, openly with such topics as "Intentional Experiences (*Erlebnisse*) and their 'Contents'," and "Elements of a Phenomenological Elucidation of Knowledge." This sounded much more like the proper concern of a psychology of experience and of knowledge than of "apophantics" and "formal ontology." Quite a few felt that this was nothing but a relapse into the now discredited psychologism.[1] To understand the reason for this seeming about-face

[1] See, for instance, C. S. Peirce in his only explicit reference to Husserl in *Collected Papers* 4.7 (1906):
How many writers of our generation (if I must call names, in order to direct the reader to further acquaintance with a generally described character – let it be in this case the distinguished Husserl), after underscored protestations that their discourse shall be of logic exclusively and not by any means of psychology. ... forthwith become intent upon those elements of the process of thinking which seem to be special to a mind like that of the human race, *as we find it*, to too great a neglect of those elements which must belong as much to any one as to any other mode of embodying the same thought.

means to understand the basic motivation for the genesis of Husserl's phenomenology.

The idea of a pure logic has at times been misinterpreted as an attempt to separate logic completely from all contact with psychological phenomena and with psychology. That this cannot and must not be done is precisely Husserl's point in the new studies. Even the ideal logical entities are given to us only in experiences, although experiences of a special kind. No philosophical and critical logic can therefore ignore them. This would seem to imply that what was needed was a psychology of the ways in which we experience logic, in fact a psychology of thinking. But psychology of thinking, especially of the type prevalent in Husserl's early days, was entirely unfit to satisfy the needs of the new logic.[1] Thus experimental studies on speed of problem solving or on logical or general intelligence are hardly apt to throw much light on the question of how we know about the laws of logic. What Husserl wanted was a descriptive study of the processes in which the entities studied in pure logic are presented. In one rather secondary passage of the introduction to the second volume of the *Logische Untersuchungen* he had even characterized the new study, now named "phenomenology," in Brentano's fashion as descriptive psychology.[2] But as early as 1903 he tried to correct this rather unfortunate self-interpretation.[3] For descriptive psychology as such, much like descriptive anatomy or geology, is interested only in actual facts of experience as they have been and can be observed in real individual cases. Instead, Husserl's intent was a description of the ideal types of logical experience corresponding to the ideal logical laws. Whether or not they had counterparts in actual experiences was immaterial to him. Specifically, he was interested in the descriptive analysis of various types of thinking, of various forms and degrees of intuitive consciousness, and of

It is hardly necessary to add that Peirce's interpretation of Husserl's "psychology" as restricted to the empirical human race is a fundamental misunderstanding of his intentions.

[1] Since then, partly as a result of Husserl's stimulation, there has been a considerable change. The work of the Würzburg school, the studies by Max Wertheimer on productive thinking and by Karl Duncker on problem solving, which often utilize Husserl's ideas, are cases in point.

[3] *Einleitung* § 6, *Zusätze* § 3.

[2] *Archiv für systematische Philosophie* IX (1903), 397–400.

modes of symbolic and direct representation. From the outset, this study of the pure types or essences of these experiences was to be neutral toward the question of what went on in actual cases. This was to remain the domain of the empirical science of psychology, including descriptive psychology. Instead of merely factual relationships, the new "phenomenology" was to study essential relationships that could be understood independently of actual cases, empirical or experimental. Once this had been achieved, philosophy would be in a position to account epistemologically for our supposed knowledge of the logical entities and evaluate its claims, by showing the adequacy or inadequacy for their task of the basic types of our experiencing acts.

The relationship between pure logic and phenomenology, understood as the study of the experiences corresponding to the logical entities, illustrates an insight which pervades the whole of Husserl's work, including even his early and supposedly altogether psychologistic *Philosophy of Arithmetic:* the insight that there is a parallelism between the structures of the subjective act and of its objective referent. This parallelism forms the basis for a correlative investigation under which both aspects of any phenomenon are to be studied and described in conjunction. To study one without the other would be an artificial abstraction which may have its uses, but which ultimately requires reintegration into the context of the concrete experience from which they have been isolated. This is what Husserl later on came to call the parallelism between the "noetic" (act) and the "noematic" (content).

It was at this point that Husserl began to use the term "phenomenology" extensively. Yet there was apparently nothing deliberate about its introduction. Husserl was familiar with its contemporary uses, for instance, in the case of Ernst Mach (see above, p. 9 note 2). The first time it appeared in Husserl's independent writings was in a footnote to the first edition of the *Prolegomena* (1900), where he spoke of a "descriptive phenomenology of inner experience" as a basis for both empirical psychology and epistemology. Only in the introduction to the second volume of the *Logische Untersuchungen* of 1901 did the name "phenomenology" make its appearance as the title for a new and

important discipline. But even then he characterized it misleadingly as "descriptive psychology," a characterization which
had to be recanted in the revision of that introduction in 1913.

There would however be little point in tracing the history of
Husserl's definitions of phenomenology. The important question
is what went on under the refurbished flag. For it was through
Husserl's actual analyses that the new conception received its
meaning. There was a concreteness and thoroughness about
these which Husserl probably never reached again. Starting
usually from semantic distinctions, Husserl penetrated into the
phenomena far deeper than any previous analyses had done.
Divergent views were always discussed with great patience and
fairness. Even Husserl himself continued to look back on the
second volume of his *Logische Untersuchungen* as

> not a mere program (and more specifically one of those high-flown ones
> with which philosophy is so abundantly blessed) but as attempts at really
> carrying out fundamental work on "things" (*Sachen*) immediately in-
> tuited and grasped ... which, even where they proceed by way of criti-
> cisms, do not get lost in discussions of standpoints, but leave the last word
> to the things themselves and to the work performed on them.[1]

It is for the sake of conveying at least a taste of these concrete
analyses, as well as for the interest of the topics analyzed, that
I now want to present some of their most significant results.

a. HUSSERL'S SEMANTICS – In the manner sanctioned by
the precedent of John Stuart Mill, Husserl begins his concrete
logical studies with a discussion of "Expression and Meaning."
Much of what is contained in these initial analyses has been made
obsolete by subsequent investigations. Nevertheless some of
Husserl's ideas may still deserve attention, and that not merely
for the sake of the historical record.[2] For such consideration
I would nominate the following distinctions:

α. *Meaning* and *manifestation*, i.e., what an expression
signifies (*Bedeutung*), and what it manifests about the speaker

---

[1] *Logische Untersuchungen*. Preface to the second edition (1913), p. X.
[2] The account of Husserl's semantic studies given by C. K. Ogden and I. A.
Richards, *The Meaning of Meaning* (1949), pp. 269–272, is misleading, since it is based
on the very different perspective of the London lectures, which take no specific
interest in problems of semantics. – For a selection from this study in Dorion Cairns's
excellent translation see now Krikorian, Yervant H. and Edel, Abraham, *Contemporary Philosophic Problems* (New York, Macmillan, 1959), pp. 36–44.

(*Kundgabe*). The manifesting function differs from the seman-
ticists' practical and emotive functions of language, which are
symbolic and purposive functions. Manifestation is involuntary,
and its understanding is a matter of sign interpretation by the
outsider.

β. *Meaning* and *object meant:* This distinction is revealed
particularly in cases where different meanings refer to the same
object ("Napoleon," "the conqueror at Austerlitz," "the loser
at Waterloo," etc.) and also where meanings are self-contradictory ("square circle"), hence are not matched by an object
meant, although they are not completely meaningless, as is the
pseudo-word "abracadabra." Here Husserl utilized and developed
some of Frege's ideas.

γ. *Signitive* or *"symbolic" meanings* and *intuitive meanings:*
The former point at their objects without intuitive content
(*Anschauung*), which the latter include. Not only the layman
reading a mathematical demonstration with very limited understanding thinks in merely signitive meanings; it is precisely
the accomplished mathematician who no longer needs to resort
to intuitive representation.

δ. Multiple *acts of meaning* and the one *ideal meaning* to which
they all point: This identical meaning is to Husserl an ideal
entity, not only a psychological datum.

b. HUSSERL'S DOCTRINE OF UNIVERSALS (ESSENCES)
– The conception of identical meanings for numerically separate
expressions leads Husserl to the problem of universals. But for
Husserl the significance of this perennial topic reaches much
farther. For phenomenology, now defined as the study of the
general essence of consciousness and of its various structures,
presupposes the conception of universal essences.

At this point Husserl has to face the problems discussed by
British empiricism and particularly the objections of its nomi-
nalistic wing. With Berkeley – according to some of Husserl's
remarks the philosopher whom he had studied first, and whose
arguments he always took most seriously without accepting
his conclusions – Husserl rejected Locke's unfortunate doctrine
of general ideas (after the manner of his weird general triangle
which was neither equilateral nor scalene, and yet had both these

properties at the same time). But this did not make him accept the substitutes of the nominalists, who had replaced the universals by particulars with various general functions made possible by special acts of selective attention. After careful examination Husserl concluded that Berkeley's, Hume's, Hamilton's, and Mill's solutions of the problem involved them all in absurd consequences. Worse than that, they all had taken to distorting the meaning of universal propositions. At the same time Husserl showed that there were special acts of generic experience or "ideation" which the old-style empiricism had overlooked and in which general essences were genuinely apprehended. To be sure, general essences, such as the essence "color," are given only on the foundation of the intuitive apprehension of particular examples. Nevertheless the act of ideation (the celebrated *Wesensschau*) is an original type of experience. It cannot be reduced to mere isolating abstraction or to acts of selective attention, which can do no more than pick out individual wholes and lack the capacity of universalizing.[1]

Husserl's investigations answer by no means all the questions that can be raised about the nature of universals.[2] But they do establish at least their existence to the extent of showing that the meaning of universal propositions can be satisfied only by the admission of general essences; that it presents instances in which we believe we face them directly; and that it provides important insights about the way in which they are given.

How far does this rehabilitation of the universals imply the acceptance of a Platonic realism? This charge, if such it be, has indeed been levelled against Husserl time and again. But all that Husserl had claimed at this stage was that universals were entities of their own with an existence sufficient to allow the assertion of true propositions about them. He never stated that they were real, eternal, changeless, or in any way superior to particulars. Their particular mode of existence always remained undetermined, except for the fact that it was called "ideal"

[1] Husserl's method of achieving essential insights resembles strikingly W. E. Johnson's "intuitive induction," described twenty years later in his *Logic* (Part II, Chapter VIII, section 3 ff.). There is, however, no evidence for believing that Johnson was familiar with Husserl's *Logische Untersuchungen*.

[2] The structure of general essences and of a number of related phenomena has been the subject of several studies in *JPPF*, especially by Jean Hering, Roman Ingarden, and the present author, in volumes IV, VII, and XI.

(*ideales* or *ideelles Sein*). To this should be added that later on, when Husserl adopted the view that all logical entities, along with all other objectivities, had their origin in subjectivity, he explicitly tried to show how universals are "constituted" by the subjective consciousness which derives them from the perceptual experience of particulars.[1]

c. THE INTENTIONALITY OF CONSCIOUSNESS – The investigation of the intentionality of consciousness is not only a climax in the *Logische Untersuchungen*, it contains what Husserl always considered the central insight in his phenomenological analysis of consciousness. Actually Husserl gives generous credit to Brentano for having called attention to this unique phenomenon. But that must not make us overlook the fact that Husserl transformed his teacher's conception to such an extent that the identity of the referents of the two portraits may well be questioned.

To begin with omissions from Brentano's conception:

α. When Husserl took over the conception of the directedness of consciousness toward objects, he at once dropped the idea of their immanency in the act, which Brentano himself abandoned only gradually and, in fact, along with the very term "intentional." Thus it is only in Husserl's thought that the term "intentional" acquired the meaning of directedness toward an object rather than that of the object's immanence in consciousness. Also, it was only with Husserl that the acts thus directed were called "intentions" and referred to "intentional objects," i.e., objects that were the targets of intentions, both being terms that Brentano had never used. Accordingly, from now on the expressions "intentional" and "intentionality" stood for the relational property of having an intention, or being aimed at by it.

β. Husserl no longer claimed that intentionality was the necessary and sufficient distinguishing characteristic of all psychical phenomena. In accordance with his disinterest in Brentano's chief concern, namely, the proper distinction between psychology and the physical sciences, his only concern was the investigation of a class of phenomena called "acts," which were defined by the presence of this characteristic. Thus Husserl

---

[1] See, e.g., *Erfahrung und Urteil*, § 82, pp. 396–7.

could dispense with Brentano's rather forced attempt to save the intentional character of mere feelings without referents by the distinction between primary and secondary objects – an attempt which made it possible to say that such feelings had secondary objects in the form of references to themselves. For Husserl there is no reason to deny the existence of non-intentional experiences (*Erlebnisse*) side by side with the intentional ones.

To this extent Husserl's account could be regarded as simplified and closer to common experience. However, Husserl's own analyses enrich increasingly the core sense of 'directedness to an object,' as it is implied in the terms "consciousness *of*," "perception *of*," "joy *at*," etc. One might distinguish four additional characteristics of Husserl's intentionality:

α. *Intention "objectivates":* This means that it refers the data which are integral parts of the stream of consciousness (*reell*) to the "intentional objects." These intentional objects are given normally only *through* such data, mostly characterized as sense-data (*Empfindungen*) and later by the name of *hyletic data*. It is the function of the intention to relate these data to an object which is itself not part of the act, but "transcendent" to it. Thus Husserl, in this respect not unlike Brentano, sees in intentional reference by no means a simple relationship, but a complex structure in which data are used as raw materials, as it were, and integrated into the total object which forms the pole of all these references. Identity of this object is compatible with various ways of referring to it, such as perception, thought, doubt (which Husserl called the "qualities" of the intention, as opposed to its "matter").

The whole idea of intentional consciousness as an objectivation of raw materials implies and presupposes a view of perception, as well as of other acts, which is by no means uncontested. It should be added that it is far from generally accepted among phenomenologists. Certainly it is in need of careful re-examination and re-evaluation.

β. *Intention identifies:* A further step in the objectivating function of intentions is that they allow us to assign a variety of successive data to the same referents or "poles" of meaning. Without such identifying functions there would be nothing but a stream of perceptions, similar but never identical. Intention supplies the synthetic function by which the various aspects, perspectives, and stages of an object are all focussed upon, and integrated into, identical cores.

γ. *Intention connects:* Each aspect of an identical object refers to related aspects which form its horizon, as it were. The frontal aspect of a head refers to the lateral aspects (profiles) and, least definitely, to its rear. It gives rise to legitimate expectations for further experiences, which may or may not be fulfilled in the further development of our experience, yet are clearly foreshadowed in what is given.

At this point a subdivision among the intentional acts becomes necessary which may not be sufficiently explicit in Husserl's own presentation: that between acts of *mere intention* and acts of *intuitive fulfillment.* The first group includes all those acts which blindly refer to the intentional objects when we merely think of them, yet have no clear idea of what they are like. The second group contains those acts which fill the empty forms of such intentions with intuitive content, as it were, as in perception or imagination. Obviously there are any number of transitions between these contrary opposites; for instance, between the mere thought of a regular icosahedron and its intuitive fulfillment. Now the first group, the merely "signitive" or "symbolic" intentions, always refer to such fulfilling acts as to their proper "sense," or proper destination. One might compare them with the check that refers to cash payment. Both acts are of course intentional in the larger sense of referring to intentional objects, and differ only in the way in which they refer to them. When Husserl calls the first group "intentions" and the second "fulfillments," he may give the impression that fulfillment is not really an intentional act – an impression which would be definitely misleading. There are thus two types of intentions, both having equal rights as far as their intentional structure goes: promising intentions,·which are still intuitively empty, and fulfilling intentions, which also carry intuitive content. But the two are intimately related. The first even requires the second as its complement, as it were.

δ. *Intention constitutes:* It is only in the period after the *Logische Untersuchungen* that Husserl goes so far as to ascribe to the intentions the function of actually constituting the intentional object. It thus becomes the "achievement"(*Leistung*) of the intentional acts. Hence the intentional object is no longer conceived as the pre-existent referent to which the intending act refers as already given, but as something which originates in the act. This constituting function of the intentional act can only be revealed by the method which Husserl calls *intentional analysis*. I shall reserve the consideration of the subject for the discussion of the phenomenological constitution below (p. 146), where I shall also consider its changing meaning for Husserl.

I might sum up the account of Husserl's "intention" by describing it as that component of any act which is responsible not only for its pointing at an object but also for (α.) interpreting pre-given materials in such a way that a full object is presented to our consciousness, (β.) establishing the identity between the referents of several intentional acts, (γ.) connecting the various stages of intuitive fulfillment, and (δ.) "constituting" the object meant.[1]

Some of the functions performed by Husserl's intentions, notably the objectifying, the identifying, and the constituting ones, are likely to remind the reader of Kant's analysis of experience, in which the intellect (*Verstand*), with the help of its categories, synthesizes the sense-data supplied by the perception (*Anschauung*), thus constituting identical objects within the flux of our sensations. This is by no means a coincidence, and yet, at the time when Husserl developed his doctrine of intention, he was still rather aloof from, though no longer hostile to, Kant to the degree that Brentano was. It was only during the following decade that Husserl became fully aware and proud of the parallels and common concerns he had with Kant and the Neo-Kantians, particularly of the Marburg persuasion.[2] But this

---

[1] Incidentally, Husserl uses the term "intention" not only for a component of acts but also for the relation between sign (or symbol) and its referent (See p. 104 f.); in fact this is the sense which occurs first in the *Logische Untersuchungen*. Thus the word "icosahedron" has the "intention" of the referent or "designatum," and this referent, when intuitively presented, "fulfills" the "merely symbolic intention" of the term. However, this relation between symbol and symbolized is clearly the offspring of intentional acts which establish "objective" intentionality in the field of symbolism. One might therefore consider this relationship as derivative from the intentional acts described above.

[2] Husserl's closest contact was with Paul Natorp, whose attack on psychologism had preceded his own by about thirteen years. It was in fact Natorp who in 1901 had given Husserl's more thorough-going discussion of psychologism in the *Prolegomena* the earliest and strongest recognition it received at the time (*Kantstudien* VI, 270 ff.).

fact must not make us overlook the differences. Specifically, Husserl's interpretation of the active synthesis of empirical data does not involve the idea of a priori forms to be imposed upon materials provided by merely passive sensation. Nor does it involve him in the Kantian dualism of appearance and "thing-in-itself," which results from the question of how we can justify our right to predicate our a priori conceptions of an empirical world.

Husserl's conception of intention shows, however, unmistakable traces of William James's inspiration. The matter is important enough to justify a brief digression into the relation between Husserl's phenomenology and William James's psychology.

Excursus: *William James's Significance for Husserl's Phenomenology* [1]

In the preceding chapter we had occasion to discuss the immediate outcome of James's visit to Carl Stumpf in Prague on October 30, 1882. But this was not the end of the story. Their encounter influenced also the further course of the Phenomenological Movement.

To be sure, James himself does not seem to have taken more than casual notice of the beginnings of a Phenomenological Movement. All that can be proved is that he knew Brentano's and Stumpf's pre-phenomenological statements. As far as Meinong is concerned James referred to him in 1908 as the "unspeakable Meinong," [1] an outburst explained not only by

But he had also emphasized the incompleteness of Husserl's approach and had actually predicted that Husserl's attempt to give his pure logic philosophical foundations would eventually lead him into the path of Kantian epistemology with its emphasis on spontaneity and construction. Apparently this development took place toward the end of the first decade of the new century and became manifest when Husserl adopted the Kantian term "transcendental," although modified, for the characterization of his phenomenology. Suddenly, as he described it in a letter to Natorp (June 29, 1918), Kant had become accessible to him. Yet in spite of the cordial philosophical contacts between Husserl and the Marburg school (perhaps even more cordial on Husserl's part than on Natorp's and Cassirer's) there remained a basic difference in problems and methods which Husserl himself, in an earlier letter to Natorp (March 18, 1909), tried to explain by their different points of departure, phenomenology starting "from below" with concrete phenomena, the Neo-Kantians "from above" with rigid abstract formulae, which were to be taken for granted. – See also the important information in Rudolf Boehm's introduction to *Husserliana* VII, p. XIX.

[1] Letter to Henry N. Gardiner in R. B. Perry, *The Thought and Character of William James*, II, 484 f.

James's opposition to the intricacy of Meinong's doctrine of "supposals" and of his *Objektive*, but also to his "complacent *Breite*." [1]

How far was James aware of the existence of a German professor by the name of Husserl, in whom some of the travelling Harvard students began to take an interest during the first decade of the new century? Hardly more than superficially.[2] It seems to be no longer ascertainable whether he ever read
[1] anything of Husserl's work. The appearances are against it. Walter B. Pitkin, who was on pretty close terms with James, relates in his autobiography that James, much to Husserl's lasting grief, had advised one of the great eastern publishing houses against accepting Pitkin's complete translation of the *Logische Untersuchungen*: "Nobody in America would be interested in a new and strange German work on Logic." [3] One may well speculate on what would have happened if James had taken the time to consult his friend Carl Stumpf on this "strange work."

But there is one remote and yet more lasting effect of the momentous encounter which we can now trace with considerable certainty: that upon Edmund Husserl. Students of Husserl's work have often been struck by the many parallels between his phenomenological insight into the structure of consciousness and some of the central chapters in James's *Principles of Psychology*. Thus the late Alfred Schuetz pointed out in considerable detail the parallels, or, as he put it, the coalescence between the two in such matters as the doctrine of the stream of thought, mentioning at the same time James's doctrine of fringes and that of intersubjectivity.[4]

It seems to me safe, however, to go considerably beyond a mere statement of coincidences. Of course it is well known that Husserl himself was most generous in acknowledging his debt to

[1] Oral communication from Dickinson S. Miller.

[2] The fact that, according to a communication from Andrew D. Osborn, the Husserl Archives in Louvain contain a reprint of James's articles from the *Journal of Philosophy* of 1904 ("A World of Pure Experience"), on which Husserl himself inscribed "Vom Verf." (author's gift) proves little about James's interest in Husserl.

[3] *On My Own* (New York, Charles Scribner's Sons, 1944), p. 319.

[4] "William James's Conception of the Stream of Thought Phenomenologically Interpreted" in *PPR I* (1941), 442–452. See also the paper by Aron Gurwitsch on "The Object of Thought" in *PPR* VII (1947), 347–353.

James in general terms, especially in conversation with American
visitors during the twenties and thirties. Yet with the exception   [1]
of one footnote in the *Logische Untersuchungen*, which is to be
sure very outspoken,[1] there is a conspicuous absence of specific
references to James, especially in Husserl's *Ideen*, the main
source for Husserl's conception of the stream of consciousness
– even allowing for Husserl's diminishing tendency to refer to
the writings of other philosophers. Nevertheless, references can
be found in Husserl's posthumous works, e.g., in *Husserliana VI
and VII*.

Thanks to contemporary and later documents and witness
accounts, it is now possible to piece together the story to a much
greater extent than before. Apparently it was Carl Stumpf who
first drew Husserl's attention to James. There would have been
ample occasion for such reminders, even before the appearance
of the *Principles* in 1890, during the three years between 1886
and 1889 which the two Brentano students spent together in
Halle, and which began four years after the encounter between
James and Stumpf in Prague. Besides, Husserl himself told
Dorion Cairns in 1931 that it had been Stumpf who had referred
him first to James's *Psychology*.[2] The earliest evidence of
Husserl's study of James can be found in an article of 1894 [3] where,
in his discussion of the contents of cognitive acts, he refers twice
to James's chapter on "The Stream of Thought" and specifically
to his doctrine of "fringes." In his later references to these early
studies Husserl seems to have spoken variously of his intention
to review James's *Principles* (to Alfred Schuetz), of having
discontinued the series for the *Monatshefte* in order to study
James more thoroughly (to Dorion Cairns), and even of having
abandoned his plan of writing a psychology, "feeling that

---

[1] " .... It will be apparent from the present work that James's genius-like
observations in the field of descriptive psychology of the cognitive experiences
(*Vorstellungserlebnisse*) are far from making psychologism inevitable. For the help
and progress which I owe to this excellent investigator in the field of descriptive
analysis have only aided my emancipation from the psychologistic position." (*Logische Untersuchungen*, II, 1 (Second edition), p. 208). In referring to James's anti-
psychologistic tendencies Husserl may be thinking, among other things, of the
"thoroughgoing dualism" between mind knowing and thing known in *Principles* I,
296 ff.

[2] Communication from Dorion Cairns, based on his notes about his conversations
with Husserl.

[3] "Psychologische Studien zur elementaren Logik" in *Philosophische Monatshefte*, XXX (1894), 159–191.

James had said what he wanted to say" (to Ralph Barton Perry).[1]

But apart from these oral statements, explained more or less by the occasion, there is now much more contemporary and unquestionable testimony in the shape of Husserl's confidential diary written during the so-called crisis of 1906. Here, in describing his early quandaries about the relation between the world of pure logic and that of conscious acts, and between the phenomenological and the logical spheres, Husserl put down the following sentences about his first years as a lecturer at the University of Halle:

> Then in 1891–92 came the lecture course on psychology which made me look into the literature on descriptive psychology, in fact look forward to it with longing. James's *Psychology*, of which I could read only some and very little, yielded some flashes (*Blitze*). I saw how a daring and original man did not let himself be held down by tradition and attempted to really put down what he saw and to describe it. Probably this influence was not without significance for me, although I could read and understand precious few pages. Indeed, to describe and to be faithful, this was absolutely indispensable. To be sure, it was not until my article of 1894 that I read larger sections and took excerpts from them.[2]

Unfortunately, no such excerpts seem to have survived, since Husserl himself destroyed much of the material from the period before 1900. There is, however, evidence of his studies in his copy of the *Principles of Psychology* in the Husserl Archives in Louvain, which shows intensive markings, chiefly in the first volume and specifically in Chapters IX (The Stream of Thought), XI (Attention), and XII (Conception).

But such evidence is no substitute for a concrete demonstration of James's influence in Husserl's own writings. That in the case of a thinker like Husserl such an influence could never take the form of mere passive reception goes without saying. For this if for no other reason no explicit credit could be expected in each single case. Besides, many of these influences may have been at work almost unnoticed and may simply have helped to accelerate certain developments already in progress.

Little would be needed to show traces of James's inspiration

---

[1] From diary notes of 1930, which R. B. Perry copied for me.

[2] "Persönliche Aufzeichnungen" in *PPR* XVI (1956), 294 f. The only other thinker mentioned by Husserl in this context is Meinong, but in a rather critical vein. All the more impressive is the testimony to James's influence.

in the case of such conceptions as that of the "stream of
consciousness" (Husserl's rendering of James's usual phrase
"stream of thought") after the publication of the second volume
of the *Logische Untersuchungen*, which had been in the making
in the years after 1894; the same applies to a concept like that
of the "fringe." But there is one case, possibly even more important, where James's influence is less obvious and has not yet
been noticed: Husserl's concept of intentionality.

The usual, superficially correct, story is that Husserl had taken
over the term and the general idea from Franz Brentano's
Psychologie, to whom Husserl gives specific credit, at least in the
crucial fifth of the six investigations of the second volume,
although the term makes its first appearance in the earlier one
on "Expression and Meaning." But more attentive students like
Ludwig Landgrebe [1] noticed long ago that for Husserl, in
contrast to Brentano, the term "intention" (which never
occurs in noun form in Brentano) stands for something much
more than, and rather different from, mere relatedness to an
object (as supposedly in Brentano), namely

α. for the character in our acts which allows different
acts to have identically the same object;

β. for an active and in fact creative achievement, rather
than for a passive or merely static directedness.

What was responsible for this change in Husserl's interpretation of the phenomenon with all its implications, among which
Landgrebe includes even Husserl's later idealism? Landgrebe
thinks that the germ for these distinctive features can be found
retrospectively in Husserl's studies on the philosophy of arithmetic. Without denying this possibility, it seems to me equally
important to point out what motifs in James's *Principles*
pertinent to this issue could have awakened a creative response
in Husserl's thinking.

As to the first original trait in Husserl's picture of intention,
i.e., the identifying function of intentionality, the most relevant

---

[1] "Husserl's Phänomenologie und die Motive zu ihrer Umbildung," published
first in *Revue internationale de philosophie* I (1939) and again in *Phänomenologie und
Metaphysik* (Hamburg, Schroeder, 1949), pp. 56–100. See also my "Der Begriff der
Intentionalität in der Scholastik, bei Brentano und bei Husserl" in *Philosophische
Hefte* V (1936), 75–91.

passages occur in *Principles*, Chapter XII (Conception), under the name of "the principle of constancy in the mind's meanings":

The same matters can be thought of in successive portions of the mental stream, and some of these portions can know that they mean the same matters which the other portions meant. One might put it otherwise by saying that the mind can always intend, and know when it intends, to think of the Same.–This *sense of sameness* is the very keel and backbone of our thinking (p. 459).

It also deserves mention that in James this whole problem makes its appearance in connection with his momentous doctrine of the two types of knowledge referring to the same object, the pre-predicative *knowledge by acquaintance with* it, and the predicative *knowledge about* it, a distinction which will likewise make its appearance in Husserl.

Here then is a place where James tackles the very problem which Husserl, in contrast to Brentano, came to consider as central both in the *Logische Untersuchungen* and later in his studies on the phenomenological constitution of objects. And what is particularly suggestive: he employs in this context the verb "to intend" to express an intention to think, in other words, he sees intention as a practical function applied to an intellectual act.

Later, James also refers to "conceptions" or "things intended to be thought about," which in contrast to the "flux of opinions" stand stiff and immutable like Plato's "Realm of Ideas." Here, in the "things intended to be thought about," we have almost Husserl's term "intentional object."

Finally, in developing, in opposition to a copy theory of knowledge, his own view of knowledge as a self-transcendent function, James speaks of the goal of the mind as "to take cognizance of a reality, *intend it*, or be 'about' it." Thus James actually uses, however casually, in a cognitive context the infinitive "to intend" in the active, if not yet creative, sense of aiming at, pointing, or meaning which Ludwig Landgrebe stresses as the second important difference between Brentano's and Husserl's conceptions of intentionality.[1]

---

[1] "Intending" in the sense of "pointing at" also occurs in the, for James, very important essay on "The Function of Cognition" of 1884, first published in *Mind* X (1885) and republished in *The Meaning of Truth*, pp. 1–42); the passage referred to appears on p. 23. However, in spite of some highly interesting parallels between

Again, one must not overemphasize the importance of such agreements in formulation and assert a direct loan from James on Husserl's part. But it seems reasonable to assume that, even in the case of Husserl's doctrine of intentionality, James's chapter on Conception was an important directive stimulus in the transformation of the Brentano motif.

Of course, it must always be borne in mind that James's primary interest in this area was psychological. By contrast, Husserl's concern was mostly epistemological. And eventually, whether for better or for worse, the whole development and use of the concept in Husserl's philosophy exceeded anything that can be found in James's striking but relatively incidental discussion.

d. PHENOMENOLOGICAL INTUITING ('ANSCHAUUNG' AND 'WESENSSCHAU') – For Husserl the ultimate test of all knowledge, and of phenomenological insight in particular, is *Anschauung*; its most important type is the much vaunted, often misused, and even more often ridiculed *Wesensschau*.

It is not easy to translate these German terms, or even to find approximate equivalents for them. *"Anschauung"* (looking at) differs from *Erfahrung* (experience), inasmuch as experience always refers to cases which are at least supposedly real, whereas *Anschauung* may also occur in imagination or recollection. It differs from intuition, especially in its German sense, where *Intuition* has usually the sense of an inspirational idea or an instinctive anticipation. Unless one were bold enough to launch a new literal English parallel like "in-templation," one can do little else but to speak of "direct intuition," or, using the unclaimed noun form of the verb "to intuit," of "intuiting."

But what is the new thing for which such a new term would stand? In the last and climactic *Logische Untersuchung* Husserl had tried to show that logical insight, in its most adequate and self-evident form, could not be described in terms of mere sensibility. There are elements in any logical proposition, such as negations, conjunctions, etc., without possible equivalent in sensuous intuiting, which Husserl in a rather peculiar terminology called *"categories."* There are besides such terms as "unity,"

James's and Husserl's views in this essay, particularly concerning the latter's doctrine of intersubjectivity, it seems unlikely that Husserl was familiar with this article.

"number," "similarity," to which no possible sense datum can possibly correspond. Nevertheless, it is possible to obtain full and adequate intuitive understanding of what they mean. This makes it clear that there is such a thing as non-sensuous intuiting (Husserl calls it *kategoriale Anschauung*), a fact which makes it necessary to expand the customary range of the word "*Anschauung*," as represented, for instance, even in Kant's widened use of the term ("*Anschauung* without concepts is blind, thoughts without *Anschauung* are empty").

Once this is established, even insights about general essences can be described as types of "categorial intuiting". But this intuiting of general essences (which was all that was implied in the dangerously mystifying word *Wesensschau*, certainly nothing like a mystic second sight) is not to be claimed lightly. While it does not require the massing of instances from experience or from experimentation or even restriction to real cases, the intuiting of general essences must be based on the careful consideration of representative examples, which are to serve as stepping stones, as it were, for any generalizing "ideation." It is also necessary to vary such examples freely but methodically in order to grasp essential relationships (*Wesenszusammenhänge*) between general essences, a method which Husserl considered peculiar to phenomenology. Yet eventually it is always the intuiting of the phenomena, particular as well as universal, in which all genuine knowledge finds its terminal verification.

3. Phenomenology Becomes "First Philosophy"

The analyses which I have tried to illustrate above were still oriented toward a reconstruction of pure logic. Yet it will have become clear that Husserl's new ideas had significance far beyond this limited area. Thus it is not surprising that the decade after Husserl's move from Halle to Göttingen in 1901 saw the rapid expansion of the phenomenological method. It also led to a considerable transformation and to the development of a completely new philosophical approach. It began with Husserl's repudiation of his earlier characterization of phenomenology as descriptive psychology after the manner of Brentano. Now it became the study of the essential structures of the acts and contents of consciousness, a study to be based not on mere empirical generalization but on the intuitive grasping of the essences of the phenomena, the *"Sachen."* From the very start, it was made clear that such "intuition" was not to be a merely passive waiting for an inspirational revelation. A strenuous active search would have to prepare for the "intuition," not a mere *Schauen*, but an *Er-schauen* ("intuition" achieved by effort), as the characteristic Husserlian neologism reads.

Yet during these possibly most productive twelve years of Husserl's thinking and teaching he published very little. Between the second volume of the *Logische Untersuchungen* (1901) and the *Ideen zu einer reinen Phänomenologie* (1913), Husserl's major efforts went into the preparation of lectures in which he tested his ideas before his students. Not until 1929 did some of these lectures become accessible. They allow one to reconstruct some of the determining factors in Husserl's development during these decisive years.

In the beginning Husserl was chiefly interested in concrete phenomenological analyses. In continuation of the last studies of the *Logische Untersuchungen* he now turned his attention toward various types of consciousness and particularly of knowledge in all its varieties, with special attention to its claims to validity. Thus he discussed the phenomenology of such fundamental cognitive acts as perception, imagination, image consciousness, memory, and, particularly important for the future, the consciousness of time. The lectures on time of 1905 and 1910, published a quarter century later by Heidegger, showed most concretely the fruits of Husserl's studies of intentionality, describing as they did the data of our immediate time consciousness, regardless of the question of whether such time was "objective" or real. A comparison with Bergson's philosophy of time, which was then still unknown to Husserl, could show very clearly the refinement that Husserl's analysis, based on the pattern of intentionality, had added to Bergson's more brilliant but less structured metaphysical intuitions of the "immediate data of consciousness."

But it was not until 1907 that Husserl was ready to state his new conception of phenomenology theoretically, rather than to demonstrate it in concrete applications. Partly under the challenge of professional disappointments during the year 1906,

Husserl undertook to re-examine his entire program of philosophy and to reformulate it in terms of a new critique of reason,
for which phenomenology would have to provide the foundations.
It was this program which he presented in five lectures, which
stated for the first time the program of a universal phenomenology conceived as the ultimate foundation and critique of all
knowledge. Besides, these lectures introduced under the title
"epistemological reduction" the new method of suspension of
belief as the way to secure phenomena in their pure and indubitable form, free from transcendent interpretations. It was also
significant that this first programmatic statement invoked as the
two greatest pioneers of the new approach both Descartes and
Kant. True, Descartes had been one of the exemplary philosophers even for Brentano. But Brentano had not been interested in the same teachings of the scientist-philosopher Descartes
as Husserl, and had linked his name with that of Bacon, in whom
Husserl never showed any deep interest. What amounted to a
complete innovation, however, was Husserl's espousal of Kant,
whom Brentano had always repudiated as having started the
decline of German philosophy that led to speculative idealism.
To Husserl from now on Kant was the protagonist for the critique
of reason, only that his own critique was to be even more radical
than Kant's critique of *pure* reason alone, a critique which thus
could make all philosophy, and not only metaphysics, scientific.

Husserl's celebrated essay on philosophy as a rigorous science
(*"Philosophie als strenge Wissenschaft"*) of 1911 became the
manifesto of this new philosophical discipline for a wider public,
at the same time challenging all other approaches to philosophy,
past and present, and claiming with a supreme self-confidence
that phenomenology alone could put philosophy and science on
the right course. The essay, which probably remains Husserl's
most impressive programmatic statement, reaffirmed the belief
in a scientific philosophy, and it formulated, in the style of
prolegomena, the conditions under which any future philosophy
could claim to be a science. Specifically, Husserl attacked, as
incapable of deciding questions of epistemological right, all those
"naturalistic" philosophies which, like positivism, tried to found
knowledge on an uncritical natural science and, in particular, on
mere experimental psychology. In this respect it was precisely

the so-called exact sciences which had failed to be "rigorous," and which needed a philosophical examination of their foundations to become truly scientific. One of the results of the idolatry of the physico-chemical sciences had been that science had failed to make sure of its basic concepts. It had neglected the descriptive clarification of the immediate phenomena. Phenomenology was to undertake this task. At the same time Husserl shocked the representatives of the historical *Geisteswissenschaften*, and in particular their prime philosopher, Wilhelm Dilthey, by attacking "historicism." Historicism, as Husserl saw it, had questioned the possibility of a scientific philosophy by arguments from its past failures, and ended up with a general relativism and scepticism concerning all metaphysical knowledge. Against this position Husserl maintained firmly that mere historical facts could never prove nor disprove any conclusions concerning the validity or possibility of any kind of knowledge. Then followed a solemn protest against any attempt to replace scientific philosophy by mere *"Weltanschauung,"* much as Husserl acknowledged an empirical and classifying typology of *Weltanschauung* in the manner of Dilthey as a legitimate and worthwhile enterprise. To Husserl science and scientific philosophy were essentially enterprises whose goals lay in the indefinite future and whose task was consequently unfinishable. By contrast, the goal of *Weltanschauung* was a finite one, namely to provide the individual with the unifying perspective in which he could live, hence subject to all the chances which changing perspectives would entail. Only in an indefinite future could the two fuse asymptotically, as it were. In the meantime the philosophies of *Weltanschauung*, with their largely personal foundation and validity, had better be kept strictly separate from science and scientific philosophy, with their indefeasible claims to timeless validity. The essay closed with one of Husserl's celebrated appeals "To the Things (*Zu den Sachen*)," which reminded of and contrasted significantly with such earlier slogans as the "Back to the Sources" (*ad fontes*) of the Renaissance Humanists and the "Back to Kant" of the Neo-Kantians.

There is reason to comment briefly on this phenomenological battle-cry. The call *"Zu den Sachen"* has at times been interpreted too naively as meaning nothing but "turning to objective

realities in the world outside," rather than to "subjective reflection." But this would be in conflict especially with Husserl's
later interpretation of phenomenology. What the phrase does
mean is the refusal to make philosophical theories and the
critique of such theories the primary and, at times, the all-
absorbing concern of philosophy, as does much lingustic
analysis and criticism. Analysis of meanings and opinions,
whether of common sense or of more sophisticated positions, is
not the prime objective of philosophy. Instead, what philosophy
must begin with are the phenomena and problems themselves;
all study of theories, however significant, must take second place.
The only proper way to evaluate the fittingness of such an
approach is by examining its fruits in actual insights.

Excursus: Wilhelm Dilthey and Edmund Husserl

The significance of the essay on "Philosophy as a Rigorous
Science" for an understanding of the relationship between
Husserl and Dilthey, so important in the later development of
the Phenomenological Movement, justifies a short digression on
their general relationship. It may also help to dispel some of the
legends which have arisen about it.

Contacts between Husserl and Dilthey had developed during
the first decade of the new century. Apparently it was Dilthey
who first became seriously interested in Husserl. As early as
1894 Dilthey, in his search for an adequate scientific foundation
for the *Geisteswissenschaften*, had developed the postulate of a
"descriptive and analytic psychology" in contrast to a merely
explanatory or constructive psychology, the only one available
at that time.[1] Dilthey himself never gave a systematic treatment of these "ideas," but only what may be termed preludes
for such a treatment, with the topics of life, life context, expression, interpretation, and understanding as the leading
themes. Thus it was only natural that he should be casting about
for possible aid from quarters in closer touch with active psychology. It seems more than likely that it was again Carl Stumpf,
Dilthey's helpful colleague in the University of Berlin after 1894,
who drew his attention to Brentano, and more particularly to

---

[1] "Ideen zu einer beschreibenden und zergliedernden Psychologie" (*Gesammelte Schriften*, vol. V).

Husserl. In any case, it seems that around 1904 Dilthey held a seminar on Husserl's *Logische Untersuchungen* at the University of Berlin.[1] In 1905, in presenting his "Studies for the Foundations of the *Geisteswissenschaften*" to the Berlin Academy, he took occasion to refer to the "excellent studies of Husserl," who "from a related standpoint had prepared a strictly descriptive foundation of an epistemology as a phenomenology of knowledge and thus a new philosophic discipline." A little later he went out of his way to acknowledge "once and for all how much, by way of the use of description in epistemology, I owe to Husserl's epochal *Logische Untersuchungen*." [2] Later, for reasons never stated explicitly but very possibly related to the appearance of "Philosophy as a Rigorous Science," Dilthey seems to have toned down his enthusiasm; for instance in a note "from a later period" he characterized Brentano's school as "psychological scholastics," since it creates such "abstract entities" as manners of behavior (*Verhaltungsweisen*) and contents, from which it wants to build up life. And he added: "The extreme case in this line: Husserl." [3]

Husserl's interest in Dilthey was apparently of a much more secondary nature, aroused by the unexpected response he had found from Dilthey at a time when the echo in his immediate academic environment was highly discouraging and when, according to Heinemann, he even visited Dilthey personally. Husserl had great admiration for Dilthey as a historian, as the typologist of *"Weltanschauungen,"* and even as the man who had seen, more clearly than others, what was needed to buttress the philosophically precarious position of the *Geisteswissenschaften*. Yet he considered him chiefly as a man of genius for intuition, but not of rigorous science and theory.[4] When Husserl, in his [1] programmatic essay of 1911, launched his devastating attack

---

[1] In 1931 Husserl told F. H. Heinemann that when he visited Dilthey in 1905, Dilthey "told him that this book (the *Logische Untersuchungen*) represented the first fundamentally new departure in philosophy since the days of Mill and Comte, and that he, Dilthey, regarded the fifth and the sixth essays, *On Intentional Experiences and their 'Contents,'* and '*Elements of a Phenomenological Elucidation of Knowledge,*' i.e., the return to the subject and its inner experiences, as most fruitful." F. H. Heinemann, *Existentialism and the Modern Predicament* (New York, Harper, 1958), p. 52.
[2] *Gesammelte Schriften*, VII, 10, 14, and extracts from the texts on pp. 39 ff.
[3] *Op. cit.*, p. 237.
[4] *Ideen* II, pp. 173.

on historicism as a new form of scepticism, he did not explicitly charge Dilthey with it. But he did express doubts as to how Dilthey, who had abandoned metaphysics as hopeless in view of the conflict of historical systems, could possibly believe that he was in a position to refute historical scepticism.[1] In fact, according to Dilthey himself the three types of *Weltanschauung*, to which he had tried to reduce all world views, were all equally valid, exactly as relativism was maintaining.

Husserl's *Logos* article led to a cooling off of the relationship, although in a correspondence with Dilthey, which has survived only in fragments, Husserl seems to have tried to minimize the differences: "We are preparing a new philosophy, which is fundamentally the same, starting from different angles." [2] That there were friendly relations between Phenomenology and the Dilthey school is a matter of historical record. But this must not make us overlook the fact that there was a deep-lying difference between the fundamentally empathic approach of Dilthey, groping as it was for theoretical foundations in spite of its fondness for historical flux and flexibility, and Husserl's primary interest in scientific rigor and its subsequent extension to ever widening fields of phenomena.

4. The Birth of the Phenomenological Movement and the Beginnings of Transcendental Phenomenology

The development of Husserl's own phenomenology into an all-comprehensive and basic approach to philosophy was not the only achievement of the years in Göttingen. This was also the period of Husserl's greatest influence as a teacher. To be sure, Husserl was disappointed that few of his students were ready and eager to accept his ideas when he began to present his transcendental phenomenology, particularly such phases of it as his new "epistemological reduction," the nucleus of his transcendental phenomenology. But even though these students were and

---

[1] "Philosophie als strenge Wissenschaft," *Logos* I, 323 ff., especially p. 326 footnote.

[2] Other excerpts in G. Misch, *Lebensphilosophie und Phänomenologie* (Leipzig, Teubner, 1929); also in *Philosophischer Anzeiger*, III (1929), 438. The full text is now published in German and Spanish by Walter Biemel in *Revista de Filosofia de la Universidad de Costa Rica* I (1957), 103–24.

7. Publisher's Announcement of Husserl's
Jahrbuch für Philosophie und phänomenologische Forschung

remained anything but orthodox followers, they offered him a live sounding board for his thought.

But equally strong, if not stronger, was the influence which Husserl began to exert outside Göttingen, especially in Munich, not only by his writings, but also by visits and exchanges of students and young teachers. Alexander Pfänder, Adolf Reinach, Moritz Geiger, and, for some time, Max Scheler were the leading members of this Munich group. From the contacts and occasional meetings with this independent branch of the Movement came the plan of the *Jahrbuch für Philosophie und phänomenologische Forschung*. The first idea of a journal for phenomenological philosophy goes back to Husserl's own students, who impressed it on a reluctant master as early as 1907, who then approached [1] Daubert and Pfänder in Munich. It took until 1913 for the yearbook to materialize. Beginning in 1913 it published some of the most substantial contributions to phenomenological philosophy as well as the work which initiated phenomenological existentialism, Martin Heidegger's *Sein und Zeit*. It was preceded by the joint statement quoted in the Introduction (p. 5), which restricted the phenomenological common tenets to the methods of first-hand intuiting and of essential insight.

It was significant, however, that Husserl's own contribution at the head of the first volume of the *Jahrbuch* went considerably beyond this minimum platform. Its title, *"Ideas Concerning a Pure Phenomenology and Phenomenological Philosophy,"* indicated several of these advances. Yet despite the ambitiousness of this largest of Husserl's phenomenological literary enterprises, the title made no claims to comprehensiveness; it offered merely "ideas" in the sense of first principles.[1] This applies not only to the first volume, the "General Introduction to a Pure Phenomenology," but also to the two posthumous volumes, which likewise fail to give anything like a final system.

The second item in the title that calls for comment is the phrase "pure phenomenology." The parallel to Kant's "pure reason" is not accidental. But this "First Philosophy" was to be even more basic than Kant's critiques. The adjective "pure" sets

---

[1] Interesting precedents for this kind of a title are J. G. Herder's *Ideen zu einer Philosophie der Geschichte der Menschheit* (1784 ff.) and, even more important, Dilthey's *Ideen zu einer beschreibenden und zergliedernden Psychologie* (1894).

Husserl's phenomenology, as now conceived, apart from any "impure" phenomenologies. While it is not immediately clear what these pseudo-phenomenologies are, this can be gathered from the subject-matter of pure phenomenology, namely the "pure phenomena." Pure phenomena are to be distinguished from the phenomena of such factual sciences as empirical psychology, which are limited to factual cases and their merely factual connections. It is in the interest of such purity that Husserl now develops the method of reduction, about which more will have to be said soon.[1]

Since the publication of the *Ideen*, "pure phenomenology," "the science of the essential structure of pure consciousness" (*Wesenswissenschaft vom reinen Bewusstsein*), also goes increasingly by the name of transcendental phenomenology, although this name can be found in unpublished manuscripts of September 1907 (*Husserliana* II, p. IX). The title "transcendental," of which Husserl grew increasingly fond and which clearly indicated his increasing sympathy for Kant, is nevertheless rarely explained and is by no means identical with any of its traditional meanings.[2] In the *Ideen* the implication seems to be that what is transcendental about phenomenology is that it suspends (*ausschalten*) all transcendent claims (i.e., assertions about reality other than that of consciousness itself). The fullest explicit discussion of the term occurs in Husserl's last publication, the "Crisis of the European Sciences and Transcendental Phenomenology" (§ 26). Here, he wants to assign it a wider meaning, in line with the Cartesian approach, according to which a transcendental philosophy "reaches back (*zurückfragen*, i.e., literally, "asks back for") to the ultimate source of all knowledge," with the implication that this source is to be found in the ego. In other words, it expresses Husserl's commitment to a radical subjectivism for which subjectivity is the source of all objectivities, a position which is spelled out explicitly only in the period after the *Ideen*.

The third part of the title, "phenomenological philosophy,"

---

[1] For an interesting text concerning the concept of "pure phenomenon," which had been worked out in 1917 by Husserl's then assistant, Edith Stein, under the title "Phänomenologie und Psychologie," see H. L. Van Breda, "Het zuivere phaenomeen volgens Edmund Husserl" in *Tijdschrift voor Philosophie* II (1941), 447–498.

[2] About this problem see the article by Ludwig Landgrebe, "La phénoménologie de Husserl est-elle une philosophie transcendentale?" in *Études philosophiques* IX (1954), 315 ff.

to which the *Ideen* are also meant to make a contribution, points clearly to an extension of phenomenology beyond its pure stage. But it is not quite easy to tell exactly what such a phenomenological philosophy in a comprehensive sense would include, since the existing parts of the *Ideen* do not state explicitly how we can pass beyond pure phenomenology, if at all. Apparently the third and concluding Book was to contain the full development of the idea of philosophy, which would have included metaphysics as well as other branches of it, as made possible on the foundation of the new "first philosophy," i.e., phenomenology. But this part never materialized. According to its sub-title Husserl's last unfinished work, *Die Krisis der europäischen Wissenschaften und die transzendentale Phänomenologie*, was to be an introduction to "phenomenological philosophy." But it never reached the threshold of such a final philosophy. If Husserl ever had such a philosophy, it has to be extrapolated from rather ambiguous clues and from posthumous manuscripts, as has been tried ingeniously and cautiously by Alwin Diemer, who studied the contents of the Husserl Archives in Louvain intensively.

Of the entire ambitious project only the first book, the "General Introduction to Pure Phenomenology," appeared during Husserl's lifetime. Book II, entitled "Phenomenological Studies Concerning Constitution," proved so much more difficult that after putting it through four versions Husserl laid it aside in favor of other publications; so it appeared only posthumously. The lecture course on First Philosophy given in 1923/24 may be considered as a partial realization of the original plan for Book III. What has been published posthumously as *Ideen III* is actually a part of Book II dealing with "Phenomenology and the Foundation of the Sciences," a topic which Husserl himself substituted in his later plans for Book III.

Hence, as far as theory, method, and basic insights are concerned, the first volume outweighs the others in importance. Of its four sections the first contains a concise restatement of the phenomenological doctrine of essences and of knowledge of essences, which is so basic for the understanding of phenomenology as compared with other descriptive sciences. As such this part constitutes common ground for all branches of the

Phenomenological Movement. This can no longer be claimed for the "Fundamental Phenomenological Meditation" of the second section, which includes the new and crucial theory of reduction together with the first clear statement of Husserl's phenomenological idealism. The third section, on phenomenological methodology and its problems, presents more concrete yet basic analyses of the structure of consciousness and expresses common phenomenological doctrine. With some reservations this may also be claimed for the last section, "Reason and Reality," which offers chiefly the epistemological evaluation of consciousness after its phenomenological elucidation. It centers in the problem of self-evidence and introduces the new theme of the "constitution" of reality, which is so central in Husserl's later work.

In the following sections I shall attempt to select some of the most influential ideas from this central work.

a. SELF-GIVENNESS – PHENOMENOLOGY AND POSITIVISM – In the course of his discussion of "naturalistic misunderstandings of the phenomenological conception of essences," Husserl formulates the following "principle of all principles":

Every type of first-hand intuiting (*originär gebende Anschauung*) forms a legitimate source of knowledge (*Rechtsquelle*); whatever presents itself to us by "intuition" at first hand, in its authentic reality, as it were (*sozusagen in seiner leibhaften Wirklichkeit*), is to be accepted simply for the thing as which it presents itself, yet merely within the limits within which it presents itself.[1]

There is a helpful alternative statement of this principle in the posthumously published draft of a supplementary preface to the second edition of the *Logische Untersuchungen*, telling us

not to hunt deductively (*von oben her*) after constructions unrelated to the matter in question (*sachfremd*), but to derive all knowledge from its ultimate sources, from principles seen authentically (*selbstgesehen*) and understood as insights (*eingesehen*); not to be diverted by any prejudices, by any verbal contradictions or indeed by anything in the whole world, even under the name of "exact science," but to grant its right to whatever is clearly seen, which thus constitutes the "original," or what precedes all theories, or what sets the ultimate norm. [2]

[1] *Ideen* I, § 24 (*Husserliana*, III, 52).
[2] "Entwurf einer Vorrede zu den Logischen Untersuchungen" (1913), edited by Eugen Fink in *Tijdschrift voor Philosophie* I (1939), 116–7.

Now Husserl is obviously not the first to proclaim the principle of givenness and to formulate the concept of the given or datum. Its chief place of origin is the tradition of empiricism and in particular that of nineteenth century positivism. But it has also a place in such metaphysical philosophies as Bergson's (*Les Données immédiates de la conscience*) and in William James's radical empiricism[1].

Clearly, everything depends upon the interpretation of this all too popular and too glibly used term, "the given." Even the "principle of all principles" taken by itself does not make it clear what is to be considered as immediately given or intuited at first hand. This can be fully understood only by reading the phrase in its context, i.e., Husserl's controversy with empiricism and positivism. Then, the main issue turns out to be the question whether or not universals, or general essences, can be considered as given in the genuine sense of the term. Husserl charges that at this point the positivists are the victims of a negative prejudice which prevents them from seeing that there is more than particular data, and especially sense data. Mathematical insights are the primary illustration for such additional insights, but even the very empiricist principle "that all valid knowledge depends upon experience" would be a case in point. Except for this dogmatic restriction of givenness to particular experience and the implied rejection of any intuiting of general essences and relations, however, phenomenology has no serious disagreement with positivism in its fight against unverified and unverifiable

[1] At first sight there is a striking similarity between Husserl's "principle of all principles" and James's formula for radical empiricism: "To be radical, an empiricism must neither admit into its constructions any element that is not directly experienced, nor exclude from them any element that is directly experienced." (*Essays in Radical Empiricism*, New York, Longmans, Green and Company, 1912, p. 48). But while this empiricism asserts, as against "ordinary or Humean empiricism," the experience of relations, and protests against the "pulverization of all experience by associations and the mind-dust theory," which deny all conjunctive relations, James does not modify the general characterization of empiricism (p. 41) according to which it "lays the explanatory stress upon the part, the element, the individual, and treats the whole as a collection and the universals as an abstraction." It has therefore no room for any intuiting of universals, as implied in Husserl's *Wesensschau*, but can treat them at best in the manner of "fringes" to individual conceptions (*Principles of Psychology* I, 473). Another and eventually more important limitation of James's radical empiricism, as seen from the phenomenological standpoint, is his concept of "pure experience," which, in its similarity to Mach's positivistic conception, abandons the "thoroughgoing dualism" of the *Principles* in favor of monism; thus it drops the insights into the intentional structure of consciousness, which had been so important for Husserl.

"metaphysical" nonsense. "If positivism means nothing but founding all sciences without any prejudices whatsoever upon the 'positive,' i.e., upon what is to be grasped at first hand, then it is we who are the genuine positivists." [1]

How far is this new concept of givenness an adequate foundation for the enlarged empiricism of phenomenology? Some of its features are certainly apt to arouse further questions, if not objections. Thus, the "principle of all principles" refers to the "authentic reality" (*leibhafte Wirklichkeit*) which characterizes the data of first-hand intuiting, as if they presented themselves "bodily" or in person, as the German expression suggests. Husserl ascribes such authentic self-givenness (*leibhaftige Selbstgegebenheit*) particularly to the data of genuine perception. Does this mean that the verdict of the phenomena is to be accepted at face value and that we can discount the risk of perceptual illusions? Some of the realists in the Phenomenological Movement have indeed understood the principle in this sense, implying, to be sure, that only genuine and critical intuiting can be relied upon as foolproof evidence of reality. It seems less credible that Husserl himself should be interpreted in this sense. For Husserl was very well aware that the claim to reality in our ordinary experience remained always dubitable in principle, as the subsequent steps of his transcendental phenomenology will reveal. Whatever Husserl's own final meaning is, I submit that it would be unsafe to claim for the given more than *apparent* authenticity. It would certainly be uncritical, not to say unphenomenological, to accept phenomena at their face value. Such an interpretation of the elliptical expression "self-givenness" would prejudge the issue, if not beg the question. We must remember the cautions of the final clause in the principle of all principles ("yet only within the limits in which the intuited presents itself").

There are other ambiguities in the concept of the given that need further clarification. Even phenomenology has not yet clearly distinguished between (1) the total object given, (2) its sides confronting the subject face to face, (3) the perspective aspects which these sides present from different positions (frontal, lateral, close, or removed), and (4) the sense data (Husserl's

---

[1] *Ideen* I, § 20 (*Husserliana* III, 46).

"hyletic data"), which only a special dismantling operation can extricate from our complete perceptions, although supposedly they form the building materials in our cognitive acts.

At times the whole concept of the given has been questioned as based on a naive view of our experience according to which this world of ours is made up of ready-made items that wait, as it were, to be picked up from a store counter. This query can certainly not be brushed aside. But it would not affect Husserl as much as it would the positivists, especially not the later Husserl who tried to trace the given to certain constituting acts. But all this must not make us overlook the fact that, whatever the contributions of the receiver in the assimilation of the given may be, there are some factors in the material which direct this assimilation into channels not of his choosing. It is these objective elements other than ourselves which the doctrine of givenness is meant to point out. Whatever the chances of isolating them may be, they should not be discounted without clear and compelling reasons.

b. PHENOMENOLOGY OF PERCEPTION AND SELF-EVIDENCE – Husserl's account of perception as the act which presents to us the things perceived in their (apparent) authentic reality is not his only contribution to a phenomenological analysis of this central phenomenon in the conscious life. The paradigm for his sustained study of perception has always been that of the three-dimensional thing in space. In studying its modes of appearance (*Erscheinungsweisen*) Husserl paid special attention to the fact that, while the "front" of the perceptual object is given in "adequate" manner, all its "lateral" aspects can be given only inadequately by way of perspective modifications (*Abschattungen*, i.e., literally, gradations of shading, a visual term to which Husserl gives a typically enlarged meaning). Their "backs" lack even all intuitive content and can be meant only signitively. From these modes of appearance modes of clarity and vagueness must be distinguished. Such modes are of course closely related to each other in a manner which allows us to anticipate their ways of appearance from other positions, as we move around them. It is essentially impossible to achieve adequate frontal presentation for all aspects and to fulfill all of their signitive anticipations. This is one reason why material objects can never be perceived exhaustively, in contrast to objects of inner perception, where no such perceptual shading has to be considered. For the same reason they are never given beyond the shadow of a final doubt: at least in principle they may still turn out to be illusions, after the manner in which halls of mirrors when tested by touch reveal themselves as optical illusions.

Landgrebe's elaboration of some of Husserl's studies on the genealogy of logic in *Erfahrung und Urteil* contains some highly original descriptions of the dynamic structure of perceptive acts. Here perception is considered as a pre-predicative type of consciousness which forms the foundation for predicative knowledge as articulated in judgmental acts. In the course of these analyses, Husserl distinguishes three stages of perception: (1) plain seizing and retention (*Erfassung* and *Im-Griff-behalten*); (2) explicating contemplation and explicative synthesis, in which the first categories of description are born; and (3) the seizing of the percept in relation (*Beziehungserfassung*), which includes its horizons and its relation to other objects. All these stages involve an intricate interplay between activity and passivity in perceptual receptivity.

Obviously, these brief indications cannot do more than convey a first idea of the dimensions and the freshness of this new attack upon the problems of perception. In this connection it also seems in order to mention the closely related topic of the phenomenology of self-evidence, for Husserl the supreme criterion of knowledge. This was one of the pervading themes of Husserl's thinking from the *Logische Untersuchungen* on. It is also one about which Husserl's position showed at least one remarkable shift. For in the end Husserl no longer claimed that self-evidence was a fool-proof guarantee of truth, and therefore he called for a final critique of self-evidence. But even apart from this, Husserl's phenomenology of self-evidence deserves special attention. For Husserl does not use self-evidence simply as a blind feeling which signals truth by a flash, as it were. Instead, Husserl works out distinctions between various types and degrees of self-evidence, which can largely explain why self-evidence has been so often invoked in vain and even involved us in seeming contradictions. In this connection I shall mention only the distinction between adequate and inadequate self-evidence, depending on how fully self-evidence represents its object.[1]

c. THE PHENOMENOLOGICAL REDUCTION – The phenomenological reduction brings us to a crucial point in Husserl's Pure or Transcendental Phenomenology and at the same time in the history of the Phenomenological Movement. At first sight it may seem a strange thing to find a phenomenologist talking about reductions. Was not the original motif of phenomenology a protest against such oversimplifying philosophies as naturalism, positivism, and psychologism with their "reductionist fallacies," as they are usually called in American philosophy? Clearly, the term "reduction," as introduced by Husserl in the years after the *Logische Untersuchungen*, must have a meaning different from this, coming as it does from a phenomenologist who had just pronounced the anti-reductionist "principle of all principles." It certainly does not involve any connotations of simplification or philosophical economy. What it does imply is best indicated by the literal meaning of the term: a leading back to the origins of which our all too hasty everyday thought has lost sight.

However, this is merely a preliminary indication of the real phenomenological meaning of this operation. To understand it fully we must determine its place in the pattern of Husserl's thought. In the *Ideen* the "phenomenological reduction" [2] makes its appearance when Husserl enters upon the "fundamental meditation" of phenomenology, which is to yield the pure and unadulterated phenomena that cannot be attained in the "naive" or "natural" attitude. It is at this point that Husserl turns to Descartes as the greatest model of such a radical return to what is given beyond the shadow of a doubt. Only he makes it clear that his own reduction is not to be interpreted as a Cartesian doubt, which denies, however experimentally or temporarily, the existence of the things reduced. Even the

---

[1] See the author's "Phenomenology of Direct Evidence" in *PPR* II (1942) 427–456.

[2] Husserl also knows a more general "philosophical reduction," which involves merely the adoption of a neutral position with regard to all the teachings of past philosophy (*Ideen*, I, § 18; *Husserliana* III, 40 f.).

borrowing of the term "epoché" [1] does not mean that he es-
poused the sceptic withdrawal from the world of facts in order
to play safe. The primary function of all reduction is to prepare
us for a critical stock-taking of what is indubitably given, before
our interpreting beliefs rush in.

To be sure, from the outset Husserl distinguishes at least two
stages of this phenomenological reduction:

α. reduction from mere particular facts to general essences,
which, in accordance with the adoption of the Platonic word
"eidos," he now also calls *eidetic reduction*. No elaborate instructions are given. Obviously the main point is to drop all
reference to the individual and particular. Thus all that is
involved has been described sufficiently under the heading of
intuiting of essences or "ideation." (see p. 105 ff.).

One might very well ask whether this operation really represents a leading back to origins, unless one assumes that
phenomenologically the generic precedes the specific and particular. But this is clearly far from self-evident. All that can be
safely asserted is that eidetic reduction is a step on the way to
the purified phenomena as such, without such complications as
are apt to arise from the consideration of particular cases.

β. the *phenomenological reduction proper*. For this reduction we
do receive ample directions, at least in the beginning stage. Its
main function is to free the phenomena from all trans-phenomenal elements, notably from all beliefs in trans-phenomenal
existence, thus leaving us with what is indubitably or "absolutely"
given. This is not a matter of individuality versus generality, as
in the eidetic reduction, where only the individual thisness or
thatness is eliminated. The target of the phenomenological
reduction is the characteristic of being or existence; hence it
concerns only that aspect of our world which is the object of the
"general thesis" of belief in an independent reality.

Now the first and basic instruction for this operation is simple
enough: inhibit or suspend (put out of action, "turn off") all
belief in existence that accompanies our everyday life and even

---

[1] Husserl never explicitly discusses the ancient Sceptics as the authors of this
term. There are strong indications that he adopted it as a result of his study of Raoul
Richter's *Der Skeptizismus in der Philosophie* (1903 ff.). According to Rudolf Boehm's
checking, Husserl's copy of this book shows intensive markings of the decisive passages; he corresponded with its author in 1904.

our scientific thinking. Instead, concentrate on the concrete phenomenon in all its aspects and varieties, intuit its essence (*Sosein*), analyze and describe it without any consideration of its reality. For this, at first only temporary, suspension of belief Husserl uses also the mathematical metaphor of "bracketing" (*einklammern*). No denial of existence or any idealistic assertion is involved at this stage. Moreover, such keeping in abeyance does not mean that we are simply to forget all about our beliefs in the bracketed reality. We are only instructed to stop attaching weight to them. Otherwise, the *phenomenon* of these beliefs and the mere *phenomenon* of reality as ascribed to the content of our beliefs are to be left untouched. We are merely to stop identifying ourselves with such beliefs in the sense of a definite commitment.

In a manner closely parallel to, but not identical with, Descartes' first *Meditation* the reduction thus "de-realizes" area after area of the world which was taken as real in the naive or natural attitude: the objects of our everyday reality, including our own organisms, but equally the realities maintained or substituted by the sciences, natural, social, and historical; similarly, the world of those peculiar transcendences which occur in religious consciousness (which is by no means denied); finally, even the world of pure mathematics and logic, inasmuch as its objective validity contains a transcendent claim – all are to be subjected to this universal ban on believing commitments.

If nothing more were involved than this mere suspension of belief in the sense of a believing commitment, one might well wonder why the reduction should produce such a basic change in our world as Husserl claims. In particular, Husserl's glowing promises about the new and limitless horizons of research which this operation is to open up might at first sight appear rather puzzling in their exaggeration. Yet, as we proceed, and as Husserl himself proceeds, it becomes increasingly clear that more is involved than mere suspension of existential belief. But it is not easy to determine in what these additional steps of the reduction consist. Even in his last decade Husserl was in the habit of stating that no adequate account of the phenomenological reduction had appeared as yet; in fact in his correspondence he referred to it as the most difficult thing ever attempted in philosophy, much as he insisted on its indispensableness for a genuine phenomenology against his erstwhile associates and students, assigning to it almost the role of a conversion.[1]

Thus far the best indications of what the phenomenological reduction involves beyond suspension of belief may be found in Eugen Fink's authorized article of 1934.[2] Rudolf Boehm's edition of the second part of *Erste Philosophie* (1923–24) under the title "Theory of the Phenomenological Reduction" in *Husserliana* VIII throws interesting light on an intermediate stage in its development. But while this text shows Husserl struggling with the problems of finding the proper point of departure for initiating the reduction, it contains very little clarification of the reduction itself. This proves how difficult Husserl found it to motivate his procedure adequately. It also reveals Husserl's attempt to find alternatives for the Cartesian approach to the reduction.

Perhaps the most revealing fact about the nature of the reductive operation is that Husserl, who describes it first chiefly in negative terms as the suspension of the existential belief, in his later writings indicates positively the direction toward which the reduction is headed: Reduction is not merely a moving away from the natural world but a moving toward something (*Reduktion auf* ...). The goal of this movement is none other than transcendental subjectivity. This positive aspect is of course also indicated by the title "transcendental reduction," which serves increasingly as the synonym for phenomenological reduction. It indicates that reduction has the purpose to inhibit and "take back," as it were, all references to the "transcendent" as the intentional correlate of our acts and to trace them back to the immanent or "transcendental" acts in which they have their source. Thus what happens in the phenomenological reduction seems to be something like this: We withhold not only our beliefs in reality but also those acts which give transcendent meaning to what is an integral element of our consciousness. The use of such terms as dismantling (*Abbau*) is hardly accidental.

---

[1] "Perhaps it will even become apparent that the total phenomenological attitude and the corresponding *epoché* is called upon to bring about a complete personal transformation (*Wandlung*) which might be compared to a religious conversion, but which even beyond it has the significance of the greatest existential conversion that is expected of mankind" (*Husserliana* VI, 140).

[2] "Die phänomenologische Philosophie Edmund Husserls in der gegenwärtigen Kritik," *Kantstudien* XXXVIII, 319–383.

Such an operation might well be compared with the interception of the beam in a projector, a procedure which would break up the pattern of the projected picture as it commonly appears. But it would allow us to find out about such mechanisms of the projection as the light source and the slide which it projects. While this is of course not the structure of the intentional act, there is something analogous to it in the relation between the intentional act, its "hyletic" data, and the intentional object. In his last phase, Husserl often speaks of "intentional analysis," an analysis which is to describe the way in which these hidden intentional functions work together. In fact, the terms "intentional analysis" and "transcendental reduction" seem to be practically equivalent. This too would seem to confirm the foregoing interpretation of the transcendental reduction as a means of uncovering hidden intentional acts which project transcendent objects.

How far is this kind of reduction really indispensable for phenomenological analysis? The fact that Husserl himself worked out some of his most important phenomenological studies in the *Logische Untersuchungen* apparently without performing all the steps of systematic reduction would seem to suggest that it need not be carried out explicitly. But at that time Husserl was concerned chiefly with easily accessible and static structures, where suspension of belief may be a valuable but not an indispensable device in helping us to stick conscientiously to what is given. It could be very different in the case of less obvious phenomena. Here an explicit reduction might be necessary in order to uncover the normally unconscious operations behind our consolidated world, which represents the "sedimentation" of our past intentions, to use Husserl's telling phrase. But before suggesting this method of uncovering transcendental acts, we would have to be quite sure that the transcendent world is really the result of these acts, as Husserl claims. Otherwise, the whole attempt would seem to be based on a questionable preconception, and all suggested solutions would be highly suspicious in a phenomenology whose basic principle is the unflinching acceptance of the verdict of the phenomena. Clearly, the expansion of this principle to the search for hidden phenomena requires great caution if one would escape from possible self-deception. Only if and when, as the result of such uncovering, the hidden phenomena withstand the full light that illumines the unhidden ones, can they be accepted on an equal level with them.

Excursus: Santayana's Ultimate Scepticism Compared With Husserl's Phenomenological Reduction

There is a remarkable and in fact highly instructive parallel to Husserl's phenomenological reduction in Santayana's startling use of an "ultimate scepticism" as an approach to his realm of essences. Indeed, Santayana himself was aware of it. He was even the only major American philosopher who took official cognizance of Husserl's philosophy, devoting several pages of the Postscript to the first volume of his *Realms of Being* to a brief account and discussion of the "thankless text" of Husserl's *Ideen*.[1] While he seems to put Husserl above Whitehead as far as the understanding of essences is concerned, his final objections to Husserl are those of the naturalist, which he claims to be, in opposition to Husserl's idealism or "malicious transcendentalism." However, it would seem that Santayana, in his concern with Husserl's doctrine of essences, had overlooked the fact that Husserl, as the result of his suspension of what Santayana called "animal faith," had also ended up with a realm of absolute and indubitable being no longer subject to suspension, i.e., the realm of pure consciousness. There can be little doubt that such a conception would stand no chance in the eyes of Santayana's sovereign "spirit," since he had found the unique solution of combining a far more radical scepticism as regards existence with a much more robust eventual "materialism" and with the stolid "normal madness" of a science-minded common sense.

The real differences between Santayana's ultimate scepticism and Husserl's phenomenological reduction must be understood, first of all, in the light of their different ultimate objectives. Santayana's were in many ways much less pretentious and less

---

[1] *The Realm of Essence* (New York, Scribner, 1927), pp. 171–4. – For a later expression of Santayana's interest in Husserl's "Pure Phenomenology" as an approach to existentialism, see his letter of February 9, 1948 published in *Partisan Review* XXV (1958), 632–37.

solemn than Husserl's. Even at the stage of the *Life of Reason* his interest was largely that of an observer from the sidelines, following sympathetically the progressive development of the human spirit. In the *Realms of Being* he attempted something like a liberation of the human spirit by lightening the weight of animal faith without abolishing it. So after showing, as a supreme feat, the omnipotence of scepticism, he could return to the realm of animal faith in full freedom without feeling any longer the crushing burden of its tyranny.

Compared with this enterprise Husserl's concern is one of deadly seriousness, a matter of scientific conscience and un-compromising radicalism. Truth and clarity are for him not esthetic values of a free spirit but the essential conditions of his existence. So he will neither drive his scepticism to Santa-yana's ironical extreme nor abandon it to a liberated and serene common sense that alights on material reality as one among many possible perches.

There are also significant differences in the actual practice of the suspension. In one sense Santayana's scepticism is even more radical. For it involves the actual denial of existence to everything within reach, even to the extent of asserting: "nothing given exists." It encompasses indiscriminately the objective as well as the subjective realm and brazenly challenges even the Cartesian *cogito* as nothing but a "given," without any prefer-ential status as regards its existence. Thus his ultimate scepticism leaves us with an ethereal realm of non-existing essences but nothing in which they are anchored. As a matter of fact, it seems to be with a feeling of relief that the poet Santayana jettisons the ballast of existence. Husserl, like Descartes, does not cut himself off from these last moorings, nor would he grant Santa-yana's reasons, if they were meant to be reasons, for dropping all existence.

On the other hand, the motives for Santayana's abrupt return from the "watershed of criticism" to the homelike lowlands of animal faith would command even less respect on the part of Husserl's uncompromising radicalism. In fact, as we know, he refuses ever to return to a common sense realism comparable to Santayana's about-face, which made him conceive of himself as "apparently the world's only living materialist."

d. The phenomenological residue: ego cogito
cogitata mea – At first glance, one might think that the
phenomenological suspension, like Descartes' doubt, would
affect every possible item of this world by converting it into a
pure phenomenon, and lead to a catastrophic impoverishment
of our universe. But while this declaration of neutrality trans-
figures, as it were, all the objects of our beliefs, it does not affect
the status of the believing consciousness itself and of its components: its existence is not touched by the fact that the validity
of its content remains in suspense. This indicates the range of
those phenomena for which Husserl claims a status entirely
different from that of the phenomena which can be reduced.
It is this phenomenological residue of reduction which he calls
the region of *absolute, apodictic,* or *pure consciousness.*

Husserl likes to characterize the structure of this minimum
world by articulating Descartes' *cogito* into the tripartite formula
"ego cogito cogitata." What does he include under its three
main parts?

(*1*) *The Phenomenological Ego.* It is a very revealing fact that
originally, i.e., in the first edition of the *Logische Untersuchungen,*
Husserl rejected the conception of an identical subject over and
above the intentional acts of consciousness, very much in the
manner of David Hume and other empiricists. But by the time
Husserl published the *Ideen* (1913), he had completely reversed
himself, a reversal which he acknowledged frankly in the second
edition of the *Logische Untersuchungen,* stressing at the same
time his continued opposition to any attempt at interpreting
this ego as a substance à la Descartes.[1] Obviously this pure ego
is to be strictly distinguished from the bodily organism and even

---

[1] First ed. (1901), p. 342: "Now, I must confess that I am utterly unable to find
this primitive ego (asserted by Paul Natorp) as a necessary center of conscious
reference." The second edition (1913) adds the following footnote to this sentence:
"Since then, I have learned to find it, or more precisely, I have learned not to be
diverted in the pure grasp of the given by the excesses of the metaphysics of the ego."
(*Logische Untersuchungen* II, 1, p. 361). There is definite evidence that it was the
repeated study of the works of Theodor Lipps, especially of his *Leitfaden der Psychologie,* and discussions with some of his students like Pfänder during the Seefeld
vacation of 1905, which played an important part in the growth of this new insight.
(Oral communication from the late August Gallinger, one of the participants; traces
can also be found in the "Seefelder Reflexionen" Ms. A VII 25). — For the further
development of the phenomenology of the ego see *Ideen* II (*Husserliana* IV, 97–120).

from any psychological self which has not yet been subjected to the phenomenological reduction. Later, Husserl introduced further distinctions into his theory of the ego. Thus he adopted especially Leibniz's expression "monad" to designate the concrete ego as comprising not only the immediate "vividly streaming present" (*lebendig strömende Gegenwart*), as does the pure transcendental ego, but also its "transcendent" range, comprising its past, its future, and its mere potentialities. There are even signs that in his final "egology" Husserl considered still further differentiations – indications based, to be sure, chiefly on Fink's authorized article in the *Kantstudien* of 1933 (p. 356). Actually their intricacy may well have endangered and weakened the valid core of Husserl's conceptions, particularly in the eyes of French phenomenologists like Sartre.[1]

(2) *The Cogitations.* What are the absolute cogitations in Husserl's sense? They comprise all the acts enumerated by Descartes in the second of his "magnificent" *Meditations*, such as doubting, understanding, affirming, denying, willing, refusing, imagining, and feeling. To these Husserl can now add all those intentional acts and components of acts which have been identified by phenomenological intuition and description, beginning with the intentions themselves. They can undergo a vast variety of modifications, for instance, with regard to the implied beliefs (*doxa*), parallel to the modifications of the cogitata – and Husserl contributed richly to their exploration. According to their intrinsic structure all these "cogitations" are made up of raw material (called "hyletic data" by Husserl) and of the various intentional interpretations "ensouling" it, as it were, in the constitution of the *cogitata* that appear through them. About both the data and the interpreting acts we can be absolutely certain, once we have subjected them to the phenomenological reduction. But the same does not apply to the results of the intentional interpretations, the *cogitata* or intentional objects. – It should be noted that in his later writings Husserl applies the terms "noesis" (adjective: "noetic") to the act of "cogitating," and "noema" (adjective: noematic) to its content.

---

[1] See my paper on "Husserl's Phenomenology and Existentialism," *Journal of Philosophy* LVII (1960), 73 f.

(3) *The Cogitata.* What are the cogitata in Husserl's sense? The simplest possible answer is to describe them as the referents or intentional objects of our cogitations in their capacity of being referred to: for instance, the perceived page as being perceived, the imagined author as being imagined, etc. How far do these cogitata share the absolute being of the phenomenological ego and its cogitations?

There is a sense in which they too have absolute, indubitable being. There can be no doubt that at this moment the reader is faced with the phenomenon of a white page covered with blackish oddly shaped marks, even if it should turn out that he was only in a dream or looking into a mirror. This is a pure phenomenon which could not possibly be endangered by any upset.

Yet there is also a sense in which the term "cogitatum" refers not only to an object in its capacity of being meant, but as a real object: for instance, to the page as a part of reality which supposedly exists in and of itself, and which can be manufactured, printed on, and burned in succession. What is the status of the cogitata in this fuller sense, apart from their being objects of cogitations?

e. PHENOMENOLOGICAL IDEALISM – It is in connection with the cogitata that Husserl's celebrated but controversial idealism has to be considered. To be sure, the term "idealism" does not occur in Husserl's publications as a designation for his own position prior to his *Formale und transzendentale Logik* of 1929 (p. 152). It is absent from the *Ideen*, as pointed out in Landgrebe's index of 1926 (*Husserliana* III, 433), where, however, all the passages are listed which characterize the idealistic position. Apparently Husserl came to accept the label only

[1] hesitantly after it had been applied to him by his critics. The conception itself, however, can be traced back to the lectures of 1907, although it did not become apparent in print prior to the *Ideen* of 1913. Here it occurs as early as the "Fundamental Phenomenological Meditation" of the second section. There can be no question that Husserl insists on this idealism with increasing vigor, to the extent of finally declaring it an integral part of his phenomenology. Yet he also insists that this idealism be

distinguished sharply from the traditional subjective idealism in Berkeley's style, which makes all being dependent on psychological consciousness. By contrast, Husserl's idealism ties up being with the transcendentally reduced consciousness. Whatever the final significance of this difference may be, the fact remains that for Husserl "being" exists only for consciousness, and that actually "being" is nothing apart from the meaning which it receives by the bestowing acts of this consciousness.

Would this not seem to imply that, at least in Husserl's case, phenomenology coincides with phenomenalism and that, after all, the current confusion in the subject index catalogues of American libraries between "phenomenology" and "phenomenalism" has some justification? A definite answer to this question presupposes a clear conception of the ambiguous term "phenomenalism." If "phenomenalism" means a theory under which, in the Kantian manner, we have to distinguish between appearance and thing-in-itself, then there is not the slightest excuse for identifying it with phenomenology: for it is precisely through the "appearances" that the appearing thing itself is given to the phenomenologist. The matter is different if we assert, with the negativistic phenomenalists, that nothing exists but phenomena, least of all unknowable things-in-themselves. In that case all depends on what we mean by "phenomena." Traditional phenomenalism of this type sees in the phenomena something like a series of images lined up on a film strip. Now it is one of Husserl's basic assertions that this conception of the stream of consciousness is mistaken, that the stream of phenomena has intentional structures, and that it has depth, as it were, in the sense that the immediate data of consciousness are transparent, showing behind them identical intentional cores of which they are the fluid appearances. Hence only if we interpret the phenomenalistic position in such a way that the phenomena are to comprise both the appearances and the phenomena that appear through them can it be maintained that Husserl, too, is a phenomenalist who maintains that all there is are phenomena, at least on the side of the cogitata. There still remains, however, the fundamental layer of the phenomenological ego and its cogitations, whose existence the traditional phenomenalist would hotly deny.

But now what is the evidence for Husserl's idealistic conclusion, which at first sight would seem to violate the very
principle of neutrality implied in the original formulation of the
phenomenological reduction as mere suspension of belief? Husserl
never presented the case for his phenomenological idealism in as
compact and explicit a form as Berkeley had done, much as
Husserl admired his arguments. In fact, the only major exception
he seemed to take to Berkeley's analysis concerned the latter's
phenomenalistic neglect of intentionality.

Husserl's arguments for idealism seem to fall into two classes:
deductive ones, based on the supposed self-contradictory nature
of realism, and direct phenomenological evidence, supplied by
analyses of transcendental constitution.

As to the deductive evidence, Husserl first argued that "being"
by its very meaning refers us back to acts which assign such
being, or, put differently, that being derives its very meaning
from consciousness. But he also maintained that the idea of a
reality unrelated to consciousness – and to be sure to *actual*
not only *potential* consciousness – was self-contradictory. Unfortunately, Husserl published very little to explain and to
develop these arguments, although manuscripts from the period
from 1908 to 1924 (especially those under B IV 6 of the Archive
transcripts) show sustained efforts to refute realism and to
establish the case for transcendental idealism. However, the
premises of these arguments are open to considerable doubt;
often they are true in one sense, and yet in the sense decisive for
the idealistic case they are anything but self-evident.

More important in any case would be the direct phenomenological evidence as based on the results of constitutional analyses.
This brings us to the doctrine of phenomenological or transcendental constitution, one of the central parts of Husserl's philosophy after the publication of his *Ideen*.

Excursus: Husserl and Josiah Royce

At this point Husserl's development seems to be approaching
the idealism of Josiah Royce to such an extent that one may well
be curious about the significance of this parallel and even raise
[1]   the question of possible contacts. To be sure, neither in Royce's
nor in Husserl's writings do we find any signs of mutual recog-

nition. Nevertheless, there is evidence of a certain awareness, which is worth recording. We know that Royce owned Husserl's *Logische Untersuchungen*. And according to Professor Harry C. Costello, to whom I am indebted for this information, Royce loaned it to him in 1913 "reluctantly." He also recalls "with some doubts" that Royce had marked up the margins of volume I with approvals. But it was then too late for Royce to keep up with Husserl's further development, especially the trend toward idealism.

Much more substantial is the evidence for Husserl's acquaintance with Royce. It concerns precisely the years when his idealism took definite shape. In the present context I can do no better than to quote from a letter which I owe to Dr. Winthrop Bell of Chester, Nova Scotia, who studied under Husserl in Göttingen from 1911 to 1914 after having done graduate work at Harvard:

When I went to be formally accepted by Husserl to work under him for a degree in the Fall of 1911 I found that he had his heart set on my doing ... an "Auseinandersetzung" (i.e., critical debate; my transl.) from the phenomenological point of view with a dominant American "Richtung" (i.e., trend; my tr.) in philosophy. He said, in effect, something like this: "There seems to be some doctrine known as 'Idealism' which is 'herrschend' (i.e., dominant; my tr.) there. William James's philosophical ideas seem to have developed as a hostile reaction to that – but of course from entirely the wrong angle. I know nothing about the actual teachings of this 'Idealism' or its leading representatives. But could you not take up one or more of those in the way I would have in mind?" When I began to say something about the subject and mentioned Royce's name, he, as I recall it, recognized it as one he had heard of as the leading figure in that American 'Idealism,' and began asking me about Royce. Having sat under Royce at Harvard a couple of years earlier I was able to talk more or less enlighteningly on his name. Husserl asked to see some of his works. ... I had some of Royce's books in Germany with me, and ordered the others, and was able to take to Husserl, before long, the whole imposing heap of Royce's publications. Husserl then would have nothing else than that I should do my *Doktorarbeit* on Josiah Royce. He came to entertain considerable respect for Royce – partly perhaps from the passages I had indicated to him in Royce's works, but mainly, I fancy, from what I had given of exegesis in my dissertation. I recall that at one critical session over part of my dissertation he reproved me for showing insufficient respect for Royce in the *tone* of my criticism in some point or other. "Herr Royce ist doch ein bedeutender Denker und darf nur als solcher behandelt werden." (Mr. Royce is, after all, an important thinker and must be treated as one; my tr.).

There is, to be sure, no evidence that after Bell's highly critical thesis [1] Husserl remained interested in Royce. But even so, Royce's philosophy contains enough parallels to Husserl's thought to make comparisons worth while. To mention only a few themes: Royce's theory of meaning as a purpose, which can be fulfilled by "reality," or his concern for the identity of meanings among several individuals as the basis for his theory of the social self have counterparts in Husserl's phenomenology of intentionality. At the same time, Royce's social idealism with its insistence on the role of the individual within the Absolute might have gone well with Husserl's later theory of intersubjectivity and with his idea of a community of transcendental monads.

But such affinities must not make us overlook the remaining differences in method and results. Royce's sovereign use of logic contrasts sharply with Husserl's slow approach through painstaking phenomenological analyses. Besides, Husserl's limited results can hardly compare with the bold metaphysical vision which underlies all of Royce's deductions.

f. PHENOMENOLOGICAL CONSTITUTION AND THE CONSCIOUSNESS OF TIME – It is significant that when Husserl in the *Ideen* (§ 50; *Husserliana III*, 119) introduces [1] the term "constitution" for the first time, he puts it in quotation marks without defining it. It seems safe to assume that it reflects his intensified study of and fascination with Kant's transcendentalism, and in particular its distinction between the constitutive and regulative use of our a priori concepts. This would also account for the increasingly idealistic interpretation which Husserl gave to the term. For to him "constitution" no longer means simply the mere static structure of an object, but the dynamic process by which it is built up as an object with a static "constitution" of its own.

There is a significant ambiguity about the way in which Husserl uses this term in concrete contexts. Very often it occurs with a reflexive pronoun, indicating that it is the phenomena themselves which take care of their own constitution. Yet

---

[1] An abstract under the title "Eine kritische Untersuchung der Erkenntnistheorie Josi ih Royce's" appeared in the *Jahrbuch der Philosophischen Fakultät der Universität Göttingen* 1922, pp. 49–57.

increasingly Husserl uses "constitution" as a transitive expression, implying that it is our intentional consciousness which actively "achieves" the constitution.

The general program of demonstrating the concrete constitution of the main regions of reality had been outlined at the end of the first volume of the *Ideen*. But the second volume, which according to its title was to supply "Phenomenological Studies Concerning Constitution," and which was drafted as early as 1912, was not published during Husserl's lifetime, since his attempts to improve on it entangled him in more and more complex investigations. His next larger publication, the *Formale und transzendentale Logik* of 1929, formulates the task of exploring the creative constitution of the logical world "genetically," i.e., by tracing the origins of the constituted objectivities as "sedimentations" of the acts from which they spring. To be sure, this "genetic phenomenology" was not meant as an historical enterprise destined to show the genesis of our world in chronological order, but to determine the structural order according to which the constituting acts are built upon one another. The studies on *"Experience and Judgment"* which Ludwig Landgrebe worked out under Husserl's supervision from several pertinent manuscripts give the best idea thus far of how far Husserl had advanced in uncovering the "hidden achievements" of intentional consciousness.

Compared with these later analyses those of the *Ideen* appear relatively static, giving only the sequence in which constitutive layers rest upon one another and in which they "constitute themselves" in our consciousness. They begin with the world of material things, add the constitution of the experienced body (*Leib*), and finally that of the world of personal life (*Geistigkeit*). Later Husserl distinguished sharply between an active and a passive constitution or synthesis, the second one being characteristic of perceptual experience, the first of judgment. One feature peculiar to passive constitution is its dependence on a pre-given material, the so-called *hyle*, exemplified primarily by our sense data. The existence of such material and, to a lesser degree, the whole process of passive constitution involves of course the dependence of the transcendental constitution on factors independent of the ego, and preserves at least a strong realistic element in the very heart of constitutive phenomenology. It is therefore not surprising that Husserl never seems to have felt satisfied about the status of the hyletic data and about the passive synthesis, and that he tried to trace them back to a deeper kind of constitution of a more creative or productive nature.

The major field for these ultimate efforts was the consciousness of time. Originally Husserl had inherited this topic from Brentano. But it kept growing on him until he believed that it contained the clue to the problem of constitution. His most concrete and interesting results can be found in his Göttingen lectures on the inner consciousness of time, edited by Heidegger during Husserl's lifetime, although not to his full satisfaction. This consciousness shows roughly the following structure: A primal impression (*Urimpression*) of a streaming present surrounded by a horizon of immediate "retention" of the past (to be distinguished from active recollection) and of immediate "protention" of the future (to be distinguished from active expectation). In describing retention Husserl shows with the help of a characteristic diagram how the consciousness of the present sinks off steadily below the surface and becomes sedimented in such a way that it is accessible only to acts of recollection. But these descriptive studies, of which the foregoing sentences can give no adequate idea, did not yet supply any evidence for an active constitution of time, much as they gave evidence of "passive" synthetic genesis. However, Husserl came to think increasingly that the constitution of the inner consciousness of time could throw light on the constitution of all other objectivities. The discovery of the active achievements in this process became all the more important. His studies in this direction, carried out in the thirties in close collaboration with [1] Eugen Fink, have not yet become sufficiently accessible. But some of their nature can be gathered from recent accounts, based on the use of unpublished manuscripts.[1] To be sure, they do not offer more than first indications of what Husserl hoped to demonstrate: the primal constitution (*Urkonstitution*) of the stream of time by the active hidden achievements of the transcen-

---

[1] See especially Alwin Diemer, *Edmund Husserl*, p. 143 ff., and Gerd Brand, *Welt, Ich und Zeit*, The Hague, Nijhoff, 1955.

dental ego in a process which he called *Zeitigung* (a word signifying
in current German usage the genesis of events *in time* from
any source, extended by Husserl to the production of time
itself). All other constitutions, such as the constitution of hyletic
data and of the full intentional objectivities based on these data,
were then to be derived from the transcendental ego as its ultimate productive root. Thus transcendental idealism would be
finally established.

Thus far there is no way to verify these claims concerning the
active constitutive achievements of Husserl's ego. What there
is by way of a demonstration is at best suggestive, but it hardly
establishes that all objectivities owe their being, as well as their
being known, to transcendental subjectivity. This does of course
not prevent constitutive analyses from supplying most important
insights into the way in which objectivities establish themselves
in our consciousness.

g. PHENOMENOLOGY AND PSYCHOLOGY – One of the
most important needs in the understanding of Husserl's philosophy is the clarification of the relationship between his phenomenology and psychology. On the one hand, the impression
has arisen that Husserl, in his battle against psychologism, and
even in his subsequent criticisms of the psychology of his day,
was a sworn enemy of psychology as such. On the other hand,
Husserl's return from "pure logic" to a study of subjectivity was
widely interpreted as a relapse into psychologism and, in fact,
into one of psychology's worst sins, "introspectionism."

Even Husserl himself, during the whole of his philosophical
development, did not find it easy to determine once and for all
his attitude toward psychology, and to define the exact function
which he assigned to it within the framework of his changing
conception of phenomenology. In any case, he kept stressing the
particularly close connection between the two and asserted
that his phenomenology was relevant to psychology and could
be applied to it after an appropriate change of attitude.

This much may be stated without qualifications as valid for
all stages in Husserl's development: He never opposed psychology as a whole, but only certain types of psychology which he
called naturalistic or objectivistic, i.e., psychologies which, in

mistaken imitation of the physical sciences, had tried to get rid of the essential features of the psychological phenomena. The worst of these psychologies was orthodox behaviorism. But Husserl had been close enough not only to Brentano but also to an active experimentalist like Stumpf to avoid generalizations about all psychologists. What he felt increasingly to be the need was a phenomenological psychology to fill the gap between philosophy and the best psychology of the day, but also as a privileged approach to phenomenology proper. It would have to consist in a more determined and more consistent development of the descriptive psychology or psychognostics of Brentano. Husserl's lectures on Phenomenological Psychology, scheduled for early publication in *Husserliana*, should throw further light on this conception.

Thus far, to be sure, it is not easy to pin down his interpretation of the relationship between psychology and phenomenology in a manner that would cover all periods of his development. Hence no such attempt will be undertaken here, much as this may seem desirable in the interest of a better understanding of the relationship between Husserl's phenomenological psychology and its many independent or inspired rivals among the psychologists themselves. Instead, I shall simply point out some constants in Husserl's conception of it.

α. Husserl's picture of scientific psychology was shaped principally by contemporary psychophysics and physiological psychology, whose dominating interest was to determine quantitatively and experimentally the relationships between objective stimuli and subjective responses. In this picture the "psychological" was nothing but part and parcel of a complete animal organism, on an equal level with its physical parts. Brentano's new psychology, while emphasizing the right of an analytical and descriptive approach preparatory to the genetic investigation of objective dependencies, had not changed anything fundamental in this conception. Nor had the psychology of William James done so. What Husserl postulated in its stead was a study which, disregarding the position of the psychological within the framework of a real organism, concentrated first and foremost upon the psychological phenomena as they appeared in and of themselves. Misplaced objectivism remained Husserl's basic objection even to Gestalt psychology in spite of many other affinities, beginning with the fact that Husserl, simultaneously with von Ehrenfels, had pointed out in his *Philosophie der Arithmetik*, the phenomenon of gestalt (under the name of *"figurales Einheitsmoment"*). In his later days Husserl also asserted that such a psychology needed a special phenomenological reduction similar to, but not quite as radical as, the transcendental reduction, with the assignment of bracketing at least all non-psychological entities. How far and in what manner Husserl wanted to reintegrate such a subjectivistic psychology into the context of nature as investigated by the objectivistic sciences is hard to determine. But Husserl never denied the right of an empirical investigation of psychological phenomena in its proper context. Nor did he deny the right of the experiment even in a phenomenological psychology, where it could function as an aid to our sluggish imagination, if for no other purpose.

β. A phenomenological psychology in Husserl's sense would have as its primary assignment the investigation of the intentional structures of consciousness first pointed out by Brentano. Traditional psychology, and especially the empiricist and associationist psychology under which Husserl had grown up, was dominated by the misleading pattern of consciousness as a mere aggregate of sensory data – a pattern which blocked the way to the understanding of the complex structures and functions of consciousness.

γ. Traditional psychology, in Husserl's perspective, lacked a systematic framework of basic concepts founded on the intuitive clarification of the psychical "essences." Whatever psychology had accumulated and was still accumulating by way of measuring and experiment concerning objective correlations was wasted as long as there was no clear grasp of what it was that was being measured and correlated. In Husserl's early days this applied specifically to studies such as those on speed of apperception or of memory reproduction. Not until a descriptive picture of the essences of perception or of memory was achieved could such studies be undertaken and interpreted meaningfully. Current controversies about the meaning of the measurement of so-called intelligence could provide a particularly good illustration of this problem. Phenomenological psychology as Husserl saw it was destined to supply the essential insights needed to give meaning and direction to the research going on under the flag of empirical psychology.

The following characterization may serve as a summary statement of Husserl's conception of the relationship among the three principal studies in question:

> *Pure phenomenology* is the study of the essential structures of consciousness comprising its ego-subject, its acts, and its contents – hence not limited to psychological phenomena – carried out with complete suspension of existential beliefs.
>
> *Phenomenological psychology* is the study of the fundamental types of psychological phenomena in their subjective aspect only, regardless of their imbeddedness in the objective context of a psychophysical organism.
>
> *Empirical psychology* is the descriptive and genetic study of the psychical entities in all their aspects as part and parcel of the psychophysical organism; as such it forms a mere part of the study of man, i.e., of anthropology.

5. The Final Radicalization of Transcendental Phenomenology

During the sixteen years prior to his retirement in 1929 Husserl published no major work of his own, though his yearbook brought out some of the most important studies of his associates and students. But these years, spent at the University of Freiburg from 1916 on, were by no means unproductive. It was however a time when the problems which Husserl had attacked under the heading of the phenomenological constitution grew out of hand, and when planned publications were postponed again and again. New manuscripts, addressed largely to himself, accumulated in frightening quantity. Until 1922 Edith Stein and then Martin Heidegger, at the time of Husserl's arrival already a fully established *Privatdozent* at the University, served as his assistants in his growing seminar. During these years of close contact and co-operation with Heidegger Husserl hoped increasingly that Heidegger would become his philosophical heir. After Husserl had turned down the offer of one of the main chairs of philosophy at the University of Berlin, he was enabled to enjoy the services of research assistants, whom he himself could train for their assignments. Among these, Edith Stein and [1] even more intimately Ludwig Landgrebe and finally Eugen Fink became his collaborators; it was largely due to them that the output of the Freiburg years has been preserved for later edition and publication.

The general character of Husserl's work during this period can best be studied in his last completed and authorized German publication, the *Formale und transzendentale Logik* of 1929. On the surface this book seems to return to the program of a pure logic free from psychologism. But while Husserl offers some interesting suggestions as to the further development of this pre-phenomenological project, his major concern is now to link it up with his new transcendental phenomenology by showing how the objective ideal laws of formal logic have their ultimate roots in a transcendental logic. Intentional analysis based on the transcendental reduction was to reveal them as the achievements of constituting acts. But here too Husserl usually gave only outlines of how this was to be done, rather than working it out in detail.

Yet, the new logic indicated only one dimension of the ever widening scope of Husserl's investigations. Even more basic than the problem of the constitution of logical entities in predicative form was that of pre-predicative experience, represented chiefly by perception. At the same time the radicalization of the reduction, which isolated the transcendental ego within its own immediate present, posed the problem of solipsism. The vindication of intersubjectivity now became one of Husserl's major concerns and called for a clarification of the problems connected with the constitution of the consciousness of other egos.

Husserl struggled desperately to carry out these widening plans, and at times he seems to have been severely discouraged. There is a passage in his Preface to the English edition of the *Ideen*, published in German as the concluding contribution of the last volume (XI) of the *Jahrbuch* in 1930, which gives a remarkable self-appraisal of Husserl in this phase, characteristic in its mixture of humorous modesty and pride:

Even though for practical purposes the author had to tone down the ideal of his philosophical ambitions to those of a mere beginner, he has, at least for his own person in his old age, reached the perfect certainty that he can call himself a *true* beginner. He could almost dare to hope that, if he were granted the age of a Methuselah, he might still become a philosopher. He has been able to pursue the problems of a descriptive phenomenology (the beginning of the beginning) further and further and to develop it in examples instructive at least to himself. The encompassing horizon for the work of a phenomenological philosophy has unfolded according to what may be called its main geographical structures, and the essential layers of problems and the methods of approach fitted to them have been clarified. The author sees spread out ahead of him the open space of a true philosophy in its infinity, the Promised Land, which he himself will no longer see in full cultivation. ... [The *Ideen*] will not be able to help anybody who is already sure of his philosophy and of his philosophical method, and hence has never experienced the despair of one who had the misfortune to fall in love with philosophy and who, even as a beginning student, was faced with a choice in the chaos of philosophies, yet became aware that he really had no choice, since none of these philosophies had provided for real freedom from presuppositions and none had sprung from the radicalism of autonomous responsibility for which philosophy calls.[1]

When Husserl retired in 1929, he designated Heidegger as his successor, hoping that this would lead to closer cooperation between them. It was only after Heidegger's return from Marburg to Freiburg that Husserl became fully aware of the divergence between his own and Heidegger's conceptions of phenomenology as expressed clearly enough in the first volume of Heidegger's *Sein und Zeit*. The full realization of this fact was by far the severest personal disappointment in Husserl's philosophical career. Also it soon led to a personal estrangement between the two most conspicuous figures of the Phenomenological Movement of the time. Heidegger's involvement, however temporary, in the Nazi regime during the early years of the Third Reich, though unrelated to the philosophical issues, added to Husserl's bitterness.

But in spite of this blow Husserl's retirement proved by no means the end of his philosophical activity. Foreign recognition increased. As early as 1922 Husserl lectured on "Phenomenological Method and Phenomenological Philosophy" at the University of London, yet apparently without making a lasting impression, possibly because of an approach which failed to make use of the special affinities between British philosophy and phenomenology; to a lesser degree this would also seem to hold for the article on "Phenomenology" in the *Encyclopaedia Bri-*

[1] *Husserliana* V, 161.

University of London.

Advanced Lectures in

PHILOSOPHY

A COURSE OF FOUR LECTURES

ON

"Phänomenologische Methode und Phänomenologische Philosophie"

WILL BE GIVEN BY

PROFESSOR EDMUND HUSSERL

(Professor of Philosophy in the University of Freiburg.)

AT

UNIVERSITY COLLEGE, LONDON

(Gower Street, W.C.)

ON

JUNE 6th, 8th, 9th, and 12th, 1922, at 5.30 p.m.

SYLLABUS :

LECTURE I. JUNE 6th.
(Chairman: Professor G. Dawes Hicks, M.A., Ph.D., Litt.D.)
The general aim of phenomenological philosophy. The Cartesian way to the thinking self and the method of phenomenological reduction.

LECTURE II. JUNE 8th.
(Chairman: Professor James Ward, M.A., Sc.D., F.B.A.)
The realm of phenomenological experience and the possibility of a phenomenological science. Transcendental phenomenology as science of transcendental subjectivity.

LECTURE III. JUNE 9th.
(Chairman: Professor H. Wildon Carr, D.Litt., J.P.)
Transcendental Phenomenology and the problems of possible knowledge, possible science, possible objective entities and worlds.

LECTURE IV. JUNE 12th.
(Chairman: Dr. G. E. Moore, Litt.D., F.B.A., [Editor of "Mind"].)
The complete idea of a logic as a theory of scientific knowledge and the system of all real sciences. The way to and the phenomenological philosophy of the future.

The Lectures, which will be delivered in German, are addressed to advanced students of the University and to others interested in the subject. A Syllabus (in English) of the Lectures will be obtainable in the Lecture Room.

ADMISSION FREE, WITHOUT TICKET.

EDWIN DELLER,
Academic Registrar.

8. Announcement of Husserl's London Lectures

tannica of 1927, an occasion on which Husserl tried to collaborate with Heidegger – and failed. The lectures which Husserl gave at the Sorbonne in 1929 proved more effective, especially in the long run. Here he presented phenomenology as a form of Neo-Cartesianism. Subsequently these lectures were developed into the *Cartesian Meditations,* of which however only a French version appeared during Husserl's lifetime. Other lectures which Husserl gave in Prague and Vienna as late as 1935 were of similar importance.   [1]

However, Husserl's main effort continued to focus on the development of his own restless thought. Only rarely did he succeed in reaching final formulations of his monological meditations. A typical day of the septuagenarian began with a morning walk in the company of his assistants and one or two of his close disciples, with whom he liked to discuss problems which occupied his mind. Three hours of the afternoon he spent at his desk, writing down what he had considered during the morning walk, rereading old manuscripts and reworking them. He did so no matter what his own dispositions or the worsening external circumstances were. When he found himself not in the mood, he used every effort "to get himself going," as he frankly admitted. But usually after jotting down his ideas for half an hour as they came to him, he had recaptured his inspiration.[1]

This life of ceaseless philosophic labor must be seen against the background of the general threats and tragedies of the thirties and the disillusionments, both philosophical and personal, which increasingly overshadowed Husserl's last years. As late as August, 1937, when his final illness began, he was working strenuously at his last publication, *The Crisis of the European Sciences and Transcendental Phenomenology.* His death early in 1938 spared him the fate of so many elderly Germans of Jewish descent who had failed to take the safer way into exile.[2]

---

[1] See Alfred Schuetz's account in *PPR* I (1940), 21.

[2] Two years later, when the Nazi Gauleiter of Baden decided to "cleanse" his province of the last Jews, the victims of his decree, having been notified one hour before the deportation, were taken to the concentration camp of Gurs in Southern France. Among them was the 84–year–old (Protestant) widow of the former *Rector* of the University of Freiburg, Otto Lenel, a man of outstanding international fame and of unquestionable patriotic record; she died soon after a delayed arrival in the notorious camp. It is not hard to imagine what would have been Husserl's fate, had he still been alive at that time.

It is not easy to characterize the content and the quality of
[1] Husserl's philosophizing during this last period. On the surface
one is struck by the mounting disproportion between growing
aspirations and fragmentary fulfillment. But closer inspection
of the texts reveals that there is little if any weakening in the
intensity and sweep of Husserl's thought, even though he
found it increasingly hard to give his ideas final shape and to
release them for publication. There is also the weighty testimony
of his last collaborators to the effect that Husserl was intellectu-
ally at his best up to the time of his last illness.

According to their content Husserl's writings during this
period can be divided into two groups: a more exoteric one,
motivated both by requests from the outside and by Husserl's
own desire to prepare a more direct approach to the final version of
his phenomenology than by the detours of his earlier works, but
inevitably introducing new and important ideas; and an
esoteric one, in the form of a final effort to radicalize transcendental phenomenology by demonstrating the primal constitution
(*Urkonstitution*) even of the passive elements in the phenomena
and to develop a comprehensive "teleology" of consciousness
with emphasis on its "historical" nature.

Of the esoteric studies, carried out in close cooperation with
Eugen Fink and concerned largely with the constitution of time,
very little is accessible thus far. They included such extensions
of the phenomenological enterprise as that of a "constructive
phenomenology." Apparently its major objective was to "regress"
even beyond the previously discussed phenomenological reduction, which demonstrated intuitively the origins of our
constitutions. This new phenomenology would have to "construct," or better re-construct, data not directly given ("*unge-
geben*"). Such a reconstruction could hardly be understood as
anything but an inference to constitutive acts, hidden in the
complete darkness of the ego's early growth. However, until
more and better texts about this joint work of Husserl and
Fink become available, any discussion had better be postponed.
Anyway, these last efforts had no serious influence upon the
course of the Phenomenological Movement thus far and failed to
convince even Husserl's erstwhile collaborators, who have now
abandoned the whole project.

The exoteric concern for better introductions in the interest of outsiders resulted in two attempts: (1) the *Cartesian Meditations*, based on the Sorbonne lectures of 1929, which appeared at least in an influential but not faultless French translation in 1931. (Husserl held up the publication of the German original, because it no longer satisfied him, especially after he received the criticisms of the French version voiced by his former student Roman Ingarden, criticisms which concerned particularly the conclusiveness of Husserl's case for transcendental idealism). The five *Meditations* consist in an attempt to lead the way to transcendental phenomenology through a radicalization of the Cartesian approach. Particularly in the last meditations on the problem of intersubjectivity there is much new and original material. The posthumous edition by S. Strasser (*Husserliana* I) preserves the original version. (2) *The Crisis of the European Sciences and Transcendental Phenomenology*, also a development of lectures given in Vienna and Prague in 1935. At least two parts of this work appeared during Husserl's lifetime in the Belgrade journal *Philosophia*, while the larger incomplete third part was held back for further revision, and a fourth part was never written. The existing parts of this important work have now been put together in Walter Biemel's edition (*Husserliana* VI).

Of the themes discussed in these works I shall take up only two, but both of a character which has made them very important for the development of post-Husserlian phenomenology: the problem of intersubjectivity and the conception of the immediate world of our daily living, the *Lebenswelt*.

a. INTERSUBJECTIVITY AND TRANSCENDENTAL MONADOLOGY – The solipsistic predicament of the subjectivist idealist is notorious. For his arguments are apt to prove too much. They may "subjectivize" the very partners of the discussion whom he wants to convert to his own ideas. What would be the point of arguing against them?

This predicament might beset even Husserl's transcendental idealism. For when his phenomenological reduction bracketed the entire external world inasmuch as it transcended consciousness, even the belief in the existence of other subjects was to be suspended. The subsequent discovery that the objective world was ultimately the achievement of the transcendental subject constituted by his intentional acts would seem to make the conclusion inevitable that the other ego is really only a projection of the *solus ipse.*

In spite of all his philosophical radicalism Husserl was just as little prepared to admit this as any other classical idealist. He had even battled with this problem as early as in his lectures of 1910–11. But only in the last of the *Cartesian Meditations* did he present a complete discussion of the subject in which he tried to show how the transcendental ego constitutes other egos as equal partners in an intersubjective community, which in turn forms the foundation for the "objective," i.e., the intersubjective world. Thus the intersubjective community of egos is introduced as the very presupposition of the "objective" world of common sense and of science. It is therefore a more basic level in the constitution of the world than the sub-personal and particularly the material world. This in itself constitutes an interesting reversal of the traditional way of proving the existence of others via the existence of their material bodies, and a significant contrast with Descartes' proof for the existence of a material world via his proofs for the existence of God, as well as with Berkeley's precarious *ad hoc* hypothesis of special "notions" in our minds as likenesses of other minds.

Whether this theory represents an adequate solution of the solipsistic problem is a point on which Husserl himself seems to have remained uneasy. But what about the actual phenomenological evidence for our knowledge of others? In the process of his attempted demonstration Husserl offered at least descriptive accounts that deserve attention, even if they should not add up to a valid refutation of solipsism. These accounts still make use of the traditional term *"Einfühlung"* (empathy), adopted by Husserl under the inspiration of the main proponent of empathy, Theodor Lipps, but offer by no means an orthodox interpretation of it. From the very start Husserl admitted that all our knowledge of others is to some extent indirect. The other is given us not in direct presentation but only by way of *Appräsentation,* a process which acquaints us with aspects of an object that are not directly presented. We are familiar with this process from our acquaintance with the backside of a three-dimensional body

[1]

when approaching it from its front. However, in such a case direct presentation may follow later. Not so in the case of our knowledge of others. What happens here is that when we perceive a body other than our own as "there" rather than as "here," we apperceive it at once as the body of an alter ego by way of an assimilative analogy with our own ego, an analogy which, however, is by no means an inference by analogy. In this process the analogizing ego and the analogized alter ego are "paired" in a characteristic "coupling" (*Paarung*). Thus the other ego, while not accessible as directly as its body, can be understood as a modification of our own pure ego by which we put ourselves into his body – as if we were in his place. Of course this account does not do away with the fact that according to Husserl other egos have their being only by the constituting grace of the transcendental ego. Nevertheless he insists that the other egos thus constituted are themselves transcendental and that these egos form a community of "monads," as he calls them with deliberate allusion to Leibniz's Monadology.

b. THE IDEA OF THE LIFE-WORLD ('LEBENSWELT')

The most influential and suggestive idea that has come out of the study and edition of Husserl's unpublished manuscripts thus far is that of the *Lebenswelt* or world of lived experience. Practically nothing of it was known during his lifetime. The only [1] time Husserl came close to releasing it was when he prepared the second installment of the *Krisis* articles for publication in *Philosophia* during his very last year. Yet this was clearly a conception which had occupied him during his entire last decade. Its earliest discussion in print occurred in an article by Ludwig Landgrebe published first in English in 1940.[1] In France it became known chiefly after Merleau-Ponty had introduced it in his writings on the basis of his study in the unpublished parts of the *Krisis* in the Husserl Archives at Louvain.

The interest this idea has aroused for its own sake must not make us overlook the fact that it had a very definite place and function in the context of Husserl's late philosophy. For he

---

[1] "World as a Phenomenological Problem" in *PPR* I (1940), 38–58; a slightly longer version appeared in Landgrebe's *Phänomenologie und Metaphysik* (Hamburg, Schröder, 1949), pp. 83–131.

conceived of it as one of two new avenues to transcendental phenomenology, the second one being through a critical evaluation of modern psychology. The *Lebenswelt*, so Husserl thought, would yield a particularly revealing clue (*Leitfaden*) for the study
[1] of intentionality in action. Actually the some ninety pages of the text devoted to this subject do not contain more than first indications as to the direction of this next step. Apparently even from here the approach to the "mothers," the keepers of the key to the ultimate sources of being, as Husserl called them repeatedly in allusion to a well-known episode in Goethe's *Faust* (Part II), remained anything but easy. But whatever the *Lebenswelt* might contribute to the confirmation of Husserl's transcendental phenomenology and to the unveiling of the hidden achievements of the transcendental ego, there can be no doubt that this was one of the most fertile ideas in the history of phenomenology after Husserl.

Perhaps the study of the *Lebenswelt* will appear not only as an unscientific but even as an unphilosophical enterprise, or at best as a pre-philosophical one. But no matter how it is classified, it is precisely such "matters of course" which philosophy cannot afford to neglect. Not even science can do so, if Husserl is right in asserting that some of the "crisis of European science" is due to the neglect of the *Lebenswelt* from which it has taken its start. Besides, the *Lebenswelt* presents some very definite tasks and problems for investigation. Each life-world shows certain pervading structures or "styles," and these invite study by what Husserl calls an "ontology of the life-worlds."

It should also be realized that the life-world is by no means immediately accessible as such to the average person in the "natural attitude," especially insofar as he has come under the spell of the scientific interpretation of the world. As Husserl sees it, a peculiar kind of first reduction, a suspension of science, is indispensable in order to get sight of the life-world and of its structures. In other words, even the study of the life-world is already a type of phenomenology, though this may still be a "mundane phenomenology." The importance of such a new phenomenology, destined to explore the fields of logic and formal ontology, ethics, psychology etc., is indicated, among other things, by the fact that the final arrangement of Husserl's

papers in 1935 put the manuscripts on mundane phenomenology first (under A) and those on reduction and the various
types of constitutions only under subsequent letters (from
B to E).

It would seem, then, that only after such inquiries have been
carried out will Husserl's phenomenological or transcendental
reduction have a sound basis and a proper guide. This reduction
will have to lead us back from the structures of the life-world
to the hidden functions of intentionality (*fungierende Intentionalität*). The discovery of these functions would then allow us to
trace the constitution of the characteristic features of the life-
world and of other objectivities based upon them.

The first step in this direction would be the thorough inspection,
analysis, and description of the life-world as we encounter it
before the transcendental reduction. How far was Husserl himself able to carry out this ambitious program? His earlier phenomenological studies in the field of perception and of other
intentional acts had focussed only on specific and isolated
phenomena. Nevertheless, largely under the stimulation of
William James, Husserl had always been aware of the significance of "fringes," or, as he mostly called them, "horizons"
for the phenomena as essential features of their make-up. But
only slowly did he come to see that even these horizons were not
merely open areas of decreasing clarity, but parts of the comprehensive horizon of a world as their encompassing frame of reference, without which any account of even a single perception
would be incomplete.

Now this world in the sense of an all-inclusive horizon was
clearly not the world in the sense of objective science, a cosmo-
logy, for instance. It was the world as experienced by a living
subject in his particular perspective, however distorted, hence
clearly a subjective and relative affair. The only form in which
this concept had found entrance into science was that of a
subjective environment (*Umwelt*) as introduced into animal
psychology especially by Jacob von Uexküll. The place where
Husserl himself found it most impressively illustrated was in
the account of the mythical and magic world of primitive mentality given by the French anthropologist Lucien Lévy-Bruehl;
in fact in a letter of March 11, 1935, which attracted consider-

able attention,[1] Husserl credited him with having anticipated his own conception in actual practice and thus shown the way for a true science of social and cultural problems (*Geisteswissenschaft*).

But except for such promising developments, science, especially mathematical science in the spirit of Galileo, seemed to Husserl to be blind to this whole matrix of its concepts. For in the pattern of the mathematicized natural sciences he saw nothing but selective idealizations. The meaning and the great task of the natural sciences was to achieve as much objectivity as could be attained, starting from a merely subjective ground like that of the life-world. Yet, according to Husserl, forgetfulness of this origin was responsible for the intensifying crises of recent science, both internal, in its own foundations, and external, in its relation to "life" and to man with his human values and aspirations. In Husserl's view, the only way to restore the proper balance was to realize that science was in fact nothing but a distillate, as it were, from the fuller life-world. This was the task of philosophy, of which the sciences were the specialized branches.

Husserl himself contributed at least some first directives for a phenomenological exploration of these total life-worlds. Thus, a life-world is to be conceived as an oriented world with an experiencing self at its center, designated as such by personal pronouns. Around this pole the world is structured by such peculiar patterns as "near" and "far," as "home ground" (*Heimat*) and foreign ground (*Fremde*). Its spatial frame of reference is experienced as stationary, contrary to the scientific conception of the Copernican universe.[2] To be sure, these descriptions were deliberately sketchy and programmatic. It remains to be seen whether the present enthusiasm for this conception will lead to more substantial achievements.[3]

---

[1] See Maurice Merleau-Ponty, "Le Philosophe et la Sociologie" in *Cahiers Internationaux de Sociologie*, X (1951), 62 f.

[2] Some of these characterizations remind one strikingly of Kurt Lewin's topological psychology with its conception of the "phenomenal" field. The parallel is by no means accidental in view of the common inspiration, in Lewin's case possibly from Carl Stumpf's phenomenological approach. Nevertheless, there remain significant differences.

[3] For some concrete and fruitful development of these ideas I refer to the studies by Alfred Schuetz, which will be taken up in Chapter XIII.

9. Edmund Husserl (1931)

D. IN PLACE OF AN APPRAISAL

This is not the place for a final evaluation of Husserl's achievements nor of his significance for the Phenomenological Movement. In any case, even if Husserl's own ultimate objective, the establishment of a new transcendental philosophy, should have led him into a dead end, the many inspirations that have resulted from his partial successes as well as from his failures secure him the place of the "venerable beginner" of a new way of philosophizing.

In the meantime there seems to be a more than accidental appropriateness in quoting here from Husserl's tribute to his teacher Brentano, as a prophetic self-appraisal and a preview of the further course of the Phenomenological Movement:

It cannot be decided here how far his methods and theories will keep their place. Certainly his motifs have taken on a different form in the nourishing soil of minds other than his own. But they have thus proved anew their original germinating power and vitality. To be sure, not to his own satisfaction, since he himself ... was sure of his own philosophy. Indeed, his self-confidence was supreme. His inner certainty to be on the right road and to be the founder of the only scientific philosophy was unwavering. To give fuller shape to this philosophy within the framework of the systematic fundamental doctrine which he considered secure: this was what he felt to be his vocation from within and from above. I would like to call this absolutely doubt-free conviction of his mission the basic fact of his life. Without it, it is impossible to understand Brentano's personality, and hence impossible to pass fair judgment on the man himself.[1]

SELECTIVE BIBLIOGRAPHY

Major Works

Über den Begriff der Zahl (1887)
Philosophie der Arithmetik vol. I (1891)
Logische Untersuchungen vol. I (1900), vol. II (1901); second revised edition in 3 vols. (1913)
    Translations: Russian (1909), Spanish (1929), French (1959)
"Philosophie als strenge Wissenschaft," Logos I (1910), 289–314
    Translations: Spanish (1951); French (1955) by Q. Lauer; English (Crosscurrents VI (1956), 227–46, 325–44) by the same translator – fair, not free from errors; Italian (1958)
Ideen zu einer reinen Phänomenologie und phänomenologischen Philosophie vol. I (1913); new posthumous edition in Husserliana III; vol. II and III edited in Husserliana IV and V (1952)

---

[1] "Erinnerungen an Franz Brentano" in Oskar Kraus, Franz Brentano, p. 160.

Translations of vol. I: English (1931) by W. R. Boyce Gibson – fair, not always accurate; Spanish (1949); Italian (1950); French (1950) by Paul Ricoeur – to be recommended not only for its excellence, but for a helpful introduction and new glossary. For a condensed English account of *Ideen* II and III see *PPR* XIII (1953), 394–413, 506–514 (Alfred Schuetz).

Article "Phenomenology" in *Encyclopaedia Britannica* (14th ed.), vol. 17, 699–72 – a rather free translation of a still unpublished German
[1]   original

Formale und transzendentale Logik (1929)
    Translations: French (1957) by Suzanne Bachelard
Cartesianische Meditationen (1931); published posthumously in *Husserliana* I (1950)
    Translations: French (1931, i.e., before the German original) by J. Pfeiffer and E. Levinas – some errors; Spanish (1942); English by Dorion Cairns (1960) mostly very faithful; Japanese (1956)
Die Krisis der europäischen Wissenschaften und die transzendentale Phänomenologie, Parts I and II (1936); all extant parts in *Husserliana* VI (1954)
    Translations: French (Part I and II only, in *Études philosophiques* IV (1949), 127–159, 229–301. – For a condensed English account see *PPR* XVI (1956), 380–399, and XVII (1957), 370–398 (Aron Gurwitsch)

Posthumous Publications

Erfahrung und Urteil. Untersuchungen zur Genealogie der Logik.
    Prepared by Ludwig Landgrebe (1939)
[2]   *Die Idee der Phänomenologie.* Fünf Vorlesungen (1907). *Husserliana* II
[3]   *Erste Philosophie* (1923/24). *Husserliana* VII and VIII

Monographs in French and German

BERGER, GASTON, *Le Cogito dans la philosophie de Husserl.* Paris, Aubier, 1941
    Influential introduction with excellent annotated bibliography.
CELMS, THEODOR, *Der phänomenologische Idealismus Edmund Husserls.* Riga, 1928
    A thorough critical study by a Latvian student of Husserl in Freiburg.
DIEMER, ALWIN, *Edmund Husserl. Versuch einer systematischen Darstellung seiner Phänomenologie.* Meisenheim am Glan, Hain, 1956
    A remarkable attempt to distill Husserl's final philosophical position
[4]   from his writings and posthumous manuscripts.
LANDGREBE, LUDWIG, *Phänomenologie und Metaphysik.* Hamburg, Schröder, 1949
    Contains a memorial address and three important essays on major aspects of Husserl's philosophical development.
LAUER, QUENTIN, *Phénoménologie de Husserl. Essai sur la genèse de l'intentionnalité.* Paris, Presses Universitaires, 1955
    Contains a detailed study of Husserl's full-fledged phenomenology, based chiefly on the texts published during his lifetime, and some criticisms. No attempt is made to trace the genesis of Husserl's thought
[5]   back to its pre-phenomenological origins.

Important Articles in German

BECKER, Oskar, "Die Philosophie Edmund Husserls" *Kantstudien* XXXV
(1930), 119–150
Becker was at the time comparatively close to both Husserl and Hei-
degger.   [1]
FINK, EUGEN, "Die phänomenologische Philosophie Edmund Husserls
in der gegenwärtigen Kritik," *Kantstudien* XXXVIII (1933), 319–383
An influential article, which bears Husserl's imprimatur.
——, "Was will die Phänomenologie Edmund Husserls?"
Tatwelt X (1934), 14–32
——, Article "Husserl, Edmund" in Ziegenfuss, Werner, *Philosophen-
lexikon*, Berlin, de Gruyter 1949, I, 569–576.
The wording of the text and Husserl's letter to Marvin Farber (*The
Foundations of Phenomenology*, p. 17) suggest Fink's authorship rather
than Husserl's.
——, "Das Problem der Phänomenologie Edmund Husserls"
Revue internationale de philosophie I (1938), 226–270
Part of an uncompleted book, which was to attempt an independent
interpretation of Husserl's philosophy.
——, "Operative Begriffe in Husserl's Phänomenologie," *Zeitschrift für
philosophische Forschung XI* (1957), 321–37

Large Studies in English

FARBER, MARVIN, *The Foundation of Phenomenology. Edmund Husserl
and the Quest for a Rigorous Science of Philosophy*. Cambridge, Harvard
University Press, 1943
Contains valuable reports on his early writings and paraphrases of
Logische Untersuchungen; critical of his later development.
——, ed., *Philosophical Essays in Memory of Edmund Husserl*. Cambridge,
Harvard University Press, 1940
Some expository but mostly critical essays on Husserl, often striking
out in new directions.
LAUER, QUENTIN, S.J., *The Triumph of Subjectivity. An Introduction to
Transcendental Phenomenology*. New York, Fordham University Press,
1958
Mostly a condensed and slightly rearranged version of the French work
mentioned above; some additions about other phenomenologists, which
cannot be recommended. The book introduces Husserl's main themes
up to the *Cartesian Meditations*, but omits such items as the *Lebenswelt*.
OSBORN, ANDREW D., *The Philosophy of Edmund Husserl in its Develop-
ment from his Mathematical Interests to his First Conception of Phenome-
nology in Logical Investigations* (Ph. D. Thesis, Columbia). New York,
International Press, 1934.
Contains much important material on Husserl's early development.
WELCH, E. PARL, *The Philosophy of Edmund Husserl. The Origin and
Development of His Phenomenology* (Ph. D. Thesis, University of
Southern California). New York, Columbia University Press, 1941
Deals with Husserl's work up to the *Ideen*. Extensive bibliography, not
always reliable. Not to be recommended: see *PPR* II (1942), 219–32

Articles in English

AMES, VAN METER, "Mead and Husserl on the Self," *PPR* XV (1954), 320–31

ADORNO, T. W., "Husserl and the Problem of Idealism," *Journal of Philosophy*, XXXVII (1940), 5–18

BAR-HILLEL, "Husserl's Conception of a Purely Logical Grammar," *PPR* XVII (1957), 362–69

BECK, MAXIMILIAN, "The Last Phase of Husserl's Phenomenology," *PPR* I (1941), 479–91
Discussion by Dorion Cairns (I, 492–98) and rejoinder (I, 498)

CAIRNS, DORION, "Results of Husserl's Investigations," *Journal of Philosophy*, XXXVI (1939), 236–238. (A remarkable attempt to state Husserl's 27 most important insights in capsule form).

[1] CHANDLER, ALBERT, "Professor Husserl's Program of Philosophic Reform," *Philosophical Review XXVI* (1917), 634–48

FULTON, JAMES STREET, "Husserl's Significance for the Theory of Truth," *Monist* XLV (1935), 264–306. (Perceptive introduction, aware of the difficulties.)

——, "The Cartesianism of Phenomenology," *Philosophical Review* XLIX (1940), 283–308. (Excellent comparison between Descartes and Husserl)

GIBSON, W. R. BOYCE, "The Problem of Real and Ideal in the Phenomenology of Husserl," *Mind* XXXIV (1925), 311–333

GOTESKY, RUBIN, "Husserl's Conception of Logic as Kunstlehre in the *Logische Untersuchungen*," *Philosophical Review* XLVII (1938), 375–387 (Ph. D. thesis, New York University, 1939)

HAMILTON, KENNETH G., Edmund Husserl's Contribution to Philosophy," *Journal of Philosophy* XXXVI (1939), 225–232

HOOK, SIDNEY, "Husserl's Phenomenological Idealism," *Journal of Philosophy* XXVII (1930), 365–380

KAUFMANN, FRITZ, "In memoriam Edmund Husserl," Social Research VII (1940), 61–91

LANZ, HENRY, "The New Phenomenology," *Monist* XXXIV (1924), 511–527. (By a Russian philosopher, who had published on Husserl before coming to the States)

MERLAN, PHILIP, "Time Consciousness in Husserl and Heidegger," *PPR* VIII (1947), 23–53

[2] MOHANTY, J. N., " 'The Object' in Husserl's Phenomenology," *PPR* XIV (1954), 343–53

REINHARDT, KURT, "Husserl's Phenomenology and Thomist Philosophy," *New Scholasticism* XI (1937), 320–31

[3] SALMON, C. V., "The Starting Point of Husserl's Philosophy," *Proceedings of the Aristotelian Philosophy*, XXX (1929). 55–78

SPIEGELBERG, HERBERT, Husserl's and Peirce's Phenomenologies: Coincidence or Interaction," *PPR* XVII (1957), 164–85

——, "Husserl's Phenomenology and Existentialism," in *Journal of Philosophy* LVII (1960), 62–74

STEWART, J. McKELLAR, "Husserl's Phenomenological Method," *The Australasian Journal of Psychology and Philosophy*, XI (1933), 221–31; XII (1934), 62–73

Ph. D. Theses

CAIRNS, DORION, *The Philosophy of Edmund Husserl*, Harvard University, 1933
Covers especially Husserl's later phenomenology as known at the time.
Cairns was Husserl's most trusted American student and translator.   [1]
SCHMITT, RICHARD, G., *Husserl's Phenomenology; Reconstruction in Empiricism.* Yale University, 1956

Most Comprehensive Recent Bibliographies

ELEY, LOTHAR, "Husserl-Bibliographie   (1945–1959), *Zeitschrift für philosophische Forschung* XIII (1959), 357–67
PATOCKA, JAN, "Husserl-Bibliographie, *Revue internationale de philosophie* I (1939) 374–97
RAES, JEAN, "Supplément à la Bibliographie de Husserl," *Ibid.* IV (1950), 469–75   [2]

IV

THE OLDER PHENOMENOLOGICAL MOVEMENT

A. THE PHENOMENOLOGICAL CIRCLES

There was no such thing as a definite beginning of a Phenomenological Movement, let alone a school, in Husserl's wake, just as little as there had been a deliberate and clearly marked founding of phenomenology in his own development. But around 1905 Husserl began to attract a number of students, in the beginning chiefly from Munich, who developed a kind of group spirit and initiative which led gradually to the formation of the Göttingen Circle.

Another major branch of the early Phenomenological Movement was the Munich Circle. Actually, its beginnings reach back even before that of the Göttingen group, and its importance for the development of the Movement was at one time perhaps even greater. It also continued for a longer period, without the rifts, shifts, and "defections" which mark the history of Husserl's immediate following in Göttingen and later in Freiburg. But even the Munich Circle lost most of its coherence after the First World War. In fact, compared with the intensity and vitality of the philosophizing that went on in these two circles during the ten years of the "phenomenological spring" (as Jean Hering has

---

[1] The writer confesses that in this chapter he found it particularly hard to resist the temptation to be comprehensive. Without such resistance this chapter could easily have grown into book size. Hence the problem of a selection, both fair and helpful to the Anglo-American reader, proved unusually difficult. The only obvious criterion for the choice of the key figures was the fact that Pfänder, Reinach, and Geiger, along with Scheler, were the original coeditors of the phenomenological yearbook. However, the other more important members will be identified and characterized briefly in the end, if only by way of guidebook descriptions, in the hope that some day someone will have a chance to do a better and more thorough job. The main function of this chapter will be to prepare the ground and invite further cultivation.

called it), the later Phenomenological Movement, though richer in literary output, seems to be almost shapeless and anemic. For this early period was a time of group philosophizing and of a vigorous mutual criticism which has been regrettably absent from most later phases of phenomenology.

1. The Göttingen Circle

Husserl's initial impact as a teacher in Göttingen was far from impressive. Among his earliest students ("*Urschüler*") before 1905 only the name of Wilhelm Schapp stands out today.[1] It was [1] only several years after his start in Göttingen in 1901 that he attracted a sizable number of followers with real understanding and originality. The more important ones among them had been prepared by the study of his *Logische Untersuchungen*, which Husserl had published while he was still in Halle. What fascinated them most was to discover in a climate of philosophic sterility (the two main chairs of philosophy in Göttingen were occupied by a relatively unimportant Lotze follower, Julius Baumann, and the experimental psychologist, Georg Elias Müller) an original thinker practicing with a unique persistence the direct approach to the "things," as Husserl had advocated it in his writings. It was this spirit which stirred them in turn. Hence it is not surprising that it soon carried them far beyond and sometimes away from the demanding course which the master was plotting for himself.

Four of the students who appeared in Göttingen in the summer of 1905 came from Munich, where they had received their first philosophical training under Theodor Lipps. Adolf Reinach and Johannes Daubert were the outstanding ones among them, to be followed soon by Moritz Geiger; Theodor Conrad came in 1907, Dietrich von Hildebrand in 1909, and Hedwig Conrad-Martius in 1910. But in addition to these transfers and visitors from the Munich Circle, Husserl now began to attract original and serious students from elsewhere, who often visited Munich, if only temporarily, like Wilhelm Schapp. After 1909 they were

---

[1] His first non-German student of note was William Ernest Hocking, who had been sent to him as early as 1902 by Paul Natorp (oral communication); see also [2] his autobiographical sketch in Adams, George P. and Montague, Wm. P., ed., *American Contemporary Philosophy* (New York, Macmillan, 1930), I, 390.

joined by Alexander Koyré, Jean Hering, Roman Ingarden, Fritz Kaufmann, and Edith Stein.

About 1907 these students began to form a special circle. They used to meet at least once a week for discussions and the reading of papers outside the lecture halls and seminar rooms, mostly in Husserl's absence and, as a matter of fact, with his hardly concealed disapproval. For to this lively group and to its varying membership and fringe, phenomenology meant something rather different from what it did to Husserl at this stage, i.e., not the turn toward subjectivity as the basic phenomenological stratum, but toward the "*Sachen*," understood in the sense of the whole range of phenomena, and mostly toward the objective, not the subjective ones. Husserl's phenomenology had given them firm ground for their independent philosophizing and removed the obstacles of psychophysical theory and of a poverty-stricken positivism.[1] Now they could range freely over the wide-open field of new phenomena, exploring them by untutored "intuiting" in search of their essential structures and the essential connections among them. It seems that in those days even the bouquet of wines and the scent of tobaccos served as legitimate topics for phenomenological improvisations and discussions. No wonder that Husserl himself frowned upon some of this piecemeal "picture book phenomenology," as he used to call it. Also phenomenology meant to the circle primarily a universal philosophy of essences (*Wesensphänomenologie*), not merely a study of the "essence of consciousness." It thus included ontology in Husserl's sense; and in fact it did so increasingly. To the first announcement of Husserl's phenomenological transcendentalism and idealism the group responded with growing consternation.[2] Increasingly it was the phenomenology of Reinach (who had become *Privatdozent* in 1909) which expressed the spirit of the group.

After 1910 the informal gatherings took the form of a Philosophical Society, which during this period also provided a sounding board for Max Scheler, then without an academic post. It

---

[1] Jean Hering, "La phénoménologie d'Edmund Husserl il y a trente ans" in *Revue internationale de philosophie* I (1939), 366–73, and oral communications.

[2] There survives from those days a little piece of spirited satire on Husserl's innovations in the form of a "*Phänomenologenlied*" composed by Th. Conrad at the end of the summer term 1907, during which Husserl had first presented his lectures on "The Idea of Phenomenology"; it reveals the sceptical attitude of the group; see Alwin Diemer, *Edmund Husserl*, p. 38, note.

10. Philosophische Gesellschaft Göttingen (1912)
Front Row (from l. to r.): Adolf Reinach, Alexandre Koyré,
Hedwig Conrad-Martius, Max Scheler, Theodor Conrad.
Back Row: Jean Hering, Heinrich Rickert jr., Ernst Rothschild,
Siegfried Hamburger, Fritz Frankfurter, Rudolf Clemens, Hans Lipps,
Gustav Hübener, Herbert Leyendecker, Friedrich Neumann.

should not go unmentioned that some of the young Göttingen psychologists, in contrast to the older generation, took a lively interest in the Circle as well as in Husserl's work, among them, for instance, David Katz. The war and Husserl's departure from Göttingen to Freiburg put an end to the Society. – It is hardly accidental that Husserl's numerous Freiburg students never formed a circle comparable to the Göttingen group.   [1]

2. The Munich Circle

The situation was considerably different in Munich. Here, as early as 1901, the older students of Theodor Lipps had organized a club under the name of "Akademisch-Psychologischer Verein," which had weekly meetings. Lipps himself did not attend except once per semester. From the very beginning Alexander Pfänder and Johannes Daubert were the central figures in this group. The common basis was Lipps's refined descriptive psychology, which was marred only by remnants from Herbart's constructivism and – more serious – by his pronounced psychologism. When Husserl's Logische Untersuchungen attacked Lipps specifically for his psychologism, Lipps tried to defend his position before the group. But the effect was practically the opposite of what Lipps had intended: Before long it led to something like a revolt of his closest students.

Then, as tradition has it, one day in 1902 Husserl received the visit of an unknown student of philosophy from Munich, who was said to have come all the way on his bicycle. From 3 P.M. to 3 A.M. Husserl discussed the Logische Untersuchungen with him, in whom he recognized "the first person who had really read the book." This conversation was easily the most important single event in the history of the Munich Phenomenological Circle.

Johannes Daubert, the visitor from Munich, was one of the older Lipps students, independent and penetrating, with a flair for new developments, yet at the same time so critical and even self-critical that he never published a line, nor did he even complete his academic studies. After Lipps's abortive defense against Husserl before his students, Daubert was so much attracted to Husserl's Logische Untersuchungen that he studied both volumes and found them a philosophical tonic bath ("Stahl-

bad"). Probably as a result of the Göttingen interview Husserl himself visited Munich in May 1904 and addressed the club. From now on, to Lipps's increasing dismay, the *Logische Untersuchungen* became the standard reference text of the club. In 1905 began the trek of students and visitors from Munich to Göttingen and vice versa. It was only after 1906 that Scheler, coming from Rudolf Eucken in Jena, joined the group, both receiving from and giving to it, especially since these were his most formative years. Earlier members included Adolf Reinach (before he went to Göttingen for good, there to become the center of the younger Circle), Theodor Conrad, Moritz Geiger, Aloys Fischer, and August Gallinger, along with other Lipps students less affected by phenomenology, like Ernst von Aster and the positivist Hans Cornelius. Among the younger Scheler-inspired members Dietrich von Hildebrand was the most prominent. If anything, the Munich Circle was even more gregarious than the Göttingen group, meeting frequently for regular discussions and informal study groups, in addition to the "psychological" club sessions. Otherwise the most distinguishing characteristic of the Munich Circle was the primary interest in analytic and descriptive psychology, and, partly under the influence of the genius loci of the art city Munich, a stronger interest in problems of value and of esthetics than was found in the more austere mathematical and scientific climate of Göttingen.

[1]

Note: Phenomenology and Conversion

In view of recent attention and publicity one aspect of the Older Phenomenological Movement deserves at least a passing comment: the seeming frequency of conversions to Catholicism among its members, a development that stands in marked contrast to the trend away from the Catholic Church in the preparatory phase of the Movement. Certain facts are undeniable. Especially under the spell of Scheler during his middle phase, Catholicism became almost fashionable among the religiously indifferent as well as among Protestant and Jewish members. There was the early conversion of Dietrich von Hildebrand, and, best-known, that of Edith Stein, who even joined the Carmelite Order. But the importance of these cases can easily be exaggerated. They have to be contrasted with those of the permanent non-Catholics, particularly the Protestants Pfänder, Kurt Stavenhagen, Hedwig Conrad-Martius, and Jean Hering, later a Professor of Protestant theology in Strasbourg, along with such convinced Jews as Fritz Kaufmann. As to Reinach, whose turn to philosophy of religion and war-time Protestant baptism before his death were remarkable and influential enough, there is certainly no

12. Johannes Daubert (about 1905)

11. Alexander Pfänder (1940)

13. Adolf Reinach (about 1912)

14. Moritz Geiger (about 1930)

conclusive evidence that he personally contemplated conversion to Catholicism. Geiger never showed any open interest in the religious sphere.

The truth of the matter would seem to be that the phenomenological approach in its openness to all kinds of experiences and phenomena is ready to reconsider even the traditional beliefs in the religious field in a fresh and unprejudiced manner. That Catholicism, and particularly Augustinianism with its emphasis on intuitive insight, had a marked advantage over Protestantism at the time may have been due partly to the neo-orthodox tendencies in Protestantism with their exclusive emphasis on supernatural revelation and Biblical faith.

Husserl, in spite of his early conversion to Protestantism, kept even in the religious area to his much more critical and uncommitted attitude. It must also not be overlooked that some of his more ardent French followers, such as Sartre and Merleau-Ponty, are outspoken atheists, to be sure, without claiming phenomenological sanction for this negative decision (which they might easily have tried to support by combining Husserl's suspension of belief with the idealistic interpretation of phenomenological constitution).

B. ALEXANDER PFÄNDER (1870–1941): FROM PHENOMENOLOGICAL PSYCHOLOGY TO PHENOMENOLOGICAL PHILOSOPHY

1. Pfänder's Place in the Phenomenological Movement

Especially outside Germany,[1] Pfänder is today overshadowed not only by the dominating figure of Husserl, but also by the more brilliant Scheler, the more provocative Heidegger, and, lately, the more moving figure of the convert nun and Nazi victim Edith Stein. Yet by age and seniority Pfänder outranked all but Husserl. What is more, Pfänder, who spent his whole academic life at the University of Munich, was the acknowledged leader of the Munich group, a position which resulted also from the fact that he was the most prominent student of Theodor Lipps and the first to hold a professorship in the University.

Nevertheless, Pfänder's relative lack of recognition was no mere accident. There was nothing spectacular about him, nor was there in him any of the all too common academic self-im-

---

[1] In England, since Bosanquet's review of Pfänder's contribution to the first volume of the phenomenological yearbook in *Mind* XXIII (1914), 591 f., only John Laird in his *Recent Philosophy* (Home University Library, 1936) has paid attention to him, but in a rather misleading context. As to France, Jacques Maritain in his highly critical discussion of phenomenology in *Distinguer pour unir ou les degrés de la connaissance* (1932; English translation by Bernard Wall, Centenary Press, 1937) refers at least in a footnote (p. 122 of the translation) to the "Munich school, which does not follow Husserl's neo-idealism, and whose full significance cannot be easily gauged until the work of Alexander Pfänder has been published completely." He has made a much stronger impression in Spain and Mexico.

portance and ambition. He worked at an unhurried and steady pace and published most of his works only after having submitted them to the test of prolonged presentation in his lectures. Nothing was more foreign to him than the ostentatious programs and the unfulfilled promises of first volumes, which were so typical of other phenomenologists. This makes it all the more deplorable that a prolonged illness prevented him from carrying out his final plans to consolidate his most advanced insights into systematic books. The most outstanding thing about Pfänder was his mental and moral integrity, his frankness to the point of bluntness. The originality and richness of his intuitions, his incisiveness and insistence in critical argument and discussion, yet his sympathetic and stimulating understanding of other people's ideas were unrivalled among other phenomenologists. No brilliant stylist, he wrote clearly and plainly, avoiding almost all of the technical vocabulary so characteristic of Husserl's writings. At the same time he provided a wealth of imaginative illustrations drawn with masterly and at times humorous strokes, using metaphorical language (often to the point of danger, at least in less cautious hands) for the purpose of helping the reader to find and see for himself. At the same time, his writing showed an unusual amount of systematic organization in the traditional sense. It was not without reason that Pfänder's highest praise for work well done was the somewhat old-fashioned adjective *"gediegen"* (i.e., solid).

Evidently Husserl was strongly impressed by Pfänder ever after the first Munich encounter in July 1904, particularly by his unorthodox *Introduction to Psychology*. This also explains the fact that it was Husserl who took the initiative in suggesting through Daubert the momentous joint summer vacation in Seefeld in the Tyrolese Alps in 1905. Also, it was on Husserl's invitation that Pfänder undertook to write a new logic which, developing the idea of a pure logic in the sense of the *Logische Untersuchungen*, appeared in the *Jahrbuch* in 1921. In the years between 1920 and 1927 Pfänder was the actual editor of the *Jahrbuch*. During this period the author heard Husserl referring to Pfänder as "our most substantial (*"solide"*) worker," and there is definite evidence that during the early twenties, i.e., before the advent of Heidegger, he thought that Pfänder would be the best person to succeed him in Freiburg when he retired. But it is equally clear that Husserl felt disappointed by Pfänder's apparent disinterest in the problems of the transcendental reduction and constitution, which absorbed Husserl more and more deeply.[1] Later on, Husserl used to refer to Pfänder and the Munich phenomenologists as bogged down (*stecken geblieben*) in "ontologism" and "realism," because they had ignored the new revolutionizing transformations of his own phenomenology through the phenomenological reduction. How far this impression was justified is another matter. The sad truth remains that the contacts between Husserl and Pfänder diminished and finally ceased.

2. *The Place of Phenomenology in Pfänder's Philosophy*

The underlying purpose of Pfänder's philosophy cannot be read off from his published works. It has to be inferred from them, largely with the help of the posthumous papers, now deposited in the *Staatsbibliothek* in Munich, and from personal information, all the more since, characteristically enough, Pfänder left no autobiographical self-interpretation. Besides, little of his correspondence, except for his letters to Husserl, has survived.[2]

Before turning to philosophy, Pfänder had been trained as an engineer. It was Theodor Lipps, the psychologist-philosopher, who had attracted him to philosophy. Thus it was only natural that Pfänder's first and in a sense even his deepest interest was in psychology. But the psychology to which he aspired was something quite different from the psychology of the time. It reflects largely his personal experience when in his own Introduction to Psychology he speaks of the severe disappointment which overtakes those who want to assuage their hunger for psychology with its present output:

---

[1] Thus in a letter of December 24, 1921 he wrote to Roman Ingarden: "Even Pfänder's phenomenology is at bottom something essentially different from my own. Since he has never fully understood the problems of constitution, he – though otherwise thoroughly honest and substantial (*der übrigens grundehrliche und solide*) – is drifting toward a dogmatic metaphysics."

[2] Another correspondence, apparently of considerable interest, is mentioned by Wilhelm Wirth, Wundt's successor in Leipzig, who, in his autobiography (Murchison, C., ed., *History of Psychology in Autobiographies*, Clark University Press, vol. III (1936), 283–327) expresses his indebtedness to Pfänder.

Who has not experienced a jolt in his thinking, as if he had been shunted onto a totally wrong track, when he was told for the first time that colors, sounds, smells, scents, heat, hardness, etc., were what is meant by the psychical, and that a dancing swarm (*Mückentanz*) of such elements constituted the psychical life? [1]

Thus Pfänder's revolt was directed both against a psychologism which converted the non-psychological intentional objects (*Erscheinungen* in the sense of Stumpf's phenomenology) into psychical phenomena, and against the diversion of psychology from its proper object by a false atomistic objectivism. It was however the revolt against Lipps's all-comprehensive psychologism and the discovery of Husserl's parallel battle against it which led Pfänder to Husserl.

But Pfänder's focal though not only interest was and remained a genuine widening and at the same time a deepening of psychology.[2] His first concern was a descriptive expansion of psychology by an enriched picture of its phenomena in their essential structures and relationships. Thus his dissertation of 1897 on the consciousness of the will examined critically various rival theories, beginning with those of Münsterberg and James, and concluding that the will contains a peculiar element which cannot be reduced to mere ideas and sensations.[3] This critical study is followed by the constructive analysis of his "phenomenology" of the will.[4] Here he characterizes the will as one of several species of the genus "*striving*" and indicates the central place of the active free ego in willing. These early studies of the conative phenomena reveal Pfänder's special interest in those aspects of the personality which are most significant for an understanding of man as an active and also as an ethical being. Pfänder's second and more profound interest was, however, in an interpretative psychology (*verstehende Psychologie*), aimed at gaining a deeper understanding of the life and structure of the human personality, in which he saw a living entity striving to realize creatively a pattern laid out in its basic essence. The

---

[1] *Einführung in die Psychologie* (Leipzig, 1904), p. 42f.

[2] That Pfänder was also at home in experimental psychology to the extent of constructing experimental apparatus is attested by Wilhelm Wirth (*op. cit.*, p. 289).

[3] Pfänder's criticisms of William James should be contrasted with his high admiration for G. F. Stout's *Manual of Psychology* expressed in a review for the *Zeitschrift für Psychologie und Physiologie der Sinnesorgane* XXIII (1900), 415–19.

[4] *Phänomenologie des Wollens. Eine psychologische Analyse* (Leipzig, 1900).

"synthetic" or macroscopic method which Pfänder developed for this vaster enterprise is demonstrated particularly in his last work, *Die Seele des Menschen* (1933).

But while a widened and deepened psychology of man, "the microcosm," was thus the central interest of Pfänder's philosophizing, and the one from which he derived its most important insights, it was by no means its only one. Even the most influential achievement of his lifetime, the systematic development of Husserl's pure logic freed from psychology, was actually only a side-product of his larger objective, the preparation of a comprehensive philosophy, understood as the attempt to attain terminal knowledge (*letzt-abschliessende Erkenntnis*), a knowledge which would bring a final appraisal of all our genuine knowledge, scientific and extra-scientific. The phenomenological method, as Pfänder developed it, was to provide the key for the study of these larger issues. His *Introduction to Philosophy and Phenomenology*, planned as one of his final works based on sixteen constantly modified outlines for his lectures, contained a systematic treatment of the major problems of philosophy. Even more advanced was an *Ethics*, of which at least a first draft was completed.

It is in these last drafts that Pfänder came closest to stating his conception of the goal of his philosophy in explicit form. One of his final drafts for this new phenomenological philosophy goes by the title "From Belief to Insight" (*Vom Glauben zur Erkenntnis*). By "belief" Pfänder understands here not so much religious [1] faith as any belief in matters of fact, in values, and in ideals (*Forderungen*). In his view, these beliefs had been weakened beyond repair by the inability of modern man to justify them. Nihilism was the inevitable result. But now there was no way back to naive belief. Nor was it to be found in make-believe, expressed in the "noisy affirmations of the so-called *"Kulturträger,"* who, to him, were fundamentally just as nihilistic as their opponents in spite of the "shoutings of their enthusiastic speaking choruses and their stamping the streets" – an obvious allusion to the strutting Nazi stormtroopers in Pfänder's immediate vicinity. In the face of such pseudo-beliefs Pfänder saw only one real remedy: a phenomenological philosophy, which was to dispel these falsifications and give fresh access to, and

first-hand perception of, the genuine phenomena behind these
beliefs; it was also the only hopeful way to gain new beliefs
based upon insight.

At first sight this may seem to be another belated return to
rationalism. No doubt Pfänder, no less than Husserl, believed
in the power of human reason to clarify and verify our basic
beliefs. But Pfänder rejected both the traditional rationalism
and its irrationalistic opponents. For it was not the intellect which
could obtain insights into essential structures, into values and
ideals. Pfänder's phenomenological version of reason was a
"seeing and feeling reason" (*Vernunft*) rather than a reason
which used deductive and inductive "reasoning" as its primary
tools (*Verstand*). It was equally opposed to the traditional narrow
empiricism of the Humean variety. Particularly in the fields of
our knowledge of values Pfänder stressed the inadequacy of the
merely intellectualistic approach. Likewise in his philosophy of
religion he rejected both the rationalism of the proofs for theism
and – though a sincere Protestant without piousness – the neo-
orthodox fideism à la Karl Barth, and tried to show that a
"centering down" (*Versenkung*) into ourselves and into the world
could give us intuitive access to the source of all being, God.

3. Pfänder's Conception of Phenomenology

Pfänder was not the type of philosopher who would write
special treatises on method. But he was not only fully aware
of the newness of the phenomenological approach while practicing it, he also reflected on it explicitly in retrospect.

Pfänder's phenomenology underwent a development as
Husserl's did. To understand it, one must realize that his phenomenology originated independently of Husserl's version, yet
that Pfänder, during the period of closest mutual approach and
even later, received considerable stimulation from Husserl,
although he never accepted it indiscriminately. Nor did he follow
the sharp curve into transcendental and especially into idealistic
phenomenology which Husserl was to take soon after their first
meeting. In the present context I shall simply distinguish between Pfänder's earlier conception of phenomenology as a part
of psychology, and the later one of phenomenology as the basic
philosophical method.

a. PHENOMENOLOGICAL PSYCHOLOGY – As early as 1900, one year before the appearance of the second volume of Husserl's *Logische Untersuchungen* with its first example of a phenomenology of knowledge, Pfänder had published his psychological analysis of the will under the title of a *Phänomenologie des Wollens*. The text of this Munich prize essay contained, to be sure, no definition of the term, which was not uncommon in the Lippsian circle,[1] nor does it occur elsewhere in the book. However, incidental characterizations of his method make it plain that Pfänder thought of phenomenology as "an elementary study designed to lay the foundations for a psychology of the will." Its approach will be "purely psychological," i.e., consist in exploring the experience of willing with its conscious components from the inside, as it were, without referring to its physical or physiological objective concomitants. Pfänder admits that this "subjective method," described more appropriately as retrospective rather than introspective, has its defects and dangers. But he considers it the only possible one. Phenomenology is not meant to take the place of explanatory psychology. But without the "complete and cautious recording of the conscious phenomena" such a psychology is apt to end up with distorting misinterpretations.

This conception is developed even more fully, though without reference to the term "phenomenology," in the *Einführung in die Psychologie* of 1904, which also precedes Pfänder's first personal contact with Husserl. Its main objective was to clear the way for a psychology worthy of the name by eliminating the misinterpretations and substitutions foisted on it by a false objectivism. While thus the subjective method is again stressed as the only one capable of leading us to psychological reality, objective methods are not completely rejected as far as the relationships between this reality and its physical counterpart are concerned. But before exploring the "why" we have to obtain full knowledge of the "what." Yet Pfänder does not object to the use of experimental methods in psychology. In fact, he thinks that they can be put to both subjective and objective, to descriptive and explanatory uses.

[1] Lipps himself does not seem to have used the term *"phänomenologisch"* before 1902 in his study *Vom Fühlen, Wollen und Denken*, p. 5.

His first conception of phenomenology as the subjective and descriptive study of psychological phenomena is still present in what is easily his most striking demonstration of phenomenological psychology, his contribution to the first and third volumes of the new phenomenological yearbook, the *Psychologie der Gesinnungen* (1913 and 1916). The only addition to the earlier descriptions is the emphasis upon the need of obtaining explicit insight into the essential structure of the phenomena, of their sub-species, their varieties and modifications, and their relations to psychological facts. Also, in full recognition of the evasiveness of these phenomena to the unaccustomed eye, Pfänder practices and recommends, as the best means to guide others to the necessary intuiting awareness, description by use of metaphorical language. But he stresses at the same time that mere intuiting, however active (*Erschauen*), is not enough, but must be followed up by analysis and synthesis, just as in any other scientific enterprise. Never for one moment does Pfänder suggest that phenomenology, in spite of its subjective approach, is not a strictly scientific enterprise, rigorous within the limits which the nature of the subject matter determines.

b. PHENOMENOLOGICAL PHILOSOPHY – Apparently it was only after the appearance of Husserl's *Ideen* that Pfänder began to think of phenomenology as a more comprehensive enterprise. For, contrary to Husserl's belief about Pfänder, he continued to weigh Husserl's later writings carefully. Thus he adopted such features as the phenomenological reduction, if only slowly and selectively; but he kept rejecting its idealistic use as based on insufficient evidence.[1] It is a matter for regret that the remaining dissents never led to an open and thorough discussion. Thus the two wings of the Phenomenological Movement drifted apart more than was warranted by their actual differences.

Pfänder's only published attempt to assimilate Husserl's universalized phenomenology can be found in the Introduction to his *Logik* of 1921:

To state briefly and yet intelligibly what phenomenology is and is striving for today is a request coming from many quarters, but at the moment it is

[1] See, especially his vigorous support of the penetrating study of *Der phänomenologische Idealismus Husserls* by Theodor Celms in *Deutsche Literaturzeitung* L (1929), pp. 2048–2050.

hardly possible to satisfy it here. All that can be done is to give some hints as to the subject and the task of phenomenology and to characterize the position of logic in relation to the science so characterized (p. 33).

The features stressed subsequently are:

α. viewing the objects under consideration from the perspective of the subject;

β. laying hold of the thoughts and beliefs of this subject while refraining from taking a stand on them; in so doing special attention is to be given not only to the objects thought or believed (the familiar "intentional objects"), but also to the acts of believing, to the modes of givenness, and to the modes of belief.

It is thus plain that Pfänder's version of phenomenology is anything but a mere ontological study of the *Sachen* in the sense of a simple "turn to the object," but that it tries to do particular justice to the subjective aspect of the phenomena. Besides, Pfänder states explicitly that phenomenology refrains from "posing the question of the reality of what is thus intuited, but pays attention only to the what and to the qualities," without however referring explicitly to Husserl's phenomenological reduction and its presumptive powers of opening up entirely new dimensions of phenomena. There is renewed emphasis on the need for cautious and almost reverent description of what is thus seen and, in addition, on the need of exploring the essential and necessary relationships (*Zusammengehörigkeiten*) among the phenomena. With reference to his own immediate enterprise, logic, Pfänder concludes: Epistemology, for an examination of our claims to knowledge, presupposes a thorough phenomenology; but logic, the study of the structure of our conceptual thoughts, does not depend for its own structure and validity on phenomenology, though it will benefit from a phenomenological clarification.

Thus Pfänder's first interpretation of phenomenology, clearly tentative though it was, assigned it a basic role in philosophy, but not yet a key position. This stage was reached only when Pfänder became fully aware of its potentialities for a new approach to the major philosophical problems of being, value, and ideal demand (*Forderung*), a development indicated among other things by the addition of the words "and Phenomenology" to the title of his central lecture course, "Introduction to Philosophy," the last two times he offered it. It is thus only these lectures which allow a full idea of Pfänder's final conception of phenomenology. To some extent this can be obtained from a study of his detailed and careful notes for these lectures and from the first drafts for a final book which he was planning. Here he states his approach to phenomenology in the following words:

In the course of the following presentation a certain conception of phenomenology will emerge as the self-evident basis of philosophy. This phenomenology, sometimes called the Munich phenomenology, is to be clarified here in such a way that the present account will be an introduction to phenomenology and at the same time its justification. (Manuscript, dated May 20, 1935, *Pfänderiana* 1, published in *Alexander Pfänders Phänomenologie* p. 52).

The development of this conception in the lectures took the form of a discussion of the major problems of philosophy in which, after a brief consideration of the main historical solutions by both rationalism and empiricism, the following three steps were taken in each case:

α. Clarification of meaning: This consists in determining what exactly we mean in using such terms as "thing," "cause,""force," "value," or "Deity." To this end, it is at least as important to determine in each case what we do *not* mean as to describe what we *do* mean. For it is at this stage that misinterpretations, under the influence of negativistic theories, have falsified our beliefs beyond recognition. A case in point is what Pfänder considers to be Hume's faulty phenomenology, particularly his disastrous misinterpretation of causation and of the self. There is however no intention on Pfänder's part to accept the verdict of these meanings as valid evidence of truth: common sense in its mere meanings is by no means necessarily right.

β. Suspension of belief: Next Pfänder demands a temporary withholding of belief in the reality of what we mean, using for this step Husserl's terms "bracketing" (*Einklammerung*) or *epoché*. This operation involves neither doubting nor denying. It is meant only as a provisional attitude, which simply leaves undecided whether or not the object of our beliefs is real and is given "in person" (*leibhaftig*). It also takes no stand on the truth of the objective sciences, or even on the existence of our own body and of our sense organs prior to a thorough and complete test of our right to believe in them. Quite apart from the terminological loan from Husserl, the agreement with his description of the phenomenological reduction is obvious. What is less obvious is that Pfänder's version does not go beyond a mere temporary suspension of belief, and that it does not involve a cancellation of all our intentional objectifications which takes the intentional objects back into the subjective absolute consciousness, a step which leads Husserl to his idealistic doctrine of the transcendental constitution. To Pfänder *epoché* is nothing but a safety measure against advance commitments, whether realistic or idealistic, not an opening wedge into a strange new world.

γ. Phenomenological verification: The final and decisive stage, for which Pfänder often reserves the term "phenomenology" proper, is the verification of our purged meanings in the light of actual perception. Perception is described, in terms again borrowed from Husserl, as the act in which the percept is "given in person" (*selbst leibhaftig gegeben*). But in Pfänder's case this phrase means what it says and thus assumes a thoroughly realistic connotation: genuine perception delivers to us the object of perception as it is in and of itself, in contrast to other cognitive acts, including certain pseudo-perceptions. In other words, perception properly purged has the unique power of breaking through the walls of our epistemological isolation and leading from the realm of subjectivity to the objects themselves. All the more must phenomenology pay special attention to such modifications of perception as the difference between inquiring perception (*forschende Wahrnehmung*) and its less critical and thorough forms. For it is only to the verdict of inquiring perception that Pfänder attaches epistemological significance. To such a perception the reality of the "given in person" reveals itself in a characteristic resistance. The view that resistance against our acts of will constitutes a criterion for reality is an idea which had been advocated before by such philosophers as Maine de Biran, Bouterwek, Dilthey, and, among phenomenologists, by Scheler. Pfänder, however, points out that, apart from other shortcomings of their versions, acts of will cannot supply a suitable testing device for all cases of reality. What is required instead is specific acts of probing as contained in inquiring perception. These give the object perceived a thorough shaking, as it were, and pass it as real only when it holds its own against such a crucial test. Properly handled, this test will protect perception from the pitfalls of illusions, hallucinations, and other discrediting evidence, which, according to Pfänder, endanger only an uncritical perception.

This phenomenology of perception is clearly in conflict with many of the traditional and contemporary theories of perception. Specifically it challenges the empiricist theory of perception of the Lockean variety and its intellectualistic counterpart as exemplified by Kant's view. Both can result only in declaring genuine knowledge of a real world impossible, since they have to convert the real either into a product of our imaginary belief or into a construct of our thought. Phenomenologically their basic defects are such unproven assumptions as these:

α. Merely sense data are given.

β. All sense data hold the same rank in relation to the supposedly real objects.

γ. Each perception is epistemologically equivalent to every other.

δ. Each perception contains thinking, which adds something that actually cannot be known on principle, namely an object that can never be given directly.

ε. Each perception includes an inference.

All these assumptions are erroneous in the light of a genuine and unbiased phenomenology of perception, and partly even absurd. Such a phenomenology does not deny the existence of sense data. But it does deny that they have the character assigned them by the empiricist theory. What they really represent are directly perceived objects, colors, sounds, etc. In fact, Pfänder objected from the very start even to Husserl's theory of the hyletic data as parts or "contents" of the intentional act. There is however indirect perception. For it is true that certain directly perceived objects ("sense data") are transparent, as it were, toward indirectly perceived objects, such as fabrics, things, forces, or other minds. But even indirect perception is perception, not foolproof to be sure, but safe enough for critical use. Models of different types of such indirect givenness can further illuminate the nature of this type of perception.

Another aspect of perception to which its phenomenology must pay attention is the various modes of givenness of the objects perceived, such as their partial or total presentation and their degrees of clarity. Here Pfänder is in substantial agreement with Husserl. In the same manner other modifications of the perceptual acts (whether searching or superficial, fleeting or steady, accompanied or not by various degrees of belief) are to be explored.

4. Examples of Pfänder's Phenomenology

A selection of concrete demonstrations of phenomenologizing is particularly difficult in Pfänder's case, not because of the scarcity but because of the abundance of such possible illustrations. For actually all of Pfänder's philosophy, from his psychology to his philosophy of religion, is permeated by his phenomenological approach. I shall concentrate on areas where this method has broken new ground and yielded particularly instructive results. In this context the following areas should at least be mentioned:

α. the phenomenology of striving and willing, with its distinctive characterization of the acts of will within the general field of striving (*Phänomenologie des Wollens*);

β. the phenomenology of attention with its studies on the attention profile (*Relief*) in the object of attention (*Einführung in die Psychologie*).

γ. the phenomenology of motivation, with its important distinction between urges (*Triebfeder*) and motives ("Motive und Motivation" in *Münchner Philosophische Abhandlungen*);

δ. the phenomenology of directed sentiments (*Psychologie der Gesinnungen*);

ε. the descriptive studies in characterology (*Grundprobleme der Charakterologie*);

ξ. the unpublished phenomenological materials included in Pfänder's preparations for his last philosophical works, particularly his phenomenology of perception. Most original and significant among these would seem to be his studies on the phenomenology of values and ideal demands (*Forderungen*) and those on the phenomenology of belief and faith (*Glauben*).

However, since in the present framework any attempt at

completeness would be out of place, a relatively more intensive report on selected items seems most appropriate. For this purpose I shall select three characteristic examples from different periods in Pfänder's phenomenological work.

a. THE PHENOMENOLOGY OF DIRECTED SENTIMENTS ('GESINNUNGEN') – It is not quite easy to render in English the connotations of the German word *"Gesinnung"* as used in Pfänder's study. Its denotation comprises such phenomena as love, benevolence, friendliness, and affection, on the one hand, hatred, ill-will, and hostility, on the other. Probably the best equivalent of *Gesinnung* would be "sentiment" with the qualification, however, that *Gesinnungen* in Pfänder's sense are not mere feelings, but feelings directed toward something; hence the phrase "directed sentiments" may be a more suggestive translation.

Although the phenomena thus designated are of basic importance for our daily living, for ethics, and for pedagogics, Pfänder finds them completely neglected or misrepresented by previous descriptive psychology. Consequently his first step is to show that sentiments cannot be reduced to acts such as attention, striving, or willing, nor to feelings of pleasure or displeasure, as a crude psychology of love and hatred would have it. Then, making a fresh start, he finds as common and essential features of these sentiments their function as connectors between subject and object, their centrifugal direction toward the object, and a peculiar psychic "temperature" in their flow. Taking the positive and the negative sentiments separately, the positive ones (love, etc.) are characterized by their warmth and life-giving quality, by the inner union with their objects (*"Einung"* or *"Einigung"* – a German neologism expressing less than identification in the customary sense), and by the affirmation of the object's right to exist (*Daseinsermächtigung*), whereas the negative ones (hatred, etc.) display a corroding virulence against their objects, an inner segregation from them, and, finally, a denial of their right to exist. Obviously all these labels are only metaphorical, but Pfänder finds them both suggestive and indeed indispensable.

Of even wider significance are the modifications of these

sentiments, since they turn out to apply equally to other kinds of psychical acts. There is, first, the dimension of genuineness (*Echtheit*) and spuriousness (*Unechtheit*). Spurious sentiments, which need not be morally objectionable, are those which we adopt, for instance, in play, without merely imagining them. Then there is the dimension of "reality," as distinguished from "being suspended" (*schwebend*), to be found in sentiments which are not fully anchored in the daily reality of the individual's life. Within this group of the unanchored sentiments, we meet the "superreal" (*überwirklich*) or exalted sentiments, illustrated by those of the orator who is being carried away by his own words into sentiments which are genuine, and yet curiously above and detached from his normal emotional level. Likewise there are episodic (*nebenwirklich*) feelings, showing up on the sidelines, as it were, of our central busy life, which may again be genuine, but for which we have "no time." Finally, there is the whole group of provisional sentiments, which are kept below the level of full reality by a temporary style of life, and admitted only "on approval." I shall add Pfänder's characterization of this provisional modification of the inner life as an example of such phenomenological descriptions:

When a person feels extremely insecure, weak, and valueless in his innermost being, when he is filled with diffidence, when he becomes thoroughly aware of the frustration of his demands on life. ... he lives on the whole only provisionally. He goes to sleep and gets up, always only provisionally; for: "This is still not the proper and real thing." He washes, combs his hair, and dresses, but only provisionally. He eats and drinks and does his day's work, but only provisionally. When he learns something or acquires a skill, he does so only provisionally. And only provisionally does he read books and newspapers, look at works of art, and listen to music. He enters into union with his clothes, his rooms, his furniture only quite provisionally. ...[1]

Other modifications of directed sentiments and also of other emotions occur when they are being held down deliberately or when we are in the esthetic attitude. A complete account of this unusually rich study is impossible. It is sufficient if these brief indications have given an idea of the widening of the psychological horizon which Pfänder's earlier phenomenology permits. Its ulterior value becomes apparent particularly in the later sections

[1] *JPPF*, III, 39 f.

of his study, where he takes up the question of the relations between the subject and these various types of sentiments with a
view to determining how far they are under his control.

b. THE PHENOMENOLOGY OF BASIC AND EMPIRICAL
ESSENCES – In his later work Pfänder introduced a phenomenological distinction among essences whose significance reached
far beyond the area of his immediate investigation, i.e., characterology and interpretative psychology; for it also entered his
metaphysics, ethics, and philosophy of religion. This is the
distinction between *Grundwesen* (basic essence) and *empirisches
Wesen* (empirical essence). While this doctrine may remind one
of such distinctions as Kant's and Schopenhauer's between
intelligible and empirical character, it differs from theirs by the
fact that the *Grundwesen* is nothing unknowable or knowable
only to a special metaphysical approach; for it is fully accessible
to proper phenomenological intuition.

Actually such an intuition is already at work in a field like
geometry. Here, starting for example from empirical circles with
all their inevitable irregularities, we can perceive over and above
the empirical essences the ideal or basic essence of the perfect
circle as the essence which they embody. We reach this basic
essence of the circle by a peculiar process of theoretical idealization, which consists in the recognition and elimination of the
imperfect parts and their constructive replacement in imagination, leading up to the intuitive grasp of the perfect circle as
the one toward which the empirical circles converge, as it were.
The similarity to the *good gestalt* of Gestalt psychology is obvious,
although eventually more is involved in Pfänder's conception.

Much more pertinent to Pfänder's conception is the intuition
of basic essences among living beings, which can be studied in
systematic biology, for instance, but indirectly also in pathology.
In this context Pfänder develops a whole theory of biological
knowledge. Most if not all empirical samples of a biological
species are somehow imperfect, abnormal, or distorted. Nevertheless, we are always in a position to construct the normal type
in theoretical idealization, and to recognize abnormalities as
abnormalities. Now according to Pfänder the same kind of
knowledge is possible in the psychological field: we can know

what a certain individual or a certain type of man is "at bottom," what his fully developed character, as distinguished from his undeveloped, misshapen, or distorted empirical deformation, would be like. In this manner we may see, for instance, that he is at bottom a friendly, courageous, independent being under-neath all the hostility, timidity, and dependence which he displays at the moment. Such recognition does not presuppose value judgments. On the contrary, Pfänder believes that ethical values can be understood only in terms of what is appropriate (*angemessen*) to the basic essence of its bearer in general and to his individual basic character in particular.

It is important to see that this conception of the basic charac-ter, as well as that of the empirical character of man, differs fundamentally from the idea of a ready-made character which inescapably determines man's development and behavior. Ever since his early phenomenological studies on the will Pfänder had upheld the role of the freely active ego-center (*freitätiges Ichzentrum*), which performs acts of self-determination and thus determines indirectly a large part of the life and character of the psyche. In fact, motives, as distinguished from urges, derive their motivating force from the fact that this ego "leans upon" them, chooses them, as it were. On the other hand, it is not in the power of the ego to create the basic character, much as he can shape and distort the empirical character. Thus Pfänder's doctrine of the basic essence allows him to adopt an intermediate position between the characterological determinism of older days and the character-denying dogmatism of the extreme ex-istentialists, for whom character exists only as the result of free acts.

c. THE PHENOMENOLOGY OF THE PERCEPTION OF OUGHTNESS – Pfänder's ethics[1] is based on a sharp division between the theory of ethical value and the theory of ethical demands, in a way strikingly parallel to the distinction between goodness and rightness (oughtness) among recent British moral philosophers. For each one he developed a special phenomenology with a phenomenology of ethical perception as its ultimate foun-dation. While his phenomenology of value might be of even more

---

[1] An edition of Pfänder's nearly completed *Ethik* is being prepared by Josef Duss.

immediate interest, Pfänder's last manuscript on ethics contains actually a fuller development of his phenomenology of ethical demands, since he usually did not find enough time to treat it in his lectures. From this phenomenology of the perception of ethical demands I shall present here at least a representative key passage.

Pfänder had just prepared the ground for such a phenomenology by his standard procedure of giving first a clarification of our beliefs (*Meinungen*), eliminating on the way misinterpretations of these beliefs, and of following it up by the suspension of the belief in their validity. Now he is ready for the crucial test of perception, which must supply evidence that the object of our initial and now clarified beliefs actually exists:

The answer cannot be obtained by acting after the fashion of so many laymen who hold their breath, exert pressure on their brain, and then simply talk or put down what occurs to them, but only by cautious phenomenological and critical investigation. Now an ethically obligatory demand such as 'You ought not to slander others' can be the object of mere believing, or of detailed reflection, or of imagination. ... But is there also a consciousness of obligatory moral demands in which these demands and their obligatoriness are given 'in person' and perceived? Perception means here the finding of the demands themselves. Now there certainly is such a finding of ethical demands. But it cannot be reached by looking for them in the void, as it were, in the expectation that they will confront us from there spontaneously. *Pfänderiana* 100 f, p. 32.

Indispensable conditions of such "finding" turn out to be

1. the detailed representation of the conduct under consideration and of the things affected by it;
2. the realization of the suitability or unsuitability of the conduct in question to the universal or the individual "idea of the person" (basic essence);
3. the realization of the ethical value of the imagined free performance of such conduct.

Then, after considering in detail and rejecting other possible interpretations of this act of "finding," Pfänder concludes that

what is needed for this purpose is a peculiar type of perception. named "nomological," which differs from other types of perception, theoretical as well as valuational. Nevertheless, the finding of ethical demands, like any other finding perception, can undergo modifications. It can be superficial or searching. There is such a thing as shutting one's mental eyes or repressing (*verdrängen*). Perception can be unbiased or biased by such factors as urges or prevailing opinions, which divert us from ethical demands, or by deliberate efforts to expel and destroy all oughtness. *Pfänderiana* 100 f, p. 34.

5. Concluding Remarks

Pfänder's philosophy has remained a torso. This is also true of his intended presentation and demonstration of the phenomenological method, as he had finally developed it. There is at least some hope that posthumous publications will convey the outlines of his systematic thought and of its methodological foundations. Thus far, however, his philosophical work, and in particular his whole conception of man, as expressed in his most mature work, *Die Seele des Menschen*, with its phenomenologically enriched and ontologically revitalized Aristotelian insights, has made little impact on the contemporary world. One reason may have been the climate at the time of publication (1933), for which Pfänder had no sympathy, another the plain straightforwardness of the book so characteristic of his unassuming integrity. Then, too, there is in Pfänder's writing a conspicuous absence of reference to and discussion of contemporary thinking and writing, which was apt to leave the more scientific workers in the field uninterested or dismayed.

There may be even more serious shortcomings in some of Pfänder's work. Some of the intuitions claimed by Pfänder strain the willingness and sympathy of his listeners and readers. Also, in spite of their suggestive power, Pfänder's metaphors may have been at times too bold to elicit sympathetic effort. Indeed they may even have antagonized the reader to whom no additional helps are given, as for instance in the case of Pfänder's metaphors for characterological differences. Finally, with regard to the solution of the epistemological problem by the phenomenology of probing perception, there still remains a lingering doubt as to whether it has completely broken the magic circle to which the subjectivistic phenomenological approach seems to condemn us. Probing perception, carefully applied, may greatly reduce the danger of illusion and error. But as long as these two do not become impossible in principle, phenomenological realism will find it hard to persuade more sceptical minds that the object perceived is really given "in person" (*leibhaftig*), and that we are not fooled by a phantom.

However, such unresolved doubts need not discredit the genuine insights in Pfänder's philosophizing. In particular, they do not affect the originality and thoroughness of his concrete phenomenological studies. His gifts for fresh intuiting and describing were unrivaled, and his results contain perhaps some of the most striking demonstrations of the phenomenological method in its original form. To this score his cautious assimilation of some of the features of Husserl's later phenomenology should now be added. As a former student of Pfänder, I cannot suppress the wishful thought that, once the excitement about the more spectacular protagonists of phenomenology has died down, a figure like Pfänder will re-emerge as one of the more solid representatives of phenomenology at its best.

SELECTIVE BIBLIOGRAPHY

Major Works

[1]   *Phänomenologie des Wollens* (1900)
      Einführung in die Psychologie (1904)
      "Motive and Motivation" in *Münchener Philosophische Abhandlungen*
          (1911)
      "Zur Psychologie der Gesinnungen" in *JPPF* I (1913) and III (1916)
      Logik (1921) *JPPF* IV (1921)
          Translation: Spanish (1928, 1940) by J. Perez Bances
      "Grundprobleme der Charakterologie" in Utitz, E., ed., *Jahrbuch für*
          Charakterologie I (1924), 289–335
      Die Seele des Menschen (1933)
      Philosophie der Lebensziele (posthumous edition of lecture notes) (1948);
          see *PPR* X (1950), 438–42

      Pfänders philosophical papers are now deposited in the manuscript
          collection of the *Bayerische Staatsbibliothek* in Munich under the title
          "Pfänderiana."

      Articles on Pfänder's Philosophy

      GEIGER, MORITZ, "Alexander Pfänders Methodische Stellung" in *Neue*
          Münchener Philosophische Abhandlungen. E. Heller und F. Löw, eds.,
          Leipzig 1933, p. 1–16
      BÜTTNER, HANS, "Die phänomenologische Psychologie Alexander Pfän-
          ders" in *Archiv für die gesamte Psychologie* 94 (1935), 317–346
      TRILLHAAS, WOLFGANG, *Alexander Pfänder In Memoriam* (Erlangen,
          1942) with nearly complete bibliography
          In English: SPIEGELBERG, HERBERT, *Obituary Note* in *PPR* II (1941),
[2]   263–5

6. *Pfänder's Following*

During the thirty-five years of his teaching at the University of Munich Pfänder reached a considerable number of students.

But although he was a provocative and rigorous teacher both in his courses and in his seminars, he made no effort to establish anything like a school or to impose his thought patterns on others. Nevertheless, especially after the First World War, his students began to form a closer group within the Munich Circle, which had lost its coherence when the *Akademisch-Psychologischer Verein* came to its end. Most of the older and more attached members of this group contributed to a *Festschrift* for Pfänder's sixtieth birthday. On the whole Pfänder's students have been more concerned with problems of logic and ontology, to some extent also with theory of value, ethics, social philosophy, and descriptive psychology, than with developing his conception of phenomenology. As far as careful workmanship is concerned, the names of FRIEDRICH LÖW, ERNST HELLER, and PHILIPP SCHWARZ deserve special mention, although they published but very little. Pfänder's responsibility for the work of his more prolific students is definitely limited. Among these the best known are probably Maximilian Beck and Gerda Walther.

MAXIMILIAN BECK (1886–1950), who after escaping from his native Czechoslovakia in 1938 spent his last decade teaching and writing in the United States, made a considerable impact as the editor and chief contributor of an original and vigorous philosophical magazine, *Philosophische Hefte* (1929–1936), which combined perceptive and courageous criticism with original thought. He also published two volumes of an ambitious metaphysical theory of value and a philosophical psychology, which show keen insights along with highly paradoxical theses. Without devoting much space to explicit discussions of phenomenology Beck took spirited issue with both Husserl's idealistic and Heidegger's existentialist versions of it. In his psychology he insisted, in opposition to Husserl, on the essential difference between consciousness and intentionality (as not necessarily conscious).

Major Writings

Wesen und Wert. Grundlegung einer Philosophie des Daseins (1925)
Psychologie. Wesen und Wirklichkeit der Seele (1938)
"The Proper Object of Psychology," *PPR* XIII (1953), 285–304

GERDA WALTHER (1897–   ) is no less a student of Husserl

than of Pfänder. Her contribution to the phenomenological
yearbook on the ontology and phenomenology of social com-
munities, building on ideas of Pfänder, is an unusually fruitful
and suggestive essay, especially by virtue of its careful analysis
of the acts of mutual inner union (*Wechseleinigung*) in Pfänder's
sense as the essential basis for the feeling of belonging together
(*Zusammengehörigkeitsgefühl*), a feeling which, much earlier,
had been made the foundation of social entities by American
sociologists such as F. H. Giddings.

Independently she has also ventured into such fields as the
phenomenology of mysticism in a book which, to be sure, deals
less with the various stages of mystic experience than with the
direct experience of God as a personal being. Much of this is based
on admittedly private experiences. In this connection she has
also taken an active interest in parapsychology, a field from
which Pfänder always stayed deliberately aloof. However, she
has also advocated the introduction of phenomenological
methods into this sprawling territory.

Major Writings

"Zur Ontologie der sozialen Gemeinschaften," *JPPF* VI (1923), 1–158
Phänomenologie der Mystik (1923; second revised edition 1955)
"A Plea for the Introduction of Edmund Husserl's Phenomenological
Method into Parapsychology." *Proceedings of the International Confer-
ence of Parapsychology*, Utrecht (July-August, 1953)

[1]

[HERBERT SPIEGELBERG (1904–   ). I feel that at this place a
brief personal statement about my own relation to Pfänder is in
order, the more so since Pfänder should be absolved of some of
the "deviations" of which I have made myself guilty in my own
writing. I owe to Pfänder chiefly a point of philosophical departure and whatever discipline his liberal but critical training
has imparted to me. However, in my choice of problems I have
only very rarely followed up lines suggested by Pfänder's own
philosophizing. In my epistemological conclusions I have even
seen myself forced to move considerably beyond Pfänder's
phenomenological realism in the direction of a more critical
version of his position. At this time it would be presumptuous on
my part to assert that there is a clear connnection between my
scattered publications, first in German, now mostly in English,
which have ranged from formal ontology to philosophy of law. But

it is perhaps permissible to add that I have not yet abandoned the unifying goal of a practical philosophy on phenomenological foundations which would combine the better insights of a phenomenology of values with a deepened conception of human existence].

Writings with phenomenological import

"Über das Wesen der Idee," *JPPF* XI (1930), 1–238
"Sinn und Recht der Begründung in der axiologischen und praktischen Philosophie," *Neue Münchener Philosophische Abhandlungen*. Pfänder Festschrift (1933), pp. 100–142
Antirelativismus. Kritik des Relativismus und Skeptizismus der Werte und des Sollens. (1935)
Gesetz und Sittengesetz. Vorstudien zu einer gesetzesfreien Ethik (1935)
"The 'Reality-Phenomenon' and Reality," *Philosophical Essays in Memory of Edmund Husserl* (1939), pp. 84–105
"Critical Phenomenological Realism," *PPR* I (1940), 154–76
"Phenomenology of Direct Evidence," *PPR* II (1942), 427–456
"Indubitables in Ethics: A Cartesian Meditation," *Ethics* LVIII (1947), 35–50
"Toward a Phenomenology of Imaginative Understanding of Others," *Proceedings of the XIth International Congress of Philosophy* (1953) VII, 235–9
"How Subjective is Phenomenology?" *Proceedings of the American Catholic Philosophical Association*, vol. XXXIII (1959), 28–36

C. ADOLF REINACH (1883–1917): THE PHENOMENOLOGY OF ESSENCES

1. Reinach's Place in the Phenomenological Movement

Independently of each other, the Göttingen students of phenomenology like Schapp, Dietrich von Hildebrand, Koyré, and Edith Stein, in their accounts of this period refer to Reinach, not to Husserl, as their real teacher in phenomenology. Hedwig Conrad-Martius even goes so far as to call him the phenomenologist *par excellence* (*der Phänomenologe an sich und als solcher*). But even beyond his remarkable appeal as a teacher, Reinach was developing a version of early phenomenology simpler and clearer in form and more concrete and suggestive in content than that of the "master."

Husserl himself saw in the clear-headed, warm-hearted, and widely read *Privatdozent* – the only one of his students who had joined him as a teacher at the University of Göttingen – a philosopher who had thoroughly understood and assimilated the phenomenological method in the sense of the *Logische Unter-suchungen*. In fact, in his obituary he even credited him with having aided his own progress toward pure phenomenology. The fact that Reinach himself, though in much closer personal contact with Husserl than all the other early phenomenologists, did not follow him on his way toward transcendental phenomenology as it began to take shape in those days, does not seem to have interfered with Husserl's esteem, much as it seems to have disturbed Reinach himself when he became aware of it. What Reinach appreciated in Husserl was chiefly the "cautious and thorough mode of working," not his results.

Reinach's importance for the development of early phenomenology thus exceeds all proportion to the brief span of 34 years granted him for the development of his ideas and his influence. It was his death in action in 1917, rather than Husserl's going to Freiburg, which cut short not only his own promise but that of the Göttingen phenomenological Circle.

It is therefore not surprising that Reinach never found the time to formulate a comprehensive plan of a philosophy in which the place of phenomenology could be clearly defined. One can only extrapolate from his essays and fragments – for he never published a book – a conception which would have incorporated a formal and material ontology on realistic lines. His last fragments and letters from the war indicate that it might have culminated in a philosophy of religion, defending the rights of religious experience without aspiring to supply it. It would have included a phenomenological theory of objective value and oughtness and particularly a social philosophy and philosophy of law on phenomenological foundations; for the latter Reinach, a fully trained law scholar, seemed uniquely qualified and had already laid the groundwork.

Yet the shortness of his life was not the only reason for the torso of Reinach's philosophy. Like all the other early phenomenologists he firmly believed in philosophy as a cooperative scientific enterprise to which each researcher would have to contribute patiently and unhurriedly, much in the same way as was the case in the sciences. There could be no such thing as a one-man system. What was to be the place of phenomenology, then, in such a framework?

2. Reinach's Conception of Phenomenology

Reinach had come to Husserl equipped with Lipps's psychological technique for painstaking yet flexible descriptions of subjective phenomena. Husserl's *Logische Untersuchungen* had meant for him primarily the discovery of the *terra firma* of pure logic, of the *Sachen* in the sense of the objective entities in general and of the realm of essences in particular, both of which he had missed in Lipps's initial psychologism. It was this aspect of Husserl's philosophizing which he kept developing vigorously and effectively, while Husserl himself was already veering more and more sharply toward his new subjectivism.

Reinach did not publish any detailed programmatic statement or exposition of his own interpretation of phenomenology. There survives, however, a brilliant lecture of his, "Über Phänomenologie," which he had delivered in Marburg, the citadel of Neo-Kantianism, in 1914. Before that he also gave a brief characterization of the phenomenological method in a study on the legal concept of premeditation (1912), which contains the following sentences:

Phenomenological analysis means that we are not permitted to inject the customary concepts of representation, thinking, feeling, and will in order to "build up" premeditation out of them, a process which inevitably would involve the loss of what is most essential to it. Rather do we have to make an effort to transport ourselves into the phenomenon in order to be able to render faithfully what we can vividly intuit there. (G.S. 122)

Thus the first-hand intuiting of the essential core of the phenomena formed the main feature and function of Reinach's phenomenological approach. In its emphasis on the need of transposing ourselves into the intuited object his account contains a definitely Bergsonian touch.

Compared with this statement, the Marburg lecture is not only more comprehensive but also more "intellectual." Yet even here Reinach refuses to give a connotative definition of phenomenology, but offers instead the equivalent of an ostensive definition by way of actual demonstrations of the phenomenological approach. He also makes it plain from the very start that to him phenomenology is not a new system of philosophy but a method of philosophizing required by the nature of the problems and opened up by a peculiar attitude (*Einstellung*). His examples of the new method, which range all the way from mathematics to psychological science, reveal the following major features:

α. The phenomenological method is to teach us how to see things which we have a tendency to overlook in our everyday practical attitude, and to see them in their unique whatness or essence without the customary attempts to reduce them to the smallest possible number, an attempt which can lead only to impoverishment and falsification of the phenomena. The prime objective of phenomenology is thus to lead us toward the phenomena and to clarify our conceptions of them.

β. Phenomenology does not restrict itself to taking inventories of the factual phenomena. It also wants to explore their essences while disregarding their existence. This actually involves two things – which to be sure are not yet sharply distinguished by Reinach: (a) disinterest in reality, understood as independence of the subjective observer, in contrast to the approach of a natural science like physics; in Reinach's version this change in attitude does not require the adoption of a special method after the manner of Husserl's phenomenological reduction; (b) interest in pure cases, which, as in geometry, considers ideal types, even when no example can be produced in actual experience. This would involve something like a theoretical idealization, though not Husserl's ideating abstraction or "eidetic reduction," which again is not mentioned in this context.

γ. Besides the intuiting of the phenomena and their essences, Reinach stresses one additional step: the study of the essential connections among these phenomena (*Wesenszusammenhänge*) and their laws (*Wesensgesetze*). These relations among the phenomena are determined by their very nature and are expressed in such phrases as "it lies in the nature of movement to have a substratum," "it follows from its very nature." According to Reinach, such essential connections occur not only among the formal structures of logic and general ontology but also in the structures of concrete "material" phenomena, for instance among colors in their similarities and relative positions. They are of two basic types: essential necessities and essential possibilities. To be sure, these are usually so obvious that no one pays attention to them. But it is precisely these neglected "trivialities" to which phenomenology has to give their due.

In this connection Reinach develops his theory of the *phenome-nological a priori*, which is perhaps the most characteristic feature in his philosophizing. It differs decisively from earlier conceptions of the a priori. To begin with, Reinach's a priori is not a property of propositions or acts of judging or knowing, but of states of affairs (*Sachverhalte*) judged or recognized. It is these ontological states of affairs or, more properly speaking, the connections be-tween the elements of these states of affairs (the object judged about and its property judged), which by virtue of these con-nections are the carriers of the a priori property.[1] The a priori is thus primarily an ontological, not an epistemological category.

But what does it mean that a state of affairs is a priori? Ob-viously not that we have an innate idea about it. In fact, Reinach agrees with the Kantian conception of the a priori to the extent of interpreting it as knowledge not grounded in experience, but not as knowledge without experience. He also agrees with Kant that necessity and universality are important aspects of the a priori: A priori states of affairs are universal for all possible examples, and they are necessary in the sense that the a priori property contained in the *Sachverhalt* belongs to its carrier by an essential necessity. However, any implication that this necessity is really only a necessity of thought to be derived from the organization of our understanding must be kept out. This, to Reinach, would mean sheer psychologism. His necessity is an ontological necessity grounded in things, not an epistemological one based on our understanding. Universality and necessity are for Reinach only secondary characteristics of the a priori; they follow from the more basic fact that there are essential con-nections (*Wesenszusammenhänge*) which are immediately intu-itable and which can be given with complete adequacy. Thus "a priori" means at bottom nothing but the fact that a certain property is necessarily entailed by the essential structure of an object and can hence be understood as such.[2]

Reinach also takes over and assimilates the Kantian termino-

---

[1] *Gesammelte Schriften*, pp. 6, 171, 397.

[2] One may well wonder whether under such circumstances the label "a priori" is still appropriate, since it was so definitely meant to be epistemological, applying to knowledge, and not ontological, applying to things known. To call this relationship a priori makes sense only inasmuch as it can always be known independently of inductive experience, by essential insight alone.

logy of *analytic* and *synthetic*. To be sure, he defends Hume against Kant, who, in his estimate, had misinterpreted Hume when he contrasted the latter's treatment of causal knowledge as synthetic with that of mathematical knowledge as analytic, a way of thinking entirely alien to Hume, who did not think in terms of concepts and propositions but of impressions and ideas,[1] i.e., actually of the things and relations meant. This is also what Reinach is concerned with, though not in the manner of Hume's sensationalistic conception of things as bundles of impressions. Applied to these new carriers of the a priori, the states of affairs, the term "analytic" thus refers to any property which forms an essential part of the thing, not a predicate which is included in the definition of the concept. Thus the property of having three internal angles is analytically contained in the essence triangle, yet not in its concept (defined as a plane figure bounded by three lines).[2] "Synthetic" in this sense is any property of a state of affairs which is based on the essential connections between several essences in their relations to each other, for instance, properties like similarity of one triangle to another.[3]

How far does this new interpretation of the situation affect the traditional problem of a priori knowledge? This is not the place for a definite answer to a question into which so much thinking and writing has gone, not only from rationalistic but also from empiricist and positivistic quarters. It is sufficient to refer to the case of Bertrand Russell, who, in spite of his empiricist leanings, found it impossible to defend our scientific knowledge, with its amazing inductions and hypothetical superstructures, without the support of synthetic a priori principles. But all he can suggest as their foundation is that they are needed as postulates in order to justify our procedures, not that they are

[1] *Gesammelte Schriften* p. 1 ff.

[2] For the distinction between ontologically and logically analytic and synthetic knowledge, see also Pfänder, *Logik*, pp. 202 ff.

[3] Here too one might question whether the continued use of this time-honored and time-worn terminology is advisable in a merely ontological context. For there is certainly nothing "thetic" in the relations between entities but only in our way of representing them. The important thing is to bear in mind that here the terms "analytic" and "synthetic" point to peculiar relationships among the objects of our thought, not merely among our concepts. The real question is: Do the relations which we discover among such objects contain mere accidental "side-by-sideness," which allows for nothing but matter-of-fact statements? Or do we also find among them the essential relationships which permit the type of insight designated by the term "synthetic a priori"?

based on insight. Thus there is seemingly no good reason for the adoption of these rather than other postulates. Reinach's approach suggests at least an alternative to the stalemate between an empiricism unable to justify its principle of induction and a rationalism based on dogmatic a priori principles: to go beyond the level of concepts and propositions to the phenomena they mean, to explore the states of affairs pointed at in their intuitively given structures. In some cases no structural relationship between these will be discovered; in others, insight-giving essential relationships will appear, as they do in some, if not in all, of the a priori sciences. As far as this is the case, we are in a position to buttress our precarious a priori synthetic postulates by insights that far transcend the range of an experience stripped of all features which can support "a priori knowledge."

Beyond this exploration of the essences and the essential connections among these essences Reinach did not contemplate any further assignments for the phenomenological method. Specifically, there is no indication of a need for Husserl's reductions and no claim to preferential status for the subjective phenomena of consciousness. Nor did Reinach show interest in a study of the ways in which these essences appear in consciousness. Thus for Reinach phenomenology coincided to all intents and purposes with an ontology of essences, studied in their fullest and most concrete variety.

Moreover, Reinach's phenomenology of essences is thoroughly realistic. While no explicit discussion of the issue occurs in Reinach's writings, his discussion of such entities as the mathematical or the legal ones leaves no doubt that he not only accepts the apparent epistemological independence of physical and psychical phenomena at their face value, but that he even shares enough of Platonic realism to attribute to essences and values a status independent of the knowing subject.

3. Illustrations of Reinach's Phenomenology

Reinach's pre-philosophical training had been in the field of law, although he was also at home in mathematics and in the natural sciences. It was therefore only natural that he tried to demonstrate the powers of the new phenomenological method chiefly in the field of social and legal phenomena. Among his publications an essay on premeditation in its ethical and legal significance includes a particularly illuminating piece of phenomenological psychology. But his most important and largest production was his contribution to the first volume of the new phenomenological yearbook, in which he tried to show how even behind mere positive law in its seeming arbitrariness there are "a priori" essences, essences which can throw light on the structure of positive law itself. In spite of Reinach's emphatic disclaimers, his treatise on the a priori foundations of civil law has often been interpreted as an attempt to revive the old conception of natural law. But quite apart from the question whether this would be a fatal flaw, Reinach did not mean to present his a priori law as an ideal model. It is therefore not surprising that this conception appeared to the traditional law scholars as neither fish nor fowl. It may well be that Reinach did not make it sufficiently clear to what extent his synthetic a priori in law differed from its parallels in such fields as mathematics and science. I shall therefore select from the rich content of this study only two doctrines which are comparatively independent of the complete argument and yet are samples of the fruitfulness of Reinach's approach.

a. REINACH'S THEORY OF SOCIAL ACTS − One of the most important phenomena in the understanding of the structures of civil law is the legal promise. But this legal promise has already a pre-legal essence. It has therefore to be studied in the framework of social acts in general among which it belongs. Here again the phenomenologist finds himself faced with the lack of adequate studies of phenomena which thus far have been simply taken for granted. Yet that which is "self-explanatory" in this sense is often merely something "which one has passed a thousand times and is just passing for the thousand and first time." In trying to determine the proper place for the promise, Reinach points out first that among the acts which may be called spontaneous some are characterized by an inner activity that takes place entirely within the agent, like the taking of a decision or giving preference to something, and others by being essentially directed toward other persons, like envying, forgiving, or giving commands. In this second group of "other-regarding" acts (*fremdpersonale Akte*) Reinach then subdivides further between those acts which need not be expressed or received by others, like forgiveness, and those which make sense only as expressed and received by others, such as commands, requests, admonitions, questions, answers, and communications. This second sub-group, which has essentially an addressee, Reinach characterizes as "in need of being received and understood" (*vernehmungsbedürftig*). Consequently they require a "body," an outer side in the form of a physical expression through words or gestures. It is this group which Reinach has in mind when he speaks of social acts in the proper sense. Further analysis yields such distinctions as those between (1) conditional and unconditional social acts, (2) acts with more than one agent or with more than one addressee, and (3) acts carried out in one's own name and those carried out in place of someone else, a distinction which is of special importance in the field of law. All these acts and their modifications have obviously much wider applications than to the field of legal phenomena, but little has been done thus far to utilize them for the understanding of social phenomena and the social bond as such. Reinach himself applied them only as background for his study of legal phenomena, in particular of the promise as the primary source of civil obligations and claims.

Another good example of Reinach's perceptiveness in holding up to view phenomena which had been either overlooked or misinterpreted consists of the acts to which the positive law itself owes its existence. A frequent theory identifies these acts with commands. Reinach points out that this theory does not make sense in considering legal stipulations, which do not have addressees, as opposed to commands, which are essentially addressed to specific persons; thus a stipulation which fixes the beginning of the legal personality at the completion of birth is without an addressee. Reinach identifies the peculiar act responsible for such a legal fact as "enactment" (*Bestimmung*), an act which, of course, is in need of detailed phenomenological study.

b. ESSENTIAL LAWS CONCERNING LEGAL ENTITIES –
Reinach's principal interest in his treatise on the apriori foundations of civil law concerns however not the legal acts but the

legal entities to which they refer, such as claims, obligations, property, and the like. Here his first concern is to show that they are entities in their own right which cannot be reduced to mere psychological acts or functions: such reductions would imply a legal psychologism which falsifies the phenomena. Nor are they mathematical entities, timeless and changeless, as these latter are, but peculiar temporal entities, independent of the thinker who conceives of them, and in that sense real, but all the same susceptible to such events as creation and destruction. Reinach's special interest centers in the essential laws which control these events.

There is, e.g., an essential law to the effect that a claim is terminated either at the moment of its fulfilment, or by a waiver, or, at least under certain circumstances, by repudiation. According to Reinach, this law is not based upon induction from experience. It is rather as universal and necessary as any a priori truth. And since Reinach traces such laws back to the states of affairs which they describe, he affirms that the very nature of claims controls the laws concerning their termination. One might easily think that all or some of these laws are actually analytic, even in Reinach's sense, inasmuch as the properties here mentioned are contained in legal claims as constituent elements. Yet Reinach maintains their synthetic character. For they are based on external relations between the essence "claim" and the essences "fulfilment," "waiver," and "repudiation." For a conclusive answer one would have to ask for a previous full description of Reinach's claim with all of its parts, which he does not supply. But even if the essence "claim" should include something like an "intention" of fulfilment, it would not not follow that it also includes "termination at the very moment of fulfilment" rather than, for instance, after such fulfilment has been acknowledged. Much less does the claim include "termination by a waiver" or by "repudiation" as one of its constituent elements. Thus there seems to be a good case for asserting that some of these essential laws emerge only from an examination of the essences in their mutual relationships, and hence that they are synthetic in Reinach's sense.

It should be understood, however, that Reinach did not mean to forbid positive law to interfere by its enactments with these essential relationships. Thus positive law may rule that claims do *not* terminate at the moment of fulfilment, as it may do in the case of minors, or that the waiver of the claim by its owner is ineffective, as it may do when the owner wants to cheat his creditors. But to Reinach such interference only proves that without it the essential law would prevail. This is of course rather different from the laws which we find in mathematics, where, e.g., the mathematician has no power to decree that $2 + 2 = 5$. In view of this difference, Reinach's conception may need at least further elaboration. Certainly it would have been a safer course not to claim more for these essential laws than that they call for some property as their "logical consequence," or better ontological supplement, rather than that they entail it as necessary. In other words, this would be a law of essential tendencies rather than one of essential necessities.

Whatever the significance of the essential laws in the particular case of legal entities may be, they at least throw light on the whole field of essential relationships, for which Scheler found a much wider and more momentous field in the area of ethical phenomena.

BIBLIOGRAPHY

Major Writings

Gesammelte Schriften (1921) (G.S.)
    Posthumous edition with introduction by Hedwig Conrad-Martius; includes fragments from his philosophy of religion.
Most important for Reinach's phenomenology:
    "Zur Theorie des negativen Urteils" (1911)
    "Die Überlegung: ihre ethische und rechtliche Bedeutung" (1912)
    "Die apriorischen Grundlagen des bürgerlichen Rechts" (1913)
    "Über Phänomenologie" (Lecture, 1914)

Articles on Reinach

HUSSERL, EDMUND, "Adolf Reinach," *Kantstudien* XXIII (1919), 147–49.

Studies in English

OESTERREICHER, JOHN M., *Walls are Crumbling*. New York, Devin-Adair, 1952, pp. 99–134

D. MORITZ GEIGER (1880–1937): FROM PHENOMENOLOGICAL ESTHETICS TOWARD METAPHYSICS

Moritz Geiger was another of the original co-editors of Husserl's phenomenological yearbook. While this establishes his place in the history of the Phenomenological Movement, it is less easy to tell how far phenomenology was and remained the core of Geiger's philosophizing.

The most striking thing about Geiger's work and about his philosophic personality was his range and his versatility. He was equally competent in mathematics, as demonstrated by his impressive *Systematische Axiomatik der Euklidischen Geometrie* (1924), and in a field like esthetics, where at the time of his death he was working on a large systematic work. Besides, he developed a strong interest in such areas as the philosophy of existence.[1] His early work in experimental psychology earned him even a place in the history of psychology.

The superficial impression may thus well be one of rather disconnected sallies into various areas of philosophy and science. Closer study and extrapolation from Geiger's published and unpublished writings reveal, however, at least two dominating themes. One is expressed in an essay on the "psychological" function of art, which Geiger wanted to develop into a full-sized book. It begins with the following sentences:

Isn't it strange? Here we have uninteresting people such as one can meet every day in Holland, whose nondescript physiognomies we pass by without paying any attention: Along comes Rembrandt and depicts them in all their plainness – and now we stand gripped and delighted before the painting of the Night Watch, and before those commonplace people who shock us in life. ... How does this happen? What is the nature of the psychical process which achieves such miracles, which produces effects that differ in quality from anything we experience elsewhere, and that can be compared only with being gripped (*Ergriffenheit*) by religious feeling and metaphysical insight?[2]

The answer to these questions, combined with the related concern to keep the genuine esthetic experience free from gushing sentimentalism, was Geiger's philosophical objective in esthetics;

---

[1] At least a fragment of his rather original though relatively unpretentious conception of it has survived. See "An Introduction to Existential Philosophy" *PPR* III (1943), 255–78.

[2] *Zugänge zur Ästhetik*, p. 67.

phenomenology was the prime method for preparing the answers. Geiger's other major stake was in science, a stake much higher, in fact, than that of most other phenomenologists. He accepted its results and even its interpretations within scientific limits at face value. But he did not think that science could stand completely on its own feet. He maintained that it contained metaphysical patterns which it was apt to neglect and which philosophy was to explicate and to clarify. Unfortunately he was prevented from formulating such a metaphysics for science, except by way of critical studies. In this area Geiger was much less inclined to expect the answer from a merely phenomenological approach.

Husserl's estimate of Geiger varied, largely in accordance with his own development. He obviously had a high regard for Geiger's work as a phenomenological psychologist, expressed for instance in a footnote to *"Philosophie als strenge Wissenschaft"* in connection with Geiger's critical phenomenological survey of the problem of empathy (*Einfühlung*). In the twenties, however, after Geiger had published his first two descriptive studies in the *Jahrbuch*, Husserl decided that only "one fourth" of Geiger's philosophizing was really phenomenological.

Geiger himself, in his generous and genial way, never stopped crediting Husserl with the initiation of a new way of philosophizing. But he did not conceal the fact that, along with the other Munich phenomenologists, he failed to see the conclusiveness of Husserl's idealistic interpretation of phenomenology, and that he considered the realist's position phenomenologically more than defensible.

Geiger was the first among the original phenomenologists who was in direct contact with American philosophy. As early as 1907 Geiger, then already a *Privatdozent* in Munich, had come to the States for a year, studying chiefly at Harvard and meeting James and Royce. In 1926 he was guest professor at Stanford University, an appointment which was repeated in 1935, and also attended the Sixth International Congress of Philosophy at Harvard, where he read two papers of considerable phenomenological interest. His last and permanent stay in the States came after 1933, when Vassar College made him chairman of its Department of Philosophy, after the Nazis had deprived him of his chair at the University of Göttingen because of his Jewish ancestry. When he died suddenly of a heart attack after three years of intensive teaching, his friend Ralph Barton Perry delivered the memorial address.

What was probably most characteristic of Geiger was his quick grasp and his perceptive and imaginative way of attacking problems. Yet Geiger's work, cut short by his premature death at 57, remained usually too tentative and disconnected to add up to a unified philosophy. It is rather characteristic that so many of the titles of his best and most original studies precisely in the area of phenomenology went by such titles as "contributions to," "a fragment on," or "approaches to." In his remarkable ability to adopt and describe different attitudes, as he does particularly in his last works, he seems to be fighting a certain disinclination to "take a stand." In fact, his later work shows that he was not even sure how far he could identify himself permanently with the phenomenological attitude, much as he continued to think it indispensable for an attack on such areas as metaphysics.

Geiger was at his best in his concrete phenomenological studies, where his sensitive touch, his wide culture, his curiosity, and his clear and at the same time lively presentation allowed him to penetrate deeply, without always reaching the bottom. These assets, combined with his outgoing and liberal personality, account for much of the personal appeal which he had both at home and abroad, and which did much to make him one of the most successful spokesmen of the older phenomenology.

1. Geiger's Conception of Phenomenology

Geiger left no systematic book or statement on phenomenology. His interest in it developed out of his early psychological studies under Lipps. After some important experimental work under Wilhelm Wundt[1] he had undertaken a descriptive and classificatory doctoral dissertation on the elementary and complex feelings (1905). Here he used repeatedly the term "phenomenological" for an approach which postponed the study of the conditions and the significance of a phenomenon in favor of exploring its intrinsic characteristics, very much in the manner Pfänder had done this five years earlier in his *Phänomenologie*

---

[1] See E. G. Boring, *A History of Experimental Psychology*, pp. 339 642.

des Wollens. He developed this conception of phenomenology considerably after a semester in Göttingen. Then in 1907, in a book-size study under the unexciting title of "Methodological and Experimental Contributions to the Theory of Quantity," he showed concretely, partly on the basis of considerable experimental work on such well-worn topics as the Weber–Fechner laws, that without a clarification of what we mean to measure all experimental shrewdness and sweat are wasted, and that such clarification can be expected only from the kind of studies undertaken by Husserl in his *Logische Untersuchungen*. In addition, Geiger now introduced the distinction between act and object, thus far overlooked in the theory of sensation, and showed that this distinction made all the difference for the meaning and correctness of these laws. Furthermore, Geiger pointed out the "a priori relationships" among objects as well as among acts, calling "phenomenology" primarily the study of these relationships among objects and thus actually identifying Meinong's *Gegenstandstheorie* with Husserl's phenomenology, an identification for which, to be sure, there was scant justification at the time in Husserl's own writings, but which was typical for the way he was interpreted by the early Göttingen and Munich Circles. In fact, in his *theory* of phenomenology Geiger always seems to have given preference to a *Gegenstandsphänomenologie* as dealing with *Sachen* in the sense of intentional *objects*. But even in the "Contributions" he mentioned, if only in a footnote, *Aktphänomenologie*, the phenomenology of acts, a field in which Geiger himself did much of his later phenomenological work. As he conceived of it in the particular context, phenomenology was to be in relation to psychology what geometry was in relation to the physical sciences. This is the conception of phenomenology which is also implied in Geiger's first contribution to the new phenomenological yearbook. His study on phenomenology of esthetic enjoyment made it plain that he expected phenomenology to describe the essential features of this psychological phenomenon and its essential laws, not on the basis of deduction or induction, but of an intuition of the essential types and relationships.

Perhaps the only occasion when Geiger tried to formulate his conception of the phenomenological method more explicitly was in an essay on Pfänder's method (1930), an essay which, while characteristic of Pfänder's conception during Geiger's Munich years (1904–1923), is perhaps even more characteristic of his own conception, except for certain modifications and additions to be mentioned below. This essay, which re-emphasizes the role of phenomenology as a method and represents perhaps the first deliberate attempt to state the principles of the Munich Circle as distinguished from Husserl's, stresses particularly the following points:

α. universal empiricism without the restrictions of British sensationalism and Machian positivism, in favor of a pure unprejudiced description of the phenomena, based on the recognition of a maximum of givenness;

β. wariness of all distorting reinterpretations of the phenomena by a reduction to "nothing but," i.e., to simpler phenomena already known, in the name of what in English-speaking countries is called Occam's Razor;

γ. opposition to nominalism in favor of the recognition of general essences, to be found and intuited on the basis of the individual phenomena;

δ. realism in line with the original objectivism of phenomenology and its willingness to accept the verdict of the phenomena as given in the "immediate attitude."

However, while this is common ground for all the older phenomenologists, it is not the last word in Geiger's own conception of phenomenology. For this, one has to take account of Geiger's particularly close contact with the latest developments in science, beginning with the theory of relativity. It was apparently his respect for science which convinced him that there are limitations to the phenomenological approach, and that phenomenology with its a priori truths held the key only for the subjective or phenomenal world, while science was concerned with the "transphenomenal" world which it found itself forced to construct along different lines, denying for instance ultimate reality to the phenomena of color and sound *as given*, and even to the separate phenomena of space and time as we experience them. But this willingness to accept the scientists' verdict in matters of objective reality did not mean that Geiger embraced the position of an objectivist naturalism. True, Geiger displayed a characteristic tendency to approach problems such as that of the nature of reality from the foundation of basic attitudes (*Einstellungen*) which would seem to be beyond argument. But upon thinking through the implications of both naturalism, which tried to account for knowledge of the external world in mechanical terms, and of the "immediate attitude," which he here identified with phenomenology,[1] he found that they both became involved in serious contradictions. The phenomenological approach in particular in its immediate form results in perplexities like the following:

α. It cannot seriously claim that external perception reaches objects out in space as they really are. At best it can give us their appearances, as it does when it shows us the moon as a disk, which is supposedly all we see in the immediate attitude. And this is nothing but a mental and hence subjective object. Nevertheless, this mental object appears out in space, not "in us." But its "projection" outward is incomprehensible.

β. Gaps, like the notorious time gap in sense perception caused by light and sound waves, make it impossible to claim that we perceive objects outside us as they are at the time when their messages reach us.

Does this mean that Geiger acknowledged permanent limits to the phenomenological approach? In his Harvard paper (1927) he suggested that both the naturalistic and the phenomenological method had to be superseded by a metaphysical method, which alone would be in a position to solve such problems as that of the status of essences. In the book of 1930, however, which was to precede a larger work on metaphysics, Geiger seems in the end to suggest that phenomenology could become self-corrective by means of certain modifications, of which, unfortunately, he gave no clear indications. Thus what at first sight may look like a fatal retreat of phenomenology to an investigation of mere subjective phenomena or appearances and like a revival of critical realism, may eventually mean not more than an amendment of the phenomenological approach, based on evidence which ultimately also goes back to phenomenological sources.

[1] *Die Wirklichkeit der Wissenschaften und die Metaphysik.* – See also his English paper "The Philosophical Attitudes and the Problems of Essence and Subsistence," read at the Sixth International Congress of Philosophy at Harvard in 1927.

What becomes clear on such occasions is that at this time Geiger was very much attracted by Nicolai Hartmann's "critical ontology," which adopted phenomenology as an essential part of epistemology and yet tried to limit it to the phenomenal range, while claiming for ontology the means and the right to attack the "transphenomenal" range and to make a final evaluation of human knowledge. It is Geiger's final indecision on these points which leaves us with doubts as to his ultimate trust in phenomenology as a universal philosophical method. But at least he faced some of the more disturbing aspects of recent science, which other phenomenologists have by-passed too quickly. These and other puzzles of external knowledge indicate some of the unfinished business of phenomenology, which cannot be postponed indefinitely.[1]

2. Illustrations of Geiger's Phenomenological Analyses

In certain areas of knowledge Geiger considered the phenomenological approach inapplicable. This is true, for instance, of mathematics. Thus Geiger's own impressive axiomatics of Euclidean geometry could be considered phenomenological only in the sense of an a priori study which bases its axioms upon an attempt to capture the structure of mathematical objects by definitions and axioms related to essential structures (*Wesensdefinitionen* and *Wesensaxiome*), not merely arbitrary definitions.

The concrete studies to which Geiger himself applied the term "phenomenological" were in the fields of esthetics and psychology. Actually his conception of esthetics as a study of the esthetic object would have called for a non-psychological approach which disregarded the esthetic acts. But Geiger found it indispensable to clear the way to the esthetic objects by phenomenological studies of the acts in which they appeared. Only thus was it possible to keep out pseudo-esthetic material smuggled in by amateurish spectators, whose inclusion falsified the whole approach to esthetics. For Geiger, politically a genuine democrat, objected to a false democratism which saw no difference between the sentimentalist effusions of a person who used art simply as a drug and the self-disciplined and discriminating

[1] For a more recent phenomenological attack on these problems see the author's article on "Critical Phenomenological Realism" in *PPR* I (1940), 154–76.

contemplator of art. In particular he objected to the corruptions and caricatures of esthetic experiences which had resulted from Fechner's "experimental esthetics" in its consideration of any type of experience, provided that it involved pleasure, no matter of what kind.

Geiger's descriptive studies on the way to this goal included such topics as elementary and complex feelings, the consciousness of feeling, and the problem of empathy of moods(*Stimmungseinfühlung*), a field where he even made some use of experimental procedures. But his most important and most explicit study in the phenomenological psychology of esthetics concerned the experience of esthetic enjoyment. I shall try to convey at least a first idea of his most significant findings in this area.

THE PHENOMENOLOGY OF ESTHETIC ENJOYMENT – Geiger's chief concern in his unusually rich though limited study is to put the often discussed subject of esthetic enjoyment into the wider context of enjoyment in general, which is commonly thrown together with such related phenomena as pleasure, joy, etc. Actually the larger part of the study is devoted to the study of general enjoyment. Preliminary clarification shows that, while all enjoyment is pleasurable experience, not every pleasurable experience is enjoyment; for instance, the sudden relief from an awkward obligation is not enjoyment. Enjoyment must also be distinguished from joy, one of the main differences being that in the case of joy it makes sense – a sense that Geiger studies in detail – to inquire about its motives, which it does not in the case of enjoyment, although enjoyment, too, has essentially an intentional object of its own. Then the question of what kind of objects can essentially be enjoyed is taken up, with the result that, while by their very nature logical concepts, numbers, or relations cannot be enjoyed, any object or state of affairs presented with a certain intuitive fullness can. As to the act of enjoyment itself, the following features are pointed out as characteristic: In contrast to an act like striving, enjoyment is a centripetal experience in which we listen for the object in a receptive mood. Compared with an act of approval (*Gefallen*), which implies taking a stand, enjoyment means the abandonment of such a stand in favor of a self-surrender to the object.

And in contrast to such peripherally rising experiences as rage or desire, enjoyment is ego-centered in the sense that it arises in the immediate vicinity of the enjoying self. Besides, again in contrast to joy, the focus of the experience of enjoyment is in the ego, not in the object. Also, it has the tendency to fill and absorb the ego, especially in such modifications as being gripped, touched, entranced, or carried away. The question of "intensity" leads to the clarification of a dimension which had been mentioned variously before, for instance by Lipps: depth, in the sense of the intrinsic weight and seriousness of enjoyment.

It is only against this background that Geiger undertakes to find the distinguishing characteristics of *esthetic* enjoyment. No particular type of object turns out to be essentially unfit for *esthetic* enjoyment. All that is needed is a certain inner distance from the self, something which is relatively easy to achieve in the cases of sight and hearing, but harder, though not impossible, in the case of one's own bodily movements. Thus, there can be an esthetic enjoyment of such non-esthetic values as wines or even of one's own moods. Esthetic enjoyment furthermore is characterized by its focus on the intuitive abundance (*anschauliche Fülle*) of its object. Besides, in contrast to non-esthetic enjoyments, it involves forgetting about oneself and concentrating upon the object enjoyed (*Aussenkonzentration*). This concentration upon the object is actually what distinguishes the genuine esthetic attitude from the self-enjoying pseudo-esthetic attitude of the gushing dilettante, who enjoys only "himself" and his own emoting. Finally, the sense of disinterestedness in Kant's celebrated phrase "disinterested pleasure" is clarified as absence of selfish interest.

None of these descriptive characterizations are meant as attempts to define enjoyment in general and esthetic enjoyment in particular by way of their specific differences – an impossibility in Geiger's view, with which we are familiar in cases like phenomenal color. Nevertheless, an analysis like Geiger's can help in the attempt to identify the phenomena and to illuminate them.

b. THE PHENOMENOLOGY OF EXISTENTIAL DEPTH – Geiger's studies in the phenomenological psychology of esthetics were not undertaken for their own sake. They were dominated by at least two wider interests: one was esthetics as the study of artistic values, of which, however, Geiger gave not more than an outline; the other an understanding of art in its significance for human existence.

It was in the attempt to determine the peculiar significance of art for human existence that Geiger stressed an effect of art which he was also to use for distinguishing art from non-artistic enterprises: the depth effect in contrast to the surface effect. For Geiger claims that while surface effects are not incompatible with art, depth effects are essential to it. But what is meant by this strange metaphor of depth in the case of emotions?

Theodor Lipps in his *Ästhetik* had already spoken of a feeling of depth, a "depth of the object which is actually my own depth," which we project empathically into the object. But quite apart from its involvement in Lipps's psychologistic empathy theory, Geiger finds the concept of psychological depth in need of phenomenological clarification. This can be done in part by contrasting it to the surface effect. By the latter Geiger means the amusement effect, so typical of a mere thriller, of games, jokes, distorting mirrors, food, and drink, which affect only the merely "vital" or non-spiritual side of human nature. The same difference can be found in the psychology of ethics when comparing pleasure and happiness: pleasure is on the whole a surface phenomenon, happiness a depth phenomenon. The pleasures of non-art do not affect us in depth by making us happier; art does.

But this still does not give clear meaning to the metaphor of depth. In his phenomenology of enjoyment Geiger had tried to distinguish five different possible meanings of the phrase "depth of experience," all phenomenologically significant and demonstrable. It can stand for:

α. the fact that an experience is "anchored" close to the self;

β. the fact that it has its origin from a "deep" layer of the self;

γ. the fact that its point of attack is deep inside the self;

δ. the fact that it absorbs the self;

ε. the fact that the experience has a "weight" of its own.[1]

---

[1] A later attempt to disinguish such meanings of "depth" may be found in Dietrich von Hildebrand's treatise on "Sittlichkeit und ethische Werterkenntnis" Part III, *JPPF* V (1922), 524 ff.

Presumably there are connections between these meanings. But what is basic for the effect of art according to Geiger is sense γ: art attacks and grips the self in its depth, an effect which clearly presupposes a certain weight of the experience in sense ε. It may also lead to complete absorption of the self, as it does essentially in esthetic enjoyment (sense δ) and closeness to it (sense α). But what it excludes is sense β: for the esthetic experience has its origin essentially outside, in the work of art, not within the self.

Of course this whole conception implies that the ego has dimensions such as depth and breadth in a more than metaphorical sense. While Geiger does not develop and defend this conception in detail, some of his analyses, and incidentally the parallel ones in Scheler, seem to bear out the right of using such descriptions by showing their relevance in concrete examples.

c. THE PHENOMENOLOGY OF THE UNCONSCIOUS – Not without some justification has phenomenology been charged with neglecting the problems of the unconscious. Yet despite its critical cautions against the wilder hypotheses of speculative metaphysicians and psychoanalysts about the unconscious, phenomenology has never denied it. A case in point is Geiger's "fragment" on the unconscious.

Geiger's study of the problem of the unconscious is not primarily the result of his interest in psychoanalysis, of which he is of course fully aware. His major concern is psychology, more specifically the correct understanding of the nature of "psychological reality." The position he advocates, against a psychology for which the psychological is essentially conscious experience, is that the psychical is something real in its own right, independent of whether or not it is experienced, just as much as physical objects are independent of whether or not they are perceived. In contrast to the theory of the psychical as essentially conscious, this conception makes the unconscious at least possible in principle.

To show the reality of such an unconscious reality, Geiger concentrates on the phenomena of the will. Distinguishing between the phase of decision (*Willenssetzung*) and willful behavior (*willentliches Verhalten*), he admits that the former cannot but be conscious. It is in the second phase that a phenomenological analysis can reveal the occurrence of an unconscious will. There is, for instance, unexperienced willful behavior when, in carrying out a decision to go to the railroad station, we engage in all sorts of unrelated activities, such as animated conversation, without once thinking of our goal. Yet even though unexperienced, the will, according to Geiger, is still there and is rediscovered as having been there all the time when we experience it again. This case differs basically from the one where the will has died down and has to be created anew. This becomes even clearer in cases where the willful behavior has been interrupted by sleep. After awakening there is no need to initiate the willing behavior all over again. All that is necessary is to "reactivate" it, a peculiar but definite act in its own right. Such reactivation cannot be identified with a mere recollection of the former willing behavior; for such recollection will never guarantee the continuation of the action. Nor has the willful behavior when it revives the earmarks of something which has remained simply unnoticed, like the ticking of a clock, which only attracts attention when it suddenly stops. For in our case unconscious will is not merely unnoticed, but completely absent from our consciousness. A phenomenological study of the will thus reveals it as a reality, only incidentally conscious, consisting in a tendency that urges us forward. It may exist as activated or as unactivated. – Another case of unconscious will considered by Geiger is that of posthypnotic suggestion. One might of course argue that in this case the unconscious will is completely beyond the range of phenomenology and can only be reached by inference. But this would not prevent its essential possibility or its actual occurrence.

All this would hardly be sufficient to establish what the psychoanalysts designate by the word "unconscious," i.e., something which can be made conscious, if at all, only by special psychoanalytic techniques, especially when it has been previously repressed. But it does give substantiation for the concept of the "preconscious," i.e., that part of the mental life which under proper conditions can be brought to full consciousness. Geiger's phenomenological vindication of this area shows at least the possibility of psychical phenomena unaccompanied by any simultaneous consciousness.

SELECTIVE BIBLIOGRAPHY

Major Works

"Bemerkungen zur Psychologie der Gefühlselemente und Gefühlsver-
bindungen," *Archiv für die gesamte Psychologie* IV (1904), 233–88
"Methodologische und experimentelle Beiträge zur Quantitätslehre" in
Lipps, Th., ed., *Psychologische Untersuchungen* I (1907), 325–522
"Über das Wesen und die Bedeutung der Einfühlung," *Bericht über den
IV Kongress, für experimentelle Psychologie* (1911), 1–45
"Zum Problem der Stimmungseinfühlung," *Zeitschrift für Ästhetik* VI
(1911), 1–42
"Das Bewusstsein von Gefühlen," *Münchener Philosophische Abhandlungen*
(1911), 125–62
"Beiträge zur Phänomenologie des ästhetischen Genusses," *JPPF* I (1913),
567–684
"Das Unbewusste und die Psychische Realität," *Ibid.*, IV (1921), 1–138
Die philosophische Bedeutung der Relativitätstheorie. Lecture (1921)
Systematische Axiomatik der Euklidischen Geometrie (1924)
"The Philosophical Attitudes and the Problems of Essence and Sub-
sistence," *Procedings of the Sixth International Congress of Philosophy*
(Harvard, 1927), 272–278
Zugänge zur Ästhetik. (1928)
Die Wirklichkeit der Wissenschaften und die Metaphysik (1930)
"Alexander Pfänders methodische Stellung," *Neue Münchener Philosophi-
sche Abhandlungen* (1930), 1–16

Studies on Geiger

Listowell, Earl of, *A Critical History of Modern Aesthetics.* London,
Allen, 1933, pp. 83–86
[1]   Perry, Ralph Barton, *Moritz Geiger.* An Address, Vassar College, 1937

Geiger's philosophical papers are deposited in the library of Vassar
College.

E. OTHER MEMBERS OF THE GÖTTINGEN AND MUNICH CIRCLES

On the following pages I shall attempt to give at least a bird's-
eye view of the best work of some of the more important members
of both Circles. Even so these first hints will have to be highly
selective and determined largely by the tangible output in
publications rather than by historical significance. Thus the
name of Johannes Daubert (1877–1947), perhaps the most
influential member of the Munich circle, will not figure here again.
Theodor Conrad, one of the first Lipps students to go to Göttingen
and a leader among them, published but very little.[1] David

[1] "Sprachphilosophische Untersuchungen" Part I, in *Archiv für die gesamte
Psychologie* XIX (1910) 395–474; "Über Wahrnehmung und Vorstellung" in
Münchener Philosophische Abhandlungen (1911), 51–76. *Zur Wesenslehre des psychi-
schen Lebens und Erlebens* (1968).

Katz, whose phenomenological studies of color and touch have become widely known, especially among psychologists,[1] can hardly be claimed as a full member of the Göttingen Circle. The same would apply to Hans Lipps, then a student of medicine, who later on published a good deal of phenomenology of a highly personal type, leading in the direction of "hermeneutic" anthropology.[2] Among the members of the Munich circle the name of August Gallinger (1871–1959) must not go unmentioned.[3]

The order in which the following phenomenologists are introduced is merely chronological as determined by the date of birth.

WILHELM SCHAPP (1884–1965): His highly original dissertation on perception, exploring in detail the way in which physical things and phenomena which are not substantial things appear, is one of the best examples of early phenomenologizing; it also attracted considerable attention among psychologists. A lawyer by profession, Schapp produced later a pioneering study in the field of the theory of law, continuing some of Reinach's work. In a later book, dealing with man's entanglement (*Verstrickung*) in history, Schapp goes beyond the frame of "classical phenomenology" as he interprets it, i.e., as dealing primarily with logical and mathematical essences; no attempt is made to relate these new studies to more recent developments, even in Husserl's own phenomenology.

Works

Beiträge zur Phänomenologie der Wahrnehmung (1910; 2nd edition 1925). *Die neue Wissenschaft vom Recht* (1930). *In Geschichten verstrickt* (1955). *Zur Metaphysik des Muttertums* (1965). *Metaphysik der Naturwissenschaft* (1965).

KURT STAVENHAGEN (1885–1951), during his years of study in Göttingen chiefly a classicist, who had but little contact with the phenomenological Circle, did not publish philosophy until his fortieth year. Inspired by some of Reinach's posthumous fragments, his first book dealt chiefly with the phenomenology

---

[1] "Die Erscheinungsweisen der Farben" in *Zeitschrift für Psychologie* 1911, Supplementary Volume 7; revised as *"Der Aufbau der Farbwelt,"* translated by Robert MacLeod (*The World of Colour*) 1935.–"Der Aufbau der Tastwelt" in *Zeitschrift für Psychologie* (1925), Supplementary volume 11. See his autobiography in Murchison, Carl, ed., *A History of Psychology in Autobiography*, vol. IV, pp. 189–211.

[2] See especially his *Phänomenologie der Erkenntnis*, 2 vols. (1927, 1928).

[3] See particularly *Das Problem der objektiven Möglichkeit*. Eine Bedeutungsanalyse (Leipzig, 1913); *Zur Grundlegung einer Lehre von der Erinnerung* (Halle, 1914).

of religion as based upon a study of the act of taking a stand (*Stellungnahme*). He then turned increasingly to questions of social philosophy such as the essence of nationality, the home land (*Heimat*), and the phenomena of solidarity (*Einungen*), in which motifs from Pfänder's and Geiger's studies were used creatively. The motivation for these studies came partly from Stavenhagen's position as a member of the German national minority in the Baltic countries. Only in his last period, especially after the end of the second World War, when he returned to Göttingen and revived there the local interest in the older phenomenology, did he apply himself to fields like philosophical anthropology as a foundation for ethics, developing at the same time a phenomenology of vital phenomena. In spite of its incompleteness, his posthumous work on person and personality is probably his richest, showing his ability to use the methods and insights of non-Husserlian older phenomenology for original and systematic interpretations.

SELECTIVE BIBLIOGRAPHY

Absolute Stellungnahmen. Eine ontologische Untersuchung über das Wesen der Religion (1925)
Das Wesen der Nation (1934)
"Charismatische Persönlichkeitseinungen" in *Neue Münchener Philosophische Abhandlungen* (1933)
Heimat als Grundlage menschlicher Existenz (1939)
Person und Persönlichkeit. Untersuchungen zur Anthropologie und Ethik. Posthumous edition by Harald Delius (1957). Contains also a complete bibliography of Stavenhagen's publications.

HEDWIG CONRAD-MARTIUS (1888–1966), who, coming from Munich in 1910, soon became a leading member of the Göttingen Circle, then with her husband, Theodor Conrad, was the center of the so-called Bergzabern Circle, has been teaching since 1949 at the University of Munich, where she revived the interest in ontological phenomenology among an enlarged group of colleagues and students. The roster of her publications is impressive. Beginning with an acute phenomenological critique of positivism, she turned soon to problems in ontology, exploring not only such fundamental topics as being, time, space, and reality, but concrete essences such as colors and sounds in their essential characteristics. On the basis of a remarkable familiarity with the scientific literature she has also discussed problems of biology and evolution in a manner that has won her the respect of sympathetic scientists.

Following the line of Adolf Reinach, Conrad-Martius sees in phenomenology primarily a science of essences (*Wesenswissenschaft*). In fact, in her recent attempts to revive this version of phenomenology she presents it as a third form of phenomenology on an equal footing with Husserl's transcendental and Heidegger's existential phenomenology, a phenomenology concerned with the complete phenomenon (*Vollphänomen*) "world." As such it is to deal specifically with the essence of reality as a whole without bracketing it. It is also to achieve an understanding of the phenomena with regard to their grounds. Such a phenomenology will thus yield an ontology and is also considered compatible with "speculation" in the sense of a disciplined exploration of the essence of reality, without condoning "wild speculation."

In working out such ontological studies, Conrad-Martius has produced some highly suggestive, but also some rather puzzling and debatable interpretations of a wide range of phenomena. In view of the fact that these interpretations have been favorite targets for sniping at the phenomenological method as such, it should be borne in mind that they commit other phenomenologists as little as any other study published under the auspices of a series like Husserl's phenomenological yearbook.

SELECTIVE BIBLIOGRAPHY

"Zur Ontologie und Erscheinungslehre der realen Aussenwelt," *JPPF* III (1916), 345–542

"Realontologie" I. Buch, *Ibid.* VI (1923), 159–333

"Farben," *Festschrift für E. Husserl*. Halle, 1929, pp. 339–390

Der Selbstaufbau der Natur. Hamburg, H. Goverts, 1944

Preface to Adolf Reinach, *Was ist Phänomenologie?* München, Kösel, 1951, p. 5–17

Die Zeit. München, Kösel, 1954

Das Sein. Ibid., 1957

Der Raum. Ibid., 1958

"Phänomenologie und Spekulation" in *Rencontre-Encounter-Begegnung* Festschrift für F. J. J. Buytendijk. Utrecht-Antwerpen, 1957, p. 116–128

Festschrift Hedwig Conrad Martius in *Philosophisches Jahrbuch der Görresgesellschaft*, vol. 66 (1958)

Includes a complete bibliography.   [1]

DIETRICH VON HILDEBRAND (1889–   ), after a start in Munich one of the leading students in Göttingen, then teaching philosophy at the University of Munich until the advent of the Nazis, since then a professor at Fordham University, did most of his phenomenological work in ethics and social philosophy. His ultimate concern is the area of religious values, determined largely by his outspoken commitment to Catholic Christianity. Methodically his approach derives mainly from Adolf Reinach. Eventually he identifies the phenomenological method with a metaphysical analysis of essences, and no longer distinguishes it from the method of "classical" philosophy at its best. Phenomenologically his most substantial work is contained in his contributions to the phenomenological yearbook. They are based to a considerable extent on the work of Scheler, with whom Hildebrand was closely connected, particularly during Scheler's Catholic phase. As an example of Hildebrand's phenomenological work, I want to point out briefly two of his most original and influential conceptions:

α. The doctrine of the adequate value response, a development of some of Scheler's earlier suggestions. Hildebrand distinguishes acts of noticing (*Kenntnisnahme*) and acts of taking a stand (*Stellungnahme*), such as joy or indignation at something. The second group is always directed toward states of affairs and responds to certain qualities in them, notably to their values. In this response these acts purport to be appropriate to or required by these values. Not all of our value responses are appropriate in this sense. For instance, to be gripped by a nursery rhyme or to be annoyed by a fatal accident are "inadequate" value responses. It should be noted that Hildebrand gives credit for this doctrine to Husserl's still unpublished lectures on ethics.

β. The conception of value blindness as a partial explanation of seeming disagreement in valuations. In studying this phenomenon Hildebrand points out and explores in detail three types of such insensitivity: (a) total moral value blindness, where the moral predicates are meaningless to the person thus afflicted; (b) partial moral value blindness, in which there is only blindness to certain types of moral values, such as the higher and subtler ones; (c) moral blindness in classifying, i.e., inability to subsume actual behavior under the types with which the valuer is otherwise familiar. To be sure, no detailed criteria for these distinctions are given. But they open up a field which requires a good deal of further exploration from the phenomenological as well as from the epistemological and psychological angle.

SELECTIVE BIBLIOGRAPHY

"Die Idee der sittlichen Handlung," *JPPF* III (1916), 126–252
"Sittlichkeit und ethische Werterkenntnis," *Ibid.* V (1922), 462–602
Metaphysik der Gemeinschaft (1930)
Der Sinn philosophischen Fragens und Erkennens (Bonn, 1950)
Sittliche Grundhaltungen (1933); translated as *Fundamental Moral Attitudes* (1950)
Christian Ethics (1953)
Graven Images: Substitutes for True Morality (1957)
    See especially the second essay ("Substitutes and Other Moral Deformations") with further studies on value blindness.
    For a comprehensive account of his work see Schwarz, Baldwin V., "On Value," *Thought*, XXIV (1949), 655–76   [1]

JEAN HERING (1890–1966), an Alsatian student of philosophy and Protestant theology, later an important New Testament scholar, launched some of the most provocative ideas in early phenomenological ontology, particularly by his compact essay on neglected differences in the field of essences. His plea for individual essences deserves special mention. Later, after the reunion of Alsace with France, he became one of the ablest interpreters of phenomenology to the French world.

SELECTIVE BIBLIOGRAPHY

"Bemerkungen über das Wesen, die Wesenheit und die Idee," *JPPF* IV (1921), 495–543
Phénoménologie et philosophie religieuse (Études d'histoire et de philosophie religieuse. Strasbourg, 1925)   [2]

EDITH STEIN (1891–1942), Husserl's last important Göttingen student and first assistant in Freiburg, has become almost a legend, largely because of her personality, her conversion, her membership in the Carmelite order, and her end in the Nazi concentration camp of Auschwitz. In her considerable philosophical output, her strictly phenomenological work must be kept apart from her later outspokenly Thomistic philosophy, in which, however, she tried to incorporate some of Husserl's non-idealistic phenomenology and a good deal of Reinach's, Pfänder's,

Scheler's, Conrad-Martius's, and Heidegger's thought. From her purely phenomenological period her brilliant dissertation on empathy,[1] her studies on psychical causation, on individual and community, and on the State, which grew out of her collaboration with Husserl, are especially noteworthy.

After her conversion she soon transferred her philosophical allegiance to Thomist philosophy. It clearly expressed more than a merely impersonal diagnosis when she explained the growing interest in Thomas Aquinas in the following words:

> This is a time which is no longer content with methodical considerations. People have lost their moorings and are in search of something to hold on to. They want concrete, material truth which proves itself in actual living. They want a "philosophy of life." This is what they find in Thomas.[2]

Important though her phenomenological dowry has been in the construction of her great posthumous work on *Finite and Eternal Being*, phenomenology has here mainly a supplementary role as a handmaiden of Thomism. Basic are the specifically Thomist categories of act and potency, of form, matter, and substance, rather than common concepts such as essence and existence.

SELECTIVE BIBLIOGRAPHY

Zum Problem der Einfühlung (1917)
"Beiträge zur philosophischen Begründung der Psychologie und der Geisteswissenschaften" (I. Psychische Kausalität, II. Individuum und Gemeinschaft), *JPPF* V (1922), 1–284
"Eine Untersuchung über den Staat," *Ibid.* VII (1925), 1–124
"Husserls Phänomenologie und die Philosophie des hl. Thomas von Aquino," *Husserl-Festschrift* (1929), 315–338
Endliches und ewiges Sein. Versuch eines Aufstiegs zum Sinn des Seins. Published posthumously in *Edith Steins Werke*, II (1950)

Translations

Writings of E. S. Selected, translated, and introduced by Hilde Graef. Newman Press, Westminster, Md., 1956
Only the last section (IV) deals with her philosophical writings. Good Bibliography.

Articles in English

COLLINS, JAMES, "Edith Stein and the Advance of Phenomenology." *Thought* XVII (1942), 685–708

---

[1] See Gordon Allport, *Personality* (1949), p. 533.
[2] "Husserls Phänomenologie und die Philosophie des hl. Thomas von Aquino," *Husserl Festschrift*, p. 329.

FRITZ KAUFMANN (1891–1958): *see* Chapter XIII, p. 633

ALEXANDRE KOYRÉ (1892–1964), born in Russia, who had come to Göttingen via Paris, from where he brought the news of Bergson's intuitionism, has worked and published chiefly in the areas of history of philosophy and, later, of history of science. Here his approach by empathic understanding of the problems, rather than by an eager search for influences, reflected to some extent the phenomenological method and proved particularly fruitful in the cases of Plato, Anselm of Canterbury, Galileo, Descartes, and (especially) Jacob Böhme. Of more direct significance for the cause of phenomenology was his role as a link between German and French phenomenology in the early twenties.[1]

Koyré himself states his relationship to Husserl in the following terms:

I have been deeply influenced by Husserl, probably learnt from him, who did not know much about history: the positive approach to it, his interest for the objectivism of Greek and medieval thought, for the intuitive content of seemingly purely conceptual dialectics, for the historical – and ideal – constitution of systems of ontology. I inherited from him the Platonic realism that he discarded; the anti-psychologism and the antirelativism.[2]

SELECTIVE BIBLIOGRAPHY

"Bemerkungen zu den Zenonischen Paradoxien," *JPPF* V (1922), 603–628 *La philosophie de Jacob Boehme* (1929). *Études galiléennes* (1939). Complete bibliography in *Mélanges Alexandre Koyré*. L'aventure des sciences. Paris, 1964.

ROMAN INGARDEN (1893–   ), a Polish philosopher, also an early Freiburg student of Husserl, who however did not follow him on his way to transcendental idealism, has perhaps kept in closer touch with his developing thought than any other of the Göttingen students, as shown by his critical comments on Husserl's *Cartesian Meditations* (*Husserliana* I, 205–218) and by his continued correspondence with Husserl almost to the very end of his life. For this reason and even more because of the scope, the clarity, and the thoroughness of Ingarden's work,

---

[1] See Jean Hering, "Phenomenology in France," in |Farber, Marvin, ed., *Philosophy in France and the United States* (University of Buffalo Publications, 1950), pp. 70–72.

[2] Personal letter of December 10, 1953.

the present account should be considered as at best a first indication of his importance. It will have to be done over again once his major work on the *Existence of the World* is completed and accessible to non-Polish readers.

Ingarden's earlier publications dealt chiefly with such questions of formal ontology as the nature of essence, but also with fundamental problems of epistemology, partly based on his intensive study of the philosophy of Bergson. Perhaps his most original phenomenological work has been done in the analysis of various works of art, beginning with his book on the literary work of art, but extending to works of music and of the pictorial and tectonic arts. In these studies Ingarden made impressive use of the strata theory of pure logic as developed particularly by Pfänder on the basis of Husserl's first suggestions.[1] However, these esthetic studies serve at the same time a wider purpose in Ingarden's philosophy. This may be described as a sustained effort to break the deadlock in the perennial controversy between idealism and realism that had become acute again in phenomenology because of Husserl's espousal of a new transcendental idealism. Here the case of the work of art as demonstrably constituted by intentional acts and dependent upon them can serve as a particularly valuable control case for the study of other constitutions. However, Ingarden's major work consists of his direct comprehensive attack on the problem of realism and idealism, in which the published ontological parts deal with the various modes of being, with a systematic development of the main possible solutions, and with a study of the main structures of beings. The final solution will be given by a metaphysical volume which has not yet appeared.

SELECTIVE BIBLIOGRAPHY

"Über die Gefahr einer Petitio Principii in der Erkenntnistheorie," *JPPF* IV (1921) 545–568

"Intuition und Intellekt bei Henri Bergson," *Ibid.* V (1922), 285–461

"Essentiale Fragen. Ein Beitrag zum Problem des Wesens," *Ibid.* VII (1925), 125–304

Über die Stellung der Erkenntnistheorie im System der Philosophie (1925)

"Bemerkungen zum Problem Idealismus-Realismus," *Husserl Festschrift* (1929), 159–190

Das literarische Kunstwerk (1930); second revised edition (1959)

---

[1] See, e.g., René Wellek and Austin Warren, *Theory of Literature* (1942), p. 139 f.

"L'essai logistique d'une refonte de la philosophie," *Revue philosophique de la France et de l'Étranger* CXX (1935) 137–159
"Vom formalen Aufbau des individuellen Gegenstandes," *Studia Philosophica* I (1935), 30–102
"Der Mensch und die Zeit," *Travaux du IX. Congrès international de philosophie* 1937, VIII, 121–27
"De la structure du tableau," Bulletin de l'Académie Polonaise des Sciences et des Lettres, 1946
"De la poétique," *Ibid.*, 1946
"Über die gegenwärtigen Aufgaben der Phänomenologie," *Archivio di Filosofia* 1957, pp. 229–42
"The Hypothetical Proposition," *PPR* XVIII (1958), 435–50 (incomplete)
"Husserl zum 100-sten Geburtstag," *Zeitschrift für philosophische Forschung* XIII (1959), 459–63   [1]

Books in Polish

O poznawaniu dziela literackiego (On Recognizing the Literary Work), 1937   [2]
Spor o istnieniu swiata (The Controversy about the Existence of the World). 2 vols, Polish Academy of Sciences and Letters, 1947 f.; reviewed in *Mind* LXVI (1957), 269–71 (A. T. Tymieniecka)   [3]
O budowie obrazu (On the Structure of the Picture). Cracow, Polish Academy of Sciences, 1946
Szkize z filozofii literatury (Sketches on Philosophy of Literature) Lodz, 1947
Studia z estetyki (Studies on Esthetics). 2 vols. 1958; reviewed in *Journal of Aesthetics and Art Criticism* XVII (1959), 391–92 (A.-T. Tymieniecka)

Studies about Ingarden

TYMIENIECKA, ANNA-TERESA, "Le dessein de la philosophie de Roman Ingarden" *Revue de métaphysique et de morale* 1955, pp. 32–57,
———, *Essence et existence*. Étude à propos de la philosophie de Roman Ingarden et Nicolai Hartmann (Paris, 1957)
Contains a comprehensive bibliography of Ingarden's writings.   [4]
Bibliografia Praz Filosoficznych Romana Ingarden, 1915–1965. Odbitka z Ksiazki R. Ingarden, *Studi z esteryki* T. II, 495–527

V

THE PHENOMENOLOGY OF ESSENCES: MAX SCHELER
(1874-1928)

"The first man of genius, the Adam of the new Para-
dise ... was Max Scheler."

José Ortega y Gasset, *Obras Completas* IV, 510*

1. Max Scheler's Place in the Phenomenological Movement

There can be little question that in the early twenties before
the advent of Martin Heidegger Max Scheler was in the eyes of
the German public the number two phenomenologist; in fact to
many he was more – a star of the first magnitude whose dazzling
light revealed more than the prominent member of a new school:
a philosopher of the age. Fortunately it is not my assignment to
discuss the validity of such contemporary estimates. Mine will
be merely to describe and to evaluate Scheler the phenomenologist, leaving aside as far as possible the overflow of Scheler's
boundless energies and ideas into fields like sociology, politics,
and education. For Scheler was certainly more than a phenomenologist. It may even be asked to what extent, in the last analysis,
he was a phenomenologist. Scheler's impact on the Phenomenological Movement as a whole, however, is an indisputable
historical fact. Besides, he probably did more for the spread of
the entire Movement abroad, especially in the French- and
Spanish-speaking world, than any other phenomenologist. This
alone secures him a central place in the history of the Movement.

Partly as a result of this fact some oversimplifying legends
have sprung up which see in Scheler merely Husserl's foremost
pupil and collaborator. It seems therefore appropriate to record
at the very start the most important facts about their relationship
and about their mutual estimates of each other.

Scheler's academic education had already been completed, and
he had started to lecture as a *Privatdozent* in Jena, when he first
met Husserl. Scheler's own account of this meeting is as follows:

15. Max Scheler

When the present writer made the acquaintance of Husserl at a party for the collaborators of *Kantstudien* given by Hans Vaihinger in Halle in 1901, a philosophical discussion ensued regarding the concepts of intuition (*Anschauung*) and perception. The writer, dissatisfied with Kantian philosophy, to which he had been close until then (he had for this reason just withdrawn from the printer a half completed work on logic), had come to the conviction that what was given to our intuition was originally much richer in content than what could be accounted for by sensuous elements, by their derivatives, and by logical patterns of unification. When he expressed this opinion to Husserl and remarked that this insight seemed to him a new and fruitful principle for the development of theoretical philosophy, Husserl pointed out at once that in a new book on logic, to appear presently [i.e., the *Logische Untersuchungen*, volume II], he had worked out an analogous enlargement of the concept of intuition (*kategoriale Anschauung*). The intellectual bond between Husserl and the writer, which has become so extraordinarily fruitful for him, dates back to this moment.[1]

Husserl's side of this characteristic story with its implied claim of independence and simultaneous discovery is not known. In fact, during his lifetime Husserl never referred to Scheler in his publications. Yet he did recommend Scheler to Theodor Lipps when Scheler wanted to transfer his lecturership from Jena to Munich.[2] When Scheler, after leaving Munich in 1910, put in repeated appearances in Göttingen, he made but little personal contact with Husserl, but all the more with his students. Nevertheless, he became one of the four original co-editors of Husserl's yearbook, along with Reinach, Pfänder, and Geiger, although he never took a very active part in its management. Correspondence from the following years reveals a growing reserve on Husserl's part, though he never stated its reasons openly. There is, however, enough explicit and implicit evidence to show that Husserl's opinion of Scheler, never too high from the start, dropped in proportion to Scheler's quickly rising fame. It is not hard to understand the basic objection of the rigorous philosopher Husserl to Scheler's rapid output with its mixture of brilliant ideas and inadequate development. Soon he began to see in Scheler more of a danger than an asset to his own aspirations. Conversationally he even referred to Scheler's phenome-

---

[1] Witkop, Philipp, ed., *Deutsches Leben der Gegenwart* (Berlin, Wegweiser Verlag, 1922), pp. 197–8.

[2] This fact transpires from a letter of Scheler to Husserl, dated March 5, 1906, now in the Husserl Archives in Louvain. Husserl's letter seems to have been written at Scheler's request.

nology as "fool's gold" (*Talmi*), compared with the genuine gold of solid phenomenology.[1] In one of his letters to Ingarden (April 19, 1931, i.e., three years after Scheler's death) he even called him, along with Heidegger, one of his two "antipodes."

On the other hand, Scheler's attachment to Husserl also diminished, as his own philosophy began to take shape. Even during his visits to Göttingen in 1910 and 1911 he had been quite outspoken in his criticisms of Husserl. Tension was bound to increase when Scheler, who had left the Neo-Kantian atmosphere in Jena, realized that Husserl, more and more attracted by Kantian transcendentalism, was passing him in the opposite direction. Thus in 1916, in the preface to the book edition of his most important work, *Formalism in Ethics and Material Ethics*, Scheler made it plain that, while he and the other collaborators of the phenomenological yearbook shared with Husserl the same methodological consciousness, he diverged widely not only in *Weltanschauung* and concrete insights, but also in the more specific interpretation and application of the phenomenological approach. Later on Scheler stated his disagreements in even more explicit form. Yet he never ceased to acknowledge what in his eyes constituted the true originality of Husserl's phenomenology, and to express his indebtedness to it.

There is thus clearly no basis for seeing in Scheler the leading student and first heir to Husserl's phenomenology, and for crediting or blaming Husserl for what Scheler made of it. On the other hand, it should be realized that other members of the Older Movement, while far from uncritical of Scheler's methods and views, had a much higher opinion of his work than Husserl. Especially the Munich and Göttingen phenomenologists not only acknowledged his brilliance, but never questioned his status as a phenomenologist, even when they remained critical of his lack of thoroughness, clarity, and organization. Heidegger, who came to know him in the twenties, in dedicating his Kant book to Scheler after his death, paid tribute to the "relaxed power" (*gelöste Kraft*) of his mind. Nicolai Hartmann, himself to be sure on the outskirts of the Movement, judged that it was Scheler's wealth of problems that had brought to phenomenology its grand sweep (*grosser Zug*), and raised it into a spiritual

---

[1] Overheard by the present writer at an informal student gathering in 1924.

movement of which he was both the vanguard and the leader.

Under these circumstances the proper answer to the question of Scheler's place in the Phenomenological Movement must come from a fuller study of his conception of phenomenology and of his concrete contributions. But before doing this I shall consider the basic motivation behind Scheler's thinking and show how this motivation is related to his philosophy in general and to his phenomenology in particular.

2. Scheler's Basic Concerns

It takes little reading in Husserl and Scheler to realize that Scheler's fundamental quest in philosophy differed basically from the search for rigorous science which characterized Husserl's original enterprise. Scheler had no ambition to found a new [1] science such as phenomenology. For him such a science was at best a means, a new approach that would help him find new answers to perennial questions as well as to acute crises.

Much of the difference between Husserl's and Scheler's approach was certainly one of personality and temperament. There was in Scheler little of the desk scholar who followed a regular routine and stayed as far away from the issues of his day as circumstances would permit. Scheler's philosophical habitat was the café house. He philosophized with an intense sense of living in and for the age, an age of crisis and transition which he had diagnosed as such long before the First World War. To Scheler the most acute expressions of this crisis were social and economic. This explains, among other things, Scheler's persistent interest in sociology. Perhaps the most symptomatic of any of Scheler's titles was in this respect the one which he gave to the second edition of his early philosophical and sociological essays: "Of the Overthrow of Values." By this overthrow of values Scheler understood primarily the replacement of the Christian value pattern by that of the bourgeois capitalistic age, a change which has been seen and acknowledged equally by other non-Marxist thinkers like Max Weber, Werner Sombart, and Ernst Troeltsch. The main characteristic of the new pattern was the spirit of rational calculation and mere utility, as impersonated in the type of the "bourgeois," with his boundless acquisitiveness, his will to dominate nature, and his indifference to quality in favor of mere quantity.

This did not mean that Scheler saw the solution of the crisis in a return to medievalism. What he envisaged, none too concretely to be sure, was a new form of Christian socialism.[1] But the real reform would have to start with man, the individual, and specifically with his sense of values, whose perversion, as Scheler saw it, was merely intensified by secular socialism. To Scheler the lever for such a regeneration could only be a revitalization of ethics. But Scheler was keenly aware that such a regeneration could no longer be achieved by a mere return to ethical common sense after the model of most British moral philosophy. The challenge to such an ethics by thinkers like Nietzsche had been much too serious, and had undermined its foundations too deeply. A much firmer reconstruction was needed to buttress and rebuild them. Nevertheless, Scheler hoped that a reconstructed ethics could rehabilitate and revive some of the Christian values, particularly those of humility and reverence. He also wanted this ethics to reveal the sham of some of the modern pseudo-values born merely of a spirit of *ressentiment* bent on detracting what was beyond one's reach and on glorifying what was within it. Such a renewed ethics would enlist the best energies of the past, especially those of an Augustinian Christianity with its emphasis on Christian love and the sense of eternal order. The means for such a reconstruction were to be supplied by the new phenomenology.

Ethics was and remained the axis for Scheler's philosophizing. It was to provide not only pious formal generalities but principles that could guide the individual in concrete situations. On this point he took issue even with Nicolai Hartmann, who wanted to keep ethics out of the battles of the day.[2] Yet this did not blind Scheler to the historical and sociological relativities, which he studied with increasing seriousness. The values of personality

---

[1] *Vom Ewigen im Menschen; Gesammelte Werke* V, 396 ff.

[2] See the preface to the third edition of the *Formalismus* (*Gesammelte Werke* II, 23). The manuscript adds the following telling sentences: "After all, ethics is damned serious business (*eine verdammt "blutige Sache"*), and if it is unable to give me directives how 'I' ought to be and to live right now in this social and historical context – alas, what good is it? (*'ach, was ist sie dann?'*) ... It is precisely the business of philosophy to bridge it (the gap between eternity and the now and here), however indirectly." (*ibid.*, p. 611).

were for Scheler the supreme ones, superior to all impersonal values. For this reason Scheler even came to label his position as ethical personalism. It was to oppose equally an individualism which denied what Scheler considered the basic fact of solidarity, and a collectivism which deprived the person of his individual responsibility.

Another social problem of the time about which Scheler became vitally concerned was that of European nationalism. Scheler's first public expression of this interest – only too successful – in his book on *The Genius of War and the German War*, dashed off during the early months of the First World War, created the understandable impression that Scheler was glorifying war as such and was a German imperialist of the worst order. While it would be silly to deny that the book contained some of the typical and some of the worst expressions of nationalist self-righteousness,[1] it should not be overlooked that even then "the spiritual unity of Europe" was Scheler's ultimate concern and the basis of his final proposals for a unification of Western continental Europe.[2] It should also be remembered that toward the end of the First World War Scheler had already adopted a position which he himself called a pacifism of intention (*Gesinnungspazifismus*) based on Christian principles. In fact he argued the case for this new pacifism in a lecture before the top officers of the German army of the Weimar regime, relating it specifically to Kant's proposals for perpetual peace.

However, the real problem for Scheler was how to rebuild the spiritual unity of Europe on the basis of a new sense of solidarity, which seemed to him impossible of achievement without a moral conversion, i.e., an act of repentance on an international scale. In Scheler's view only the values of ancient civilization combined

---

[1] According to Nicolai Hartmann (*Kantstudien* XXXIII (1928), p. XV), Scheler himself later repudiated his war books most outspokenly.

[2] It would seem that this book represents the only basis on which Scheler is today still under the suspicion of being a proto-Nazi, prevented from joining the Party merely by his early death and his mixed ancestry. For the sake of setting the record straight, it should therefore be mentioned that as early as 1925 Scheler foresaw an age of equalization (*Ausgleich*) in which racial desegregation and mixture would be not only inevitable but a possible gain, and that he warned specifically against the "foggy ideologies of the racist mass movements which, in ignorance of the European reality and drunk with imaginary absolutistic race aprioris, obscure our world perspective in every direction, and which do not comprehend a world situation that makes a new solidarity of the European nations imperative." "Die Wissensformen und die Bildung," in *Philosophische Weltanschauung* (Bonn, Cohen, 1929), p. 89 f.

with those of an Augustinian Christianity could provide the foundation for such a deeper solidarity. He missed this spirit in the nationalistic narrowness of our historians and even of most modern philosophers. He hoped that it would unite even Catholics and Protestants, Rome and Stockholm. But to Scheler the center of the problem continued to be the development of a new philosophy with a deeper conception of man.

The problem of man and of redefining and remaking him was indeed one of Scheler's central themes. As he himself put it in retrospect:

Since the first awakening of my philosophical consciousness the questions: 'What is Man? And what is his place in the universe of being?' have occupied me more deeply and more centrally than any other philosophical questions.[1]

And he adds that he has now happily discovered that most of the problems which he had attacked in his philosophy had their focus in the problem of a philosophical anthropology.

Obviously such an anthropology means much more than what it has come to signify in contemporary physical and social science. Its purpose in Scheler's case is to determine man's nature and place in relation to the universe as a whole. It therefore demands at the same time a metaphysics able to determine the nature and meaning of reality itself. The connection becomes clear if we read one of his climactic statements about the meaning of reality in the preface to the second edition of his *Formalism in Ethics* (1925):

The most essential and important proposition which this work wants to defend and to convey as completely as possible is this: that the final meaning and the final value of this whole universe is in the last resort to be measured by the amount of pure being (not of achievement) in personalities, by their greatest possible goodness, by their fullest a- bundance, by their most complete development, and by their purest beauty and inner harmony – personalities upon whom all the energies of the cosmos at times converge and to whom they surge.[2]

Ethics and philosophical anthropology are thus the persistent central concerns of Scheler's philosophy. What was the function of his phenomenology in their pursuit? I shall try to answer this

---

[1] *Die Stellung des Menschen im Kosmos*, p. 9.
[2] *Gesammelte Werke* II, 16; see also "Die Wissensformen und die Bildung" (1926) in *Philosophische Weltanschauung* (p. 103), where Scheler expresses the same general idea in terms of his new metaphysics of drive and spirit.

question by first tracing the role of phenomenology in Scheler's development.

3. Phenomenology in the Development of Scheler's Philosophy

A comprehensive philosophical biography of Scheler is still impossible. Fortunately, the present context requires only an account of the development of his phenomenology. Even such a limited account must, however, take note of the fact that, although born in Munich, he received his university education in Jena under the major guidance of Rudolf Eucken, whose activistic "new idealism," dedicated to the cause of a spiritualized culture, had found a considerable response even outside Germany and particularly in the United States. Another teacher of his was Otto Liebmann, the Neo-Kantian, known for the slogan "Back to Kant." Scheler actually taught in Jena for seven years during this pre-phenomenological period. His first publications reveal his intense interest in questions of ethics and particularly in the problems of the place of work (*Arbeit*) in life. The thesis on the transcendental and psychological method, which he submitted in support of his request for admission as a *Privatdozent* (*"Habilitation"*), shows his dissatisfaction with both of these as interpretations of the "work world" (*Arbeitswelt*) and his effort to develop Eucken's "noological method" as an alternative. But while some of Scheler's ideas about the role of the spirit in his later philosophy can be traced back to Eucken, Scheler seems to have abandoned this effort around 1900, i.e., about the time when he first met Husserl. There is surprisingly little mention of Eucken in Scheler's later writings, and most of it is critical. Apparently his increasing interest in phenomenology coincided with a growing emancipation from Eucken's philosophy, resulting in the final transfer of his lecturership from Jena to Munich, his native city. There the free spirit in which the Munich Circle applied the new phenomenological approach had a particular appeal for him. But only after he had arrived in 1907 did he join the group and begin to philosophize in the phenomenological manner. Moritz Geiger, one of the members of this group most sympathetic to him, described this period of Scheler's life as follows:

In Munich Scheler found the method which was congenial to him: with surprising·speed he became at home in it, and from then on the fountains of his mind flowed ceaselessly. What attracted him to phenomenology was not the analysis and separation of the phenomena carried out in strictest discipline, which had found its most incorruptible model in Alexander Pfänder. Scheler, who rushed ahead with his characteristic brilliance, was not made for checking and counter-checking. For him something different was essential in phenomenology: he had discovered in it a method of intuition. Actually, Scheler had been aware of the importance of intuition in philosophy even before he went to Munich. For it was he himself – as always sensing the approach of new movements – who had discovered Bergson and persuaded the publisher Diederichs (in Jena) to start a German translation of his works. However, the intuition advocated by Bergson was more a modification of Schelling's "intellectual intuition" than a real method for concrete philosophical research. Phenomenology gave Scheler such a tool. Its primary objective was to grasp what is given. It allowed, and even made it a duty, to intuit plainly and simply, prior to constructive systematizing and to genetic considerations. From now on Scheler's many-sidedness came into its own. After he had stripped off the constructivism of his earlier days, it became apparent that no one possessed the capacity for such intuition ("*Schau*") to a higher degree than Scheler; but also that no one was equally exposed to the danger inherent in phenomenological intuition, as in every intuition, that what *seems* to be intuited and what has been seized without proper examination is taken for something *really* intuited.[1]

In 1910, after three years during which he was developing his new ideas before a growing circle of students, Scheler had to resign his Munich position for reasons unrelated to his teaching. During the following nine years he lived as a private scholar in Berlin and Göttingen, giving only occasional lectures. But these were the years when Scheler prepared his major phenomenological works, based in part on his Munich lectures, especially his *Formalism in Ethics*, a work which came out in two installments in volumes I and II of Husserl's *Jahrbuch*, and his largest study in phenomenological psychology, the phenomenology of the feelings of sympathy. He also wrote and published two volumes of essays which included some of his most acute phenomenological studies, e.g., on *"Ressentiment"* and on the idols of self-knowledge. During the First World War he also composed at top speed his book on "The Genius of War and the German War." He even served semi-officially on diplomatic missions to Switzerland and the Netherlands.

These were also the years when Scheler formally rejoined the

---

[1] "Zu Max Schelers Tode" in *Vossische Zeitung*, June 1, 1928.

Catholic Church, in which he had been baptized at eleven, but [1]
from which he had drifted away during the following thirty
years. Yet even during the six years of his active Catholicism,
its sacramental parts seem never to have meant anything to
him,[1] and he was often considered only as a mere "volunteer"
of the Church.

After the war Scheler returned to the academic life and was
appointed to a special chair for philosophy and sociology at the
revived University of Cologne, where he taught for nine successive years from 1919 to 1928. Along with his teaching, Scheler
published in 1921 the first volume of his major work in
phenomenology of religion, entitled *Vom Ewigen im Menschen*
("Of the Eternal in Man"), which was to be followed by two more
volumes under the comprehensive title, "Religious Renewal."
But only one year later, in 1922, he left the Church. What was
the reason for this abrupt change? Personal difficulties in
connection with his second divorce and remarriage have been
suspected. But quite apart from the irrelevancy of such explanations in the present context, much more pertinent changes in
his convictions clearly influenced his decision. Among these one
has to distinguish changes in his estimate of the Catholic Church
and more basic ones in his philosophic views. As to the first,
Scheler himself stated the main reasons for his shift as follows:

(1) The slow and painful realization that even my initial anti-Scholastic
and anti-Thomistic version of Augustinianism was really incompatible
with the dogmatic philosophy of the Church. It was, as I came to realize
slowly and painfully, a complete error of "modernist" theology to
consider Thomist philosophy as separable from ecclesiastical dogmatics.
For today even the ontological validity of the principle of causation, the
methods of metaphysics, and those for obtaining knowledge of God by
causal inference (not only the belief that such knowledge is possible) are
dogmas.
(2) the threat to the individual from the existence of institutions
designed for the purpose of salvation, whose dogmas are bound to suppress
independent thought and to cause rigidity of religious consciousness even
among believers;
(3) the deification of the founder of the religion, introduced into Christianity by St. Paul, a process which removes him from the ranks of the
people and at the same time deprives his demands of their human significance, thus undermining the sense of personal responsibility;

---

[1] See Dietrich von Hildebrand, *Zeitliches im Lichte des Ewigen* (Regensburg,
Habbel, 1932), especially p. 362.

(4) the alliance between dogmatic metaphysics and positivism, both of which stifle genuine metaphysical thinking;
(5) the most dreadful weapon: the prohibition even of doubt concerning propositions and matters relevant to faith as being sinful, a prohibition which dogmatizes and petrifies a certain metaphysics.[1]

Of the reasons for the shift in his philosophical position Scheler left only a partial account. Thus in the preface to the third edition of his *Formalism in Ethics* he stated that changes in his metaphysics had made it impossible for him to claim any longer the title of a theist, and that these changes were due to expansions of his views on philosophy of nature and anthropology. Scheler's last work, the Darmstadt lectures on *"The Place of Man in the Cosmos"* (1928), which were to be followed by his book on Philosophical Anthropology, makes it possible to suspect that these reasons were related to the introduction of his new dualism between the power-charged urge (*Drang*) and the powerless spirit (*Geist*), whose evolutionary struggle constituted the cosmic drama. Here God was no longer "a spiritual and in His spirituality omnipotent personal God," but the ground of being which realized itself in man through his commitment to the ideal of *"Deitas."* Scheler also stated that it was precisely his unchanged ethical insights which had led to a revision of his theological beliefs. One may suspect that Scheler's struggle with the problem of theodicy, which according to his editor Maria Scheler was one of the starting points for this revision,[2] had its basis in some of these ethical insights, and that they made it impossible for him to accept any longer the justification of evil by man's fall, to which he still subscribed in *Vom Ewigen im Menschen* (1921). Nicolai Hartmann, after 1925 Scheler's colleague in Cologne, to whose diagnosis Maria Scheler subscribes, speaks of the "gravity of the problem of reality" (*die Schwere des Realitätsproblems*) as the most important factor which enforced changes in Scheler's philosophy, and mentions not only "the problem of ontology" but the claims of the "lower non-spiritual" powers. In view of such plausible explanations there is certainly no need to seek other than philosophical reasons for his final shift.

Scheler's sudden death of a heart attack in 1928, even before

[1] *Die Wissensformen und die Gesellschaft*, p. 84. Footnote.
[2] Editorial Postscript to *Gesammelte Werke* V, 456.

he could begin his teaching at the University of Frankfurt, to which he had been called, prevented the completion of his culminating works on philosophical anthropology and metaphysics. During his Cologne years Scheler was at least able to complete, as an introduction to the metaphysics, a voluminous book under the title of "The Forms of Knowledge and Society," [1] which actually combined two works: his sociology of knowledge, in which Scheler defined and defended the rights of his metaphysics both against an extreme sociologism and against the authoritarianism of the church; and a second work, entitled *"Knowledge and Work,"* "a study of the value and the limits of the pragmatic principle in our knowledge of the world," in which he fought for the place of metaphysics against science, a science whose "pragmatic" character (taking the word in the sense of Charles S. Peirce) Scheler admitted and stressed, but to which he attributed an objective and approach entirely different from that of metaphysics. Aside from this work Scheler published a vast number of minor essays in the fields of ethics and sociology, most of which have appeared in various collections of his essays.

During this period references to phenomenology as such and, what was more significant, attempts to support his findings by phenomenological methods diminish conspicuously. But there [1] is no indication that in his metaphysical, anthropological, and sociological work Scheler meant to abandon phenomenology, though he did abandon some tenets for which in his earlier works he had claimed phenomenological backing. This suggests the question: What was his understanding of phenomenology?

4. Scheler's Conception of Phenomenology

Scheler himself never claimed that his own version of phenomenology differed significantly from that of the early Husserl or from that of the Older Movement. Certainly he never did so programmatically and aggressively. Nevertheless, close examination reveals increasing peculiarities, which may also account for some differences in results.

In part these differences may be explained in the light of the expectations which Scheler attached to the new Movement as a

---

1 *Die Wissensformen und die Gesellschaft* (Leipzig, Der Neue Geist Verlag, 1926).

whole. For he saw its main destination in the development and utilization of impulses which Nietzsche, Dilthey, and Bergson had given to modern thought long before Husserl. In other words, Scheler conceived of phenomenology as the great tool which could bring about a decisive reform of our *Weltanschauung*. Speaking about this transformation, he expressed his hope for the new movement in prophecies like the following:

It will be like the first step into a flowering garden of a man who had stayed for years in a dark prison. This prison is our human environment confined by an intellect that has turned toward the merely mechanical and whatever can be mechanized. The garden is God's colorful world, which we see opening up before us and greeting us brightly, if only from a distance. And the prisoner is European man of today and yesterday, who plods along sighing and moaning under the burden and who, with his eyes fastened to the ground and weighed down by his body, has forgotten his God and his world.[1]

During his lifetime Scheler discussed the nature of phenomenology and the phenomenological method as he conceived of them only incidentally in his publications. The most important of these discussions occur in his *Formalism in Ethics*. There exists, however, among his posthumous papers a group of fragments which were meant to go into a separate book on phenomenology and epistemology. In fact, one outline for this book includes not only a formal part, devoted to methodological and epistemological questions, but also a "material" part in which the applications of phenomenology to such areas as the external world, the "inner" world, the social world, the world of biological life, and metaphysics were to be taken up in systematic sequence.[2] For Scheler, in this respect not unlike Husserl, rejected the idea of a "picture book phenomenology," and was by no means averse to a phenomenological system based on the structural articulation of the phenomena.

But only the "formal" part of the projected book has been discovered in ostensibly final though incomplete form. Probably Scheler believed that in this text, actually composed before Husserl had published his *Ideen*, he was stating common phenomenological doctrine. But he clearly based this formulation

[1] "Versuche [einer Philosophie des Lebens" (*Vom Umsturz der Werte*, II, 181); *Gesammelte Schriften* III, 339.

[2] *Schriften aus dem Nachlass* (Berlin, Der Neue Geist Verlag, 1933) I, 464–5; *Gesammelte Schriften* X, 516 f.

on his own understanding and practice of it. To begin with, what he saw primarily in phenomenology was not a method in the sense of a set of mental operations but a peculiar attitude or way of viewing (*Einstellung*). In this attitude we enter into an immediate intuitive relationship with the "things" (*Sachen*), a relationship for which he also used the phrase "phenomenological experience" (*phänomenologische Erfahrung*). Actually Scheler insisted that phenomenology is "the most radical empiricism and positivism ever developed." It opposes chiefly a rationalism which either presupposes abstract principles or the uncriticized results of science (scientism), or which is preoccupied with the question of finding indirect criteria of knowledge. But phenomenology is equally opposed to a narrow empiricism which restricts experience to sense-experience. "Phenomenological experience" is not concerned with "things" of any type, but with a very special kind of facts. Scheler's peculiar doctrine of the three types of facts distinguishes between natural facts, scientific facts, and phenomenological or pure facts. The latter are pure intuitive contents given in immediate experience, without regard for possible reality, just as they present themselves immediately in independence of our positing beliefs or disbeliefs. By contrast "natural facts" are the facts of our naive beliefs in everyday things and events as expressed in our usual "Ptolemean" frame of astronomic reference; "scientific facts" replace this by the more sophisticated framework of a Copernican construction. Phenomenological facts or "whatnesses" (*Wesenheiten*) are always fully given and are hence beyond the range of all possible illusion. For there is here, it would seem by definition, no possible difference between what is merely symbolically meant and what is intuitively given: there is complete coincidence (*Deckung*). These facts are also in a new and peculiar sense a priori, i.e., independent of what can be given by inductive and particularly by causal knowledge. This new sense of the a priori includes obviously all of the immediate data of our untutored experience in all their qualitative richness.

A particularly important aspect of Scheler's phenomenological experience is its de-symbolizing quality, i.e., its role as a guide away from symbolizing thought to the symbolized self-given phenomenon. In contrast to symbol-dependent enterprises such as science, Scheler conceived of phenomenology as the concerted effort to go from the symbols back to the things, from a conceptual science and a civilization contented with symbols to intuitively experienced life. In this he sympathized particularly with Bergson and dissented from a conception like that of Ernst Cassirer, who saw in man primarily the symbolic animal. For Scheler this was at best a one-sided interpretation of man. The danger of symbolism lay in the tendency of symbols to displace and to conceal the phenomena.

The following may be considered the three main positive characteristics of the phenomenological approach as understood and practiced by Scheler:

α. *"Erleben,"* i.e., intuitive experience "lived through," as it were, and aiming at the same time to penetrate to the given itself; it thus represents an intensified form of living in contrast to its merely passive forms;

β. attention to the "what" (the *essentia*), while suspending the question of the "that" (the *existentia*);

γ. attention to the a priori, i.e., to the essential connections which exist between these "whats."

In connection with the second point it should be added that Scheler, in accord with the Husserl of the *Logische Untersuchungen*, never distinguished between the "eidetic reduction" (from the particular to the universal essence) and the "phenomenological reduction" (from existence to mere phenomenal whatness). Scheler's "what," when freed from the "that," was neutral even to the distinction between universal and particular.

Among additional features in Scheler's phenomenology which deserve discussion, some actually claim less for the new method than other phenomenologists had done:

a. THE DOCTRINE OF THE 'PHENOMENOLOGICAL CONTROVERSY' ('PHÄNOMENOLOGISCHER STREIT') – Scheler realized that the problem of communication arises in phenomenology even more than in connection with other philosophical approaches: what if one phenomenologist claims to see something and the other denies it? Scheler's answer is: The only meaning of a phenomenological discussion is to make the partner, whether reader or listener, intuit what according to its very essence is accessible only to intuition. Definition of the phenomena, according to Scheler essentially impossible anyhow, offers no easy solution. In fact Scheler stresses that "phenomenological philosophy is the very opposite of all quick-settling (*schnellfertige*) philosophy by mere talking. Here, one talks a little less, remains more silent, and sees more – even that part of the world which can perhaps no longer be talked about." But this does not pre-clude that only one of the two disputants is in a position to see the facts of the case. Thus phenomenological controversy is "deeper and more radical" than any other argument. It is, however, "not beyond settlement except where, as in the case of merely individually valid truths, there is no sense in disputing." [1]

Such scepticism might give the impression that Scheler was ready to surrender the cause of self-evident knowledge and hence of phenomenological intuition. After all, what guarantee have we that perception itself will not eventually turn out to be mere illusion? Scheler's reply to this objection is that only if there is veridical perception can there be illusion. This is true particularly if we try to explain the illusionary character of perception by resorting to our knowledge of brain events, etc. Besides, one of Scheler's students has shown that to every illusion there belongs essentially a type of perceptual disillusionment (*Enttäuschung*). In other words, there could be no illusion without veridical perception.[2]

b. THE IDOLS OF SELF-KNOWLEDGE – Brentano, in substantial agreement with Descartes, had asserted the self-evidence of inner perception. Husserl, who in the *Logische Untersuchungen* (II, 1, p. 230) had questioned this assumption, had nevertheless asserted that the transcendental ego, once it had performed the phenomenological reduction, was infallible.

Yet Scheler, for whom Husserl's transcendental phenomenology had no meaning, questioned the self-evidence of inner

1 "Phänomenologie und Erkenntnistheorie" III; *Gesammelte Schriften* X, 391 ff.
2 Herbert Leyendecker, *Zur Phänomenologie der Täuschungen* (Halle, Niemeyer, 1913), Abschnitt III.

perception on a much vaster scale. For to him inner perception, or more specifically self-knowledge, was as susceptible to illusion as was external knowledge; in fact, Scheler thought it to be even more exposed to such illusion. In an attempt to demonstrate this, Scheler went back to Bacon's general doctrine of the idols of knowledge with an investigation of the sources of illusions in the field of self-knowledge. These are in part scientific, in part pre-scientific. Without attempting to give a systematic list of them, I shall mention here

α. illusions due to the psychologist's tendency to imitate the physical scientist;

β. projections, i.e., illusions which comprise not only the attribution of internal processes to the outside world but also the attribution of outside processes to ourselves;

γ. illusions due to subconscious mechanisms such as Freud's repression, of which Scheler gives a phenomenological interpretation;

δ. illusions coming from the presence or absence of a terminology for the phenomena under investigation;

ε. illusions due to our tendency to treat self-observation as a mere imitation of other types of observation.[1]

c. THE PHENOMENON OF RESISTANCE AS THE CRITERION OF REALITY – If in the preceding points Scheler seemed to be more cautious than other phenomenologists, he was considerably bolder in others. Thus he believed that the phenomenological method is by no means permanently neutral in epistemological matters, but that it can establish the case for epistemological realism. To be sure, Scheler did not have time to state his theory of reality and of the perception of reality in a systematic and definitive form. But he succeeded in separating the problems with considerable acuteness in his essay on "Idealismus – Realismus." [2]

Scheler never questioned that there is a reality independent of consciousness. It reveals itself by a peculiar phenomenon, that of resistance (*Widerständigkeit*). But resistance to what? According to Scheler it is not the intellect which experiences it. It is rather our active, spontaneous, volitional life to which resistance is "pre-given," and with it reality itself. It is therefore not in perception proper that reality is experienced "in person"

---

[1] "Die Idole der Selbsterkenntnis" (*Vom Umsturz der Werte*, II,1–134); *Gesammelte Schriften* III, 215–292.

[2] *Philosophischer Anzeiger* II (1928), 255–324.

(*leibhaft*), but in a pre-perceptive practical attitude. Hence reality is to Scheler relative to our practical interests, and in a sense a pragmatic affair. Obviously much in this unfinished theory stands in need of further clarification and development. But it seems worth recording that Scheler was the first phenomenologist to state in print the case for a phenomenological realism as an alternative to a merely neutral phenomenology and to the idealistic phenomenology on which Husserl insisted more and more.

d. SCHELER'S PHENOMENOLOGICAL REDUCTION – As little as in Pfänder's case would it be justified to charge Scheler with complete neglect of Husserl's cherished transcendental or phenomenological reduction. It is another question whether he interpreted it in the same manner as its originator. In any event, Scheler's conception changed as did Husserl's, to be sure in a direction which led the two even farther away from each other than they had been at the start.

When Scheler first appealed to the reduction as a means to distill the phenomenological or pure facts from the natural and scientific world, he apparently believed he reflected merely Husserl's conception,[1] although his characterization of it differed not insignificantly from Husserl's. More important, however, is the difference in goal, i.e., the attainment of pure essences of any kind, not only of the essences of absolute consciousness. Later, Scheler became openly critical of Husserl's conception, especially as it had crystallized in the *Ideen*. Specifically, he took exception to the lack of clarification of the meaning of existence prior to its bracketing. But that did not mean that Scheler himself abandoned the phenomenological reduction. Instead, he found a new and more significant function for it in the context of his metaphysical enterprises, namely as part of the spiritual act by which man can free himself from the immersion in the world of factual reality and even break the power of reality over himself. For his deliberate "no" can inhibit the vital urge to which the phenomenon of resistance, and with it reality itself, is relative.[2] On the other hand this reduction is

[1] See, e.g., "Phänomenologie und Erkenntnistheorie" (*Gesammelte Schriften* X, 394.
[2] See *Vom Ewigen im Menschen* (*Gesammelte Schriften* V, 86); *Die Stellung des Menschen im Kosmos*, p. 63.

also an expression of the positive love of essences, which are revealed by it in their pristine purity. It hardly needs repeating that both the nature and the function of such a metaphysical act have little if any connection with Husserl's conception.

It should not go unmentioned that in 1922, to be sure only in the apologetic context of a second preface to his *Vom Ewigen im Menschen,* Scheler distinguishes between two kinds of phenomenology: "descriptive phenomenology" and "phenomenology of essences" (*Wesensphänomenologie*).[1] The former he also called a reconstructive phenomenology, designed to lead back from metaphysical or religious systems to their intuitive basis, a method to which Scheler assigns universal application ("a maid of all work"), and which he considers to be essentially relativistic. By contrast, the phenomenology of essences, while avoiding all assertions about actual existence, is charged with securing absolute insights into the what or essence of whatever is intuitively given in experience. To be sure, Scheler makes no attempt to keep these two types of phenomenology strictly apart. In actual practice they seem to coincide with different stages in the application of the phenomenological approach, the first one being of a merely preparatory nature and applicable only where previous thought has blocked the way to a direct and unbiased approach to the essences. It is the exploration of these essences which remains the foremost task of Scheler's phenomenology.

What is the place of such a phenomenology within the framework of philosophy as Scheler conceived it? He certainly did not identify the two. And he did not even assert that the phenomenological attitude could provide the answer to all the problems of philosophy or of life. Thus he considered it constitutionally unfit to answer questions of reality. These can be decided only (1) by factual experience, notably by the factual sciences, which can provide nothing but probable knowledge, (2) by metaphysics, which aspires to provide absolute knowledge about reality itself, or (3) by revelation, for which Scheler, at least in his earlier writings, reserved a place in his philosophy of religion. Nevertheless it seems safe to say that for Scheler phenomenology remained the necessary if not the sufficient condition for the

---

[1] *Gesammelte Schriften* V, 13 ff.

fruitful discussion of all philosophical issues, even those of a trans-phenomenological metaphysics. Unfortunately, there is little hope of finding out what additional sources of knowledge for metaphysics Scheler had in mind.

How far can the introduction of the phenomenological attitude secure to philosophy as a whole the status of genuine if not scientific knowledge? This was after all Husserl's great hope and promise.

To convert philosophy into a rigorous science was certainly not one of Scheler's primary objectives. This does not mean that Scheler's philosophy was anti-scientific or incompatible with scientific method, as is often believed and asserted. On the contrary, as far as empirical science was concerned, Scheler utilized its findings perhaps more than any other phenomenologist. But philosophical knowledge as he saw it differs in nature from mere scientific knowledge. It is essentially "absolute," in a sense still to be explained, possessing its own "rigor," different from that of the sciences.[1] In order to appreciate this conception of philosophy one has to relate it to Scheler's general theory of knowledge and particularly to the typology of knowledge which he developed in connection with his sociology of knowledge.

Scheler's growing interest in sociology has often been misinterpreted as a tendency to subordinate philosophy to sociology. But Scheler never stopped protesting against a sociologism which would make truth a function of social variables. His real purpose in studying the sociology of knowledge was to find out to what extent the concrete realizations of knowledge were socially determined. But he never granted to these variables any other significance than that of accounting for the perspective-slanted selections from the realm of truth. Truth itself remained unaffected, and social factors could account at best for its varied appearances and distortions in our eyes.

The most characteristic and important distinctions among types of knowledge that Scheler introduced were based on its different objectives:[2]

---

[1] "Vom Wesen der Philosophie" in *Vom Ewigen im Menschen*; *Gesammelte Schriften* V, 73 ff.

[2] Without raising the question of a possible influence I would like to point out the striking parallel between the two main types of knowledge according to Scheler (1. and 3.) and Bertrand Russell's distinction between power-knowledge and love-knowledge in *The Scientific Outlook* (New York, Norton, 1931), pp. 261 ff.

α. Knowledge for mastery and achievement (*Herrschafts- oder Leistungswissen*). According to Scheler it is precisely "positive" modern science which is animated by this practical motive. This explains Scheler's intense interest in the "great intellectual movement of pragmatism," with which he was familiar through William James's writings, and of which he gave one of the longest and fairest European appraisals.[1] In fact, Scheler believed that the pragmatist interpretation of knowledge was correct as far as mere scientific knowledge was concerned. It failed only as an account of metaphysical or "absolute" knowledge. For to Scheler scientific knowledge has only relative validity: it selects what is controllable or manipulable in the phenomena, i.e., their merely mechanical aspects, which can be utilized in the construction of machines. Specifically, the picture of the world obtained by the merely mechanical sciences is relative not only to such factors as the limited receptive powers of our physical organism for certain stimuli, but also and chiefly to the technical purposes we adopt, which call for the selection of a minimum of technical means (principle of least action). This is also true of the attempt of science to substitute an efficient system of symbols for a picture of the things for which these symbols stand, thus by-passing the question of the essence of the phenomena. Mechanical knowledge and science thus understood are therefore perfectly valid and justified, but only within the limits of their restricted objectives, i.e., relative to the purposes of practical control; in other words, science has pragmatic relativity.

Despite this relativity of science based on its selectiveness, Scheler by no means rejected scientific knowledge as such. "No weakly Romanticism of the Christian or Indian variety will extinguish the living torch of science." At the same time it must be admitted that its "flames" will never be able to give man

that guiding light through life whose quiet glow alone can feed this torch: *humanitas* and the type of knowledge which it presupposes. Even when positive science should be completed, man as a spiritual being would still be absolutely empty. In fact he might relapse into a barbarism compared with which all the so-called primitive nations were Hellenes. ... For barbarism supported systematically by science would be the most dreadful of all conceivable barbarisms.[2]

[1] Thus the subtitle of the large second part of *Die Wissensformen und die Gesellschaft* ("Erkenntnis und Arbeit") reads: "A study of the value and the limits of the pragmatic principle in knowledge."

[2] *Die Wissensformen und die Gesellschaft*, pp. 237 f.

β. There is thus for Scheler a second type of knowledge whose primary objective is "cultivation" (*Bildungswissen*). Scheler developed his ideas about this type of knowledge only rather sketchily, notably in a lecture on the forms of knowledge and education but also in his articles on educational reform. At times this type of knowledge seems to fuse with the third one, to which it forms merely a transition. Its major objective is clearly the full development of the personality as such.

γ. For the last and highest type of knowledge Scheler chooses the rather puzzling and easily misleading expression "knowledge for salvation"; misleading, for there is no indication that, as in Buddha's or Schopenhauer's case, such knowledge is meant to save us from the misery of existence – an estimate of the world which Scheler by no means shares. Actually this third knowledge is characterized by its role in serving the cause of the entire world and its development; as such it is even called knowledge for the sake of God. As to ourselves, such knowledge lets us participate in the "source of all being" and unites us with it. Thus it constitutes salvation only in the sense that it delivers us from "tension" or "original conflict" which ties us to ourselves. But Scheler never states clearly in what exactly this conflict consists, or how the new knowledge is able to relieve it. All he does is to refer us to the "irrestible urge of all beings to be in knowing contact with a reality intuited as super-powerful (*übermächtig*) and holy." [1]

However, the most important feature of this last type of knowledge is that it aims at the essence of its object, not at its practical or symbolic aspects. This is where philosophy, as distinguished from the practically motivated sciences, has its rightful place. Scheler's separation of philosophy from science does not mean that he expects philosophy to be less scientific in the sense of a lack of objectivity. For it aspires to "absolute knowledge," free from the relativities of science with a merely pragmatic orientation, which is bound to change as varying practical interests determine its perspectives of relevance. It is another question how far philosophy and particularly metaphysics in this sense have any chance of achieving Scheler's objectives, as he, with striking confidence, claims they can. As far as his

---

[1] *Die Wissensformen und die Gesellschaft*, p. 64.

own metaphysical achievements are concerned, Scheler died too soon to present them in a form which would allow one to test his claims fairly.

There is, however, even more to Scheler's conception of philosophy than the desire for "absolute" knowledge of essences, i.e., for knowledge that is not relative to pragmatic interests. Scheler's momentous essay "On the Essence of Philosophy" adds in its very title the significant phrase "and the Moral Prerequisite of Philosophical Knowledge." [1] While for Scheler philosophy is autonomous knowledge, free, or at least as free as possible, from such presuppositions as those of historical knowledge (traditionalism), scientific knowledge (*Scientifismus*), and a dogmatic common sense, it does have personal prerequisites, which are actually of a moral nature. They consist primarily in "love of being" in the sense of the desire to participate by knowledge in the essential nature of beings other than oneself. In this sense, if in no other, love, according to Scheler, has to precede knowledge. Such love requires rising above the level of our habitual setting, humility on the part of our natural self in freeing ourselves from our merely accidental nature, and control of our natural inclinations. Without such self-discipline no knowledge adequate to its object can be expected. Love and humility are also the prerequisites for the discovery of what Scheler, even before Heidegger, stated as the point of departure of all philosophy: the wonder at the fact that there is not nothing but something, a fact which only he who has looked into the abyss of nothingness can really appreciate. [2]

In the end philosophy is defined as "insight, rigorously self-evident in nature, into essences and essential relationships, accessible by way of concrete examples, not to be increased or destroyed by induction, valid a priori for everything contingent, in the order and hierarchical sequence in which such essences are related to 'absolute being' and its essence" (V, 98). Surely such a conception of philosophy is one of the most ambitious ever formulated. One might well wonder how far it is at all within our reach. In order to determine this, one would certainly

---

[1] "Vom Wesen der Philosophie und der moralischen Bedingung des philosophischen Erkennens" in *Vom Ewigen im Menschen*; *Gesammelte Schriften* V, 61–100.

[2] "Vom Wesen der Philosophie" in *Vom Ewigen im Menschen*; *Gesammelte Schriften* V, 93.

have to discuss fully Scheler's conception of the Absolute and our chances of knowing it. But this would not affect the right and the fate of Scheler's phenomenology of essences, much as this phenomenology is presupposed and even incorporated in his conception of philosophy. Absolute knowledge and especially metaphysical knowledge of existence in Scheler's sense is clearly not an integral part of the phenomenological insight into essences, even if this insight does affect metaphysics.

5. Scheler's Phenomenology in Action

In what follows an attempt will be made to illustrate as concretely as a second-hand report can what Scheler's phenomenological approach meant in actual practice. Completeness being out of the question, the examples will be chosen chiefly for their representativeness, their instructiveness, and their substantive merit. For this reason I shall concentrate on Scheler's middle period, when his phenomenological interest was most pronounced. But I shall omit some of the better known doctrines which Scheler himself emphasized, such as his doctrine of the person as an ontic unity of acts (*Seinseinheit*) which is essentially non-objectifiable. Although this doctrine forms the climax of Scheler's ethics, occupying the second half of his magnum opus, and the center of his philosophy, I can see comparatively little phenomenological foundation for it, especially since Scheler does little if anything to substantiate his sweeping and often astonishing pronouncements in this area. Here Scheler's eagerness to reach metaphysical conclusions and to derive practical applications seems to have gotten the better of his phenomenological caution. More serious are the omissions of his perceptive and suggestive analyses of such phenomena as reverence and humility, of his phenomenological studies on the consciousness of our own body, death, and freedom, on the feeling of shame, and on ethical models and leaders, which were published posthumously.

a. VALUE AND OUGHTNESS

(*1*) *The Intuitive A Priori* – Scheler's first and major interest in applying the phenomenological approach concerned ethics. The way to its reconstruction and development as he envisaged it led via a phenomenology of value in general and of ethical values in particular. Such a phenomenology was also to make ethics immune to the threats of psychological, sociological, and historical relativism.

For a German philosopher of the time, particularly for one who like Scheler had grown up in the Jena tradition, the obvious point of departure for such an undertaking was Kant. Now Kant had indeed rescued ethics from the relativism of a merely empirical approach by deriving it from a priori principles. But he had done so by a merely formal ethics which, especially in the sense in which it was interpreted by the Neo-Kantians, provided no clear and definite solutions for concrete problems and hence could not function as a definite guide for actual conduct. It is for this reason that Scheler found it necessary to begin his reconstruction with a critical examination of the "colossus of steel and bronze," Kantian formalism, in an attempt to show that apriorism need not be merely formal, but that it may equally well be based on the non-formal values which thus far were the exclusive domain of empirical ethics. The synthesis was to be found in phenomenological ethics.

Scheler's first step in approaching his objective was to identify and examine the hidden presuppositions of Kant's formalism. In his *Critique of Practical Reason* Kant had objected to all moral rules with any kind of content on the ground that content could only consist in objects of desire, that such desires were necessarily empirical, that this would make ethics essentially subjective and relative to such desires, and subordinate all our actions to the rule of self-love and happiness, hence to our lower nature. In challenging these assumptions, one of Scheler's major points was the distinction between objects of desire (*Ziele*) or goods (*Güter*) and values (*Werte*), values being the good-making characteristics in a goal or good which by no means coincide with it. While Scheler admitted that objects of desire are merely empirical, variable, and subjective, he denied that the same is true of the values carried by them. For these he claimed a basis and dignity quite different from merely a posteriori experience, namely phenomenological intuiting and intuitive insight.

What exactly are these values as distinguished from goals and goods? Scheler has often been interpreted as saying that values are general essences, ideal entities hovering over the empirical world of ethical experience like so many Platonic Ideas. Actually Scheler assigned to them neither the status of individuals nor that of universals. They are given as the contents of immediate intuition in concrete cases of ethical experience, once we attend to the value characters in their pure "whatness" (*Was*) regardless of their existence. It would seem, therefore, that such "whatness" is as un-Platonic as any other property that is carried by the objects of our concrete experience.   [1]

It should also be realized that what Scheler means by calling the intuiting of such values a priori is not that they can be found without any experience. What he does mean is that insight into value can be obtained by contemplating the mere content of a value experience, disregarding the question of whether this initial experience is factually correct. We may be entirely mistaken about the nobleness of a specific deed. But intuition can still show us that the nobleness which we believed we saw in such a case is a higher value than clever speculation. We need not even wait for the occurrence of concrete cases in actual experience: Imagined cases can serve us equally well. A priori insights are insights into the properties of experienced objects which depend merely on their essence, regardless of their exemplification in concrete cases of experience.

(2) *Non-Formal ('Material') Values* – By no means does Scheler deny or neglect formal properties of and relations among values, which Brentano had expressed in axioms like the following:

> "the existence of positive values has itself positive value"; or:
> "the existence of positive value ought to be realized." (III, 102)

And since Scheler interprets statements about such properties and relations as synthetic judgments a priori, they are certainly not without interest for the moral philosopher.

But of much greater importance and originality is what Scheler has to offer on the subject of non-formal or "material" values and on the laws applying to them. Here the most important task is the identification of the basic value qualities. These Scheler groups into the following four classes, clearly on the basis of previous phenomenological exploration:

α   Values of the pleasant and unpleasant. These occur in objects attuned to beings endowed with senses. Since these senses differ, different things may appear pleasant and unpleasant to different types of individuals, while the values themselves remain constant.

β.   Values of "vitality," a group which constitutes Scheler's original addition to the traditional list of value qualities. Chief examples are the noble (*edel*) and vulgar (*gemein*), illustrated primarily by higher and lower breeds of plants or animals and expressed in greater or lower vitality, health, youthfulness, etc. In this Scheler clearly attempted to assimilate the new values which Nietzsche had tried to make all-important.

γ.   Values of the spirit (*geistige Werte*). These are unrelated to the circuit of organism-environment. Among them Scheler distinguishes the esthetic values of beauty and ugliness, the values of right and wrong, and the values of pure knowledge for its own sake.

δ.   Values of the holy and unholy. They represent a type of value exemplified in certain "absolute objects." Obviously the carriers for this value have to be found in the religious sphere. Its chief representatives are on the human side the saint, in the superhuman range Divinity, for which only the phenomenology of religion can give the proper setting. (II, 125–30)

Even in Scheler's original text the six-page list of these non-formal values is so condensed and sketchy that it calls for further development and, more important, for critical analysis. Nevertheless, its suggestive influence and power was and still is considerable.

One characteristic and original feature of this list is that, except for the values of correct (*richtig*) and incorrect (*unrichtig*), it does not mention the specifically moral values. The explanation is that for Scheler these are values that appear on a different level: they attach to acts which realize the before-mentioned values, and realize these in the right order. The moral act is therefore essentially directed toward non-moral values, and the moral value appears only, in Scheler's picturesque expression, "on the back" of acts which attempt to realize them.

Now Scheler does not leave these values side by side on an equal level. Like Franz Brentano, he believes that there is an order of preference or precedence among them. The "vital" values ought to be preferred to the pleasure values, the spiritual to the vital ones, and the religious to the spiritual ones, since they are "higher" in rank. This relative rank is to Scheler a matter of intuitive insight too. It is manifested by criteria such as the following:

α.   Enduringness in the sense of an intrinsic tendency to last longer. Happiness, as compared with mere evanescent pleasure, or love, in comparison with mere transitory liking, may illustrate the significance of this criterion.

β   Indivisibility in the sense that higher values cannot be divided up among several persons as the lower ones can. However, they can be shared to a much greater degree than the lower ones and need not be sliced up in order to be equally enjoyed.

γ.   Relative independence of other value qualities. Thus the useful, according to Scheler, depends for its value on the pleasant, but the value of the pleasant in its turn is founded on the values of vitality, and these ultimately on those spiritual values which to Scheler make life worth living.

δ.   Depth of satisfaction (*Befriedigung*) as contrasted with mere intensity. These two dimensions are described in detail in Scheler's analysis of the stratification of the emotional field.

ε.   Relative independence of the experiencing subject's organism. Thus the values of the pleasant are to a particularly high degree dependent upon the possession of senses and sensuous feelings, which are less important in the case of the "higher" values, if not exactly unimportant.

In Scheler's belief, these criteria enable us to establish a clear-cut hierarchy of values according to which the smallest quantity of a higher value is still preferable to the highest quantity of its immediate inferior. One may well wonder whether the order among the non-formal values need be so rigid, and even whether it follows from Scheler's own criteria as stated above. Yet it remains true that greater flexibility would have had to be bought at the price of greater complication in actual decisions.

(3) *Value, Ideal Oughtness, and Moral Oughtness* – Scheler's ethics is opposed to Kantian ethics in one more respect: it rejects Kant's emphasis on laws and imperatives as the fundamental facts of moral consciousness. Against this view Scheler asserts the primacy of the phenomena of value.

This does not mean, however, that Scheler would deny the phenomena of oughtness. On the contrary, he introduces a much more differentiated pattern of the normative phenomena. Thus, in addition to distinguishing sharply between the phenomena of value (*Wert*) and oughtness (*Sollen*), Scheler tries to demonstrate in considerable detail the basic difference between mere ideal ought-to-be (*ideales Seinsollen*) as it had been asserted, though merely in passing, by Henry Sidgwick, and a moral ought-to-do (*ethisches Tunsollen*), as expressed particularly in the experience of duty and obligatoriness. However, Scheler challenges the tradition according to which the moral ought constitutes the highest form of the ethical consciousness. Action based on the sense of the moral ought, i.e., of duty, lacks the generous spontaneity of the truly ethical act. For duty presupposes, as Kant had pointed out and Scheler concurs, an inclination on the part of the subject to oppose the ideal. For this reason it is also relative to the intensity of these obstreperous inclinations. This cannot be said of the ideal ought-to-be, which merely depends on the underlying values and actually forms the foundation of the moral ought. The ideal ought, not the moral ought, is the indispensable foundation of moral conduct.

Here too Scheler's original distinction required and still requires further elaboration and verification. His pronounced antagonism to the idea of duty may well appear as biased and exaggerated.

b. The phenomenology of cognitive emotion – From a consideration of value and oughtness as objective correlates of our moral acts Scheler turns to the experiences in which these phenomena are given. Phenomenologically the sections dealing with these acts may prove to be the most noteworthy of his ethics. Scheler's main effort here is to use phenomenology for the purpose of breaking down the rigid disjunction between reason and emotion, cognitivism and emotivism, which had put the cognition of value, and particularly of non-formal or material value, into such a precarious if not hopeless position.

The key to Scheler's solution is to be found in his phenomenology of feeling. For the whole rationalist tradition, feeling, with the significant exception of Kant's feeling of awe, represented the quintessence of utter subjectivity. What Scheler now undertook to show was that there is a large number of feelings which have an "objective" character and differ fundamentally from the merely subjective feelings, which in the past had been taken as representative of all feelings. Actually Scheler was not the first to attempt such a rehabilitation of the emotional life. He himself gives generous credit to St. Augustine and, more specifically, to Pascal as his predecessors. Pascal's program of an "order" or "logic of the heart" based on "reasons of which the intellect is ignorant" was in fact one of Scheler's main inspirations. Now he tried to put this conception on a phenomenological basis and to apply it to ethics.

He begins by a fundamental distinction between feelings as mere states of mind without any referents, exemplified most characteristically by moods like elatedness or depression, and feelings which have referents beyond themselves. Feeling in the latter sense has the same structure as any other "intentional" act in which we are conscious of something, including our own states. Among these functional feelings the feelings of value, in which qualities such as agreeableness, beauty, and goodness are given, constitute a distinctive and distinguished case. They are basic even for such specific reactions as joy *about* or indignation *at* something. To these "feelings of value" (*Fühlen von Werten* or *Wertfühlen*), in contrast to the mere states of feeling and to other non-cognitive types of intentional feeling, Scheler ascribes genuine cognitive function. What is more, Scheler makes a determined plea for the objective validity of these feelings, inasmuch as they are based not merely on rash and impulsive reactions but on careful study of the facts of the case and a responsible weighing of their values.

c. ETHICAL ABSOLUTISM AND RELATIVITY – In a sense this is of course "absolutism," and Scheler does not hesitate to call it so. But this does not mean that he denies all "relativity" in the field of value and our experience of value. Actually one of his main goals is to determine the exact sense and the range of cultural and historical relativity and to account for the "palette with the overturned paintpots" with which a superficial survey of human valuations confronts us. He does this by pointing out factors other than the subjective relativity of the values themselves, which may explain them. This enables him to distinguish types of relativity which do not affect the objectivity of the values themselves:

(*I*) *Variations in the Valuations or Acts of Value-Experience*, which he calls, none too felicitously, the *ethos*. Among the many factors responsible for the *relativity of the ethos* Scheler studies especially, and with considerable psychological acuteness, the

[1] factor of *ressentiment* – a phenomenon for which even the German language had to borrow the label from the French – held responsible by Nietzsche for the Jewish-Christian "slave morality." In Scheler's interpretation it consists of the feeling of revengeful impotence which substitutes pseudo-values of its own making for the genuine values which it is unable to reach. In addition to making a genuine phenomenological study of this mechanism, Scheler now makes use of this concept against its very introducers. Thus he tries to show that not Jewish-Christian ethics but precisely the modern bourgeois morality is the result of *ressentiment* – *ressentiment* against the Christian ethics of love. For to Scheler love is an expression of inner strength rather than of impotence. Compared with love, even altruism and humanitarianism appear to Scheler to be born of the inability to face, and the desire to escape from, one's own self. This ingenious reversal of Nietzsche's theory provides an apt illustration of Ernst Troeltsch's characterization of Scheler as the "Christian Nietzsche."

(2) *Relativity of Ethics* in the sense of variations in our opinions about ethical matters. Some of these opinions are merely implicit in our unarticulated beliefs, some are explicit in the form of ethical theories. Scheler never contests their variability. But such variety in our opinions is obviously no proof of a variation in the values to which these opinions refer.

(3) *Relativity of Types of Actions*, i.e., variations due to change in our way of seeing units of action. These ways are relative to varying social institutions. Thus theft or adultery presupposes a certain organization of property or of sex relations. In societies which have not yet introduced property and marriage, the actions which presuppose them could not even occur.

(4) *Relativity of the Practical Morality* (morals) of people, which, to a considerable extent, varies independently of people's beliefs of what is ethical and hence is not a clear sign for relativities of type (2). High criminality is no proof of low "ethics"; it may mean the opposite.

(5) *Relativity of Customs* in which, to some extent at least, ethical beliefs are expressed. Their different and varying forms are to be distinguished from the deeper identities which may be embodied in them.

d. THE PHENOMENOLOGY OF SYMPATHY – One of Scheler's most original and influential analyses of phenomena related to the general area of experience of ethical value occurs in his book on sympathy, love, and hatred.[1]

Actually the main purpose of the first and most influential part of this work is largely negative. It tries to show that sympathy, the foundation of several important conceptions of ethics, such as Adam Smith's and Schopenhauer's, is a phenomenon fundamentally different from love, and that it is incapable of supporting a satisfactory social ethics, despite the fact that under some very definite conditions sympathy does have ethical value.

The book begins with a comparative phenomenological analysis of sympathy, laying special emphasis on phenomena in this area which had been neglected in earlier accounts. In particular, Scheler points out the difference between sympathy and similar acts directed toward persons with whom we sympathize. Such acts are, for instance, the realization (*Auffassung*) or understanding (*Verständnis*) – no sharp distinction between these two is drawn – of others' emotions, and the imitative feeling (*Nachfühlen*) in which these emotion are imaginatively presented, without being fully lived over again. Neither of them as such

---

[1] The original title was *Phänomenologie der Sympathiegefühle und von Liebe und Hass*. The additions of the second edition, to a considerable extent metaphysical and scientific (psychoanalytic) in nature, were apparently responsible for the change in title to *Vom Wesen der Sympathiegefühle*.

implies or entails genuine sympathy. In fact, understanding may occur without sympathy and without imaginative empathy. But even sympathy itself has to be distinguished from acts of feeling, whose peculiar nature is usually not even noticed. There is, for instance, immediate solidaric feeling (*unmittelbares Mitfühlen*) with someone else's sorrow, i.e., a joint or parallel feeling, a feeling essentially impossible in the case of his physical pain or pleasure, which cannot be shared to this extent. There is furthermore a type of contagious transmission of the same feeling from one to the other in a crowd. Again this does not mean any sympathy with the other. Finally there is a type of unity feeling (*Einsfühlung*) in which a group of people feel themselves united "as one" by something like an *esprit de corps*. Such unity feelings can be found in totem consciousness and mystic ecstasies. The latter must also be distinguished from the complete identification which Scheler diagnoses in pathological mass-psychoses.

In contrast to these phenomena, real sympathy is concerned with the other person's feelings as those of a distinctly other individual, not as in any sense fused with those of the sympathizer. In feeling sympathy with the joy and the suffering of the other, one does not substitute oneself for him or melt together with him, but one respects him as a separate personality.

Beyond this, however, the first third of the book contains very little positive description of sympathy, although a good deal of light falls on it in the course of subsequent genetic, metaphysical, and historical considerations. Here one has to remember that Scheler's main purpose in offering this study of sympathy was to supply a foil for his phenomenology of love and hatred, i.e., the more basic phenomena for ethics.

To love and hatred too Scheler applies the method of confrontation, but he also tries to add positive descriptions. But while the contrast, especially that with sympathy, throws interesting light on the phenomena of love and hatred, the positive characterization is less differentiated and seems distorted by Scheler's preconception of love as an experience concerned with values. Despite this limitation, Scheler supplies significant suggestions about the highest types of love. Specifically he describes love as not static, but as "movement" in the sense of an act that tends from one condition to another, namely from the lower to the higher value in the object loved, in such a way that love leads to the "flashlike effulgence" (*Aufblitzen*) of the higher value. To be sure, love does not mean a creative transformation of the object or person loved but rather of the lover. Nevertheless, it is oriented toward possibilities of enhancing value in the loved one for his own sake. Such love is spontaneous, not reactive. Sympathy does not form the foundation of such love; the fact is rather that such love is the basis of sympathy.

The emphasis on this dynamic tendency of a love which tries to develop rather than merely to recognize and to preserve existing values would seem to be a significant addition to the understanding of such phenomena as *agape*, a love that does not simply desire to obtain the more perfect – like the Platonic *eros*, which looks up to what is already lovable – but a love which loves what is not yet lovable for the sake of what it might become.

e. KNOWLEDGE OF OTHER MINDS [1] – Scheler's discussion of our knowledge of other people contains another characteristic and very influential example of his phenomenologizing. Again he begins by the negative demonstration that neither an account of this knowledge by analogical inference nor one by empathy is at all adequate. That an inference by analogy from our introspective experiences will not do has been made clear by animal psychology, notably by the study of apes as described by Wolfgang Köhler, and likewise by a baby's unquestionable recognition of the attitudes and acts of grown-ups with which it cannot possibly be familiar from its own previous experience. Besides, the bodily motions which form the supposed basis for such an analogical inference differ when observed optically in other people's bodies and when experienced in our own bodies, i.e., chiefly through kinaesthetic sensations. Then there is the fact that we seem to notice emotions and attitudes even in animals such as fish and birds, whose entire pattern of physical motion is different from ours. As to the empathy theory, which Theodor Lipps had used as a maid of all work, Scheler points out that it cannot account for the difference between merely imagi-

---

[1] For this item see also the critical account by Alfred Schuetz, "Scheler's Theory of Intersubjectivity ..." in *PPR* II (1942), 323–41.

native and esthetic empathy on the one hand and cognitive empathy on the other, which is supposed to show us the reality of other people's minds, not only an imaginative projection. Finally, Scheler points out that in the case of historical knowledge we seem to know about other minds even without knowing anything about their physical organisms and motions.

Thus Scheler sees no alternative to acknowledging direct perception of other selves, a perception no less direct than that of our own selves, and, in principle, even that of material objects. He has no doubt that we can see immediately "the other's joy in his smile, his suffering and his pain in his tears, his shame in his blushing, his entreaty in his folded hands, his love in the glance of his eyes, his rage in his gnashing teeth, his threats in his clenched fists." We never perceive the other person's body in isolation. We never see merely his eyes: we also see his gaze. We see a complex whole (*einheitliche Ganzheit*) consisting of the expression and what it expresses. The theory that all we can perceive directly is the other person's body is not even consistent. Logically it should lead to the conclusion that all we can perceive are the sense data referring to his body. There is no better reason to admit that we perceive other people's bodies than that we perceive their minds. This does not mean that our perception of other people's minds is infallible, or that it is ever complete. In fact, Scheler repeatedly points to a certain area of absolute privacy (*Intimsphäre*) of a person which is impenetrable to other people's scrutiny.

With this rejection of the traditional theories of our knowledge of other minds Scheler combines the thesis that originally our social consciousness contains only a neutral stream of experiences, not yet assigned to either ourselves or to others; furthermore, that our immediate tendency is to ascribe these to others rather than to ourselves, since we live more in others than in ourselves. In any case, according to this theory the self and the other are discovered only as a result of a process of differentiation in the neutral primordial stream. I submit that much of this theory goes considerably beyond the scope of direct phenomenological verification.

f. PHENOMENOLOGY OF RELIGION – Scheler's ambition was to work out a phenomenology of the essential structure of any religion (*Wesensphänomenologie der Religion*). For such a phenomenology Scheler outlined three objectives:

α.   the analysis of the essential features of the Divine (*Ontologie*);
β.   the study of the modes in which the Divine appears;
γ.   the study of the religious acts in which the appearances of the Divine are given. The "revelation" which this implies does not mean a supernatural event. For Scheler is concerned only with the field of "natural theology."

Scheler does not commit himself to the Thomist division between the natural and the supernatural. On the contrary, Scheler's religious philosophy is emphatically anti-Thomist and tries to revive the more intuitive Augustinian approach. Specifically, he discounts indirect demonstrative proof (*Beweis*) in the scholastic manner and tries to guide toward direct intuition which can show the phenomenon itself (*Aufweis*). This implies that phenomenology must very often try to awaken and to actualize religious acts which exist in the reader in undeveloped form, otherwise simply referring to them would be of no avail.

Scheler's main interest in the developed parts of his phenomenology of religion concerns the study of the religious acts. However, this required at least a minimum characterization of the religious object including the essential nature of the Divine toward which the religious acts are directed. In this context Scheler refers repeatedly to Rudolf Otto's *The Idea of the Holy* as a particularly successful piece of phenomenological description without the official label "phenomenology" attached to it. The essential attributes of the Divine as they emerge from these considerations are absoluteness – an attribute which, to be sure, does not guarantee actual existence, but does imply complete independence – superiority to all other beings, universal efficacy, and holiness, the attribute which describes divine perfection in terms of its values. From these fundamental attributes Scheler derives such additional aspects as spirituality (*Geistigkeit*) and personality.

The experiences in which this Divine essence is manifested to the religious person are two closely connected receptive acts: the experience of his individual nullity (*Nichtigkeit*), expressed in the phrase "I nothing, You everything," and that of being His creature (*Geschöpflichkeit*), implying "I am not nothing absolutely, I am a creature of God." A being as relative and dependent as man has thus characteristic experiences showing him his essential condition of being the effect of a power not himself (*Gewirktheitserlebnis*). In fact, according to Scheler's interpretation, these experiences lead us back immediately to the awareness of an absolute being who is the source of this experience. Later on Scheler also maintains that we can experience ourselves as reflections and, as it were, mirror images of a creator, once we penetrate reflectively into the roots of our spiritual nature.

Scheler thinks that additional support for these insights can be derived from a study of certain specifically religious acts which, to him, differ essentially from all other personal acts. Among these he distinguishes acts addressed to oneself (*religiöse Eigenakte*) such as centering down (*Versenkung*), repentance, etc., and other-addressed acts (*religiös-soziale Akte*) such as entreaty, thanksgiving, praise, veneration, obedience, and the like. Such religious acts are characterized by the fact that by their very essence they cannot be satisfied or "fulfilled" by any finite object of experience. At the same time they are deeply rooted in the very nature of man.

How far does the occurrence of such acts constitute valid evidence for the existence of a Divine object as their correlate? Scheler's claim is: "Only a real being with the essential characteristics of the Divine can be the cause of man's religious dispositions." Here then is an interesting modification of the Cartesian proof for the existence of God from the idea of God, an idea which can be explained only by a real God. However, Scheler denies that it is a *Beweis* (proof) in the usual sense; instead it is meant as an *Aufweis*, a pointing up of what everyone can discover directly by following the direction of the pointer.

An unbiased appraisal of Scheler's phenomenology of religion is impaired by the fact that soon after he had published it he found it necessary to modify it even in parts as central to his work as his accounts of the Deity. It is not easy to determine the full extent of these modifications, since Scheler did not have the time to restate his views in a new edition or separately.

Nevertheless, it is safe to assert that he did not, as is sometimes asserted, adopt a Nietzschean atheism. Yet it is true that he came to reject the theistic conception of God as a personal, omnipotent spirit. Invoking as his predecessors both Spinoza and Hegel – with questionable credentials, I may add – he now interpreted God as a being who is only in the process of becoming real and whose only place of realization or "deification" is man. Obviously this is not pantheism, which also has been ascribed to the later Scheler. For Scheler's "deification" occurs only in those rare and unique situations where the blind urge to life and the powerless spirit, now called Deity, interpenetrate. In answer to the objection that such a God in the making is an unsatisfactory if not an intolerable conception, Scheler replied that metaphysics is not an insurance service for the weak who are in need of crutches: "In the place of the relation of distance – the result of childlike thinking and weakness, as it is construed in the objectifying and hence evasive relationships of contemplation, adoration, and the prayer of entreaty – we for our part put the elemental act by which man pledges himself for the Deity, and identifies himself unreservedly with its spiritual intentions." [1]

Such a position, reminiscent of the earlier Bergson and, perhaps even more so, of Samuel Alexander, stood of course in glaring contradiction not only to any Christian theology, but also to Scheler's own earlier views. For here Scheler had insisted on the necessity of conceiving God as an absolute being, both perfect and personal, an insight for which he had even claimed the dignity of an "essential insight" (*Wesenseinsicht*).[2]

6. Toward an Appraisal of Scheler as a Phenomenologist

On the whole Scheler's rating in the Anglo-American world has not been very high. Even some phenomenologists in the States have repudiated him, not only on the basis of his presumptive political sympathies but also because of his "attacks on scientific philosophy" and his "dogmatic defense of selected articles of faith" (Marvin Farber). Much of this hostility may be the result of insufficient acquaintance with Scheler's prolific work. The

---

[1] *Die Stellung des Menschen im Kosmos*, p. 112.
[2] See for instance *Der Formalismus und die materiale Wertethik*, p. 412; *Gesammelte Schriften* II, 407.

access to his most important writings, especially to his ethics, is still not easy, particularly for those who have to depend on translations. Instead of defending Scheler against these unfair criticisms, I have therefore tried simply to present some of the relevant evidence and to leave it to the reader to pass a more informed verdict or, even better, to turn to the sources.

But this is no excuse for avoiding all critical evaluation. Scheler's total philosophy, of which only the barest outlines could be drawn, can and must be omitted from appraisal here. Only its phenomenological aspect has to be considered.

It would be hard to deny Scheler's genius as an original practitioner of the phenomenological method. He had few if any rivals in the choice of significant and promising areas for its application. Also, his ability to see relevant differences and shades in the phenomena which others had overlooked is unique. But not all of his discoveries and insights seem to be sufficiently underpinned. Many of them were apparently not yet exposed to the cleansing fire of critical doubt and to the attempt to think through alternative perspectives and interpretations. Scheler was too often in a hurry. Phenomenology was for him only a stepping stone on the way to his ulterior objectives. In the dazzling outpouring of his overflowing mind he was too prone to mistake his first flashes for final insights. This often led him to make excessive claims for his final conclusions as based upon phenomenological evidence, almost in inverse proportion to the care he had spent in testing them. It is therefore not surprising that Scheler found himself forced to repudiate some of his most cherished findings in a manner which was perhaps as creditable to his integrity as embarrassing to his ambitions. This is true particularly of his phenomenology of religion, where he had claimed evidence "as clear as sunlight" (*sonnenklar*) for positions on which he had to reverse himself so completely that his reversal was apt to discredit his phenomenological claims even in other areas.

When Scheler describes his insights, he is generally more impressive in showing negatively what a certain phenomenon is not than in pointing out positively what it is. This relative absence of positive descriptions is explained to some extent by his expressed belief that ultimately no positive definition or even description of genuine phenomena is possible, and that only direct intuiting can do justice to them. Yet whatever the legitimacy of this position may be, Scheler fails too often to give his reader the leads which he needs and has a right to expect in order to catch up with his guide.

Some of this may be blamed on Scheler's way of writing, which does not always make for easy reading. Next to pages that are brilliant in their suggestiveness and concreteness there are others which with their apodictic claims shock the critical reader who has not yet become spellbound. And too often the fireworks of footnote digressions prove more distracting than illuminating. Even Scheler's best work bears too often the earmarks of incomplete revision.

Scheler's phenomenological work is strikingly illuminating but uneven. It has to be read sympathetically and critically at the same time. If approached in this spirit, it contains some of the most stimulating anticipations, if not yet final insights, which phenomenology has thus far yielded.

7. Scheler's Following

Scheler's permanent influence cannot be measured by his academic following alone. True, his lectures attracted vast audiences. But his academic career was too brief and intermittent for the formation of a school. Nevertheless, even during his Munich years he gave decisive stimuli for the later phenomenological work of DIETRICH VON HILDEBRAND and HERBERT LEYENDECKER.

The years in Cologne gave him much greater scope. At least two of his students there deserve special mention. One, the South African philosopher HENDRIK G. STOKER, prepared a noteworthy monograph on conscience considered primarily as the expression of the evil in man, a study which Scheler himself recommended particularly for its phenomenological insights.[1]

The most impressive and independent of Scheler's Cologne students, however, was PAUL-LUDWIG LANDSBERG (1901-1944), whose major interests, to be sure, were not in phenomenology for its own sake, and whose writings show few attempts to use it

---

[1] *Das Gewissen, Erscheinungsformen und Theorien* (Bonn, Cohen, 1925).

deliberately. Even more than in Scheler's case the needs and problems of the hour, and particularly those of the generation after the First World War, claimed Landsberg's efforts. To satisfy them he studied historical phenomena such as the Platonic Academy and the world of the Middle Ages, which he interpreted as idealized types. His major systematic work was directed toward a philosophical anthropology, of which he published at least prolegomena.[1]

Landsberg's most mature and significant piece was perhaps an essay on the experience of death and on suicide, which appeared posthumously in French.[2] It reflects his personal plight as an active opponent of the Nazis and later as a refugee in France, who finally fell into the hands of the Gestapo, yet refused to take his own life, and died in a concentration camp. This essay shows him to have been much closer to the Catholic position than Scheler, although he never took the final step of conversion.

SELECTIVE BIBLIOGRAPHY

Major Works

Zur Phänomenologie und Theorie der Sympathiegefühle und von Liebe und Hass (1913); second edition under the title *Wesen und Formen der Sympathie* (1923)
  Translations: French (1928), Spanish (1943), English, *The Nature of Sympathy* (1954) by Peter Heath – at times rather free, but faithful to the main meaning; the Introduction by W. Stark is often quite misleading.
Der Formalismus in der Ethik und die materiale Wertethik (1913, 1916)
  Translations: Spanish (1940), French (1955)
Abhandlungen und Aufsätze (1919); second edition under the title *Vom Umsturz der Werte* (1923)
[1]   *Vom Ewigen im Menschen* (1921)
Die Wissensformen und die Gesellschaft (1926)
Die Stellung des Menschen im Kosmos (1928)
  Translations: Spanish (1929), French (1951), English (Beacon Press, to
[2]   appear soon).

Posthumously Published

Philosophische Weltanschauung (1928)
  Translations: English (1958) under the title *Philosophical Perspectives* by Oscar A. Haac – good, except for technical passages.

[1] *Einleitung in die philosophische Anthropologie*, Frankfurt, 1934.
[2] *Essai sur l'expérience de la mort*, Paris, 1940.

Schriften aus dem Nachlass I (1933)
Gesammelte Werke Francke, Bern, 1954 ff..
Scheler's works, published and unpublished are now appearing in a comprehensive edition by Maria Scheler, of which 4 volumes (2, 3, 5, and 10) have come out thus far. It contains valuable editorial comments and indexes. [1]

Monographs in German and French

DUPUY, MAURICE, *La Philosophie de Max Scheler*. Son évolution et son unité. 2 vols. Paris, Presses universitaires, 1959
Comprehensive, scholary work; biographically not quite adequate.
——, *La Philosophie de la religion chez Max Scheler*. Ibid., 1959
This collateral study deals perceptively and critically with Scheler's early phenomenology of religion.
GURVITCH, GEORGES, *Les Tendances actuelles de la philosophie allemande*. Paris, J. Vrin, 1930
Chapter II ("L'intuitionisme émotionel de M.S.") contains a detailed analysis of Scheler's phenomenological philosophy.
KRÄNZLIN, GERHARD, *Max Schelers phänomenologische Systematik*. Leipzig, Hirzel, 1934.
Not without value, but not very penetrating; often quite critical. Extensive bibliography.

Important Articles

HARTMANN, NICOLAI, "Max Scheler" *Kantstudien* XXXIII (1928), IX–XVI
SCHUETZ, ALFRED, "Max Scheler" in Merleau-Ponty, M., ed., *Les Philosophes célèbres*. Paris, Mazenod, 1956, pp. 330–35

Studies in English

BECKER, HOWARD, "Some Forms of Sympathy: A Phenomenological Analysis," *Journal of Social and Abnormal Psychology* XXVI (1931), 58–68
BECKER, HOWARD and DAHLKE, HELMUT OTTO, "Max Scheler's Sociology of Knowledge," *PPR* II, 310–22
BUBER, MARTIN, "The Philosophical Anthropology of Max Scheler," *PPR* VI (1946), 307–21
CLARK, MARY EVELYN, "A Phenomenological System of Ethics," *Philosophy* VII (1932), 414–430, VIII (1933), 52–65 (Clear and sensitive account)
COLLINS, JAMES, "Scheler's Transition from Catholicism to Pantheism," in Ryan, John K., ed., *Philosophical Studies in Honor of the Rev. Ignatius Smith O.P.*, Westminister, Md., Newman, 1952. p. 179–207
FARBER, MARVIN, "Max Scheler on the Place of Man in the Cosmos," *PPR* XIV (1954), 393–400 (Misleading)
GUTHRIE, HUNTER, "Max Scheler's Epistemology of the Emotions," *The Modern Schoolman* XVI (1939), 51–54
HAFKESBRINK, HANNA, "The Meaning of Objectivism and Realism in Max Scheler's Philosophy of Religion: A Contribution to the Understanding of Max Scheler's Catholic Period," *PPR* II (1942), 273–291. (Clear and sympathetic; written by a German student of Moritz Geiger). [2]

HARTMANN, WILFRIED, *Max Scheler Bibliographie*, Stuttgart, Bad Cann-statt. Friedrich Frommann Verlag, 1963

McGILL, V. J., "Scheler's Theory of Sympathy and Love," *PPR* II (1942), 273–291 (One-sided and often unfair)

OESTERREICHER, JOHN M., "Max Scheler and the Faith," *Thomist* XIII (1950), 135–203

SCHILPP, PAUL A., "The Doctrine of 'Illusion' and 'Error' in Scheler's Phenomenology," *Journal of Philosophy* XXIV (1927), 624–633

SCHILPP, PAUL A., "The 'Formal Problems' of Scheler's Sociology of Knowledge," *Philosophical Review* XXXVI (1927), 101–120

SCHILPP, PAUL A., "Max Scheler 1874–1928," *Philosophical Review* XXXXVIII (1929), 574–588

SCHUETZ, ALFRED, "Scheler's Theory of Intersubjectivity and the General Thesis of the Alter Ego," *PPR* II (1942), 323–347

SCHUETZ, ALFRED, "Max Scheler's Epistemology and Ethics," *Review of Metaphysics* XI (1957), 304–314, 486–501 (Best concise account thus far of Scheler's main phenomenological doctrines).

SCHUSTER, GEORGE N., "Introductory Statement to a Symposium on the Significance of Max Scheler for Philosophy and Social Science," *PPR* II (1942), 269–272 (The papers introduced by this statement are of very unequal value and omit Scheler's phenomenology and ethics).

WILLIAMS, RICHARD HAYS, "Scheler's Contributions to the Sociology of Affective Action, with Special Attention to the Problem of Shame," *PPR* II (1942), 348–358

Ph. D. Theses

KÖHLE, ECKHARD JOSEPH, *Personality*. A Study according to the Philosophy of Value and Spirit of Max Scheler and Nicolai Hartmann. Columbia University, 1941; published Trenton N. J., 1941. Bibliography

MUNSTER, RALPH F. W., *The Development of Ethics in the Philosophy of Max Scheler*. A Study in Personalistic Phenomenology. Duke University 1953

[1] SCHNEIDER, Rev. MARIUS, *Max Scheler's Phenomenological Philosophy of Values*. Catholic University, 1951

VAN TUINEN, JACOB, *The Phenomenological Ethics of Max Scheler*. University of Michigan, 1936

WALRAFF, CHARLES, S., *Max Scheler's Theory of Moral Obligation*. University of California, 1939

WELCH, E. PARL, *Max Scheler's Philosophy of Religion*. University of Southern California, 1934

Most Comprehensive Recent Bibliographies

DUPUY-MAURICE, La *Philosophie de Max Scheler*, pp. 741–8

KRÄNZLIN, GERHARD, *Max Schelers phänomenologische Systematik*, pp. 84–97; also Ziegenfuss, Werner, *Philosophenlexikon*, Artikel "Scheler, Max"

VI

MARTIN HEIDEGGER (1889–   ) AS A PHENOMENOLOGIST

1. On Understanding Heidegger

The name of Martin Heidegger overshadows the present scene not only of German but also of Continental and Spanish-American philosophy. This very fact implies an enigma, at least to the Anglo-American world. What can account for the still growing fascination with a thinker of Heidegger's type? Certainly not the volume of his published production. Besides, his largest work, [1] *Sein und Zeit*, is a torso, and according to his own recent announcement it will for ever remain so. Yet it confronts its reader with a language and a style of thinking more demanding, if not actually forbidding, than most other philosophy, present or past. And while some of the circumstances surrounding Heidegger's way of life are highly unconventional compared with those of the typical German university philosopher, neither his personality nor his appearance are sufficient to account for his impact on the academic and non-academic world.

It would be misleading, however, to think that Heidegger has never made an impression on Anglo-American thinkers. A measure of this impression may be found in the tribute which an analytic philosopher like Gilbert Ryle once paid to Heidegger in a review of his magnum opus, which in spite of its severe strictures and negative conclusions contained such sentences as the following:

> I have nothing but admiration for his special undertaking and for such of his achievements in it as I can follow. ... He shows himself to be a thinker of real importance by the immense subtlety and searchingness of his examination of consciousness, by the boldness and originality of his methods and conclusions, and by the unflagging energy with which he

tries to think beyond the stock categories of orthodox philosophy and psychology.[1]

It is also worth mentioning that after Sidney Hook's return from a study trip in Germany in the early thirties John Dewey expressed to him considerable interest in Heidegger, particularly in his conception of the human situation and in his concept of concern (*Sorge*), to which there are indeed not a few parallels in Dewey's own thought.[2]

Another approach to Heidegger's thinking is suggested by the present vogue of Paul Tillich's *Systematic Theology*. For Tillich himself has acknowledged the decisive influence which Heidegger's thought has had on his work since 1924–25, when the two were colleagues at the University of Marburg, i.e., during the time when Heidegger's *Sein und Zeit* was in the making.[3] Heidegger's impact was even stronger in the case of Rudolf Bultmann, whose so-called "demythologization" (*Entmythologisierung*) of New Testament theology is arousing increased interest even outside Germany.[4]

But the fundamental paradox remains. To resolve it fully one would have to consider not only the voice which has aroused such an amazing echo but also the acoustic conditions for its reception in Germany and in other parts of the world. Even before that, a clear and complete presentation and interpre-

---

[1] *Mind* XXXVIII (1929), 355–370.

[2] Personal communication; see also his Portrait: "John Dewey," *The American Scholar* XVII (1948), 108.

[3] "In Marburg, in 1925, I began work on my *Systematic Theology*, the first volume of which appeared in 1951. At the same time that Heidegger was in Marburg as professor of philosophy, influencing some of the best students, existentialism in its twentieth century form crossed my path. It was years before I became fully aware of the impact of this encounter on my own thinking. I resisted, I tried to learn, I accepted the new way of thinking more than the answers it gave" (Kegley, Charles W. and Bretall, Robert W., eds., *The Theology of Paul Tillich*. New York, Macmillan, 1952, "Autobiographical Reflections," p. 14). — See also Paul Tillich, *The Interpretation of History* (New York, Scribner, 1936), p. 39 f. — Tillich's theology stresses, for instance, the distinction between Being and "a being" very much as Heidegger did from *Sein und Zeit* on; see Paul Tillich, *Systematic Theology* I (1951), p. 163 ff.; *Love, Power, and Justice* (1954), pp. 18 ff. Also, Tillich's whole conception of ontology, whose subject is described as *being*, as distinguished from the sciences which deal with *beings*, reflects Heidegger thought. To be sure, thus far Heidegger has steadfastly refused to identify Being with God, as Tillich now does.

[4] Here Heidegger's existential interpretation is used as a means to determine just what the non-mythical sense of the Biblical text implies. See Dinkler, Erich, "Existentialist Interpretation of the New Testament," *Journal of Religion*, XXXII (1952), 87–96; Macquarrie, John, *An Existentialist Theology. A Comparison of Heidegger and Bultmann* (London, SCM Press, 1955).

tation of Heidegger's entire philosophizing, as far as publicly accessible, would be indispensable. Such an assignment would be a staggering one. It must be left to those who are prepared to submerge themselves in Heidegger's writings to the extent of pondering them line by line like any classical text that requires interpretation by a commentary, yet without giving up their critical attitude toward his weird if impressive style.

Luckily, the needs of the present enterprise are more limited. For all it requires is to determine the connection between the Heideggerian enigma and the Phenomenological Movement, on whose development Heidegger has exerted such a fateful and almost fatal influence. This calls merely for the discussion of the phenomenological aspect of his work. To be sure, it cannot be taken for granted that such a separation is feasible. But this possibility is at least suggested by the fact that Heidegger himself has dropped all references to phenomenology from his later writings.

The most formidable hurdle for any attempt to understand Heidegger, particularly the Heidegger of the decisive middle period, is no doubt linguistic. No reader without an exceptional command of German can expect to fathom the sense and the full connotations of Heidegger's language. The delay in English translations is clearly related to this primary difficulty. But even the native German finds himself all too often stymied by Heidegger's way of writing, which would almost call for a translation into ordinary German. For Heidegger has a way of not only forming new terms based on obsolete root meanings, but of using existing words for new and unheard-of purposes without providing a glossary as a key or introducing his new uses by explicit definitions. Thus even the German reader has really no alternative to learning Heidegger's vocabulary just as he learned his mother tongue, i.e., by watching its uses and by trial and error. We shall see later that the problem of language is actually the one which has blocked Heidegger's main attack on his central problem.

The difficulties of Heidegger's style would seem to deepen the enigma of his impact. It therefore seems worth pointing out that it was not until the appearance of *Sein und Zeit* that Heidegger's literary style had fully developed. Hardly any of his peculiarities occur in his earlier publications, such as his thesis on Duns Scotus. In fact, his initial success and reputation was built mainly on his lecturing in Freiburg and Marburg and on the expectations it had aroused. It was only on this foundation that the publication of *Sein und Zeit* in volume VIII of Husserl's phenomenological yearbook made such a deep impression. That the style of Heidegger's teaching differed considerably from that of his writing can be gathered from the recent publication of some of his lecture courses. They show little of the knottiness of the central sections of *Sein und Zeit*. In fact his lecturing is characterized by its "clear and deliberate way," to which even a master of clarity in the Anglo-American world like Ralph Barton Perry testified after attending one of his classes. Also in personal contacts, in his calm plainness and unassuming direct-ness, Heidegger presents a striking contrast not only to his pontifical manner of writing and carefully timed desk perform-ance, but also to the aloofness typical of too many German scholars, a contrast which may have contributed to making his amazing and often mystifying message all the more effective.

However, Heidegger's philosophical significance will have to rest on his publications. There is no way of getting around these. Few, if any, second-hand accounts can pave the way to them. Almost all of those now available in English are marred by the mere fact that they are found in the misleading context of ac-counts of existentialism, which Heidegger repudiates. Most of them fail to realize the development in Heidegger's thinking. And they are even less adequate as introductions to the pheno-menological aspects of Heidegger's work. Thus the challenging problem of providing a real introduction to Heidegger's thinking remains unsolved to this hour. In stating this I do not mean to imply that it can be solved, especially at this stage when im-portant evidence is still missing. Yet the attempt ought to be made, if only for the sake of better relations between the main philosophical currents of our time.

There is one final suggestion which I would like to offer before turning to my limited assignment, all the more since it has a bearing even on the development of Heidegger's attitude toward the phenomenological approach. Since Heidegger's Hölderlin studies began to appear in 1936, it has become manifest that poetry holds a unique place in Heidegger's thinking. In 1954 a little volume "From the Experience of Thought" appeared in which two short poems of his own surround a sequence of reflections consisting of mood-setting half-sentences, striking in their imagery, on one page, and quasi-Presocratic aphorisms on the opposite page. They suggest a synthesis of the styles of Hölderlin and Parmenides, Heidegger's main guides in recent years. This turn to poetry provides perhaps the best clue to Heidegger's secret. It suggests at the same time that he is fundamentally much closer to the poets of the world than to its pure philosophers. Coleridge, Thoreau, and T. S. Eliot are more congenial to him than even a philosopher-poet like Santayana.

2. Heidegger's Place in the History of Phenomenology

How far is Heidegger's thinking rightfully to be included in the history of the Phenomenological Movement? This question, which is of considerable importance for the present enterprise, is usually not even raised; nor is it easy to answer it.[1] The accepted story, especially among outsiders, says that Heidegger is Husserl's legitimate heir, as evidenced by his succession to Husserl's chair in Freiburg; that consequently Heidegger's philosophy represents the rightful development of Husserl's phenomenology; and that the case for or against phenomenology can be settled by looking at its logical outcome in Heidegger's work. But there are also those who, partly because of their better knowledge of Husserl's final repudiation of Heidegger's thinking, and perhaps also from a desire to acquit phenomenology of responsibility for Heidegger's philosophy of existence, see in him merely a corruptor of, or even a deserter from, "orthodox" phenomenology.

The history of Heidegger's association with phenomenology is almost entirely the history of his association with Edmund Husserl. His contacts with Scheler in the later twenties came at a time when Scheler's interest in phenomenology as such had weakened considerably, and when philosophical anthropology

---

[1] See however Delfgaauw, B., "La phénoménologie chez Martin Heidegger," *Études philosophiques IX* (1954), 50–56, and Hyppolite, Jean, "Ontologie et phéno-ménologie chez Martin Heidegger," *ibid.* 307–14.

was their main common concern. No serious contacts with the Munich Circle seem to have occurred.

A final appraisal of the relationship between Husserl and Heidegger presupposes first of all adequate knowledge of the facts. To be sure, important evidence, such as the complete Husserl-Heidegger correspondence, is still inacccessible. But enough material is available to reconstruct at least the outline of the story. As far as Husserl's side of the relationship is concerned, it has all the earmarks of a personal tragedy, where fault-finding would be as futile as it would be silly. Besides, most of it is irrelevant to our story, which concerns only the temporary association and final estrangement between two thinkers too independent-minded and too committed to their distinctive tasks to allow more than a temporary association. There is, however, need for a simple recording of the chronological facts in this relationship.

Apparently there were no personal contacts between Husserl and Heidegger during the Göttingen period. True, Heidegger's interest in Husserl was strong enough to make him wish for a chance to study under him personally. But financial necessities prevented this and forced him to complete his studies at the University of Freiburg in his native state of Baden.[1] When Husserl arrived in Freiburg in 1916, Heidegger had not only completed his academic education under Heinrich Rickert, but had been admitted to the faculty as a *Privatdozent*, whose inaugural lecture on July 27, 1915 dealt with the concept of time in historiography. The preface to his habilitation thesis on Duns Scotus, in which he acknowledged Husserl's help in connection with his request for a publication grant, suggests that the first personal meetings occurred immediately upon Husserl's arrival. But it was apparently not until the end of Heidegger's military service during the First World War and the beginning of his full scale teaching that closer contact was established. Heidegger was therefore never Husserl's pupil in a sense of the term which would justify the expectation of a special personal loyalty to Husserl, any more than this could be expected of the Munich phenomenologists. Moreover, Heidegger was an established scholar in his own right, with a record of several publications,

---

[1] Oral communication.

before he had ever met Husserl. However, from then on an intense philosophical and personal relationship and friendship between the full professor and the young *Privatdozent* began to take shape, particularly after Heidegger had become Husserl's assistant in his academic duties. In order to fully understand this relationship one has to realize that Husserl started his Freiburg teaching with an almost entirely new group of students, Edith Stein being the only candidate for the Ph.D. degree, soon to become his private assistant, who had come with him. What was even more important, Husserl's philosophical development since the publication of the first volume of his *Ideen* with its new idealistic interpretation of phenomenology had left him practically isolated. All the more anxious was he to attract mature students and scholars as collaborators in the tasks of coping with an ever increasing number of new problems and of organizing the accumulating piles of his manuscripts. Husserl soon discovered the originality and vigor of his new colleague. At the same time, Heidegger's lively interest in phenomenology aroused in him hopes for close co-operation, especially after his forthcoming retirement, and of Heidegger's eventual succession to and continuation of his own work where he would have to leave off. It is probably an unanswerable question how far Heidegger himself gave encouragement to this hope. However, the fact that Heidegger identified himself with the cause of phenomenology is manifest from the very titles of his lectures from 1919 on, when he first announced a course on "Phenomenology and Transcendental Philosophy of Value," the latter meaning clearly the Neo-Kantian value theory of Heinrich Rickert. From then on until his transfer to Marburg as full professor in 1923, Heidegger offered every semester courses and seminars in whose titles the word 'phenomenology' occurred. This continued even during the five momentous years which he spent in philosophical independence at Marburg. During the first semester after his return to Freiburg as Husserl's successor, he again announced phenomenological seminars. All the more conspicuous is the total absence of the word from Heidegger's academic offerings after that, except in connection with a course (in 1930–31) on Hegel's *Phänomenologie des Geistes*.

There is parallel evidence in Heidegger's publications. The

Duns Scotus book of 1916, without expressing an explicit commitment, displayed intense interest in Husserl's phenomenology and an attempt to use it for a historical interpretation. *Sein und Zeit*, which appeared in the phenomenological *Jahrbuch* while Heidegger was still in Marburg, and which in its separate book edition carried a special dedication to Husserl (*"in Verehrung und Freundschaft"*), contained the most pronounced espousal of phenomenology, although the specific references to Husserl are relatively rare and insignificant. However, the word "phenomenology" is missing in "Vom Wesen des Grundes," Heidegger's contribution to the *Festschrift* for Husserl's seventieth birthday in 1929, published one year after Heidegger's return to Freiburg.[1] *Kant und das Problem der Metaphysik*, appearing during the same year, uses the term only twice in relatively minor places in connection with the characterization of Kant's *Critique of Pure Reason*, which, in Heidegger's eyes, turns out to be ultimately inadequate for a task which he himself intends to complete by his new *Fundamentalontologie*. After that I can trace only two more explicit references to phenomenology in Heidegger's writings. Both occur in the *"Letter on Humanism"* (1949), which includes Heidegger's most illuminating philosophical autobiography thus far. Here, after acknowledging the relative superiority of the Marxian interpretation of history to all others (because of its awareness of the alienation and homelessness of modern man in the world) Heidegger states:

[1]

> Since neither Husserl nor Sartre, as far as I can see thus far, recognize the essential place of the historical factor (*das Geschichtliche*) in Being, neither phenomenology (*die Phänomenologie*) nor existentialism has entered the dimension in which alone a constructive debate with Marxism can take place.[2]

This statement sounds as if Heidegger had dissociated himself completely from all phenomenology, and not only from Husserl's version of it. It would, however, be rash to infer on the strength of one such passage alone that Heidegger has repudiated phenomenology lock, stock, and barrel. In the very same letter

---

[1] This *Festschrift*, whose editors are not mentioned, but which was clearly prepared by Heidegger without the cooperation of the older collaborators of the *Jahrbuch*, has no dedicatory preface, but carries a motto from Plato's *Sophistes* (254 A), Heidegger's favorite Plato dialogue at the time, which, in its characterization of the philosopher, sounds like a curious homage to Husserl.

[2] *Platons Lehre von der Wahrheit*, p. 87.

there occurs another sentence which emphasizes that he wants to "hold on to the essential help of phenomenological viewing" (*die wesentliche Hilfe des phänomenologischen Sehens*), while rejecting the "improper aspiration" to "science" (*Wissenschaft*) and "research" (*Forschung*) (p. 110). Besides, Heidegger has never rejected the Phenomenological Movement in its entirety. What, then, is the meaning of and the deeper reason for his abandonment of all phenomenological terminology? Here again it becomes important to secure more factual information about the development of the relations between Husserl and Heidegger in the period of their actual co-operation.

During Heidegger's Marburg years his direct contacts with Husserl were naturally less frequent, although Heidegger kept passing through Freiburg on the way to his ski-hut in the Black Forest. There was, however, one attempt at concrete co-operation whose failure throws considerable light on the entire relationship. Presumably as a sequel to his London lectures in 1922 Husserl was asked to write an article on Phenomenology for the 13th edition of the *Encyclopaedia Britannica*. He seems to have considered this occasion important enough to invite Heidegger to collaborate with him on a joint statement, based of course on his own draft: this would also give him a chance to make Heidegger a more active participant in the latest phase of his transcendental phenomenology. The history of this article has been described in considerable detail, though not exhaustively, by Walter Biemel.[1] In the present context the following documents deserve special attention:

α. Heidegger's unpublished independent draft of 1927, consisting of eleven typewritten pages, clearly prepared after he had already completed *Sein und Zeit*, with Husserl's annotations to it.

β. Heidegger's comments on Husserl's main draft, representing Heidegger's attempt to formulate the common ground as he saw it at the time.

Heidegger's draft is particularly instructive if compared with [1] Husserl's preceding version. For here Husserl, after a brief introductory definition, had started immediately with a dis-

---

[1] "Husserls Encyclopaedia Britannica Artikel und Heideggers Anmerkungen dazu," *Tijdschrift voor Philosophie* XII (1950), 246–280.

cussion of phenomenological psychology. Thus making the
subjective sphere his point of departure, he had moved in the
second part to the more radical form of subjective phenomenology
– transcendental phenomenology. Heidegger's draft begins with
a general introduction of more than two typewritten pages
dealing with "the idea of philosophy and the regress (*Rückgang*)
to consciousness," in which the primary concern of all philosophy
is characterized as "being qua being," which is, as we shall see,
Heidegger's one pervading theme. Parmenides is mentioned as
the first thinker to state it. Now to Heidegger the remarkable
thing is the fact that from the very start this problem has been
linked up with a reflection (*Besinnung*) upon the thought about
this "being." Phenomenology is then characterized as "the basic
realization of the necessity of a regress to consciousness, the
radical and express determination of the way and of the laws
governing the steps of this regress, and the fundamental demarcation and the systematic explorations of the field opened up
during this regress." [1] While this formulation seems to go far
toward meeting Husserl's insistence on the all-importance of
the study of transcendental subjectivity, Heidegger adds at
once: "It stands in the service of ... the question about the
being of what is (*Sein des Seienden*) in the articulated variety of
its types and stages" – an addition which establishes the connection with the theme of *Sein und Zeit*. Psychology as a positive science is then declared incapable of taking over the task of
the needed science of subjective experience in which transcendent
being constitutes itself. – After this introduction Heidegger's
draft runs almost completely parallel to Husserl's account of
phenomenological psychology as published in the rather free
translation of the original in the *Encyclopaedia Britannica*. The
published version shows that Husserl left out Heidegger's
introduction completely. Judging from his notes and bracketings,
he seems to have objected particularly to the passages in which
Heidegger characterized the goal of philosophy as concern with
Being.

---

[1] "Die grundsätzliche Einsicht in die Notwendigkeit des Rückganges auf das
Bewusstsein, die radikale und ausdrückliche Bestimmung des Weges und der Schritt-
gesetze dieses Rückganges, die prinzipielle Umgrenzung und systematische Durch-
forschung des auf diesem Rückgang zu erschliessenden Feldes bezeichnen wir als
Phänomenologie."

For the second part of Husserl's article, entitled "Transcendental Phenomenology," the Husserl Archives contain no draft from Heidegger's hand. The half-empty last page of the typescript makes it unlikely that there ever was one. There exists, however, a letter from Heidegger, dated October 22, 1927, in [1] which he attempts to define his position with regard to transcendental phenomenology and to the transcendental reduction in particular, very much along the lines of the sections in *Sein und Zeit* which discuss transcendental philosophy (pp. 207 ff.). Reading these statements, particularly in retrospect and in the light of the parallel statements and silences of *Sein und Zeit*, it seems difficult not to see how completely Heidegger had moved away from Husserl's position, how wide the gap between their interpretations of phenomenology had become, and how little of Husserl's transcendental philosophy, and particularly of his transcendental reduction, was acceptable to Heidegger. In fact Husserl's letter of December 26, 1927 to Roman Ingarden contained the statement that "Heidegger has not grasped the whole meaning of the phenomenological reduction." It is thus not surprising that the final version of the *Britannica* article does not seem to include any of Heidegger's draft. Thus the attempt to use the occasion to bring about an agreement between the two protagonists of Freiburg phenomenology had just the opposite result.

A second case of an attempted collaboration was Heidegger's editing of Husserl's Göttingen lectures on inner time consciousness, dating back to 1905 and 1910, in the volume of the *Jahrbuch* (IX, 1929) that followed immediately upon the publication of *Sein und Zeit*. Heidegger's interest in such a topic was only natural. However, his brief preface introduces these lectures merely as supplements to the *Logische Untersuchungen* without so much as a reference to Husserl's later intensified analyses. It may well be that it was this fact which left Husserl disappointed with the results of Heidegger's editing.

In spite of mounting misgivings, Husserl clung to the hope that he could win Heidegger over after his return to Freiburg. Hence he submitted his name as that of his only qualified successor. None of this hope materialized when Heidegger took over Husserl's chair in the fall of 1928. Instead, after the first two months, their contacts became less and less frequent.

Around this time Husserl also returned to an intensive study of *Sein und Zeit*, partly with the aid of his new assistant, Eugen Fink, who had been trained by both Husserl and Heidegger. His marginal comments to this work and to Heidegger's Kant book (*Kant und das Problem der Metaphysik*) reveal his growing awareness of the differences between himself and Heidegger and his suspicion of hidden attacks in Heidegger's text.[1] Apparently his main impression was that Heidegger, by substituting human existence (*Dasein*) for the pure ego, had transformed phenomenology into anthropology, the very same anthropology which Husserl had once fought in the first volume of his *Logische Untersuchungen* as a species of psychologism. The absence of any reference to Husserl's doctrine of the phenomenological or transcendental reduction and, in fact, to practically all of his recent work made him conclude that Heidegger's phenomenology had not yet passed beyond the natural or "naive" attitude, and that his philosophy was simply another form of "objectivism," "naturalism," or "realism."

Indications are that Husserl began to express his disapproval of Heidegger's phenomenology with increasing frankness soon after Heidegger's return to Freiburg. The most explicit repudiation of Heidegger's philosophizing appeared on the last pages of the terminal volume of the *Jahrbuch* (XI, 1930), notably in a *Nachwort* to the *Ideen*, which presented a slightly amplified version of Husserl's preface to the English translation by W. R. Boyce Gibson. Here, in an opening section omitted from the translation, Husserl protested against certain objections not explicitly listed, but clearly attributed to Heidegger, and declared sweepingly that all of them were

based on misunderstandings and fundamentally upon the fact that one misinterprets my phenomenology backwards from a level which it was its very purpose to overcome, in other words, that one has failed to understand the fundamental novelty of the phenomenological reduction and hence the progress from mundane subjectivity (i.e., man) to transcendental subjectivity; consequently that one has remained stuck in an anthropology, whether empirical or a priori, which according to my doctrine has not yet reached the genuine philosophical level, and whose interpretation as philosophy means a lapse into "transcendental anthropologism" or "psychologism." [2]

[1]   [1] For samples of these notes see Alwin Diemer, *Edmund Husserl*, p. 29 f.
      [2] *JPPF* XI (1930), 551; also *Husserliana*, V, 140.

This charge was pressed home further in a lecture on *Phänome-nologie und Anthropologie"* which Husserl gave in Berlin and Frankfurt in 1931,[1] though still without mentioning Heidegger's name. Here anthropologism, which Husserl characterizes as a psychologism that builds phenomenology on human existence *(menschliches Dasein),* is termed the diametrical opposite of transcendental phenomenology. Around this time Husserl also began to refer to Heidegger and Scheler as his philosophical antipodes.

These and similar developments were responsible for the fact that Heidegger dropped all references to phenomenology in his writings and lectures, perhaps also in deference to Husserl's prior claim to the term. Without a formal break, even personal contacts seem to have subsided long before Heidegger became involved in national socialism. There is no sign that Heidegger tried to alleviate Husserl's difficulties during the Nazi regime. But it should be pointed out that the humiliations meted out to Husserl as a racially Jewish member of the Freiburg faculty occurred after the end of Heidegger's official leadership of the university.   [1]

These ascertainable facts make it plain that after Husserl's denunciation Heidegger no longer considered himself a member of the Phenomenological Movement in Husserl's sense. The quiet demise of the phenomenological yearbook, whose management during these years had been chiefly in the hands of Heidegger and Oskar Becker, himself a much closer associate of Heidegger than of Husserl, is additional evidence.

But this does not settle the question whether Heidegger, in accepting Husserl's "excommunication," also meant to dissociate himself from the whole Phenomenological Movement in the wider sense. The fact that he has failed to revive the *Jahrbuch* would seem to suggest that he is at least no longer interested in its continuation. However, a final answer to this question will have to wait for the discussion of Heidegger's own conception of phenomenology and its development later on.   [1a]

3. Heidegger's Basic Theme: The Quest for Being and Time

Before we pursue further the question of the nature and function of Heidegger's phenomenology it will be necessary to

1 *PPR* II (1941), 1–14.   [2]

clarify Heidegger's general philosophy and its development, at least to an extent which will make it possible to determine and understand the place and function of his phenomenology in this wider framework.

Heidegger recently expressed the characteristic idea that every great thinker "thinks only one single thought" (*einen einzigen Gedanken*).[1] There is no difficulty about discovering such a focal idea in Heidegger's own thinking. One of its most instructive expressions occurs in a seemingly minor place, the postcript to *What is Metaphysics?* of 1934 and reads:

Man alone of all existing things ... experiences the wonder of all wonders: that there are things-in-being (*dass Seiendes ist*).[2]

There is perhaps no better way to describe the basic difference between Heidegger's and Husserl's fundamental purposes than to contrast this sentence with a parallel statement in Husserl's writings: "The wonder of all wonders is the pure ego and pure consciousness." (See p. 87). Heidegger's fundamental wonder is objective Being, Husserl's, subjective consciousness. The two problems are sufficiently connected to account for the temporary coalition between the two. But they are ultimately so far apart that Husserl and Heidegger were bound to part company. This same fundamental difference is also expressed in Heidegger's historical orientation centering in Aristotle and, later, in Parmenides, toward whom Husserl was singularly indifferent, compared with Husserl's focal interest in Descartes, whom Heidegger opposes strenuously.

Heidegger himself claims that he is the first thinker in the whole history of philosophy (including phenomenology, as Husserl deduced with amazement in his marginal comments to *Sein und Zeit*) to have raised explicitly the question concerning the sense of Being.[3] The legitimacy of such a claim presupposes clarification of its meaning.[4] Heidegger is convinced

---

[1] *Was heisst Denken?* p. 20.

[2] *Was ist Metaphysik?* Sixth edition 1951, p. 42. See also *Kant und das Problem der Metaphysik*, 2nd ed., p. 204: "We are familiar with things in being – but being itself? Are we not always attacked by dizziness (*Schwindel*) when we are to define or only to grasp such matters?"

[3] *Einführung in die Metaphysik*, p. 64.

[4] It may be well to recall that Heidegger's mystery of Being as such is not entirely unknown to other thinkers, though not to philosophers in the school sense.

that man lives usually in complete oblivion of the question of Being (*Seinsvergessenheit*). In fact, in his *"Brief über den Humanismus"* he states that *Sein und Zeit* originated from the fundamental experience (*Grunderfahrung*) of the general forgetfulness of Being, an experience which would seem to be the complement of the wonder of Being itself. It is this forgetfulness of Being which Heidegger blames for the decline and crisis of man's history on this planet.

But what precisely is the sense of this question about Being (*Sein*; lately Heidegger sometimes uses the old-fashioned spelling *Seyn* for emphasis)? To begin with, it is not Being itself, but the [1] *meaning* (*Sinn*) of Being which Heidegger wants to explore. At first sight one might think that all that is involved is the discovery of the referents of the word "Being" by a listing of its uses. As a matter of fact, especially in his recently published *Einführung in die Metaphysik*, Heidegger goes to a considerable extent into the etymology and even into the grammar of the word *"sein."* However, beginning with *Sein und Zeit* it becomes apparent, though only gradually and indirectly, that "sense of Being" (*"Sinn von Sein"*) means something much more specific. For here "sense" is characterized mainly as the final end (*das Woraufhin*) which makes a thing intelligible (p. 151). This would seem to presuppose that Being as such has a definite destination. Actually Heidegger tells us that only human existence can be with or without meaning. Being has meaning only insofar as it has import for a human being (*Dasein*),[1] "protrudes" into such a human being (*sofern es in die Verständlichkeit des Daseins hereinsteht*). It would appear, therefore, that the whole question concerning the sense of Being has a rather limited scope, since

---

A particularly striking example can be found in the following passage from Coleridge's *The Friend*:

Hast thou ever raised thy mind to the consideration of existence, in and by itself, as the mere act of existing? Hast thou ever said to thyself thoughtfully, It is! heedless in that moment, whether it were a man before thee, or a flower, or a grain of sand, – without reference, in short, to this or that particular mode or form of existence? If thou hast attained to this, thou wilt have felt the presence of a mystery, which must have fixed thy spirit in awe and wonder. ... Not to be is impossible: to be, incomprehensible. If thou hast mastered this intuition of absolute existence, thou wilt have learned likewise that it was this, and no other, which in the earlier ages seized the nobler minds, the elect among men, with a sort of sacred horror. ... The power which evolved this idea of being, being in its essence, being limitless, comprehending its own limits in its dilatation, and condensing itself into its own apparent mounds – how shall we name it? ... (*The Complete Works*. New York, Harper, 1868, II, 463 f.).

[1] I shall translate Heidegger's peculiar use of the German word *Dasein* for the thing-in-being called man (SZ p. 11), by "human being" or "human existent."

it affects only its relation to man. However, in his later writings Heidegger seems to have expanded the meaning of the question considerably. Thus the introduction to the sixth edition of *What is Metaphysics?* (1951) characterizes "sense" as the "accessible or open area in which something can be understood." Also *Sinn von Sein* and *Wahrheit des Seins* are here identified.[1] Both expressions seem to designate being in its capacity of being knowable.

A fuller understanding of the significance of Heidegger's wonder also presupposes a clear grasp of two related conceptions, that of the "ontological difference" and that of "mode of being" (*Seinsart*).

The ontological difference (*ontologische Differenz*) is the distinction between *Sein* and *Seiendes*. It is not quite easy to render this distinction in English, especially in the absence of an unambiguous participle equivalent to *Seiendes;* "what has being" or "thing-in-being" (a suggestion by B. Q. Morgan) may be the most adequate equivalent and less artificial than Ralph Manheim's "essent." It is Heidegger's contention that the neglect of this distinction is responsible for the increasing failure not only of western philosophy but even of western civilization. For they became more and more diverted from a contemplation of Being to a study of, and finally to the technical use and subjugation of, the things-in-being. Thus metaphysics, science, and technology increasingly take the place of what should properly be called ontology or the study of being. Specifically metaphysics as it has developed since the time of the early Greeks has become sidetracked almost completely into research on the things-in-being, their natures and their uses.

How far is it possible to study Being in independence of the things-in-being, as Heidegger's demand for a fundamental revision of all previous philosophy implies? There is hardly any explicit answer to this question in his published writings. The approach in *Sein und Zeit*, however, suggests that it is primarily, if not exclusively, by the analysis of a specific "thing-in-being," namely human being (*Dasein*), that Being can be understood. Thus Being appears to be a dependent attribute of things-in-being, an abstract property or dependent part. Yet Heidegger

---

[1] p. 17, see also *Vom Wesen der Wahrheit, Anmerkung* (p. 26).

seems to assign it much higher dignity, particularly in the later phases of his philosophy. For here Being assumes an active role, revealing itself to or hiding itself from thinking, and even determining the fate of the things-in-being. Metaphorically Heidegger compares it to a lightning or storm.[1] In this respect, Being reminds one to some extent of the Aristotelian and Thomist conception of existentia as an active "form." One of the crucial questions for Heidegger's philosophy of Being is how far not only the "ontological difference," but this conception of the place of Being in relation to the things-in-being is tenable. Otherwise the whole emphasis on Being at the expense of the things-in-being may amount to a case of "misplaced concreteness" (Whitehead), i.e., of hypostatizing Being into a separate entity.

Being as such, however mysterious, may at first sight seem to be a rather undifferentiated, if not monotonous, topic which hardly lends itself to very extensive and illuminating study. What relieves this possible uniformity is the fact that Being occurs in a variety of forms (Seinsarten). Even before Heidegger, German philosophers were in the habit of distinguishing, for instance, between real being and ideal being (the being of mathematical entities, of Platonic Ideas, or of values). Heidegger, to be sure, rejects, or rather ignores, these earlier divisions. Instead, he introduces such types of being as the mere occurrence of physical objects (Vorhandensein), the "availability" of daily utensils (Zuhandensein, literally: at-handedness), to which he even assigns priority in our immediate experience, and the various modes of being of man, the human being. Especially at the time of Sein und Zeit the study of the modes of being in the human being is the foundation of Heidegger's enterprise. In its course Heidegger distinguishes between such constitutions of being (Seinsverfassungen) as existence (Existenz), moods (Stimmungen), concern (Sorge), or being-toward-death (Sein zum Tode). This raises the question as to the difference between Heidegger's concept of "mode of being" and that of other qualitative charac-

---

[1] Holzwege, p. 32; Vorträge und Aufsätze p. 229. Karl Löwith, Heidegger, Denker in dürftiger Zeit (S. Fischer Verlag, 1953), p. 39, points out a strange retreat from this position between the fourth edition of What is Metaphysics? (1934), where Being is characterized as independent of the things-in-being, and the fifth edition (1940), where Heidegger states that Being never occurs without things-in-being.

teristics of the things-in-being. No explicit discussion of this fundamental concept occurs in Heidegger's published writings.[1] In its absence it seems hard to justify his determined attempt to distinguish his separation of an "ontological study of human existence" confined to the modes of being (*existentiale Analytik*) from an analytics of existence in all its qualitative features. This may not invalidate the merits of Heidegger's accounts qua selective analyses of certain features of human existence; but it makes it dubious how far what he offers can be taken as an account of the human mode of being and as indicative of being in general. Also, the lack of a clear concept of mode of Being threatens to blur the borderlines between Heidegger's "ontology" on the one hand and science – anthropology in particular – on the other. The clarification of the concept of mode of being would seem to be crucial both for an understanding and for the ultimate evaluation of Heidegger's enterprise.

While thus Being (in contrast to the things-in-being) and the modes of being (in contrast to the qualitative differences among the things-in-being) form the central theme of Heidegger's thinking, at least a second theme must be mentioned at the very start: time. It occurs as the companion of Being in the title of Heidegger's central work. Actually, it can be traced even in his writings before *Sein und Zeit*. However, Heidegger's concern with time is not independent of his primary theme, Being. For Being is to him essentially temporal. The idea of a timeless or even eternal being is for him illegitimate. Hence he also calls time in rather Husserlian but indefinite terms "the possible horizon for an understanding of Being," a formulation which implies that time is the most promising frame of reference for the exploration of Being. But Being is described not only as temporal but also as historical. The full meaning of this characterization can be understood only in the light of Heidegger's conception of history. Thus, by its essence, Being has history, a history which is actually its own doing as well as its undergoing.

If thus Being, in contradistinction to the things-in-being, and time, as its frame of reference, represent the persistent themes of Heidegger's philosophizing, it seems somewhat surprising

---

[1] For this problem see also Alphonse de Waelhens, *La Philosophie de Martin Heidegger* (Louvain, 1942), p. 309.

that Heidegger's thought, especially in his own eyes, has been subject to so many misinterpretations. These are reflected particularly in the various labels that have been attached to it. Specifically, Heidegger's philosophy has been classified interchangeably as existentialism, philosophy of existence, philosophical anthropology, metaphysics, or ontology. Heidegger himself has protested against all these labels, in some cases from the very beginning, in others only in the course of his later development, but certainly only with limited success. The facts behind these protests are briefly the following:

α. Heidegger has always disclaimed to be an existentialist or even a *philosopher of existence*. For human existence is to him neither the primary nor the ultimate philosophical problem. The belief that his is a philosophy of existence is actually the result of the incompleteness of *Sein und Zeit*. For while Heidegger planned to use his existential studies only as an entering wedge for his major problem, the sense of Being in general, the non-appearance of the later parts meant that only his analytics of existence was available. The impressiveness of the published sections was responsible for the fact that they became effective as studies of human existence for their own sake, all the more since the direction of Heidegger's next steps remained largely in the dark. In other words, in the public eye Heidegger became an existentialist despite himself.[1]

β. Heidegger has always denied being a philosophical anthropologist after the manner of Max Scheler. The impression that he is one has arisen chiefly since his Kant book, which, even more than *Sein und Zeit*, used the human being as its point of departure, and stressed Kant's interest in man as an essentially metaphysics-minded being. Even Husserl, as seen above, shared this view about Heidegger. But while some aspects of philosophical anthropology were of considerable interest to Heidegger during his middle period, he certainly used them only as stepping stones on the way to ontology.

γ. Heidegger no longer wants to be considered a *metaphysician*. The contrary impression is due particularly to his Freiburg

---

[1] See "Brief über den Humanismus" in *Platons Lehre von der Wahrheit*, p. 73; Letter to Jean Wahl in *Bulletin de la Société Française de philosophie* XXXVII (1937), p. 193.

inaugural address of 1929 on "What is Metaphysics?," to his book on *Kant and the Problem of Metaphysics*, and to his various lecture courses on metaphysics, one of which was published under the old name as late as 1953. However, after 1936 Heidegger began to announce the need of an *Überwindung* of metaphysics, a word which at first sight seems to mean a conquest or over-coming of metaphysics, but which Heidegger, who later came to regret this phrase as misleading, now connects with the German word *verwinden*, meaning literally "getting over a painful experi-ence"; he thus implies that metaphysics was a necessary phase in the history of Being.[1] What is involved for Heidegger is the distinction between Being and thing-in-being. He now holds metaphysics responsible for the fateful preoccupation with the thing-in-being (*Seiendes*), instead of with the fundamental theme of Being itself. Obviously, Heidegger's protest against being called a metaphysician has to be judged in the light of this peculiar definition and interpretation of metaphysics.

δ. But Heidegger does not even want to be classed any longer as an ontologist. At the time of *Sein und Zeit*, ontology, in con-trast to metaphysics, was characterized as the study of Being itself, and this study was described as the only worthy subject of a phenomenological philosophy. Its task was to be prepared for by a "fundamental ontology" (*Fundamentalontologie*) of human being (*Dasein*). In recent years, however, Heidegger has come to the conclusion that the old term is too closely linked up with traditional metaphysics to express his own meaning.

ε. In fact, for similar reasons, Heidegger now even rejects the very name "philosophy." This name has become so hopelessly discredited that it can no longer serve as the proper title for Heidegger's new way of thinking. For "philosophy" is in fact the "enemy" of thinking.[2] The proper name for Heidegger's philosophizing is Thought of Being (*Denken des Seins*). Never-theless it is still true even for him that such "thinking" is based on "love of wisdom." [3]

Thus in Heidegger's own eyes Thought of Being is something utterly unique and unclassifiable. We need not examine this

---

[1] *Vorträge und Aufsätze*, p. 71 ff.
[2] *Holzwege*, p. 247.
[3] "Brief über den Humanismus" in *Platons Lehre von der Wahrheit*, p. 119.

implicit claim in the present context. The question which concerns us is whether and to what extent Heidegger's thinking can still be considered phenomenology. Heidegger's silence on this point is certainly not without significance. It is, as he intimated to me in conversation, also related to his new aversion to all labels and traditional classifications. This does not yet answer the   [1] question, however, of how far not only the name "phenomenology" but also the thing is absent or has disappeared from his thought. It is this question which will concern us now.

4. The Development of Heidegger's Thought of Being

It is not only Heidegger's 'Being' which has a history. This is also true of his thinking about Being. For our purposes it will be important to trace at least its major stages.

Even a merely factual account, let alone a full understanding, of Heidegger's intellectual history would presuppose much more biographical material than is at present available, especially in the absence of almost all autobiographical statements.[1] At least in this respect Heidegger's reticence expresses the complete subordination of his personality to the *Sache*, the matter under consideration; the first personal pronoun is unusually rare in Heidegger's writing.

On the basis of Heidegger's writings I shall distinguish three main periods in his development relevant to the present enterprise. They are not marked by abrupt breaks but rather by accelerated transformations. There is a preparatory period in which Heidegger formulates his basic theme, but is still in search of an adequate method of attacking it. After the personal encounter with Husserl begins the period of the maturation of *Sein und Zeit*, in which phenomenology is the dominant methodological principle. A third period is characterized by the abandonment of the plan of *Sein und Zeit*, and by a method which no longer emphasizes phenomenology.

---

[1] Some indications about the world of his early childhood can be found in a little privately printed autobiographical sketch, *Der Feldweg*, written after his sixtieth birthday. More significant data, especially about his later philosophical development, can be derived from the *Brief über den Humanismus* and from the chronological notes to the smaller essays and lectures published since *Sein und Zeit* in front or in the back of these publications.   [2]

a. PREPARATORY PERIOD – The *Feldweg* depicts Heidegger as the little son of the sexton of St. Martin's church in
Messkirch, Baden, "whose hands often rubbed themselves hot
in ringing the church bell ... which had its peculiar relationship
to time and temporality." It is generally known that until 1911
Heidegger was first a novice in a Jesuit seminary in Freiburg.
As to the reasons for and the form of his leaving, no authentic
information is available. It is not even known whether and to
what extent his obvious move away from the Catholic Church
has led to a formal severance of his ties with it. In any event,
lately Heidegger has protested vigorously against being classed
as an atheist.

For one piece of significant information about his philosophical
development I am indebted to Martin Heidegger personally:
The first philosophical book, put into his hands casually by one
[1]   of his teachers at the Seminary, that made a lasting impression
on his mind was a doctoral dissertation on the multiple meanings
of being in Aristotle (*Von der mannigfachen Bedeutung des Seienden nach Aristoteles);* its author was Franz Brentano. It would be
hard to understand how this comparatively dry though most
scholarly and acute treatise could have affected Heidegger so
deeply, unless the question of the meaning of Being had already
been simmering in him at that early period.

Heidegger did his Ph. D. work under the supervision of Heinrich Rickert in Freiburg. Even before its completion in 1913
he published a critical survey on recent research in logic for a
Catholic magazine.[1] It showed his familiarity with the whole
range of logical studies, including even the mathematical logic of
Russell and Whitehead. Husserl is mentioned repeatedly. Thus
he writes:

We would like to assign far-reaching significance to Husserl's circumspect
and most felicitously formulated investigations. For they really broke
the spell of psychologism and set in motion the clarification of principles
mentioned before (p. 466).

Besides, Husserl is credited with having at the same time
"founded" phenomenology (the "study of the meaning of acts")
theoretically "and having done successful work in this difficult

---

[1] *Literarische Rundschau für das katholische Deutschland* XXXVIII (1912),
465–472, 517–524, 565–570.

area" (p. 520). Heidegger's Ph.D. thesis dealt with the theory of judgment according to psychologism, much in the free Neo-Kantian spirit of the Freiburg philosophy of the time. The sections published in two instalments in one of the leading philosophical periodicals of the day[1] show solid workmanship in the traditional style. Here Heidegger identifies psychologistic elements not only in Wilhelm Wundt but also in Franz Brentano and the later work of Theodor Lipps. Husserl's critique of psychologism is mentioned only in passing at the very start of the thesis in words almost identical with those of the earlier survey.

The year 1912 also saw the publication of a brief article, "Das Realitätsproblem in der modernen Philosophie," in the Catholic *Philosophisches Jahrbuch der Görresgesellschaft* (XXV, 353–363) on the problem of reality in modern philosophy. Its main ostensible purpose is a discussion of the critical realism of Oswald Külpe, the founder of the Würzburg School, recommending with minor reservations his epistemological work to the attention of Aristotelian Scholastics, with whom Heidegger still seems to identify himself. Perhaps even more important is the fact that the article expresses for the first time Heidegger's concern with the problem of Being, though in the traditional form of the epistemological problem of reality. Against a cavalier dismissal of this problem he insists that "the energetic liberation (*Sichlosringen*) from the leaden deadweight (*Bleilast*) of a supposed truism (*Selbstverständlichkeit*) is a necessary condition for a deeper realization of a task which calls for solution." Also the article presents in detail the case against Humean and Machian "conscientialism" (*Konszientialismus*) and against Kantian phenomenalism in a way which makes Heidegger's later tacit refusal to follow Husserl's phenomenological idealism much more intelligible. Again Husserl's name appears only once in a footnote in connection with the critique of psychologism in logic.

The momentous thesis which Heidegger submitted on the occasion of his admission as a *Privatdozent* to the University of Freiburg in 1915 dealt on the surface with a merely historical subject: *Duns Scotus' Doctrine of Categories and Meanings.*

---

[1] *Zeitschrift für Philosophie und philosophische Kritik* CLV (1914), 148–172; CLVI (1915), 41–78.

However, it is noteworthy that in choosing a medieval thinker Heidegger picked Duns Scotus, an "individual thinker with unmistakably modern features" (p. 12), rather than Thomas Aquinas. The main basis for his study was the so-called "*Grammatica speculativa*," incidentally the very same text which had attracted Charles Sanders Peirce on his way to his "phenomenological" studies of the categories, so much so that he called himself a Scotist realist[1], but which since then has been traced back by Martin Grabmann – who gives high praise to Heidegger's acute interpretation "in the terminology of phenomenology" – to an otherwise unknown magister Thomas of Erfurt.[2]

The contents of Heidegger's seemingly rather specialized and remote study are of much greater significance for his development than would appear from the title. For it shows Heidegger in full transition not only from scholastic philosophy but even from Rickert's transcendental philosophy to Husserl, in fact not the Husserl of the *Logische Untersuchungen* but of the *Ideen*. This is all the more remarkable since at that time Heidegger was not yet in personal contact with Husserl, although the concluding chapter may have been written after Husserl's arrival in Freiburg. Actually, Heidegger's first book shows more of the letter and the spirit of Husserl's early phenomenology than any of his later writings. Besides, it reveals in retrospect remarkable indications of Heidegger's entire later development, although it still maintains connections with his scholastic and theistic past.

It is true that on its face the book carries a dedication to his main academic teacher, Heinrich Rickert (*in dankbarster Verehrung*), and that it often uses the language of his philosophy. Also, while intimating considerable reservations, Heidegger still expresses great hopes for the theory of value (Preface and p. 235), a term which he has since then rejected with increasing vehemence. However, a glimpse at the index of persons reveals that, while both Rickert and Husserl are the most frequently quoted authors, there is even a slight edge in favor of Husserl. In addition to that, Husserl's decisive importance is stressed not only for the "pure logic and theory of meanings" (p. 14 footnote

---

[1] Charles K. McKeon, "Peirce's Scotistic Realism" in Wiener, Philip P. and Young, Frederic H. eds., *Studies in the Philosophy of Charles Sanders Peirce* (*Harvard University Press*, 1952), pp. 238–50.

[2] *Mittelalterliches Geistesleben* (München, Max Hueber, 1926), I, p. 116 ff.

1), but also for the "phenomenology of the noetic acts" (p. 102). Intentionality in Duns Scotus is interpreted in Husserlian terms (p. 130). Finally, Husserl's statements about "pure consciousness" are cited as "giving a decisive preview (*Durchblick*) of the richness of consciousness" and as "destroying the often pronounced opinion about the emptiness of consciousness in general" (p. 234, footnote).

These appraisals, in combination with the extensive programmatic statements in the introductory and concluding chapters, offer considerable clues as to the reasons for Heidegger's turn toward a Husserlian phenomenology, including even its emphasis on the subjective. In his by no means uncritical account of medieval philosophy Heidegger stresses its lack of methodical consciousness, its missing urge and courage to ask questions independent of authority, and the absence of a connection between abstract principles and concrete life:

The Middle Ages lack what makes the characteristic of the modern spirit: the liberation of the subject from his ties with his environment, the firm establishment in his own life. ... For medieval man, the stream of his peculiar life with its manifold entanglements, diversions, and reflections in its varied and widely ramified conditioning is mostly buried (*verschüttet*), and is not recognized as such. (p. 8)

True, Heidegger makes a strong plea for the scholastic method, but only because it includes "elements of phenomenological intuiting (*Betrachtung*), perhaps more than any other" (p. 11). He also points out that "at least insofar as it is permeated by the genuine spirit of Aristotle" it is oriented toward descriptive content rather than toward an empirical and genetic explanation. But he also admits that its metaphysical way of thinking cancels and even makes impossible the "phenomenological reduction." Ultimately, Heidegger stresses the need for intensified study of the scholastic psychology, which is anything but psychologistic and is favorable to a study of the phenomena of intentionality. Its theory of meaning represents a good case of a going back to the subjective act of signifying. Then he adds revealingly:

I consider the philosophical, in fact the phenomenological exploration of the mystical, ethico-theological, and ascetic literature of medieval scholasticism as particularly urgent for decisive insight into the basic character of scholastic psychology (p. 15).

In this context Heidegger reveals his plan of a study of Master Eckhart's mysticism (p. 232 note).

Thus it is strikingly clear that at the time of the thesis Husserl's emphasis on subjectivity fitted in extremely well with Heidegger's reservations against, and criticisms of, scholastic philosphizing. It provided for Heidegger the modern balance against the traditional scholastic objectivism from which he came. Presumably this was another reason why he had chosen Duns Scotus as a symbol for his new enterprise.

Finally, the Duns Scotus book foreshadows Heidegger's next phase by linking it with his basic theme: Being. For in spite of the need of a subjective logic to supplement the objective logic of scholasticism he announces the ultimate need of a translogical *metaphysics* (the word is printed in bold face) as the real optics (*eigentliche Optik*) of philosophy, which is to go beyond the logical problems of categories and meanings. For the first time a brief footnote (p. 237) expresses the hope of an early, more detailed study about Being, Value, and Negation, which is to include basic definitions (*prinzipielle Festsetzungen*). Here is the nucleus of *Sein und Zeit*. But there are also other signs of future developments, e.g., in the demand for a breakthrough through the totality of the knowable to "true reality" and "real truth" (p. 236).

The Duns Scotus thesis also announces the theme of history. The "living spirit," which is said to underlie the whole logico-epistemological sphere with its problems of categories and meanings, is said to be essentially historical. A historical philosophy of this living spirit, as Heidegger seems to envisage it in conclusion, would embrace both philosophy and mysticism. For philosophy as a mere rationalistic structure is powerless, while mysticism as mere irrationalistic *Erleben* is purposeless. It will have to come to terms with the most powerful historical *Weltanschauung*, that of Hegel, whose name ends the book, as a motto from him had opened it.

Time and history also form the subjects of Heidegger's inaugural lecture on "The Concept of Time in Historiography." Here an even more basic motif of Heidegger's later work is stated, although its connection with the problem of Being is not yet visible to anyone but the informed. For ostensibly it is only historiography which is under consideration. The time concept of history is, however, contrasted sharply with that of natural science in a way which shows Heidegger's familiarity with the science of Einstein and Planck. As distinguished from the latter, historical time is characterized as heterogeneous and qualitative, since condensed or "crystallized" in the life of historical beings; it is not identical with the time of the mere chronicle of events. This too would seem to point toward a more subjective type of time, as lived in human existence. There is however no explicit reference to phenomenology in this lecture.

Thus the basic themes of Heidegger's phenomenology, Being, time, and history were already formulated when Heidegger came in personal contact with Husserl. Also, in addition to these goals, Heidegger had already decided that a subjective approach in the manner of Husserl's phenomenology was the most important extension of the Aristotelian-scholastic methods needed for a successful approach to these problems. But not until Heidegger took up full scale lecturing after the end of the First World War was it manifest that he wanted to be counted as a phenomenologist rather than as a follower of Heinrich Rickert.

b. THE PHENOMENOLOGICAL PERIOD – I have already recorded the external facts of the subsequent period in Heidegger's development as far as his relationship to Husserl personally is concerned. But I have not yet attempted to show their meaning in the light of Heidegger's philosophical growth.

No adequate information about the content of Heidegger's phenomenological courses and seminars between his first Freiburg lectures and *Sein und Zeit* is available. Hence there would be little point in speculating about the meaning of their announced titles. Heidegger himself indicates, however, that as early as 1919–20 he had introduced his analysis of environment (*Umweltanalyse*) and his "hermeneutics of factual existence" (*Hermeneutik der Faktizität*) in a course entitled "Selected Problems of Pure Phenomenology." This makes it plain that from the very start Heidegger took the liberty of interpreting and developing phenomenology in his own way and for his own purposes. It also stands to reason that his subsequent courses discussed further themes of *Sein und Zeit*, which he started writing in 1922.[1] Thus very soon Heidegger's phenomenology took on a very different character from Husserl's and even from the one he seemed to be advocating in the Duns Scotus book.

To trace these differences in detail would require a complete analysis of *Sein und Zeit*. I shall merely point out some of the major peculiarities of this astonishing torso, comparing it particularly with Husserl's approach.

α. Perhaps the most striking thing for anyone who comes to *Sein und Zeit* from a reading of Husserl's studies is the complete difference in language and terminology. Even apart from the form of expression, very rarely does there seem to be a similarity of concerns or overlapping of topics. Specific references to Husserl's writings are surprisingly few, probably less in number than in the much shorter Duns Scotus book, and they take up only minor items, mostly from the *Logische Untersuchungen*. The reductions, both eidetic and transcendental, Husserl's major concern since his *Ideen*, are not even mentioned by name. However, apart from the dedication, Husserl is given general credit in a paragraph which states that

the following investigations would not have been possible without the ground laid by Husserl, whose *Logische Untersuchungen* meant the breakthrough to phenomenology.

In a footnote to this paragraph Heidegger also acknowledges his personal indebtedness to Husserl, who had made possible his further progress (*einige Schritte vorwärts*) by "familiarizing" him "during his Freiburg apprenticeship (*Lehrjahre*) with the most diverse areas of phenomenological research by intense (*eindringliche*) personal guidance and by the freest possible access to unpublished studies." (p. 38). However, a study of Husserl's manuscripts published since then or otherwise known to me provides little evidence that Husserl's unpublished writings have influenced Heidegger's work except by way of challenge.[2]

What is responsible for Heidegger's implicit rejection of some

---

[1] Information given on the cover of the record "*Zum Atomzeitalter*" (1955).

[2] The reference to *Ideen* II (*Sein und Zeit*, p. 47 footnote) represents a good example of such stimulation. This raises the question of possible influences in reverse from Heidegger on Husserl. If at all, these have hardly been conscious ones. At most one might suspect that such concepts as that of the *Lebenswelt*, or even the use of the term "existential" in Husserl's later manuscripts, may be an unconscious assimilation of some of Heidegger's motifs. See also Alwin Diemer, *Edmund Husserl*, p. 65 f.

of the basic tenets of Husserl's later philosophizing? Ultimately the answer has to be given in the light of Heidegger's basic theme, Being, and of the question how far Husserl's method of reduction could have helped him in determining the meaning of this Being. As far as the eidetic reduction to general essences is concerned, one might perhaps think that Heidegger was heading for an interpretation of Being as such, and hence that he could not object to the eidetic method of generalizing abstraction. But one of his first theses is that Being has not the nature of a genus (p. 3). As a "transcendental" concept in the old scholastic sense it "transcends" the customary categories, hence no kind of generalization would be able to reach it. Besides, Heidegger makes a special point of emphasizing that Being, particularly in the case of human being, is fundamentally individualized, something which is easily ignored in any Platonizing approach.

As to the phenomenological or "transcendental" reduction, even in the form of mere bracketing of existence, the explanation is perhaps even easier to find. For the reduction consists primarily in suspending, at least temporarily, the question of whether any given phenomenon has being. How can such a method help in exploring the nature of Being? Even though Husserl believes that it ultimately can, it would seem rather strange to approach such a problem by first looking away from it. Also it is certainly true that in performing the reduction Husserl took little time to first establish what it was that he suspended when he bracketed "existence" and concentrated on "pure phenomena" only. In other words, for Heidegger's undertaking eidetic and transcendental phenomenology were at best useless, at worst falsifying, when existence and being were at stake. Apparently Heidegger tried on occasion to divert Husserl from his stubborn insistence on the reductions, but to no avail. Yet, for unstated reasons, he did not see fit to bring the issue out into the open.

Nevertheless, there are passages in *Sein und Zeit* where this difference nearly comes to the surface. And at least on one such occasion Heidegger intimates the deeper reasons for his avoidance of traditional terminology, including that of Husserl's phenomenology with its concepts of consciousness (*Bewusstsein*), subject, and personality. As he puts it, they are all characterized by a "strange insensitiveness" (*Bedürfnislosigkeit*) to the question of Being in the things designated by the word "being" (in German the word Bewusst*sein* actually includes the component "being"). For although in comparison with Dilthey and Bergson "the phenomenological interpretation of personality is fundamentally more radical and transparent, it does not reach the dimension of the being of *Dasein*." (p. 47). It is at this point that Heidegger's new hermeneutic phenomenology is ready to step in.

Thus emphasizing the differences in approach and development between *Sein und Zeit* and Husserl's thought should of course not minimize the common themes and perspectives which a more penetrating study would be able to bring to the surface. Even though Heidegger avoids demonstratively such terms as "intentionality," the phenomenon it designates is omnipresent in his concept of "being-in-the world." Even more obvious is the common interest in such topics as "world" and "time." This is certainly more than a coincidence. But without further evidence than the texts there is very little chance to determine the kind and amount of influences.

β. In spite of the obvious differences, even Heidegger's new phenomenology shared with Husserl's version at least the general area of departure, namely man himself, if not in the form of the conscious subject, at least in that of human being (*Dasein*). For the strategy of *Sein und Zeit* consists in an attack upon the meaning of Being by way of an analysis of the being of man, inasmuch as he is the privileged entity who is concerned about his being and has thus a certain understanding of Being, however defective, from the very start. Man is thus fundamentally "ontological," i.e., thinking about the "*on*" (being). So the plan of *Sein und Zeit* in its first half provides for an analysis of this human being. This half is subdivided into three sections, of which only two have been published, the first being a preparatory analysis of human being for its ontological structure, the second giving a fundamental (*ursprüngliche*) analysis of this being in its relation to temporality. The third section, whose publication has now been abandoned for good, was to furnish the transition from human being and human temporality to time and Being itself; here human being was no longer to function as the exclusive clue to Being. The second half of the work, also abandoned, was to be reserved for a "phenomenological destruction" of the history of ontology based on the analysis of temporality, and was presumably meant to supply a confirmation of the conclusions of the systematic first half by means of a critical interpretation of three decisive chapters of the history of philosophy.

This approach, beginning from human being and leading to Being itself, reflects at least to some extent Husserl's primary emphasis on subjectivity, as developed in the *Ideen* and in his later writings. It differs from these, however, by the substitution of human being for pure consciousness. What is the real meaning of this substitution, and what is the relationship between these two conceptions? Here lies perhaps the decisive difference between Husserl's and Heidegger's phenomenologies.

Heidegger's concept of human being is closely linked up with his concept of existence, although strictly speaking existence (i.e., the "possibility of being or not being oneself") is only one of several basic features of human being. It is at this point that Heidegger's phenomenology makes its momentous and fateful contact with the philosophy of existence, which, going beyond Heidegger's own intentions, has since led almost to an identification of phenomenology and existentialism. There is thus far no way of telling what led Heidegger to the adoption of his new concept of existence, which differs basically from the scholastic use (opposed to essence), as it is found even in Heidegger's Duns Scotus book. It seems likely that the study of Kierkegaard (which became widespread in Germany after the First World War and which was promoted further by Jaspers' account of him, even before Jaspers himself had fully developed his philosophy of existence) had a good deal to do with it.[1]

But even more important is an understanding of the purpose of Heidegger's analysis of existence. For Heidegger wants it to be understood that this analysis is not to be a full-fledged study of human existence in the sense of Jaspers' philosophy, for which Heidegger uses the German adjective *"existentiell."* His own analysis is meant to be *"existential,"* a new coinage in German, which is supposed to convey the idea that human existence is to be studied only for its "categories," not for its *what* or nature,

---

[1] See, e.g., *Sein und Zeit*, p. 338. Actually, Kierkegaard's name appears only three times and relatively late in *Sein und Zeit*, and then merely in an incidental manner (pp. 190, 235 note, 338).

since this is all that is needed for the proposed approach to Being in general. To be sure, Being for Heidegger is the decisive part of human being, so much so that he is not even sure whether there is an essence of man over and above his being: For "The essence of human being lies in existence" (p. 42). In view of this, one may well doubt whether there would be anything left for a philosophy of existence after Heidegger's analytics of existence had carried out its task. Existence, as Heidegger sees it, is anyhow a non-theoretical affair, which can be handled only by actual existing, not by any kind of theoretical analysis (p. 12).

But this does not yet explain Heidegger's reason for replacing consciousness by human being. Heidegger's answer is that Husserl's conscious ego, as well as that of Descartes, leaves the question of the being of such consciousness completely unanswered.[1] This may seem somewhat surprising since Husserl, although he "brackets" the being of the whole "transcendent" world, insists all the more on the "absolute," "apodictic," and indubitable being of pure consciousness, without, to be sure, elaborating on what such absolute being involves. What Heidegger seems to be missing must be the discussion of the "meaning" of being as he himself supplies it, something which has to do with the objective of consciousness in its constitutive functions. Though in his last stage Husserl seems to have considered such problems explicitly under the heading of teleology, this certainly does not amount to anything comparable to Heidegger's analytics of human being.

While Heidegger thus believes he is even more radical than Husserl himself with his return to the transcendental ego, he is in another sense unwilling to go so far. Perhaps this can best be illustrated from Heidegger's comments on the following sentence in Husserl's draft of the *Encyclopaedia Britannica* article: "If I carry out the (transcendental) reduction for myself, I am not a human ego." In his comment Heidegger underlines "I am" and "not" and adds, "or perhaps I am precisely that, in its most specific, most amazing (*'wundersamst'*) existential possibility." In the margin he also asks: "Why not? Isn't this activity a

---

[1] *Sein und Zeit*, pp. 46, 207 f. This point is also made with great emphasis in Heidegger's comments on Husserl's *Encyclopaedia Britannica* article (*Tijdschrift voor Philosophie*, XII, p. 274).

potentiality of man...?" Here is the deepest root of the growing disagreement: For Husserl, man is an entity constituted by his consciousness; for Heidegger, consciousness, even in its sublimated phenomenological form, is conversely an activity of man, constituted by him. Without presuming to rule on the merits of the case, I submit that the ultimate difference is based on a difference of focus: Husserl is interested primarily in the epistemological aspect (How do we know about man?), Heidegger in the "ontic" angle (What is Being and what are the foundations for philosophizing and phenomenologizing in the midst of it?). Heidegger undertakes to shift the center of gravity of phenomenology by making human being, rather than consciousness, its hinge. For those who do not share his ontological concern, this amounts indeed to an entirely new phenomenology with an anthropological foundation. The phenomenology of *Sein und Zeit* is still subjectivistic to the extent that it makes man its point of departure. But this is certainly no longer a transcendental subjectivity in Husserl's sense.

γ. Still another point about Heidegger's position in *Sein und Zeit* deserves discussion here, especially in view of the fact that Heidegger by-passes Husserl's method of reduction: his attitude toward phenomenological or transcendental idealism.

Husserl's marginal notes to *Sein und Zeit* make it plain that to him Heidegger's philosophy appeared to be nothing but another type of realism, related even to the old scholastic realism of Thomas Aquinas, from whom, he thought, Heidegger had not yet freed himself completely. Heidegger himself certainly does not acknowledge any such attachments, but rather claims that his new approach unhinges the whole stalemated problem of realism and idealism, which relates the issue to the question of dependence upon consciousness rather than upon human being. But apart from rejecting Husserl's point of reference Heidegger admits a realistic element in his concept of *"Erschlossenheit,"* i.e., literally, the unlockedness or accessibility in the things as encountered in our world. He opposes realism only insofar as it is supposed to imply the reducibility of Being to things-in-being (p. 210 f.) – hardly one of the customary interpretations of realism. A few pages later he denies specifically that reality, in the sense of physical and cultural things, is dependent upon human being.

He does assert, however, that "only as long as there is human being, i.e., the ontic possibility of understanding of being, is there ("*es gibt*") such a thing as "Being." Unless the "*es gibt*" is interpreted in a Pickwickian sense, this certainly sounds like idealism at its strongest. It should be added, however, that since then Heidegger has interpreted this statement in the sense that "only as long as human being is," i.e., man as the "clearing" of Being (*die Lichtung des Seins*), does Being hand itself over (*übereignet sich*) to man.[1] Hence the "*es gibt*" must have meant literally "*giving itself*," not "occurring," in which case Being might well precede and survive the "gift-stage."

Clearly, this cannot be considered a satisfactory adaptation of Husserl's transcendental idealism. Heidegger's later development completely removes the seeming traces of the transcendental idealism of this period.

δ. The above discussion of *Sein und Zeit* merely means to bring out aspects that have bearing on Heidegger's general development. Hence, instead of the problematical attempt to summarize its other theses, of which I shall select later those that illustrate his phenomenological method, I shall simply try to indicate the stage at which Heidegger leaves his reader at the end of the published two sections of the first half of the work.

The preparatory analysis of human being in the first section, starting from man's everyday existence, had led to a determination of the "meaning of Being" (*Sinn des Seins*) of human being for which Heidegger uses the term *Sorge* (concern). The second section had attempted an interpretation of human being as a whole by introducing the element of time in the form of temporality, i.e., the time-structure of our existing. In fact, temporality was now called the "meaning" (*Sinn*) of concern (*Sorge*), which had previously been called the being of human being. Thus the published sections of the work reach at least Heidegger's first objective: the determination of the meaning of one type of Being, the Being of the potentially most revealing thing-in-being, man. This leaves other types of Being undetermined. More important, it leaves the climactic question of the meaning of Being in general still unanswered, much as one can surmise that the temporality of human being was meant to be

---

[1] "Brief über den Humanismus" in *Platons Lehre von der Wahrheit*, p. 83.

the bridge to "Time and Being," the announced topic for section III. The last pages of the published part dismiss the reader with a string of questions, which may at first seem to be merely rhetorical, aimed at intensifying the reader's expectation. In retrospect, however, one notices certain ominous undertones of indecision as to the best possible way to attack the major question. In fact, we are told in the end that there is no chance of settling the controversy about the interpretation of Being, since thus far it has not even been stirred up (*entfacht*).

But if *Sein und Zeit* is incomplete, one might at least think of it as a complete and final treatment of a more limited subject with the more appropriate title "Human Being and Temporality" (*Dasein und Zeitlichkeit*, actually the title of section II). The difficulty with such a restrictive interpretation is that too often in the development of these sections we are told to wait for the final dénouement of points discussed merely in a preliminary fashion. In view of this fact the question arises whether Heidegger's later work can in some way provide the missing capstone for the impressive arch which he built in *Sein und Zeit*.

Heidegger's contribution to the *Husserl-Festschrift* of 1929, "Vom Wesen des Grundes," is ostensibly not directly related to *Sein und Zeit*. It is not easy to determine the exact place of this study, which is unusually compact and far from easy to interpret. It certainly does not elucidate the meaning of 'ground' in any customary sense. The essay follows the pattern of *Sein und Zeit*, inasmuch as it approaches the problem of ground by way of the study of *Dasein*, particularly in the form of what Heidegger now calls "transcendence," namely the self-transcendence of man in the direction of a world. This transcendence itself is traced back to man's freedom, which might make one think that Heidegger wants to derive the world from a free act of the human being, which would amount to a kind of existential idealism. But this is not the case. For freedom, as Heidegger soon adds, consists, paradoxically enough, in letting the world take its own course (*Waltenlassen*), which sounds more like an act of giving freedom than of having it. The final analysis of the free act of grounding reveals human being as not only projecting the world (*Weltentwurf*), but as having been taken over by the world (*Eingenommensein*). In fact, human being is now conceived of as being in the midst of being other than human being. Thus, while human Being still appears as the primary access to such concepts as "ground" and "Being," it is now ontologically imbedded in being and certainly not equipped with any kind of constitutive function and superiority as it is in transcendental idealism.[1]

About one year after his return to Freiburg Heidegger delivered his celebrated and perhaps most widely quoted inaugural lecture, *"What is Metaphysics?"* Ostensibly it still advocates a revival of metaphysics, which is to include the exploration of the ground of the things-in-being. Indeed, the postscript of 1934, and even more the introduction of 1951, show to how many misinterpretations his formulation of the basic question of metaphysics ("Why is there something and not rather nothing at all?") had given rise. The impression was certainly defensible that Heidegger was on the way to a reconstruction of metaphysics in its most comprehensive sense, rather than to its reorientation around the problem of Being in contrast to the things-in-being. This, among other things, may account for his later efforts at "overcoming" or "getting over" metaphysics.

The lecture itself fits into the approach of *Sein und Zeit*, in its move from human being to Being. But it views the problem of Being from a new side, namely from its contrast to nothingness. According to Heidegger, nothingness itself, puzzling though it is, becomes accessible in the fundamental experience (*Grunderfahrung*) of human existence called anxiety, in which the things-in-being seem to retreat or flee away from us. To Heidegger this metaphysical experience is actually a part of human being, in fact the fundamental event in human experience, so much so that he even states that metaphysics is human being itself. Thus it is still the subject in the form of man, with his questions and experiences, that seems to supply the privileged approach to Being as such.

In 1929 Heidegger published his third book, *Kant und das Problem der Metaphysik*. To some extent this may be considered as an installment of the projected first section of the second half of *Sein und Zeit*, which was to furnish a "phenomenological destruction" of the three major ontologies that Heidegger

---

[1] About the "misleadingness" of this essay as seemingly dealing with the metaphysics of things-in-being, see *Der Satz vom Grunde* (1957), p. 84.

considered to be the main obstacles to his fresh start. But as it stands, the book seems to have been conceived independently and can be considered as a kind of historical prolegomena to *Sein und Zeit* as a whole. It is the first of those historical interpretations which in a unique way combine painstaking documentation in securing the original texts with admitted violence in their use. It is also a first example in Heidegger's writing of the form of dialogue between himself and the great philosophers of the past which is so characteristic of Heidegger's later philosophizing.

Seen in a wider context, the Kant book means simply an indirect corroboration and reinforcement of Heidegger's main plea in *Sein und Zeit*, the need of a "fundamental ontology" of human being, focused on the phenomenon of temporality, as the foundation for a genuine philosophy and metaphysics. To this extent it does not represent any significant shift in Heidegger's development. Nevertheless it is a highly instructive piece, particularly if compared with a fuller and less forced view of Kantian philosophy.

Revealing, for instance, is the interpretation of the *Critique of Pure Reason* as an attempt to lay the foundations of a metaphysics based on the nature of man. Man is now defined not as an a priori ideal subject, however empirically imperfect, but as finite, chiefly because his knowledge is primarily *Anschauung* – the latter a view well in line with phenomenology, but perhaps questionable in the light of Kant's view of the relation between *Anschauung* and *Begriff* – and because this *Anschauung* is non-creative and dependent on something already in existence (p. 31), hence derivative – a view which indicates again the realistic element in Heidegger, if not in Kant.

Another distinctive feature of Heidegger's interpretation of Kant is the decisive weight he attaches to the synthetic imagination (*Einbildungskraft*) as the root of the synthesis between intuition and thought, particularly in connection with the problem of the doctrine of the transcendental schema. Equally important is the role given to time for an understanding of the workings of the synthetic imagination.

But the most important aspect of the book is the explanation Heidegger gives for the disappearance of the synthetic imagination from the second edition of the *Critique of Pure Reason*.

For Heidegger sees in it a sign of Kant's retreat (*Zurückweichen*) from the implications of his own approach: he cannot bear the realization of the subjective character of the subject (p. 194). "To question one's way (*Hineinfragen*) into the subjectivity of the subject, the 'subjective deduction,' leads into darkness." In the attempt to lay a subjective foundation for the *Critique of Pure Reason* Kant had actually undermined it: the foundations threaten to cave in and to reveal the abyss (*Abgrund*) of metaphysics. Regardless of how clear and convincing this interpretation is, one of the implications of Heidegger's concluding critique of Kant's approach is that it indirectly reveals the failure of the subjective approach, so basic to Husserl's phenomenology of subjectivity, which had led Husserl to increasing interest in and admiration for Kant. To Heidegger, subjectivism was now a failure, in view of the essential finiteness of man, i.e., the dependence of his *Anschauung* on powers not in himself. And Kant's failure spelled Husserl's failure as well.

Finally, there is the fact that the book, dedicated to the memory of Max Scheler, contains a discussion of Scheler's idea of a philosophical anthropology as an alternative foundation for metaphysics. This is rejected in favor of the "fundamental ontology" of *Sein und Zeit*, which alone is said to make possible an understanding of the finiteness of man. Thus, although there are indications of further developments in Heidegger's thought, the fundamental approach to Being through human being remains unchanged. Yet no basic progress beyond *Sein und Zeit* is apparent from Heidegger's publications during the twenties.

After 1929 the roster of Heidegger's publications shows another conspicuous gap. The early thirties were the period of his temporary but intense involvement in the affairs of the Nazi regime. In the present context his political expectations and early disillusionment are without immediate significance. What is significant, however, is the fact of his association with a political movement as activistic and violent as Nazism. It is true that authentic existence, as Heidegger conceived of it at the time, called for resoluteness (*Entschlossenheit*, a word which in customary German has exclusively voluntaristic connotations). But beyond the meaning of an orientation toward death (*Sein zum*

16. Martin Heidegger (about 1930)

Tode), Sein und Zeit had failed to define the kind of life this would spell.[1]

Quite possibly during these years Heidegger had the strange illusion that not only could his own philosophy assimilate some of the Nazi ideology but also that he could offer the latter a more adequate philosophy than Alfred Rosenberg's "Myth of the Twentieth Century." The grotesqueness of this error does not [1] make the spectacle of this episode any more edifying.

The only separate publication from this period is Heidegger's Rectoral Address of 1933, entitled oddly enough "The Self-assertion of the German University." The revealing part about it is the reinterpretation of science in the context of the new political pattern as he conceived of it. The address contains Heidegger's supreme appeal to the will as the lever for shaping man's destiny in his universe and, in the case of science, for unlocking the essence of all things. What is more, the universe now appears so antagonistic to man that this address expresses the closest approximation to explicit atheism that can be found anywhere in Heidegger's writings.[2] In a sense this speech, to- [2] gether with similar utterances from this period, represents the high watermark and possibly the turning point of Heidegger's trust in the capacity of human being to force Being to surrender its secret. Nietzsche's will-to-power is its symbolic expression. The failure of Heidegger's excursion into the political world spells not only the end of his activism but also of his trust in human being and the powers of subjectivity as embodied in the will.

c. UNDER THE SIGN OF HÖLDERLIN – To what extent has there been a break in Heidegger's thinking since *Sein und*

---

1 There is a characteristic story of a student of Heidegger who emerged from one of his lectures with the exclamation: "I am resolved: Only I am not sure on what." See K. Löwith, "Les Implications politiques de la philosophie d'existence de Heidegger" in *Les Temps Modernes* II (1946), 347.

2 "If that is true which Friedrich Nietzsche, the last German Philosopher who passionately sought God, said, namely that 'God is dead' – if we have to accept seriously the forsakenness of modern man in the midst of the things-in-being ... then the perseverance of the Greeks before the existing world, initially in the spirit of admiration, now becomes a completely unsheltered exposure to the hidden and un-certain, i.e., the questionable." Science now becomes an "inquiring, unsheltered perseverance (*Standhalten*) in the midst of the uncertainty of the things-in-being as a whole" (p. 12 f.). By contrast, Heidegger's reinterpretation of Nietzsche in 1943 (*Holzwege* 1950, p. 293 ff.) leaves us wholly uncertain as to his own position. It is perhaps not insignificant that Sartre, who labelled Heidegger an atheist, was in Freiburg around the time of this Rectoral Address. [3]

Zeit and, more particularly, since the end of his involvement in politics? Certain changes, such as the disappearance of the term phenomenology, are manifest. But do they justify the belief that Heidegger came to reverse himself? The case for such an interpretation has been stated most strongly by as informed a critic as Karl Löwith.[1] However, Heidegger himself asserts that there is no such break. Certainly he has not repudiated *Sein und Zeit*, but keeps referring to it as if he considered it his most permanent and presumably his greatest achievement.

I shall begin by presenting the concrete evidence for the view that there have been serious shifts in Heidegger's thinking, sufficient to set his later period apart from what was described earlier.

There is, first of all, the postponement and apparently now the abandonment of the plan of publishing the missing parts of *Sein und Zeit*. Heidegger's own explanation for this reversal is that the third section of the first half of *Sein und Zeit*, which, under the title of *"Zeit und Sein,"* was to furnish the final answer to the question of the meaning of Being, was "held back" (hence, it seems to have existed) at the time of the publication of the first sections "because thinking failed in the attempt to express adequately the turning *(Kehre)* – from '*Sein und Zeit*' to '*Zeit und Sein*' – and did not reach its goal by using the language of meta-
[1] physics."[2] It is not exactly easy to appraise the difficulties for which language alone is here held responsible. But it is hardly insignificant that what Heidegger was most worried about in the context of this quotation is the danger of a subjectivistic interpretation of *Sein und Zeit*. Thus, he is anxious to stress the need of a thinking that "leaves behind subjectivity" and the idea of "achievements of subjectivity" (p. 69 f.), which seemed to be suggested particularly by the concept of an existential project *(Entwurf)* introduced in connection with the hermeneutics of human being.

Heidegger adds that the lecture *Of the Essence of Truth* "conceived and read in 1930 but not printed until 1943," throws a "certain light" on the thinking of his decisive "turn" in *Sein und Zeit* to Time and Being. The modesty of this claim and in fact

---

[1] *Heidegger, Denker in dürftiger Zeit*, Chapter I.
[2] "Brief über den Humanismus" in *Platons Lehre von der Wahrheit*, p. 72.

the delay in the publication of the lecture is possibly explained by a note at its very end to the effect that it was to be supplemented by a second lecture "Of the Truth of Essence": But "this lecture miscarried (*misslang*) for reasons now hinted at in the letter *Über den Humanismus.*" Since no specific reference to the lecture occurs in the letter, it may be inferred that it was again the inadequacy of the language of metaphysics which was at the root of this second failure.

These two striking admissions of change of plan and failure must be taken together with the evidence afforded by Heidegger's actual publications in the years since 1933. These consist almost exclusively of lectures and smaller essays, which in recent years (since 1950) have been combined in book form. They also in- [1] clude the edition of some important courses and even a little volume of poetry and aphorisms (*Von der Erfahrung des Denkens*). There is however at present no promise of a book which could take the place of the missing parts of *Sein und Zeit*. [2]

On the other hand, there is a surprising widening in Heidegger's range of interests. There is particularly a seemingly sudden [3] new interest in fine art, music, and particularly in poetry, which was conspicuous by its absence in the earlier period. This became manifest almost abruptly after the end of Heidegger's excursion into politics, and expressed itself particularly in the sequence of his commentaries on some relatively neglected and difficult poems of Hölderlin, the Hellenizing German Romantic, on Rilke (whom he rejects in spite of obvious affinities), and on the recent poet Georg Trakl. Besides, Heidegger reveals an intense interest in the nature and meaning of technology. This increased range of topics, however, by no means indicates an abandonment of his original concern, rather its pursuit into new areas.

The present context does not call for a detailed account of all these efforts but merely for an attempt to point out some of the pervading features and results of this ongoing period, sufficient to determine its relationship to the earlier outspokenly phenomenological phase in Heidegger's development.

To begin with more external characteristics, Heidegger's writings of this period are not only shorter but more rounded within their more limited scope. They show a deliberate attempt to avoid the traditional terminology of philosophy, yet try all

the harder to squeeze all the juices of literal meaning out of
the old word shells, and sometimes even to instill new life into
them. Many terms and concepts, especially the more technical
ones, disappear from his vocabulary. Others are reinterpreted and
even re-spelled, such as existence (now: *Ek-sistenz*) or *Sein* (often:
Seyn), and some are added, such as *Ge-Stell* for the products of
technology, or *dingen* as the mode of being of the "thing"
(*Ding*). On the whole, the fewer new terms Heidegger uses, the more
he overloads the existing ones. The style is less involved, and
especially the lectures display a clarity of organization and even
of diction which makes them perhaps the best introduction to
Heidegger's entire thought. One senses an intensified need for
communication and contact with the audience, especially in the
lectures. This does not mean that their sense is easy to assimilate.
Even now there is very little attempt to prove points in any
traditional sense of the word by "for's" and "because's."
"Nothing can be proved in this area, but some things can be
shown." [1] One does not even notice a sustained effort to show
them. Instead, we find mostly the bare pronouncement of a
"truth" which, if it does not ask to be accepted on the writer's
say-so, makes high demands on the reader's sympathetic efforts
at understanding and verification.

Perhaps the most startling change in the content of Heidegger's
later thought is that Being, the distant goal of *Sein und Zeit*,
suddenly appears to be so close and manifest that hardly any
special approach or method seems to be needed to discover it,
once we have stopped running away from it. After the 438 pages
of *Sein und Zeit*, which constantly stressed our utter ignorance
of the meaning of Being, in fact our unawareness of the question,
and which made Being seem the darkest possible mystery, to
be approached via human being and even via the experience of
nothingness, it now appears that Being is essentially open and
unconcealed all the time and that we have direct access to it,
provided we do not forget it. Yet even Heidegger says that we
live in, and in fact are nothing but, a "clearing" (*Lichtung*) in the
midst of Being, which seems to imply that around this clearing
Being is still a dark jungle. What is more, it is not given to
human being or thinking to force its way into Being, but it is

[1] *Identität und Differenz*, p. 10.

primarily Being itself which reveals itself to thinking by its own initiative, its speaking to us (*Zuspruch*). Man can do nothing but either resist or accept it in "mellow tranquillity" (*Gelassenheit der Milde*). It is significant that in this context Heidegger often uses a German expression which comes very close to the equivalent of grace: *Huld*, i.e., graciousness, or *Gunst*, i.e., favor of Being.

The clearest expression of this new interpretation of thinking as mostly receptive is to be found in Heidegger's lectures on *Was heisst Denken?* of 1951–52. It is for this reason also that Heidegger now calls man, in a language reminding one of Rilke, the "shepherd" or "guardian" of Being, whose main function it is to watch "the house of Being," namely language. *"Was heisst Denken?"* distinguishes four senses of the question about the meaning of thinking, based upon various meanings of the word *"heissen"* in German, which comprises "meaning" and "bidding." To Heidegger the most important of these meanings is "What bids us to think?" The answer to this is none other than: Being itself. Thinking thus loses its character of a spontaneous activity and consists instead in an acceptance and listening to the voice of Being.

It is part of the same pattern that thinking now moves into the immediate neighborhood of poetry. And while Heidegger still distinguishes between the thinker who "says" Being and the poet who "names" the Holy,[1] the latter is certainly not the inferior, and at times it would even seem the superior, of the thinker. There are actually places where even thinking appears as one of the offshoots of poetry. It needs to keep close to poetry, which is its "good" and hence its healthy (*heilsam*) danger, as opposed to itself, its "evil" danger, and to philosophy, its "bad" danger. [2]

It is obvious that this type of thinking leaves little room for anything like a method. Actually, logic in Heidegger's new sense means something entirely different from the traditional logic, in which he sees practically nothing but the precursor of *"Logistik"* or mathematical logic, another branch of modern technology. It is obvious that this must also affect the idea of phenome-

---

[1] *Was ist Metaphysik?* Nachwort, p. 46.
[2] *Aus der Erfahrung des Denkens*, p. 15.

nology as a philosophical method which approaches its object in
the spirit of research. For no method is called upon to enforce the
revelation of truth, at best it can prepare the way of truth in
the thinker.

One other element in Heidegger's later period, closely related
to this Being-centered approach and of considerable importance
for his new attitude toward phenomenology, is his attack on
subjectivism and subjectivity in philosophy. This should be
contrasted with his plea for the need of subjective studies as a
supplement to the objective logic of the categories in the Duns
Scotus book.[1] *Sein und Zeit* represented an effort to substitute
human being for the subject of pure consciousness, but it still
approached Being from the same direction. Now "not only every
kind of anthropology and every subjectivity in the sense of man
as a subject has been left behind, as it was already in *Sein und
Zeit* ... but the way of the lecture undertakes to think by beginning from this new ground (the *Da-sein*)." [2] *Da-sein* in this
new sense, in which the hyphen makes the first syllable emphatic,
is no longer human existence in its relation to the world but
rather to what is there, i.e., Being in its openness or "truth,"
something into which man can enter.[3]

Perhaps Heidegger's strongest condemnation of subjectivism
develops out of his critical discussion of Nietzsche's philosophizing. For he sees in it an extension of Descartes' way of
thinking. Descartes' *ego cogito*, which is also Husserl's foundation
stone, becomes to Heidegger the symbol of the modern age. It
represents an insurrection against Being as such, converting all
things-in-being into objects for a subject and ultimately sucking
them into subjectivity. As a result they are reduced to mere
perspectives under the control of the value decisions of the will-
to-power.[4] In spite of his high regard for Nietzsche as a thinker,
Heidegger thus sees in him the climax in the revolt of subjectivism.

---

[1] "Without taking account of 'subjective logic' it does not even make sense to
talk about immanent and transcending ("*transeunt*") validity. ... Objectivity
(*Gegenständlichkeit*) makes sense only for a predicating subject, without which it will
never be possible to bring out the full meaning of what is meant by validity (*Geltung*).
(*Die Kategorien- und Bedeutungslehre des Duns Scotus*, pp. 234 ff.).

[2] *Vom Wesen der Wahrheit*, p. 27.

[3] *Was ist Metaphysik?* Einleitung (1951), p. 13.

[4] *Holzwege*, p. 241.

A case may be made for the view that Heidegger himself reversed his attitude toward the will during the period of his Nazi involvement. At first the will to a vaguely conceived national destiny had seemed to him also the guide to Being. His disillusionment with this final outburst of the will, coupled with his return to a poet as contemplative as Hölderlin, may well have something to do with his final repudiation of all types of subjectivism. No wonder the turn away from phenomenology, at first only in the form of a rejection of Husserl's transcendental subjectivism, now confirmed his disinterest in any kind of subject-centered approach.

One other change around this time made likewise for Heidegger's latest disinterest in phenomenology. Up to the time of his Rectoral Address of 1934, Heidegger had never displayed any fundamental reservations or objections to the idea of science in the German sense of the word, which comprises both the natural sciences and the social and historical studies (*Geisteswissenschaften*). Nor did he object to Husserl's idea of philosophy as a rigorous science. He used to insist that the special sciences are dependent branches of philosophy, and that, if completely emancipated from philosophy, they become degenerations of philosophy. But even in the address of 1933 science appears as one of the highest possibilities of human existence. Besides, Heidegger has exerted a highly stimulating influence on several scientific studies, chiefly the sciences of man.[1]

This attitude toward science changes with *Holzwege*, where for the first time science as such comes under attack. Heidegger now states that in science, as contrasted with art, no original truth is found but merely the development of what is already known (p. 50). An even more serious stricture against science follows as a result of Heidegger's attack on modern technology, in which he sees nothing but an outgrowth of the modern metaphysics of the will, an attack which is related to Heidegger's earlier analysis of the things of our daily environment by such concepts as utensil (*Zeug*). Thus modern science, along with the totalitarian state, is interpreted as a necessary consequence of modern

---

[1] See especially *M. Heideggers Einfluss auf die Wissenschaften*, Festschrift zu seinem 60. Geburtstag. Bern, 1949.

technology, on which science is said to be based.[1] It is an even more serious charge that science is called a degeneration of "thinking," since it does not really think at all.[2] Besides, the "startling" realization is said to emerge that the sciences cannot comprehend what is meant, for instance, by nature, by history, and by language. Only reflective meditation (*Besinnung*) can do that.[3] It is obvious that Heidegger's increasingly anti-scientific tone is also apt to affect the cause of any philosophy like phenomenology which aspired to be scientific, or at least to cooperate with science.

What is the upshot of Heidegger's long search for Being?

α. The only definitive and deliberately simple answer is that Being is "Itself" (in connection with Being Heidegger often writes the German pronoun *es* for Being with a capital E). Most other statements about it would have to be merely negative.

β. Among the various characteristics of Being, the outstanding one is its "truth." Truth, however, is interpreted by Heidegger on the basis of a literal dissection of the Greek word *"a-letheia"* as un-hiddenness (*Un-verborgenheit*) or openness. Nevertheless, Being is apparently not given without any concealment (*Bergen*); it also seems to have a tendency to hide and to withdraw. Its openness is a clearing, but apparently a clearing in a dark forest, full of *Holzwege* (blind alleys).

γ. The revelation of Being in its truth is its own doing. It should therefore be conceived as an active rather than as a passive process, and Being as in a sense self-determining. Thus Heidegger uses the German intransitive verb *'ereignen'* (to happen) in a new transitive manner to indicate that Being makes things happen. All that our thinking can do is to "let Being be" (*Seinlassen*).

δ. Being is temporal, not timeless or eternal. Although Heidegger has failed to present the demonstration of this thesis in *Sein und Zeit*, he clearly holds to the view that the two are inseparable.

---

[1] *Holzwege*, p. 267; *Vorträge und Aufsätze*, pp. 45 ff.
[2] *Was heisst Denken?* p. 4.
[3] "Wissenschaft und Besinnung" in *Vorträge und Aufsätze*, p. 66.

ε.   Being has a history in the sense of a development. This   [1]
     history of Being is perhaps the main explanation of the
     seeming inconclusiveness of Heidegger's search. In reading
     his *Einführung in die Metaphysik* (1935) one receives at
     first the impression that here at last Heidegger has
     found the saving word: namely that Being is presence
     (*Anwesenheit*). However, closer inspection reveals that
     even this is at best the answer of the Greeks. It therefore
     describes merely the Greek phase in the history of Being,
     in which only one of its temporal dimensions had been
     considered. It has been followed by other phases, the
     most fateful one in recent times when Nietzsche conceived
     of Being as an expression of the will. Thus all the changing
     views of Being are actually parts of Being itself. Such an
     answer raises, to be sure, the further question as to the
     connecting link between all these events in the history of
     Being: What is it after all that allows us to ascribe them
     all to one and the same substratum, Being?

ζ.   Heidegger's most recent discussion of Being also suggests
     that it is the ground of all things-in-being. Being itself,
     however, is groundless.[1]

η.   Perhaps the most significant feature of Being in Heideg-
     ger's most recent accounts of Being is its interdependence
     with man: Man needs Being, and Being needs man. Both
     belong together.[2] It hardly needs spelling out how much
     such an astonishing estimate can add to the stature of
     man at the price of the autonomy of Being. Nevertheless,
     this view suggests a final balance between the two poles,
     Being and man, the objective and the subjective.   [2]

To what extent are such results adequate answers to Heidegger's great initial question, even in his own sense? At times
one might feel that he himself does not want an answer, but
prefers to leave the question open with all its tantalizing mystery,
and that a "genuine shipwreck" (*echtes Scheitern*) on the rocks of
the question would satisfy him very well (SZ 148). The last
dictum of *Was heisst Denken?*, especially in the form of the lecture
as published separately in *Vorträge und Aufsätze*, seems to imply

---

[1] *Der Satz vom Grund*, p. 205.
[2] *Der Satz von der Identität*, p. 22 ff.

that we are not even yet ready to receive an answer. We are at best on our way, in the *"neighborhood"* of Being. Now it may well be that we are not yet ready. But how about Heidegger himself? How can he tell us that we are close to the answer unless he himself knows it? Thus far he has not revealed to us that he does, and the only chance is that it is to be found in his desk, in that section of *Sein und Zeit* which he is no longer willing to release.

5. *Heidegger's Conception of Phenomenology*

Thus far we have studied merely the role of phenomenology in the history of Heidegger's thinking without trying to give a full idea of what he means by it. It is now time to fill this gap. We shall do so by first taking account of Heidegger's own interpretation of phenomenology and then by observing it in action in some of its more instructive applications.

There would seem to be little point in discussing Heidegger's conception of phenomenology prior to *Sein und Zeit*. For the references to phenomenology in the Duns Scotus book suggest that at that period Heidegger believed himself to be in complete agreement with Husserl's interpretation of it. By contrast, *Sein und Zeit* reveals that Heidegger had gone considerably beyond Husserl, and that he was fully aware of it. We shall therefore begin with an analysis of the phenomenology of *Sein und Zeit*. Subsequently we shall discuss Heidegger's later methodology, with a view to determining how far this can still be considered as phenomenological.

a. HERMENEUTIC PHENOMENOLOGY – Heidegger introduces his own conception of phenomenology in the second (methodological) chapter of the introduction to *Sein und Zeit*, after having stated in a first chapter "necessity, structure, and prerogative of the question of Being." But before characterizing this phenomenology itself, he discusses a task whose solution he considers indispensable before the question of Being can be attacked with any chance of success: the so-called destruction, also named the "phenomenological destruction," of ontology.

The need of such a purge is a consequence of Heidegger's conviction that no fresh start can be made until we have identified and neutralized the metaphysical preconceptions which falsify the very formulations of our philosophical problems, in fact even the description of our phenomena. Words such as "consciousness," "subject," or "substance" are the results of metaphysical theories which have vitiated our whole approach to the phenomena. In this respect even Husserl's phenomenology is still too naively dependent on tradition and anything but free from presuppositions. It is the task of phenomenological destruction to liberate us from unconscious servitude to our metaphysical past.

However, the iconoclastic term "destruction" is not to be understood in the merely negative sense of a repudiation of all tradition or of any kind of ontological nihilism or relativism. Instead, "destruction" is characterized as a loosening up of the hardened tradition and the removal (*Ablösung*) of the screens (*Verdeckungen*) for which tradition is responsible. Destruction in this sense has actually a positive referent, the primordial (*ursprüngliche*) experiences from which the tradition was formed, and which constitute its birth certificates. It is in this sense that Heidegger intends to "destroy" the history of ontology at the three decisive crossroads of western philosophy, Kant, Descartes, and Aristotle (in that order), in an obvious attempt to retrace and reverse the steps these thinkers had taken. It is, however significant that in the outline of *Sein und Zeit* Heidegger postponed this destruction to the second half of the work, which has shared the fate of Part I, Section 3. Apparently it was thus not phenomenology which presupposed the destruction, but destruction which presupposed the phenomenology of the original experiences.

What, then, is phenomenology in Heidegger's sense? In the published parts of *Sein und Zeit* Heidegger offers two conceptions of phenomenology, the more developed one actually only of a preliminary nature (*Vorbegriff*), the definitive one, called the idea (*Idee*) of phenomenology, unfortunately sketched only in a passing manner which appears to be a prelude for a fuller treatment, presumably in the missing parts of *Sein und Zeit*. Thus the preliminary concept still is, to all intents and purposes, Heideg-

ger's most explicit formulation of his own conception of phenomenology.[1]

From the very start Heidegger made it amply clear that what
he understands by phenomenology in *Sein und Zeit* was not
identical with what Husserl meant by it, and that he claimed the
right to develop it on his own beyond the stage it had reached
with Husserl. To be sure, he saw in Husserl's phenomenology the
indispensable foundation for such a development, but significantly enough, in this context he mentioned only the "breakthrough" to phenomenology in the *Logische Untersuchungen*,
not the *Ideen*, its developed form. Even more significant, he
states that it is not the essential thing about phenomenology
to be actual as a philosophical school ("*Richtung*") : "Potentiality
stands higher than actuality. To understand phenomenology
consists in seizing it as a potentiality." (p. 38) Also, to Heidegger phenomenology is neither a "standpoint" nor a "school":
[1]   it cannot ever become one "as long as it understands itself."
For:

> The term "phenomenology" means primarily a concept of method. It
> does not characterize the qualitative content (*das sachhaltige Was*) of
> the objects of philosophical research, but the mode of approaching them
> (*das Wie*). . . . The title "phenomenology" expresses a maxim which can
> be formulated thus: "To the things themselves!" – in contrast to all the
> unsupported (*freischwebenden*) constructions, the accidental findings, the
> blind acceptance of concepts verified merely in appearance, and the
> pseudo-questions which, often for generations, strut about (*sich breit-
> machen*) as "problems." One might reply, however, that this maxim is
> after all pretty obvious (*reichlich selbstverständlich*) and, besides, an
> expression of the principles of all scientific knowledge. One does not
> understand why this triviality should be included explicitly under the
> head (*Titelbezeichnung*) of a type of research. It is indeed a 'triviality'
> (*Selbstverständlichkeit*) which is at stake, one which we want to approach
> more closely insofar as this is relevant to the elucidation of the method of
> this treatise (p. 27 f.)

Heidegger's preliminary account of this seemingly "trivial"
method takes its characteristic point of departure from an
analysis of the word "phenomenology" in which the two components "phenomenon" and "logos" are distinguished and inter-

---

[1] The one contained in his counter-draft to Husserl's *Encyclopaedia Britannica*
article (see p. 280) was hardly meant to be much more than an attempt to help Husserl
in the formulation of his own conception, in a manner that seemed to Heidegger more
effective; witness the occurrence of the term "consciousness" in this definition, a
term which Heidegger had already eliminated at the stage of *Sein und Zeit*.

preted first separately. The result differs from Husserl's interpretation so vastly that it might be well to start here by contrasting the two.

When Husserl took up the term "phenomenology," as shown in Ch. III (p. 103) he gave no explicit definition or discussion of what he meant by "phenomenon." It was only as his idea of phenomenology crystallized into something distinctive and fundamental for philosophy that he felt the need for a redefinition. After abandoning Brentano's sense of the term in *Logische Untersuchungen* (II, 1, p. 371), he assigned to it a precise meaning, first in his momentous lectures on the "Idea of Phenomenology" of 1907, and then in the Introduction to the *Ideen*. Here the "pure phenomena" of the new phenomenology are described as non-individual, i.e., as the general essences of empirical phenomena obtained by the eidetic reduction, and, in addition to that, as non-real, refined by the phenomenological reduction, which had bracketed their reality. Consequently, their ontological or metaphysical status was deliberately left undecided at the start, while the final word was that they owed their being to consciousness.

No such neutrality, let alone dependence upon consciousness, is implied in Heidegger's concept of phenomenon. Instead, "phenomenon" is here interpreted as "what shows itself," more specifically even as "what shows itself in person (*das Sich-an-ihm-selbst-zeigende*) or what is manifest (*das Offenbare*)." This manifestness does not preclude the possibility that at times Heidegger's phenomenon hides behind a misleading appearance. But it is clear that it is not the distillate of special reductive operations. It is rather an autonomous entity with powers of its own, independent of and prior to our thinking.

However, this does not mean that Heidegger simply returned to the colloquial use of the word "phenomenon" as used in ordinary discourse and also in science. True, Heidegger took cognizance of the common (*vulgär*) sense of the word as one among several others, notably one which applies to the empirical world, and which is presumably also the "phenomenon" of natural science. From this Heidegger distinguished the "phenomenological concept of phenomenon" as that of a phenomenon which "first and foremost" (*zunächst und zumeist*) does *not* show itself but remains hidden as the meaning (*Sinn*) and ground (*Grund*) of what shows itself (p. 35).

Hence the "phenomenological phenomenon" requires much more by way of direct demonstration and verification than a merely descriptive phenomenology, which Heidegger mentions only in passing, and for which he seems to have little use. It calls for a method which makes us see what is normally hidden and forgotten. Now "logos," the second component of the word "phenomenology," means in Heidegger's intensifying interpretation of its literal meaning a method of making us see what is otherwise concealed, of taking the hidden out of its hiding, and of detecting it as "unhidden," i.e., as truth (*a-letheia*).[1] Thus phenomenology in the genuine sense of the word becomes to Heidegger the method of uncovering the hiding, or "interpretation" (*Auslegung*), which he also calls the methodical meaning of phenomenological description. (p. 37).

Now the primary phenomenon which needs uncovering in this sense is Being, the victim of our usual forgetfulness of the "ontological difference" between Being and the things-in-being. In fact, for Heidegger the science of Being of the things-in-being or ontology is declared possible only as phenomenology. Moreover, although no further reason is given, it turns out that for Heidegger even the converse holds: according to its content phenomenology coincides with ontology. Having gone so far, Heidegger finally concludes that philosophy itself is nothing but "universal phenomenological ontology based on the hermeneutics of human being (*Dasein*)," which by implication makes phenomenology the one and only philosophical method.

Quite apart from the startling boldness of this deduction, the idea of such a phenomenological ontology contrasts sharply with Husserl's conception. For to Husserl, at least at that time, the name "ontology" stood not for the science of the Being of things-in-being, but primarily for a branch of his pure logic, i.e., the eidetic science of the pervasive categories of all things-in-

[1] He is, however, not the first to suggest this. See Nicolai Hartmann, *Platos Logik des Seins* (Marburg, 1909), p. 477. – As to the philological soundness of this interpretation see now Paul Friedländer, *Plato* I, Ch. XI: Aletheia. For Heidegger's etymology and etymologizing philosophy of *logos* see also *Was heisst Denken?* pp. 120 ff., 170 ff. and *Vorträge und Aufsätze*, pp. 257 ff. Husserl's meaning of "logos," as developed in *Formale und transzendentale Logik*, deals only with the several strata of logical entities.

being (formal ontology), followed by "regional" ontologies dealing with the supreme categories of each science in their different essential natures. True, in Husserl's conception even these ontologies had to be underpinned by phenomenological derivation from original intuitions. But such a phenomenologically supported ontology was clearly restricted to a limited area of the things-in-being rather than to Being as such. Heidegger's is restricted in a very different sense, inasmuch as it deals only with a certain feature of all things-in-being. Presumably he would leave Husserl's problems completely to the sciences.

But what exactly is the new type of interpretation which Heidegger's phenomenological ontology demands? It is in this connection that the term "hermeneutics" appears in Heidegger's phenomenology, which also goes by the name of "hermeneutic phenomenology." Hermeneutics is not a new term. It has its origin in Biblical exegesis and has also been applied to the interpretation of historical documents; Dilthey, to whom Heidegger pays repeated tribute, brought the word into prominence. But as Heidegger now uses the term it no longer refers to documents or symbolic expressions, but to non-symbolic facts of the real world, to human being or *Dasein*. In fact it is the interpretation of this particular type of being for which Heidegger reserves the term "hermeneutic." Only indirectly is hermeneutics relevant to ontology in general, since it deals with *Dasein*, i.e., that type of being which provides the foundation for the interpretation of Being in general (p. 47).

What does it mean to "interpret" such a non-symbolic fact as human being? Interpretation aims at the meaning of the thing interpreted. It therefore presupposes that what is to be interpreted has meaning. Now it is one of Heidegger's basic assertions that human being has meaning in a sense which admits of interpretation. For human being is essentially related to its own being as that which is "at stake" for it: "The essence of being consists in its being toward" (*Zu-sein*) (p. 42). That "toward which" human being exists consists, to be sure, primarily in a possibility, notably the possibility of being authentic or inauthentic. Hence in this orientation toward possibilities beyond itself, human being is capable of an interpretation which identifies these possibilities ahead of itself by determining its "what-for" (*woraufhin, um-zu*).

But human being is not only *capable* of such interpretation, it also demands it. For just as Being has a tendency to fall into oblivion, so human Being has an inherent tendency to degenerate. Heidegger calls this in German *Verfallen*, which may be understood in the sense of decay but also of infatuation and escape, a characteristic of the everyday mode of human being from which hermeneutic phenomenology has to take its start. This also explains why hermeneutic interpretation has to swim, as it were, against the current, and to use a certain violence, as Heidegger candidly admits.

This poses the problem of how such an interpretation can actually be carried out and what its criteria are. Heidegger himself points out that understanding and interpretation depend on certain preconceptions. Thus every interpretation of ordinary items in daily life is related to a frame of relevance (*Bewandtnisganzheit*) which embraces it (*Vorhabe*), implies a preview (*Vorsicht*) looking toward anticipated meanings, and requires conceptual patterns for it (*Vorgriff*) (p. 150). Heidegger admits that this procedure is anything but free from presuppositions, and that it has all the earmarks of a vicious circle. He maintains, however, that the anticipations of hermeneutic interpretation are not determined by chance ideas or popular conceptions but by the "things themselves." He makes no attempt to link this procedure with general scientific methods other than those used in the historical studies. But it would not seem too difficult to relate it to the logic of hypothesis, if not to the use of heuristic concepts.

Hermeneutic phenomenology may thus be defined as a method of bringing out the normally hidden purposes of such goal-determined things-in-being as human beings. It presupposes, of course, that these beings possess such a purposeful structure; but there seems to be no reason why this presupposition should not be verifiable and also actually verified. Hermeneutics thus uses methods which go beyond mere description of what is manifest and tries to uncover hidden meanings by anticipatory devices. It is almost surprising that they are not compared and contrasted with the techniques of psychoanalysis in its attempts to uncover the unconscious. One can only suspect that for Heidegger these would be of much too conceptual or theoretical a nature, and lacking in a sufficiently basic interpretation ot human being within the total frame of Being.

To be sure, all this still concerns only the preliminary concept of Heidegger's phenomenology. It leaves the question of its definitive concept unanswered. As to this, the only clues which Heidegger supplies in *Sein und Zeit* occur in a section close to the end of the existential analysis of human being (p. 357 ff.). Here, after temporality has been diagnosed as the final "sense of the Being of human being," Heidegger tries to apply this new insight to various human enterprises, among them science. And since, especially at this stage, Heidegger still considers phenomenology a science, this interpretation has bearing on phenomenology as well. Science, or more specifically theoretical scientific activity, is here interpreted as a modification of our usual circumspect concern with our environment. In this activity our practical interests are either neutralized or overlooked. However, no application of this general interpretation of science to the science of phenomenology is given. It stands to reason that it would show even the phenomenological approach as a restriction of the concrete meaning of everyday living. On the other hand phenomenology might be at the same time the very kind of scientific interpretation which could reveal the limitations of the merely scientific approach.

In what sense and to what extent, then, can hermeneutic phenomenology claim to be phenomenology in the original sense of the term? Quite apart from the element of violence needed in the kind of interpretation Heidegger performs, it certainly goes beyond the "immediately" given, if immediacy means manifest givenness. It requires anticipations which go beyond it, as any explanatory hypothesis does, and requires extrapolation beyond what is directly present. Certainly this is phenomenology in an enlarged sense. Whether in spite of this it should be acknowledged as genuine phenomenology must largely depend on how far it is possible to underpin its extrapolations to the meanings of the phenomena by intuitive verification of a more than merely private and persuasive nature. To what extent has Heidegger succeeded in doing this?

b. HERMENEUTICS IN ACTION – This section will attempt
to supply some representative examples of hermeneutic phenomenology, concentrating on those which have achieved a certain
notoriety. Without question Heidegger's most substantial phenomenological analyses occur in *Sein und Zeit*. No attempt will
be made to render the argument of this work, although we shall
follow its sequence of topics. It will, however, be well to recall
Heidegger's methodological strategy. He starts with a "preparatory analysis of human being," which takes its departure from
what is given "first and foremost" (*zunächst und zumeist*) in
our everyday existence (*Alltäglichkeit*). It is only on this foundation that he advances to a level of interpretation which digs
down to the deeper origins of meaning (*ursprüngliche existentiale
Interpretation*).

The main difficulty in the presentation of the following examples is due to the extreme condensation of Heidegger's accounts. Rarely, if ever, does he give descriptions in the sense of
the earlier phenomenologists. He mostly points at the phenomena
by means of new, provocative and, at times, stunning terms
which keep even the native German groping his way toward a
tentative understanding.

(*1*) *Ipseity* ('*Jemeinigkeit*') *and* '*Existence.*' Heidegger begins
his analysis with the provocative sentence:
"The thing-in-being whose analysis is our task is we ourselves.
The being of this thing-in-being is each one's "mine" (*je meines*)."
(p. 41). To this personalized character of being Heidegger then
attaches the synthetic label *Jemeinigkeit*, which, translated
literally, would amount to something like "each-his-ownness."
"Ipseity" has at least dictionary status and might do for our
purposes. What does it involve?

Heidegger's conception is clearly related to Kierkegaard's
picture of the single existing individual in his ultimate loneliness,
although Heidegger does not mention him in this context. However, Heidegger is not interested in this aspect for its own sake,
but for the sake of ontology. His main point is the fact that
human being in its "ipseity" is "related to" (*verhält sich zu*) man's
own personal being, to which it is "handed over" (*überantwortet*).
This is interpreted immediately in the sense that human being

is directed *toward* this, its own being (*Zu-sein*) and that it is this being which is at stake for it in its living – in fact that such being is its only stake. (This interpretation is as essential to Heideggers' ultimate objective as it may seem questionable to a more sceptical reader. For even if ipseity should prove to be one of the fundamental characteristics of human being, does it follow that essentially it is preoccupied by the question of Being, and primarily of its own being?)

From ipseity with its concern for one's own being Heidegger also derives the insight that human being is always oriented toward future possibilities of its own. For the fundamental possibility of choosing these possibilities, especially the possibilities which he calls "to be oneself or not to be oneself," i.e., to assume one's authentic way of being or to dodge it, Heidegger introduces the term "existence," in a sense which clearly differs from all previous usages, Scholastic as well as Kierkegaardian. It is in this sense that we are to understand Heidegger's key sentence: "The essence (*Wesen*) of human being lies in its existence," i.e., in its possibilities to choose different ways of being. One might well wonder whether this is not an over-statement, since even possibility presupposes at least some actualization as its base. In fact, later characterizations make it clear that "existence" in this narrowest sense does not exhaust the "essence" of human being but that it also includes such actualized characteristics as facticity (*Geworfenheit*) and falling-for (*Verfallen*), about which we shall hear more.

In considering Heidegger's concept of "existence" one must not overlook the fact that after *Sein und Zeit* he introduces one more sense of the term, namely as man's "standing in the clearing of being," as "being open for the openness of being," or as "standing in the midst of being" in such a way that he has access to being.[1] Heidegger's new spelling of the term, "Ek-sistenz" in his later writings, which first appears in *Vom Wesen der Wahrheit* (1943), is a typical attempt to resurrect the etymological literal sense of a

[1] To be sure, Heidegger does not seem to admit that there has been such a shift. Thus in the *Nachwort* to *Was ist Metaphysik?* (Sixth Edition, 1951, p. 14) he maintains that even in *Sein und Zeit* existence meant the "openness of the human being, who stands open for the openness of being" and that he "stands in this openness by enduring it" (*ausstehen*). A similar unacknowledged reinterpretation takes place in the case of concern (*Sorge*), which is no longer confined to human being, but referred to being as such.

word. Even more startling is the characterization of human being as "ec-static," i.e., as "standing in the clearing of being"; in fact now man himself is called the "clearing of being." [1] No derivation, phenomenological or otherwise, of this transition from the first to the second interpretation is given. It reflects the change from the hermeneutics of human being to the "thought" of Being.

(2) *Being-in-the World.* Possibly the most important structural characteristic considered in hermeneutic phenomenology is being-in-the-world (*in-der-Welt-sein*). For human being, as Heidegger understands it, does not, and even cannot, occur except in the framework of an encompassing world with which it belongs together, into which it finds itself inserted. This is not simply a matter of a part-whole relationship, where the human being is encased in the world like a box within a box. The relationship is much more intimate. Both are what they are only in being related to one another.

If thus being-in-the-world is the basic structure of human being, consciousness and particularly knowledge are only modifications of this underlying fundamental relationship. However, within this close-knit relationship Heidegger distinguishes three components: (1) world, (2) that which is in the world, (3) the relation of being "in." They are analyzed at first separately.

Under the heading of "worldliness" (*Weltlichkeit*) of the world Heidegger investigates the world of daily experience in contrast to the derivative world of science. It has its center in human being and coincides with our subjective environment (*Umwelt*) or milieu insofar as it is experienced. Heidegger shows impressively how the things within this world are given primarily not as physical objects, which simply occur "before our hands" (*vorhanden*), but as usable things or utensils (*Zeug*), which refer to possible applications within a practical world and are thus "handy" (*zuhanden*). Things of this type refer to one another and form systems of mutual reference of meaning.

While not entirely novel, these analyses represent perhaps one of the most interesting and fruitful parts of hermeneutic phenomenology. They have influenced particularly the attempts of phenomenological psychopathologists such as Ludwig Bins-

---

[1] "Brief über den Humanismus" in *Platons Lehre von der Wahrheit*, p. 69.

wanger to understand the world of psychopathic personalities in its inner coherence. World and worldliness embrace and support the otherwise unrelated intentional structures distinguished by early Husserlian phenomenology. Yet it must not be overlooked that Heidegger's own interest in these structures is only transitional, since he uses human being only as his point of departure for the analysis of its Being, not as its destination.

(3) *The Impersonal ('People')*. An even more influential example of hermeneutic phenomenology occurs in connection with the analysis of the carrier, the "who," of human existence in the world. It begins with an important discussion of the ego – an unreliable guide for hermeneutics – and of social existence in a shared world. After that, in less than four pages, Heidegger gives one of the most impressive accounts of everyday personal existence in its tendency to escape from itself and to fall into inauthentic being (*Verfallen*). As such it accepts the guidance and control of the subject signified by the impersonal pronoun "one" or "people" (the German *"man"*). Thus "one" is constantly concerned about keeping at the proper distance from other people, yet at the same time in a state of subservience which allows the other to determine the form of his existence. "One" wants to keep close to the average. Other possibilities of existence are levelled down by our constant regard for what "people" do. Thus the "one" takes over the load of our personal existence, makes us exist in a dependent and inauthentic fashion. Human existence is first and foremost that of "one," not of "self."

There are, to be sure, plenty of precedents and successors for this interpretation among writers both philosophical and non-philosophical. Sociologists will inevitably be reminded of G. H. Mead's concept of the "generalized other." But quite apart from the problem of the exact meaning of his conception, its general framework is quite different. And so is its evaluation: Mead is concerned with the evolutionary problem of the social matrix from which the individual self arises. For Heidegger it is a matter of describing a form of inauthentic social existence in which the individual tries to escape into an impersonalized average existence. The problem of authentic existence hardly seems to arise for Mead. – David Riesmann's concept of other-

directedness would be a more pertinent recent equivalent of
Heidegger's "people."

"Naked is he (the concrete man) flung into the world . ."
William James in *The Sentiment of Rationality*

(4) *Moods and 'Facticity.'* Before Heidegger, moods (in
German "*Stimmungen*," i.e., literally "attunements") may have
been of some interest to psychologists and phenomenologists
of feeling. But in contrast to the "intentional" or referential
feelings, moods were usually considered as merely subjective
affairs, of no cognitive significance beyond their own whimsical
occurrence. This changes in the light of Heidegger's hermeneutics.
Now that human being has been found to be inserted into a
world with meanings centered in it, and now that the center of
this world has been considered, the question of their relation
is raised, i.e., that of man's existence within such a world. For
this relation Heidegger uses the equivalent of the English 'being
there,' i.e. *Da-sein*, this time spelled with the two components
of the word separated and hyphenated in the obvious intention
of reviving their literal meanings. For we are there in this world
in the sense of finding ourselves in a peculiar fundamental
situation (*Befindlichkeit*). It is Heidegger's contention that we
can find out about the meaning of this fundamental situation
by interpreting certain fundamental moods. Strangely enough,
the moods which he selects are not so much those where we are
"in tune," but those that show us out of tune (or "sorts,") such
as fear and anxiety. What they reveal is Being as a burden.
Even the elated moods reveal this by way of liberating us from
this burden (p. 134). (Why this interpretation is the correct one,
and not rather its opposite, is never discussed. There is,
after all, the buoyancy of those who seem to be supported by the
surge of something like a vital élan, whose absence is revealed in
the depressive moods).

The burden of human existence as thus manifested according
to Heidegger consists in the poignant fact that human being
"is and has to be," "whence and whither, however, remain in
the dark." This is obviously the feeling expressed in the well-
known lines of Edward Fitzgerald's *Omar Khayyam*:

I came like water, and like wind I go
Into this Universe, and Why not knowing
Nor Whence, like water willy-nilly flowing.

For this situation of facticity Heidegger coins the striking though ponderous word *"Geworfenheit,"* which would have to be rendered by a passive participle of verbs like to throw, to fling, or to cast. However, to Heidegger "thrownness" is not a mere brute fact: it represents an intimate part of our way of being, even though it is usually pushed into the background. Moods also give access to certain characters of our world as a whole, of our social being, and of our existential possibilities. Thus threateningness or dreadfulness is revealed to us in the mood of fear or dread.

In none of these interpretations does Heidegger ever raise the question whether and to what extent moods are reliable guides for an understanding of the world, even if they should be good clues for the interpretation of our own feeling about it. This question is all the more urgent since some moods are taken as signs of the opposite of what they seem to attest. No matter how significant one considers these interpretations, the question of their limitations is inescapable.[1]

(5) *Anxiety and Nothingness.* Few items in Heidegger's philosophy have given rise to more protests and even ridicule than these. Anxiety (*Angst*), as Heidegger sees it, is the most revealing of all the fundamental situations (*Grundbefindlichkeiten*). But what does it reveal? In order to appraise this, one must consider Heidegger's distinction between anxiety and fear in their hermeneutic significance.

Fear is characterized as a mode of human being in which we are afraid of something more or less definite, notably the dreadful. Its stake (*worum*) is human being itself. The function of fear is to expose us to the threatening in a way which makes us concerned. This characterization by function, in which the directional aspects, the source, and the stake of the experience are stressed, whereas its intrinsic nature is not even mentioned, constitutes a good illustration of the difference between hermeneutic and descriptive phenomenology.

[1] O. F. Bollnow in his book *Das Wesen der Stimmungen* (Frankfurt, Vittorio Klostermann, 1942) gives an important critical development of Heidegger's analyses with very different results.

By contrast, anxiety is described as the condition which is behind our everyday escape into (small) talk, curiosity, and ambiguity. What threatens us here and makes us flee is "nothing in particular," something which is "nothing and nowhere." Ultimately Heidegger diagnoses the object of anxiety as the world as such and our whole position in this world. In such a state of anxiety the world appears with the peculiar character of uncanniness (*Unheimlichkeit*). The "nothing" revealed by the anxiety of *Sein und Zeit* thus consists of the uncanny indefiniteness of the world as a whole and of our being in the world.

The interpretation of anxiety and of the nothing to which it refers is pushed somewhat further in the lecture *Was ist Metaphysik?*, which has attracted particular attention. Here the "nothing" serves as a direct foil for Being itself, Heidegger's real concern in his seeming preoccupation with nothingness. Anxiety is now interpreted as a pulling away from the nothing. He identifies this nothing with the things-in-being in their entirety. In this experience they seem to drop away from us and to hold us off at the same time. It could perhaps be compared with the experience of agoraphobia, in which the more distant objects seem to recede from us, or with the pattern of the expanding universe according to the latest astronomic views. It is this peculiar movement which to Heidegger makes the essence of what is commonly called "nothing." Hence Heidegger's nothing is not an entity but an event or character which attaches to the world in the peculiar mood of anxiety. For this event Heidegger coins a special verb from the noun nothing, *"nichten."* It is therefore unfair to charge Heidegger with having hypostatized the nothing, while it is true that he denies the origin of the term from negation or from a process like annihilation. Against the background of this experience Being stands out all the more clearly and poignantly. It is another question how far the character of nothingness is the necessary obverse of the experience of Being, as Heidegger implies.

Even more startling and provocative is Heidegger's formula for man's position in relation to this "nothing": "Human being is suspension (*Hineingehaltenheit*) into the nothing"; or "man is the stand-in (*Platzhalter*) for the nothing." The second, quaintly striking formulation seems to suggest that the nothing is a phenomenon which depends on human beings and could not be without them. The first, even more daring, assigns to the nothing the status of a surrounding medium. Both convey the idea of a unique distinction of man as a being who stands not only in the midst of being, but also finds himself exposed to the possibility of non-being, and who in this sense can transcend the mere fact of his being.

(6) *Concern ('Sorge') as the Fundamental Structure of Human Being.* Thus far the hermeneutics of being-in-the-world with its various expressions has not yet supplied the pervading clue by which Heidegger would like to make human existence intelligible, and which he calls the Being of human being. It is the function of the phenomenology of anxiety as the fundamental mood of the human situation to bring out this structure. Anxiety is always concerned about the existential possibilities of human being caught by its facticity and trying to escape into everyday existence. Human being thus shows a threefold directedness: (1) it is ahead of itself toward its future possibilities (*Sich-vorweg-sein*); (2) it is already involved in its factual being (*schon-sein in ...*); (3) it is lost in the world of its daily occupations (*sein bei ...*). For this threefold structure Heidegger uses the German word *Sorge*. It can best be rendered by the much more appropriate "concern," "care" being a more dubious equivalent, since Heidegger, none too successfully, wants to exclude all connotations of worry. Concern, then, is at the root of all our dealings, especially our practical dealings and aspirations in our everyday life, our willing and wishing. It shows man as primarily reaching out into the future, as tied to his past into which he finds himself "thrown," and as diverted by the world of his present.

> "On the dialectical or ideal (not biological) relation of life to death I think Heidegger is splendid."
> George Santayana, *Letters*, p. 381.

(7) *Death.* All the preceding analyses are included by Heidegger among the preparatory ones. One of the most characteristic examples of existential interpretation on the deeper level (*ursprünglich*) is that of death. Compared, for instance, with

Scheler's posthumously published analysis of death[1] it might
seem rather meager. Thus Heidegger never attempts to describe
the way in which the process of dying constitutes itself, however
inadequately and distantly, in human consciousness. Yet, what
Heidegger is interested in is not the phenomenon of death, but
its role as the event which "completes" human existence. Thus
he identifies and characterizes death only as the most authentic
possibility of human existence, the one in which existence itself
becomes impossible. Human existence is essentially "existence
toward death." This does not mean that death is the goal of
human existence. But it does mean that it is oriented toward it,
at least by way of anticipation.

Much about Heidegger's interpretation of man's attitude
toward death as the ultimate possibility which ends all possibility, and about his attempts to escape it is impressive. Nevertheless, one wonders why facing this possibility in stern
resoluteness should be his one and only authentic possibility.
True, Heidegger is not obsessed by the physical or theological
aspects of death. Nevertheless, he does not even consider any
alternative authentic possibilities of human existence, such as
the fulfillment of a life project in the spirit of Goethe's *Faust*
or the supreme unconcern about death of Spinoza's wise man.

The same pattern can be observed in Heidegger's hermeneutics
of conscience, of guilt, and of resoluteness (*Entschlossenheit*), a
word which in its German literalized meaning expresses to
Heidegger a certain type of openness (*Erschlossenheit*). A somber
preoccupation with necessary failure, with guilt and futility
(*Nichtigkeit*) seems to permeate this whole section of *Sein und
Zeit* more than any other part of the book. However, Heidegger
always refuses to put these interpretations into a theological
framework. This very fact may have made them all the more
attractive to theologians, who could look upon them as independent confirmations of their revelational diagnoses of the
human condition.

(*8*) *Temporality*. With the subject of temporality we reach
the point or "horizon" from where Heidegger hopes to answer
not only the question of the meaning of human being but of Being

---

[1] "Tod und Fortleben" in *Nachlass* I, p. 1–52; *Gesammelte Werke* X, 9–64.

itself. The published parts of *Sein und Zeit* lead at least far enough to show how time is rooted in human existence in the form of "temporality."

Temporality is introduced as the "meaning" of the concern (*Sorge*) which makes up the Being of human being. It is not exactly easy to determine what "meaning" signifies in this context. Indications are that what Heidegger has in mind is something like a frame of reference or "horizon" for the projects of human existence; but there also seems to be the connotation of a final purpose (*woraufhin*), which makes our secondary projects possible (p. 324). However, there is a clear parallelism between temporality in its three phases of future, present, and past, and the three aspects of *Sorge* in which we are ahead of ourselves toward the possibilities of future existence, are immersed in the facticity of our past, and "fall for" the escapes of our present.

In the pattern of temporality Heidegger assigns priority to the future, which he interprets, in accordance with one literal meaning of the German word *"Zukunft,"* as that which comes toward us. This future is even said to originate our present and our past. Another feature that goes with this is that temporality is not properly a thing-in-being. It is not even correct to say that time "has" being. Rather does it "temporalize" itself. The German word which Heidegger uses in this context, *"zeitigen,"* is not completely new. In ordinary contexts it stands either reflexively for the coming into being (*sich zeitigen*) or transitively for the bringing into being of various things as time goes on. But one could certainly not say that time itself is the result of *Zeitigung*.[1] While Heidegger does not give any definition of the term, one gathers that time has a mode of being completely its own. It almost sounds as if time produced itself like a causa sui, since it does not seem to originate from human beings or from Being in general.

Temporality is also characterized as "ecstatic." There are no signs that Heidegger wants this term to be understood in the

[1] As mentioned before (p. 149) the term appears also in an extended sense, in the manuscripts, mostly unpublished, of Husserl's later period, which deal with the deepest layer of constitution in consciousness, the constitution of time. Whether the term drifted from Heidegger to Husserl must remain an open question. Certainly, if so, it has changed its meaning in the process.

traditional sense of a mystic ecstasy. Rather does he think of an intensified literal meaning of the word, in the sense of standing beside itself (*ausser sich*), which is used to convey the idea that human being in its temporality is always reaching out beyond itself, that it is beyond itself, i.e., in the future which "comes toward" it, that it goes back to its past facticity, and that it meets its present. Thus future, past, and present are also called the "ecstasies" of temporality (p. 329). Temporality, at least in the form in which it is the backbone of human being, does not consist of unrelated phases, but forms a dynamic system of references in which one form implies the other.

There is of course still a considerable gap between the mere temporality of human being and the time of Being in general. But it stands to reason that what Heidegger has in mind is a certain parallelism between the time structures on both levels. In view of the incompleteness of Heidegger's philosophy of time it would be hard to evaluate it as to its originality and its adequacy. According to his own testimony, it has grown chiefly out of his dialogue (*Gespräch*) with Aristotle, Augustine, Kant, and Hegel. However, he rejects Bergson's ideas with almost surprising violence. Perhaps the most original feature of Heidegger's conception is the emphasis on the prerogative of the future. To be sure, certain ideas of Whitehead, of John Dewey, and of G. H. Mead could be related to it without too much effort. Heidegger's interpretation, however, differs very significantly from Husserl's descriptive phenomenology of our inner time consciousness as contained in his Göttingen lectures of 1905, which Heidegger edited and published one year after the appearance of *Sein und Zeit*.

To what extent can temporality be accepted as the sense of human existence in any ordinary meaning of the word "sense"? It would hardly do to say that the passage of temporality and time makes up the sense of human being. At best one might understand it as the setting or raw material of our being. It is hard to shake off the impression that in these sections Heidegger is so preoccupied with the more general ontological problem that he no longer cares for an intelligible interpretation of human life rather than for what function temporality may have as a clue to the structure of Being as such.

(9) *Historicity*. Before Heidegger, phenomenologists had attached only limited and secondary importance to the problem of
history. Husserl had even launched a vigorous attack on historicism as one of the many forms of contemporary relativism. This,
however, did not mean that he wanted to ignore history completely. Thus the phenomenological "platform" of 1913 had expressed the idea that phenomenology would be in a position to
utilize the insights of the earlier philosophy much more fully
than ever before. Husserl himself, in his selective way, had tried
increasingly to relate his enterprise to the previous history of
thought and to justify it in this light.

From the very start Heidegger's attitude toward history was
of a very different nature. Historical studies were one of his first
major interests. As a Catholic theologian he had immersed
himself not only in Thomism but also in its sources in Aristotle,
in Augustine, and in the mystic tradition of Master Eckhart. In
the philosophical atmosphere around Heinrich Rickert he had
then developed an intense interest in German idealist thought
from Kant to Hegel and particularly in Nietzsche. But he had
also become deeply interested in the problems of history as such,
of historiography, and of its theory, particularly along the lines
of Wilhelm Dilthey. Later on, especially during his Marburg
years, his interest spread backwards to Plato and to the very
beginnings of Greek thought in the Pre-Socratics (a term which
Heidegger detests). If there is any area which he has comparatively neglected, it is that of Anglo-American philosophy.

As early as his inaugural lecture of 1915, Heidegger had taken
up the problem of historical time as distinguished from the time
of the physical sciences. It now found its proper place in the
existential analysis of human being. Later developments have
made it clear that he assigns to history a major place in the
structure not only of the things-in-being but also of Being itself.
We noted before that his strongest objection to Husserl has been
the latter's lack of a sense of history.

It would be misleading, however, to see in Heidegger's interest
in history simply an increased accent on historical studies within
phenomenology. Actually the very translation of Heidegger's
vocabulary involves a problem for the proper understanding of
his real concern. German has at least two terms for history,

"Geschichte" and *"Historie."* Since the latter is somewhat old-fashioned and obsolete, Heidegger reserves it for the merely antiquarian study of the past, in which he does not want to have any part. *"Geschichte,"* however, which usually has no substantially different meaning, is interpreted by Heidegger in the literal sense derived from the German word *geschehen*, i.e., to occur or to happen. Hence it is used to express the actual happening of historical events, or history in the making. It is tempting to coin for this second "historicity" an artificial term like "occurrency" or "proceedingness."

However, the important thing is to understand the phenomenon so designated as Heidegger interprets it. The historicity of human being consists primarily in the individual's fate (*Schicksal*) based on his own resolvedness (*Entschlossenheit*) within an inherited yet chosen frame of possibilities. There is both impotence and freedom in such an existence. The foundation of historicity is the temporality of human being as outlined above. As was the case with temporality, the center of gravity of historicity lies in the future. For human being is oriented toward the future, ultimately toward man's only authentic possibility, death. From this final "shipwreck" it is thrown back to its facticity, which gives it pastness (*Gewesenheit*). In taking over the inherited possibility of its 'thrownness' (*Geworfenheit*) it can become instantaneous (*augenblicklich*) in its time (p. 385). Resolvedness allows us to recapture the past in the form of a tradition, which is in a literal sense a re-petition or re-acquisition (*Wieder-holung*).

In mentioning these aspects one has to admit that an attempt to convey a concise picture of Heidegger's hermeneutics of historicity is particularly risky, not only because of its unusually top-heavy formulation, but also because of its position at the end of the published part of *Sein und Zeit*, thus presupposing the assimilation of the essentials of the preceding interpretations. Hence it would make little sense to attempt an evaluation, however tentative, of the phenomenological merits of these analyses. Even without that it is possible to acknowledge the originality of Heidegger's attack upon the problem of history's place in human existence. It keeps away equally from a blind worship of history as an enslavement to the past, and from a futile rebellion against it. Even though it leaves too many obscurities and ambiguities, it points the way toward intensified phenomenological studies of the historical consciousness and history's place in human existence.

c. PHENOMENOLOGY IN HEIDEGGER'S PHILOSOPHY SINCE 'SEIN UND ZEIT' – The fact that the term "phenomenology" has practically disappeared from Heidegger's writings since *Sein und Zeit* has been mentioned above. It is perhaps even more significant that even his own expression 'hermeneutics' no longer occurs. Does this mean that the phenomenological method and its hermeneutic modification have disappeared along with these terms? That this is not entirely the case may be gathered from the passage in the *"Brief über den Humanismus"* quoted on p. 279, which reaffirmed the "essential aid" of phenomenological seeing while rejecting the "improper aspiration to science and research." The real question is therefore to what extent and in what sense phenomenology can still be said to be a decisive factor in the structure of Heidegger's thought. The answer to this question depends chiefly on an adequate understanding of Heidegger's new approach to Being, for which he uses the plain German word *Denken*. Besides, we shall have to consider Heidegger's new attitude toward method in general, as expressed in his ideas about "ways of thinking" (*Denkwege*).

What does Heidegger in his later writings mean by "thinking"? Certainly nothing like the techniques of abstract reasoning as studied by logic in the technical sense, which Heidegger repudiates as a form of mere technology. Even more important is the fact that he does not conceive of thinking in the way Kant and Husserl did, namely as the opposite of *Anschauung* or intuiting and as restricted to concepts. The main task in clarifying the phenomenological status of Heidegger's *Denken* is to determine the place of what, in the phenomenological tradition, had been called intuiting (*Anschauung*) in the structure of *Denken*.

Denken, after having been introduced as the main correlate to Being and Truth in a rather casual fashion, finally became the subject of Heidegger's lecture course of 1951 and 52, published in 1954. Here the way in which Heidegger tried to elucidate the structure of thinking is based partly on etymology, partly on the translation of a fragment from Parmenides.

The etymological approach leads to the interpretation of thinking as *Gedanc* (a medieval German word), *Andacht* (i.e., literally, worshipful meditation), and *Dank* (i.e., thanksgiving). By *Gedanc* Heidegger understands the "collected, all-collecting remembrance" also identified with *Gemüt* or heart, very much after the model of Pascal's *logique du coeur*. Actually Heidegger regards logico-rational thought as a narrowed-down version of *Gedanc*, which includes remembrance (*Gedächtnis*) in the sense of holding fast to what is collected. It also implies affection (*Zuneigung*) of the heart toward what is made present by thinking in the sense of a thanks-giving or listening reverence toward the things to which we are indebted. All these hints, based on intensified interpretations of root meanings, add up to a conception of thinking as an intent and reverent meditation with our whole being on what makes the content of our thinking. "Being mindful" might be the nearest English equivalent of such a conception.

The approach via the Parmenides text uses a passage usually translated as "It is necessary to say and to think that Being is" (fragment 6). Without following Heidegger's highly characteristic discussion all the way, I shall concentrate on his interpretations of the terms 'saying' (Greek: *legein*) and 'thinking' (Greek: *noein*). *Legein* is understood primarily as making something lie (or appear) before us (*vorliegen lassen*); *noein* is taken to mean not merely a receptive process but an active taking before us: we take something into our heed or guard (*in die Acht*), leaving it, however, exactly as it is (D 123 f.). The two are inseparable parts of thinking. Taking something into our heed is described as making what lies before us come toward us. It is not a reaching out (*Zugreifen*) toward it (D 127) nor any attack upon it. More important, it is not a matter of concept (*Begriff*). Thus while "thinking" thinks in accordance with the things, it thinks without concepts; according to Heidegger this is true even of thinking in the sense of Aristotle.

What can be derived from these characterizations, which never add up to a sustained description of what goes on concretely in a specific case of thinking? Clearly, this thinking is anything but a methodical procedure for which definite rules could be prescribed. It is a matter of the whole human thinker, including his heart as well as his intellect, insofar as this distinction is still permissible. It seems to be neither completely receptive nor spontaneous, but in any case it stands under the commanding guidance of the object of thought, i.e., Being, which determines its content.

Is it possible to identify such a non-conceptual thinking simply with intuition in the old phenomenological sense? No explicit statement for or against such an interpretation can be found in Heidegger's own writings. In answer to a personal inquiry Heidegger intimated that he avoids the terms *"Anschauung"* and *"Intuition"* chiefly because of their past associations, among them, it may be assumed, with Husserl's *Wesensschau*. It should also be noted that the operations of thinking as characterized above are hardly those in which we are actually cognizant. At best these operations precede or follow cognition. The etymological interpretation of thinking in the sense of "being mindful" and the one based on the Parmenides text, according to which thinking makes its object lie before us, seems to refer to a phase which prepares actual cognition, while "taking under one's guard" describes one that follows it. However, even though Heidegger's account of thinking does not mention the cognitive phase explicitly, he certainly does not exclude it. But is this sufficient ground for asserting that thinking is identical with the phenomenological intuition?

Heidegger's later writings contain little reference to method in the traditional sense. But there is all the more frequent reference to a motif which is actually a translation of the Greek word *methodos* (i.e., "way after") namely, "way of thinking" (*Denkweg*). These *Denkwege* occur particularly in two types. One of them carries the German title *Holzwege*, i.e., forest paths or roads that chiefly serve the lumbermen but to everyone else are nothing but blind alleys; whence '*auf dem Holzweg sein*' means colloquially 'to be on the wrong track.' Heidegger uses this word as the title for six long essays seemingly without mutual connection. Only in his mystagogic prologue does he hint that the lumbermen and the rangers (*Waldhüter*, reminding us of the "guardians of Being") "know" these paths. The *Feldweg*, however, designating a private winding country path through the fields, is used by Heidegger as the title of a charming autobiographical reminiscence.[1] This path seems to assume almost the role of a messenger of truth and even of a comforter to man. Thus, in the unarticulated language of the things around the *Feldweg*, "God is finally God." Yet the last message of the *Feldweg* remains in a resigned chiaroscuro: "The message (*Zuspruch*) is now quite distinct. Is it the soul that speaks? Is it the world? Is it God? Everything speaks of resignation to the same thing. ... It grants the inexhaustible power of the simple" (*das Einfache*).

None of Heidegger's later "ways" has the nature of an easy royal road or even of a normal highway. They are all byways. There is no assurance as to their destination nor any claim to universal validity. And there is no clear prescription telling us how to use them. Thinking consists in a being "underway," which actually builds the way.[2] It is also a lonely way. And Heidegger even seems to doubt the advisability of making this way "publicly visible." Thus "thinking," even insofar as it is in our power and not simply a response to the initiative of Being, is clearly nothing that can be put into the form of a method to be taught and learned.

There are other characteristic proofs for this conclusion. In his decisive attempt to force the proper translation and interpretation of the Parmenides text quoted above Heidegger speaks about the necessity of a leap, the leap of a single glance (*Blick*) which catches sight of what Parmenides meant. This almost sounds like Kierkegaard's celebrated leap into faith. Apparently we can prepare for such a leap. But Heidegger does not tell us how (p. 141). One can only tell what he sees in such a leap. But reasons and counter-reasons are ineffective. More recently Heidegger, playing on the double meaning of the word "*Satz*" in German as "proposition" and as "leap," even used such fundamental logical propositions as the "law of sufficient reason" and the "law of identity" as starting points for a leap into Being whose abruptness does not allow for any methodical approach.[3]

Another indication of the non-methodical character of the new "thought" is Heidegger's repudiation of the term "research."

---

[1]
[1] See also *Holzwege*, p. 194; *Vorträge und Aufsätze*, p. 184.
[2] *Was heisst Denken?*, p. 164.
[3] *Der Satz vom Grund*, p. 95 f., 157; *Identität und Differenz*, p. 24 f.

To him research is the mark of modern science, which is characterized by a certain preconception (*Entwurf*) of its field and by its method. The researcher becomes actually a technician in the service of the conquest of the world by the subject man. Reflection (*Besinnung*), which Heidegger contrasts to this research as the proper task of philosophy, apparently cannot be described in terms of a clear and teachable method.[1] Even more indicative of this non-methodical character of the new kind of thinking is its affinity with poetry, as Heidegger conceives of it and even practices it. It would exceed the possibilities and needs of this discussion to give an account and attempt a clarification of what Heidegger means by poetry. But it is clear that it goes far beyond the creation of a merely imaginative world. Poetry not only finds truth, it even establishes it, says Heidegger, using one of his favorite but enigmatic words "*stiften*." It "names" the Holy, and is thus the road toward the Divine and indirectly toward God.[2] In any case, poetry is a parallel enterprise to thinking, in its highest achievements even superior to thinking. At times Heidegger now seems to think of thinking itself as merely a form of poetry.[3] Certainly there are no longer any sharp borderlines between them. And both seem to be much more under the guidance and control of Being than of man, the poet or thinker.

This poses the question of whether there are any tests for this kind of thinking. Heidegger himself raises it in connection with one of his boldest, most forced interpretative translations. Here he admits that no scientific proof is possible, but he also rejects mere faith. Instead, "Thinking is the poetry (*Dichten*) of truth of Being in the historical dialogue of the thinkers" (*geschichtliche Zwiesprache der Denker*).[4] This dialogue is a recurrent motif in Heidegger's philosophizing. But it is obviously not so much dialogues among contemporaries which he has in mind. Some of these, like the meeting between Heidegger and Ernst Cassirer in 1929 were memorable events.[5] But they have hardly modified or tested anyone's beliefs, but were chiefly public confrontations.

---

[1] *Holzwege*, p. 69; translated by Marjorie Grene in *Measure* II, 269 ff. See also *Vorträge und Aufsätze*, p. 45 ff.

[2] *Was ist Metaphysik?* Nachwort (1934), 6th edition, p. 46.

[3] *Aus der Erfahrung des Denkens*, p. 25; *Holzwege*, p. 343.

[4] *Holzwege*, p. 302 f., 343.

[5] See, e.g. Hendrik J. Pos, "Recollections of Ernst Cassirer" in P. Schilpp, ed., *The Philosophy of Ernst Cassirer*, pp. 67–69; *Sein und Zeit*, p. 51 f.

The dialogue which is the testing ground for Heidegger is that with the texts of the great thinkers of the past, to whose interpretation he seems to have turned as his favorite approach to the problems. However, a dialogue in which the real partner is silenced from the very start offers little guarantee that we shall hear anything but an echo of the speaker's own voice. In fact, Heidegger himself seems to be aware that his own interpretations are by no means valid for all times nor, for that matter, for anyone else but himself.[1]

What has become at this stage of Heidegger's earlier interpretation of phenomenology, notably of his hermeneutics? We remember that the ground for such a phenomenology was laid by the so-called phenomenological destruction. Even without using the name, Heidegger has continued this technique, especially in his *Holzwege*, where, for instance, the discussions of Nietzsche and Anaximander offer excellent examples of it. Here a searching interpretation of the texts serves as preparation for a more original approach to the phenomena.

It is less easy to say what has become of the hermeneutic method of *Sein und Zeit*. For it is not only the term that has disappeared: human being, the one and only subject of such interpretation, no longer constitutes the privileged topic of Heidegger's investigations. The themes of his later thinking are no longer taken from such a limited area, but include not only works of art but also aspects of Being itself. This means that interpretation no longer takes the exclusive form of uncovering the true purposes of human being. But this does not mean that interpretation as such is abandoned. To be sure, it is not Being itself or truth which requires *Auslegung*. Now it is primarily texts which form the starting points for Heidegger's own philosophizing. Their interpretation had been a constant concern of Heidegger's lectures and seminars, beginning with his Aristotle interpretations of 1921/22. The first large-scale example to reach the wider public was the Kant book. The explanation of Hölderlin's poetry, beginning in 1936, applied this interpretation to a new area. *Holzwege*, especially in the case of the fragment from Anaximander, gave a first sample of Heidegger's interpretation of Pre-Socratic texts, which were followed by the Parmenides

---

[1] *Was heisst Denken?* p. 110.

interpretations in *Was heisst Denken*? But how do these interpretations differ from the scholarly interpretations of the philologisus? True, Heidegger often begins with a careful study of the texts. But he wants his analysis to be clearly distinguished from merely philological interpretation, for which he shows little taste or respect. For he is not afraid of doing violence to his texts in order to "understand" a thinker better than he has understood himself, whether his name is Kant or Plato. "In contrast to the methods of historical philology, which has its own task, a thinking dialogue is subject to different laws." [1]

Whatever the methods and limitations of these new interpretations of given texts may be, in what sense can they be claimed to be phenomenology, even if they should still be hermeneutics? The answer must depend on the extent to which they still deal with phenomena, even if this term is understood in Heidegger's own sense of "what shows itself by itself." It could hardly be claimed that texts as such, poetic or otherwise, are such phenomena. Hence it would be rather inappropriate to describe their interpretation as genuinely phenomenological.

How far, in fact, do Heidegger's last writings deal directly with phenomena? The "unhiddenness" of Truth and Being would seem to make hermeneutic interpretation superfluous. On the other hand "truth," being merely the "clearing" within Being, leaves enough darkness around it to challenge the hermeneutic thinker. However, as long as Heidegger himself does not offer such a hermeneutics of Being and of Truth, and especially as long as he does not do so explicitly and in some detail, it would be premature to label his present preludes to it as a hermeneutics of Being.

It should also be noticed that Heidegger's thinking has now abandoned all pretense of being "scientific." The hermeneutic phenomenology of *Sein und Zeit*, even in its "definitive concept," still tried to be science and seemed to maintain Husserl's original aspirations toward a rigorous science. How far this amounts to a difference in Heidegger's actual procedure. rather than to a difference in his self-interpretation is another matter. But it highlights again the degree to which Heidegger has drifted

---

[1] *Kant und das Problem der Metaphysik.* Preface to the 2nd ed., 1950.

away from his original conception of phenomenology and his
hopes for it.

In conclusion, I should mention the fact that in September
1953 I had a unique opportunity to interview Martin Heidegger
personally about his present attitude toward phenomenology.
Without quoting his words, I feel entitled to render the sense of
his answers as follows: Heidegger frankly admitted and restated
his rejection of transcendental phenomenology. But he did not
express any intention of dissociating himself from the Phenomenological Movement, as far as its general intentions are concerned.
Nor did he say or imply that any substantial change in his
methods had taken place since the publication of *Sein und Zeit*,
particularly not with regard to such innovations as the phenomenological destruction and phenomenological hermeneutics. As
far as the abandonment of *Sein und Zeit* is concerned, he intimated
that the new approach from Being to human being by no means
excluded the earlier one from human being to Being. In fact
he stated that if he ever should rewrite *Sein und Zeit* he would try
to combine the two approaches. In other words, for Heidegger
this is a matter of a both-and, not of an either-or.

I shall not attempt to discuss this self-interpretation in the
light of the evidence already presented. In any event, Heidegger
did not deny the obvious shift in his approach. He thus confirmed
my conjecture that phenomenology, understood as the hermeneutic interpretation of human being, has lost its priority in the
pattern of his thinking. How far there can be any such thing as a
phenomenology within the framework of the later approach
must remain an open question. Heidegger does refer to the
"essential aid of phenomenological seeing." However, there are
no conspicuous examples of it in his later writings except those
strewn in among his interpretations of texts. This is one reason
why no illustrations of this later phenomenological thinking will
be added here. Heidegger's original phenomenology remains
that of *Sein und Zeit*.

6. *Toward an Appraisal of Heidegger's Phenomenology*

I began the attempt to introduce Heidegger's phenomenology
by a remarkable tribute taken from Gilbert Ryle's review of
Sein und Zeit. It would, however, be misleading to conceal the

fact that in spite of his sympathetic approach to Heidegger's text he came out with a rather disastrous estimate of his pheno-menology. His final conclusion concerning its significance for the entire Phenomenological Movement seems worth pondering even in retrospect:

It is my personal opinion that qua First Philosophy Phenomenology is at present heading for bankruptcy and disaster and will end either in self-ruinous Subjectivism or in a windy Mysticism. ... I hazard this opinion with humility and reservations, since I am well aware how far I have fallen short of understanding this difficult work.

At least to some extent this modest prophecy, read with all its qualifications, has come true. It has proved so at least for that part of the German phenomenology of the thirties with which Ryle was acquainted (he clearly was not with Scheler). For Husserl's radicalized subjectivism failed to produce the promised final systematic statement in a version that satisfied the master himself sufficiently to authorize publication.

As to Heidegger's phenomenology, Ryle anticipated remarka-bly the trend toward an increasingly mystic approach. And since Heidegger had captured the minds of most German phenomenologists and "stolen the show," as it were, his final abandonment of the label "phenomenology" can be interpreted as the liquidation if not as the bankruptcy of the Movement. The fact that even Husserl's erstwhile assistants, Ludwig Land-grebe and Eugen Fink, have declared phenomenology a closed chapter could be considered as the final confirmation of the prophecy.

But whether or not it has proved correct, more important than the prognosis is the diagnosis, which in Ryle's case is more than debatable. The following attempt to evaluate Heidegger's phe-nomenology is not meant as an assessment of his philosophizing as a whole. Its limited objective will be (1) to determine to what extent Heidegger's philosophy was really phenomenology and hence can be taken as representative of phenomenology as such: (2) to point out the peculiar strengths and weaknesses of Hei-degger's phenomenologizing.

a. TO WHAT EXTENT IS HEIDEGGER A PHENOME-NOLOGIST? Clearly Heidegger never was a phenomenologist in the strictest sense defined by Husserl's subjectivist transcendentalism with its idealistic implications, even though, especially at the time of *Sein und Zeit*, he rejected traditional realism. In particular, he never accepted the phenomenological reduction in Husserl's sense.

As to the strict sense of phenomenology, in which attention to the ways of givenness becomes essential (sense γ), the hermeneutic analyses of *Sein und Zeit* hold at least considerable implicit interest. This is particularly evident in the interpretation of moods as revealing more or less indirectly the fundamental situation of human being.

It may be more dubious whether Heidegger's phenomenology fits into the framework of a phenomenology in the wider sense, which emphasizes the insights into essences (sense β). For hermeneutic phenomenology intends to treat human existence as each one's own, although one might say that in the final analysis it still gives a diagnosis of human existence in general. It should also be mentioned that quite often Heidegger speaks of certain features as "essentially" belonging to Being or thinking, and even refers to essential laws, which would seem to imply that he at least practices eidetic phenomenology even if he does not want to preach it.

It is, however, by no means clear whether Heidegger belongs any longer unconditionally within the framework of the Phenomenological Movement in the widest sense α. The first test, acceptance of intuiting as the ultimate source and test of all knowledge, could be justified probably even in the case of Heidegger's later philosophy of thinking, in which phenomenological seeing is appealed to as an essential help, if not as the substance of his approach. What is more questionable is whether he still identifies himself actively with the Phenomenological Movement, even if he does not dissociate himself from it completely. Perhaps the real question is whether Heidegger still recognized the survival of such a Movement at all. Certainly he himself does not give evidence of any active interest in its continuation or revival.

Summing up, we must remember: Phenomenology was for Heidegger fundamentally only a means for the solution of his basic problem. This means proved to be only partially effective. It never was an integral part of his philosophy. Heidegger had come to Husserl's phenomenology with his task all laid out. In the days of his emancipation from scholastic and transcendentalist philosophy (Rickert), and especially after meeting Husserl, he thought that a hermeneutic phenomenology of human being (in contrast to Husserl's descriptive phenomenology of pure consciousness) offered the best chance for the solution of his problem. His failure to win over Husserl to this approach and the ensuing rift between them were factors in his retreat from phenomenology in the technical sense. More important was the realization that the approach to the problem of Being via an analysis of human being was not the hoped for master key to the riddle of Being, since the transition from the temporality of human being to the time of Being itself could not be made. It was this retreat from the prerogative of the subjective in the sense of the human which entailed his detachment from phenomenology with its primary interest in the given as given. Phenomenology, insofar as it is still a part of Heidegger's recent approach, is no longer its decisive part. It was fundamentally nothing but a phase in his development. No wonder he now seems disinterested in its present and future.

This conclusion does not discharge us from an evaluation of Heidegger's concrete phenomenological achievements. In what follows I shall therefore offer some observations on the points that seem to me relevant to such a more detailed appraisal beyond the incidental remarks that have been made in earlier sections of this chapter.

b. STRENGTHS AND WEAKNESSES OF HEIDEGGER'S PHENOMENOLOGY – There can be little question that in his hermeneutic phenomenology Heidegger has attacked a variety of phenomena, such as fear, anxiety, and concern, which had not been taken up before by phenomenologists, and that he has brought out some of their aspects and characters in a way that shows his unusual perceptiveness and penetration.

Nevertheless, Heidegger's accounts of these phenomena, taken as phenomenological descriptions, are often meager, chiefly because he usually limits himself to attaching to these phenomena striking and evocative names instead of determining their constituent elements, their varieties, and their comparative characteristics. This lack is clearly related to the fact that Heidegger considers the task of a mere description of manifest phenomena to be superfluous. The concern of his hermeneutic phenomenology is to uncover the hidden phenomena and particularly their meanings. However, the question seems legitimate whether in this regard Heidegger does not share the naiveté of many explanatory sciences which overlook the fact that what is manifest is not always thoroughly perceived, assimilated, and understood in its structure and its varieties. It is for such reasons that the descriptive basis for Heidegger's interpretations is often too narrow.

This raises the whole question of the rights of hermeneutic phenomenology. Difficult though it may be, Heidegger's program of a phenomenology that attempts to investigate the hidden aspects of the phenomena (the "phenomenological" phenomena) is more than justifiable, particularly if it can succeed in making them directly accessible rather than leaving them in the realm of merely hypothetical explanations which can be only indirectly verified. This applies particularly to the hermeneutic interpretations of human being and existence. Doubts concerning them apply more to the practice than to the principle of this obviously ambitious and difficult enterprise. Rarely if ever does Heidegger seem to consider the possibility of interpretations other than his own. And often, for instance in his discussion of moods, one cannot overcome the impression of a biased approach which prevents him from considering alternatives. Never does he seem to feel the need of showing his readers his criteria. There is a finality about his monumental and oracular pronouncements which ignores the question of evidence and strains the critical sense of all but the devotees.

If one recalls the caution-and carefulness which characterized the work of the early phenomenologists, one cannot help being amazed at the blitheness with which the new phenomenology takes, for instance, the manifestness (*Offenbarkeii*) of Being for granted. The seeming qualification that Being also tends to hide, or that we are forgetful of it, does but little to relieve the stunning boldness of the claim. If we are also told that it is Being itself which plays this game of hide and seek on a cosmic scale, it seems hard to avoid the impression of a fantastic drama without personal protagonists. Surely, in the name of a critical phenomenology such claims must not go unchallenged.

Lack of patience with the critical reader leads to what is perhaps the severest handicap of Heidegger's phenomenology: the difficulty of its formulation and transmission. In raising this point one must not minimize the creative originality and power of Heidegger's diction and style. If these qualities alone could determine the rank of philosophy, there would be no question in my mind that Heidegger's achievement is unique. There is a certain grandeur in his writing, even if in places but one step separates the sublime from the ridiculous.

But there are requirements for philosophical language other than style. Heidegger himself, who has thought deeply about language, has an extremely high conception of its nature and capacities. Perhaps its most exalted formulation is implied in the statement: "Language is the house of being. In this house man has his abode." [1] It is for this reason, too, that ultimately poetry, in preference to the non-verbal arts, receives such a preferred rank in Heidegger's thinking.

In view of this estimate it is all the more significant that precisely difficulties of language, the "house of being," have blocked the way of *Sein und Zeit* beyond its published parts and have apparently interfered even with the development of Heidegger's second approach in *Vom Wesen der Wahrheit* (see p. 311). To be sure, it is the language of metaphysics which failed, not language as such. But what language can supplant it? Hardly the language of the poet, who "names the Holy," but does not "tell Being," as the "thinker" is expected to do.

This difficulty leads to the even more serious, and in a sense gravest, crux of Heidegger's phenomenology: its communicability through language. Heidegger's obvious intent to awaken and even to shock his reader into a realization of the phenomena has all too often defeated his own purpose. The squeezing and bending of existing words by literalizing their meanings, whether etymologically justified or not, without additional guidance to the reader by way of definitions or examples, is apt to create a twilight of uncritical semi-understanding among the gullible, and of hostile misunderstanding among the more critical. True,

---

[1] "Brief über den Humanismus" in *Platons Lehre von der Wahrheit*, p. 53.

phenomenology has always had to face the problem of devising new terms for new phenomena. But it has never been enough to coin such terms without also introducing the reader to the new phenomena. Precisely this is one of the functions of a descriptive phenomenology. Lack of patience and empathy with his readers is the worst weakness of Heidegger's hermeneutic phenomenology. It reduces it to a more or less private enterprise or esoteric cult. Yet it would seem to me that this is by no means an irremediable weakness, and that it should be possible to salvage a good deal of Heidegger's insights by a less reckless and violent approach to the problem of communication. It may well be that the success of French phenomenology, including its Heideggerian ingredients, is due to greater concern for this problem.

One final doubt is raised by the approach of Heidegger's later writings. Phenomenology in its early stage was characterized by its courageous attack on the things themselves, regardless of previous opinions and theories. There is in Heidegger an increasing tendency to go to the "things" by way of classical texts and by an interpretation based primarily on etymology and at best secondarily on an appeal to the phenomena. It is thus again the secondary world of books and traditions which gets between the "things" and their fresh intuition. To be sure, it would be a sad loss if phenomenology should deprive itself completely of the insights of the past, which now also include the insights of the earlier phenomenologists. But it would be just as fatal if "going to the sources" should again assume the sense of going to the texts, instead of going to the phenomena. The way from *Sein und Zeit* to *Was heisst Denken?* shows an alarming tendency in this direction.

Once in the twenties, in one of his exuberant moods at the height of his cooperation with Heidegger, Husserl exclaimed: "Phenomenology, that is Heidegger and me." Had it been so, Ryle's prophecy would indeed have come true. But here, as in Husserl's case, I shall invoke Heidegger's own words with which he vindicated his independence of Husserl in *Sein und Zeit*: "The essence of phenomenology does not consist in its actuality. Higher than actuality stands potentiality."

Later chapters will tell the story of the development of these unexhausted potentialities.

7. Heidegger's Following and Phenomenology

Compared with the academic influence of other phenomenologists such as Husserl and Scheler, Heidegger has unquestion-
ably the largest following. Even some of Husserl's Freiburg
students like LANDGREBE and FINK have come so much under
the influence of Heidegger that a recent bibliography of German
philosophy of existence may be justified in including them among
his "immediate students." [1] Others include OSKAR BECKER,
F. J. BRECHT, WALTER BRÖCKER, HANS GEORG GADAMER,
GERHARD KRÜGER, KARL LÖWITH (the last two among his
keenest critics), WILHELM SZILASI, his Freiburg successor, and
KARL-HEINZ VOLKMANN-SCHLUCK. Beyond them there is a
widening circle of thinkers inside and outside Germany who are
more or less his disciples in the non-academic sense. [2]

It is another question whether these followers practice Hei-
degger's phenomenology. No sweeping answer to such a question
should be given without detailed conscientious examination.
However, on the whole, there is in the literature of the Heideg-
gerians little explicit reference to phenomenology. Some of
Oskar Becker's studies, particularly his earlier ones, those of
Karl Löwith, and in a wider sense perhaps even those of O. F.
BOLLNOW would seem to be most phenomenological in character.
So is the work of the Swiss psychiatrist LUDWIG BINSWANGER,
which owes much to both Husserl and Heidegger, though he
finally emancipated himself even from Heidegger.

Then there is the question of the extent to which Heidegger's
followers have maintained the level set by the master. It is one
thing to practice a thinking as unique and self-willed as Heidegger's. It is another matter to duplicate it without imitating the
mannerisms of the master and especially the artificialities of
his language. Unfortunately, the result has been too often
turgid imitation, combined with an uncritical worship of the
words of the master.   [1]

---

[1] O. F. Bollnow, *Deutsche Existenzphilosophie* (Bern, Francke, 1953).
[2] Werner Brock, the editor of *Existence and Being*, is one of these. – See also the
list of contributors to the two *Festschrift* volumes published on the occasion of
Heidegger's 60th birthday.

SELECTIVE BIBLIOGRAPHŸ

Major Works

Die Kategorien- und Bedeutungslehre des Duns Scotus (1916)
Sein und Zeit. I. Hälfte (1927) (SZ)
   Translations: Spanish (1951) by José Gaos; French (excerpts from the
[1]   second section in *Qu'est-ce que la métaphysique?* (1938) by H. Corbin.
"Vom Wesen des Grundes" in *Festschrift für E. Husserl* (1929)
   Translations: French (1930 and 1938) by H. Corbin
Kant und das Problem der Metaphysik (1929)
[2]   *Translations*: French (1954) by W. Biemel and A. de Waelhens
Was ist Metaphysik? (1929) – Nachwort (1944); Einleitung (1951)
   Translations: French (1931 and 1938); Spanish (1933); English (1949)
   by R. F. C. Hull and Alan Crick in *Existence and Being*, edited by
   Werner Brock[1] – a careful, conscientious effort. The "Einleitung,"
   translated by Walter Kaufmann, appeared in his *Existentialism from
   Dostoevsky to Sartre* (1957), pp. 207–21
Die Selbstbehauptung der deutschen Universität (1933)
Hölderlin und das Wesen der Dichtung (1936)
   Translations: French (1938); English (1949) by Douglas Scott in
   Existence and Being – fair.
Vom Wesen der Wahrheit (1943)
   Translations: French (1949) by A. de Waelhens and W. Biemel;
   English (1949) by R. F. C. Hull and Alan Crick in *Existence and Being* –
   good.
Platons Lehre von der Wahrheit (1947)
[3]   Contains also the "Brief über den Humanismus" to Jean Beaufret.
Holzwege (1950)
   Translations: English (1951), second essay only, by Marjorie Grene in
   Measure (1951), 269 ff.
Einführung in die Metaphysik (1953)
   Translations: English (1958) by Ralph Manheim – on the whole reliable
   and readable, though not as close to the original as possible.
Was heisst Denken? (1954) (D)
Aus der Erfahrung des Denkens (1954?)
Vorträge und Aufsätze (1954)
Was ist das – die Philosophie? (1956)
   Translations: English (1958) by W. Kluback and Jean T. Wilde with
   German text added.
Der Satz vom Grund (1957)
[4]   *Identität und Differenz* (1957)

---

[1] "Existence and Being," a title not used by Heidegger himself, characterizes
very well the poles of his thinking, but is hardly indicative of the content of a volume
two thirds of which consist of Brock's helpful paraphrase of *Sein und Seit*, followed
by the translation of four original essays in the last third. These essays, selected by
Heidegger himself for the occasion and even prefaced by a brief "Note" (p. 249),
are a puzzling combination, especially if meant as an introduction for Anglo-American
readers, since two of the four essays are interpretations of Hölderlin poems, which
are put before the two metaphysical essays. Heidegger himself seems to be merely
concerned lest they be considered as "contributions to research in the history of
literature and esthetics," which he deprecates, pleading merely that the four
essays "arose from a necessity of thought."

Monographs in French and German

BIEMEL, WALTER, *Le concept de monde chez Heidegger*, Louvain, Nauwe-
laerts, 1950
Careful analysis of a central concept in Heidegger's thought against the
background of the problem of Being, based chiefly on his earlier work.
FÜRSTENAU, PETER, *Heidegger, Das Gefüge seines Denkens*. Frankfurt,
Klostermann, 1958
A well-informed attempt to show the unity of Heidegger's thought
from *Sein und Zeit* to the latest works.
GAOS, JOSÉ, *Introducción a el Ser y el Tiempo de Martin Heidegger*. Mexico,
1951
LÖWITH, KARL, *Heidegger, Denker in dürftiger Zeit*. Frankfurt, Fischer,
1953
A series of three penetrating studies on the development of Heidegger's
thought, pointing out important changes in his later work.   [1]
DE WAELHENS, ALPHONSE, *La philosophie de Martin Heidegger*. Louvain,
Institut supérieur, 1942
Thus far the most detailed study of Heidegger's central works up to
1942, focussing on his existential analytics, but including a discussion
of its phenomenological features.
——, *Phénoménologie et vérité. Essai sur l'évolution de l'idée de vérité chez
Husserl et Heidegger*. Paris, Presses Universitaires, 1953
The second and larger part of this perceptive study deals with the fate
of the idea of truth in Heidegger's thought, including his later works.

Large Studies in English: [1]

GRENE, MARJORIE, *Martin Heidegger*. New York, Hilary, 1957
An informed but not altogether sympathetic brief interpretation,
omitting a number of central doctrines. The connections with phenome-
nology are hardly mentioned. Important passages are given in both
German and English.
LANGAN, THOMAS, *The Meaning of Heidegger. A Critical Study of an
Existentialist Phenomenology*. New York, Columbia, 1959
An attempt to show the unity of Heidegger's work. Its phenomenolo-
gical aspect is only named but never explained   [2]

Articles in English   [3]

CERF, WALTER, "An Approach to Heidegger's Ontology," *PPR* I (1940),
177–90
DELIUS, HARALD, "Descriptive Interpretation," *PPR* XIII (1953), 305–23
EARLE, WILLIAM, "Wahl on Heidegger on Being," *Philosophical Review*
LXVII (1958), 85–90

---

[1] The Anglo-American reader will find considerable help in the Heidegger
chapters of several books on existentialism, especially in Allen, E. L., *Existentialism
from Within*; Blackham, H. J., *Six Existentialist Thinkers* (1951), Ch. V.; Collins,
James, *The Existentialists* (1952), Ch. V.; Kuhn, Helmut, *Encounter with Nothingness*
(1951) (where especially the connections between phenomenology and existentialism
in Heidegger are discussed very helpfully in Ch. VIII). But few of these much too
comprehensive accounts are free from factual errors.

356   THE GERMAN PHASE

FARBER, MARVIN, "Heidegger on the Essence of Truth," *PPR* XVIII
[1]   (1958), 523–32
FREUND, E. H., "Man's Fall in Heidegger's Philosophy," *Journal of
Religion* XXIV (1944), 180–87
GLICKSMAN (GRENE), MARJORIE, "A Note on the Philosophy of Heidegger," *Journal of Philosophy* XXXV (1938), 93–104 (Student impressions
from Freiburg 1931–2).
GRAY, J. GLENN, "Heidegger's "Being," *Journal of Philosophy*, XLIX
(1952), 415–22. (Clear account of Heidegger's later philosophy)
——, "Heidegger's Course: From Human Existence to Nature," *Journal
of Philosophy* LIV (1957), 197–207
——, "Heidegger Evaluates Nietzsche," *J. of History of Ideas* XIV
(1953), 304–9.
HINNERS, RICHARD, "The Freedom and Finiteness of Existence in Hei-
degger," *New Scholasticism* XXXIII (1959), 32–48
KAUFMANN, F. W., "The Value of Heidegger's Analysis of Existence for
Literary Criticism," *Modern Language Notes* XLVIII (1933), 487–91
KRAFT, JULIUS, "The Philosophy of Existence," *PPR* I (1941), 339–58
Discussion by Fritz Kaufmann I, 359–64 and rejoinder 364–5.
LÖWITH, KARL, "Heidegger: Problem and Background of Existentialism,"
Social Research XV (1948), 345–69
——, "M. Heidegger and F. Rosenzweig on Temporality and Eternity,"
PPR III (1943), 53–77
MARX, WERNER, "Heidegger's New Concept of Philosophy. The Second
Phase of Existentialism," *Social Research* XXII (1953), 451–74
MERLAN, PHILIP, "Time Consciousness in Husserl and Heidegger," *PPR*
[2]   VIII (1948), 23–53
RICHEY, CLARENCE W., "On the Intentional Ambiguity of Heidegger's
Metaphysics," *Journal of Philosophy* LV (1958), 1144–48
SCHRADER, GEORGE, "Heidegger's Ontology of Human Existence,"
Review of Metaphysics X (1956), 35–56
SCHRAG, CALVIN, O., "Phenomenology, Ontology, and History in the
Philosophy of Heidegger," *Revue internationale de philosophie* XII
(1958), 117–32
STERN, GUENTHER (ANDERS), "On the Pseudo-Concreteness of Heideg-
ger's Philosophy," *PPR* VIII (1948), 337–71
STRASSER, STEPHEN, "The Concept of Dread in the Philosophy of Hei-
degger," *Modern Schoolman* XXXV (1957), 1–20
TAUBES, S. A., "The Gnostic Foundations of Heidegger's Nihilism,"
Journal of Religion XXXIV (1954), 155–72
TINT, H., "Heidegger and the Irrational," *Proceedings of the Aristotelian
Society* LVII (1957), 253–68
TRIVERS, HOWARD, "Heidegger's Misinterpretation of Hegel's Views on
Spirit and Time," *PPR* III (1943), 162–68
TURNBULL, ROBERT G., "Heidegger on the Nature of Truth," *Journal of
Philosophy* LIV (1957), 559–65
WEISS, HELENE, "The Greek Conception of Time and Being in the Light
of Heidegger's Philosophy," *PPR* II (1942), 173–87
WERKMEISTER, W. H., "An Introduction to Heidegger's 'Existential
[3]   Philosophy'," *PPR* II (1941), 79–87

Ph. D. Theses

GLICKSMAN (later GRENE), MARJORIE, *The Concept of Existence in Contemporary German Philosophy.* Radcliffe, 1935

HINNERS, RICHARD C., *Heidegger's Conception of the Question "What is the Meaning of to-be?" in Sein und Zeit.* Yale, 1955

MALIK, CHARLES M., *The Metaphysics of Time in the Philosophies of A. N. Whitehead and M. Heidegger.* Harvard, 1937

RICHARDSON, s.j., WILLIAM J., *Heidegger. Through Phenomenology to Thought* (1963)

STAVRIDES, RIA, *The Concept of Existence in Kierkegaard and Heidegger.* Columbia University, 1952

TWEEDIE, DONALD F. Jr., *The Significance of Dread in the Thought of Kierkegaard and Heidegger.* Boston University, 1954

VERSENYI, LASZLO, *Heidegger's Theory of Truth.* Yale, 1955

WYSCHOGROD, MICHAEL, *Kierkegaard and Heidegger. The Ontology of Existence.* Columbia University, 1954; London, Kegan Paul, 1954

Most Comprehensive Recent Bibliography

LÜBBE, HERMANN, "Bibliographie der Heidegger Literatur 1917–1955," *Zeitschrift für philosophische Forschung* XI (1957), 401–52   [1]

VII

PHENOMENOLOGY IN THE CRITICAL ONTOLOGY OF
NICOLAI HARTMANN (1882–1950)

1. Hartmann's Relation to the Phenomenological Movement

The right and the need to include Nicolai Hartmann in an
account of the Phenomenological Movement are by no means
beyond dispute. His inclusion will have to be justified by his
actual significance for the development of the Movement,
regardless of his own ambivalent relationship to it. In any event,
the widespread picture of Hartmann as one of the central figures
in the Phenomenological Movement badly needs revision in the
light of the ascertainable facts.

It is true that it meant one of the most impressive gains for
the Movement when in 1921 the Marburg-trained Neo-Kantian
and successor to the chair of Paul Natorp publicly expressed his
solidarity with the actual work of *"die Phänomenologie"* – though
he made reservations as to its methodology – and even used
phenomenology as the basis for his "metaphysics of knowledge." [1]
But Hartmann always kept at a philosophical distance from the
Movement and from its main representatives. The reasons for
this aloofness were not merely geographical. The two years from
1923 to 1925 during which he shared the department in Marburg
with Heidegger did not lead to a closer and more fruitful contact,
especially since Heidegger's sweeping success as a teacher actually
undermined the position of his older colleague. [2]

[1] *Grundzüge einer Metaphysik der Erkenntnis*, p. V.
[2] Communication from Professor Paul Friedländer, now in Los Angeles, one of
their colleagues at the time. – See also Robert Heiss in *Nicolai Hartmann: Der Denker
und sein Werk* (Göttingen, Vandenhoeck & Rupprecht, 1952) p. 18 ff.: "When Hartmann and Heidegger were together in Marburg, a joke made the rounds to the effect
that occasionally the two wanted to have a discussion. But it did not work out. When
Heidegger came to Hartmann in the evening, he was the first to talk. But after
hours, toward midnight, Hartmann would take over, and precisely when Hartmann

17. Nicolai Hartmann

Hartmann's contacts with Max Scheler were much closer. Scheler's ethical writings had been Hartmann's point of departure in the development of his own *Ethik*. So when Hartmann joined him at the University of Cologne in 1925, hardly without Scheler's active support, their connections became even more direct and intense. [1] However, in those years Scheler was less interested in phenomenology for its own sake, and other concerns, chiefly metaphysical, provided the main link. There were also some occasional contacts with members of the Munich Circle, particularly with Moritz Geiger, who felt closest to Hartmann. On the other hand, there is no evidence that Hartmann ever established personal contact with Husserl. Hartmann always objected to Husserl's idealism, the very idealism which had driven him away from Neo-Kantianism to phenomenology. And Husserl never acknowledged Hartmann as a genuine phenomenologist; privately in his correspondence he even referred to Hartmann as a dazzler (*Blender*). Conceivably Husserl also resented Hartmann's defection from the Neo-Kantian idealism of Natorp, for whom he entertained a warm admiration. And in a letter to Ernst Cassirer (April 3, 1925) Husserl denounced Hartmann's utterly mistaken dogmatist metaphysics, for which phenomenology in a completely misunderstood form supposedly furnished the foundations.

Besides, even Hartmann himself, for all his repeated compliments to "the phenomenologists" as his nearest philosophic neighbors, never identified himself with them as a group. At times, especially in his later works, he criticized not only Husserl but "the phenomenologists" in rather sweeping fashion. Some of these criticisms reveal considerable oversights and misunderstandings which make it doubtful that Hartmann was fully abreast of what was going on inside the Movement. As to himself, he never went beyond proclaiming the need for a phenomenology

---

was fully awake, Heidegger became tired. So they did not get together and could not get together because their times were too different. .... Only few know what a shock Heidegger's activity in Marburg was to Hartmann, and only much later did he confess it to others. Perhaps the greatest shock was that he met in Heidegger a philosophical thinker whom he recognized as one of high rank, yet from whom he could not learn." Hartmann discusses Heidegger's ideas in a number of places, usually with restraint, but with negative results. Heidegger comments on Hartmann's *Metaphysics of Knowledge* only by way of a footnote in *Sein und Zeit* (p. 208), where he simply asserts that it is inadequate to comprehend human being (*Dasein*).

[1] See particularly Hartmann's obituary for Scheler in *Kantstudien* XXXIII (1928), IX–XVI.

as a first step in his new approach, and practicing it as such more or less explicitly in his major works. But this phenomenology was clearly not the phenomenology of "the phenomenologists." Nevertheless, the extent of its use explains why Hartmann is so widely classified as one of them. This fact alone is reason enough for including a discussion of Hartmann's phenomenologizing in the present account of the wider Phenomenological Movement.

An additional reason for including Hartmann is the unusual interest he has aroused in the Anglo-American world, where he has been introduced very often as a phenomenologist and even as one close to Husserl. Actually, more of Hartmann's work than of any other phenomenologist, including Husserl, has been translated into English. Besides, it is Hartmann's most phenomenological though possibly not his most important work, the *Ethics*, which makes up the bulk of these translations.[1]

2. Hartmann's Philosophical Objective: Critical Ontology

The impact of Nicolai Hartmann's work is due to a number of factors. No other German philosopher of the 20th century has published as impressive a series of major systematic works. At his death in 1950 he had prepared imposing tomes on nearly every field of philosophy. The seeming gap of a philosophy of religion may well be explained by his agnosticism, if not antitheism, as it reveals itself in several places, without ever becoming aggressive.

In spite of the astonishing volume of his work Nicolai Hartmann was no mere quantity writer. Every book had gone through several drafts. There is no padding in his compact chapters and

---

[1] The story behind the translation of the *Ethik*, which came out in 1931, only one year after that of Husserl's *Ideen*, likewise in Muirhead's Library of Philosophy, is not without interest. For its first stimulus was an extended discussion of the book in an article in the *International Journal of Ethics* ("A Critique of Ethical Realism") of 1929 (XL, 179–210) by Sidney Hook, who had opposed its principles vigorously, while admitting that this was "the most impressive statement of intuitive ethical realism in print" and that it constituted "the most important treatise on the subject in the present century." It was this review which attracted the attention of Stanton Coit, one of the leading members of the Ethical Culture Movement, who was impressed both by its comprehensiveness and by its "realism." It may not be altogether gratuitous to surmise that Hartmann's pronounced elimination of all theistic elements from ethics, to the extent of emphasizing the conflicts between ethics and religion, had something to do with the appeal of this German work for an Ethical Culturist, who about the same time had tried in vain to enlist Husserl's support for the Ethical Culture Society.

paragraphs. All are unusually well organized. His style and diction, employing mostly short sentences, are plain and clear. It is only the lack of logical connectives that often makes the sequence of his brief categorical statements sound choppy, if not dogmatic.

However, these features must not be interpreted to mean that Hartmann was primarily a system builder of unusual scope and clarity. For it was one of his central convictions that the time for such systems was past and that it was false romanticism to hanker for their return. But while he thus rejected any philosophic system in the sense of a speculative construction, he believed all the more firmly in a systematic connection among the phenomena and the problems to which they gave rise. Any kind of a philosophic system could emerge only after these had been analysed and explored. But Hartmann never claimed that he had achieved it. At times he almost seemed to delight in leaving the subject in the twilight of unsolved riddles.

Hartmann himself supplied a bird's-eye view of this kind of system as it had finally evolved in a concise article for Ziegenfuss's *Philosophenlexikon* of 1949. It is revealing also in the final arrangement of its subjects, which nearly inverts the order of his publications. For after a brief discussion of his approach he starts out immediately with ontology, his climactic achievement, followed by a philosophy of nature, a philosophy of the "spirit" (i.e., the historical world of human creations), by ethics and esthetics, with theory of knowledge and logic at the end. It almost reads like a system of philosophy in reverse.

This raises the question as to the germinal idea for Hartmann's philosophizing. It is characteristic of Hartmann's absorption in his task that his prolific literary output includes no autobiographical statement, least of all one that would reveal his guiding philosophic motivation. But even in its absence there can be little question that the dominating if not the pervading goal of his philosophizing was the development of a new critical ontology. This can be inferred even from the brief opening paragraph of the aforementioned survey, which names as the most important event of his career the "breakthrough" to a new type of ontology in 1919, after seven years of "battle" against the logical idealism of the Marburg school. Yet it was not until he had published his works on epistemology, on ethics, and on the structure of cultural phenomena (*geistiges Sein*) that he was ready to attack this task directly. This he did in an ontological tetralogy which he himself considered to be his central achievement.

What is the meaning of this new "critical ontology?" The adjective "critical" expresses more than a call to caution and self-discipline. It is a reminder of the fact that Hartmann was not only a temporary member of the Marburg school, but that in working his way toward his new ontology he had not simply brushed aside the spirit of the Kantian "critiques." [1] There is certainly nothing dogmatic about it. If anything, it expresses an attitude of scepticism in the face of the many insoluble or "irrational" problems with which the metaphysical part of ontology is beset. Still, it is not an indiscriminate scepticism, but one which tries to determine the exact limits for an ontology which can slowly and patiently prepare the ground for steady progress in philosophy.

It is not easy to tell what exactly Hartmann understands by his "ontology," which he wants to oppose to the old Pre-Kantian form of ontology. He certainly does not identify it with metaphysics. In this respect Hartmann's enterprise differs fundamentally from the many more or less fashionable attempts to resurrect metaphysics, attempts which have rarely led to more than tentative and precarious results. Superficially Hartmann's "ontology" may seem to be nothing but what it meant to Aristotle: the science of being qua being in its most general characteristics. In order to determine its actual content, however, it will be best to look first at the type of topics and problems which Hartmann takes up under the time-honored name. They comprise not only being qua being, i.e., the most general concept of what is (*das Seiende*), but existence (*Dasein*) and essence (*Sosein*), which he calls *Seinsmomente*, and the types of being designated by the adjectives "real" and "ideal," named *Seinsweisen*, all of which are discussed in the first volume of the ontological tetralogy. The second volume deals with the modes of being (*Seinsmodi*) such as possibility and actuality, necessity and accidentality,

---

[1] Perhaps the most illuminating discussion of Hartmann's relation to Kant occurs in an article entitled "This Side of Idealism and Realism" in the *Kantstudien* of 1924, which is meant as a "Contribution Toward a Separation of the Historical and the Transhistorical in Kantian Philosophy." Here he sees the permanent value of Kant's *Critique of Pure Reason* precisely in the phenomenological elements of his thought.

impossibility and unreality – particularly impressive and perhaps the most original part of the set. The next major theme is the categories, first the general ones applying to all the strata (*Schichten*) of the real world and explored in the third volume (*Der Aufbau der realen Welt*), then the special categories pertaining only to limited areas, such as nature, which Hartmann takes up in the final volume of the tetralogy, also his last complete and second largest work. Finally, there are the categories peculiar to the realm of cultural entities (*geistiges Sein*), which he discusses in a work whose publication actually preceded the ontological tetralogy.

The mere mention of these topics will make it clear that such an ontology differs considerably from what had passed as ontology before Hartmann. It covers more and less. It adds the spheres of being which have been opened up by the sciences and the new cultural studies as well as by the theory of values. But it omits the traditional metaphysical problems, i.e., the ultimate questions dealing with God and immortality, which were the prize pieces of speculative metaphysics. The fact that Hartmann abandons this earlier metaphysics does not mean that he denies its problems. Their insolubility even provides the very background for his new ontology. Hence we have no right to simply ignore them.

Ontology thus conceived constitutes really a segment of a metaphysics which is no longer simply a field for speculative treatment by a priori methods. To Hartmann metaphysical problems are those which form the horizon of scientific knowledge, and which are inescapable because of their connection with what we can know scientifically, yet which cannot be solved by the methods of science alone. Some of these problems he considers to be impenetrable and "irrational" on principle, even though they too contain an ingredient (*Einschlag*) which can be explored by the rational methods of critical ontology. This "least metaphysical part" of metaphysics is the proper field of the new ontology.

What exactly is the methodical foundation of this ontology? Hartmann is most emphatic in stressing that the new ontology has to cooperate with the sciences, that it starts from below, not from above. Does this make it an inductive metaphysics, one that proceeds by way of hypotheses and empirical if not ex-

perimental verification? Hartmann says little to encourage such
an interpretation. His metaphysical asceticism forbids him to
engage in the kind of cosmic hypotheses in which even more
empirically minded scientists and philosophers like to indulge
during their Sunday morning reveries. Nevertheless, there is no
easy answer to the question in view of the fact that Hartmann
seems to have a certain reluctance to discuss the inductive method,
The loss of Hartmann's *Logic* on his flight from Berlin to Göttingen in 1945 may account for this gap. In any event, ontology
is to Hartmann "first philosophy" only in the order of being,
but last (*philosophia ultima*) in the order of knowing. A characteristic expression of this approach is the frequency with which
Hartmann speaks about problems as being, or not yet being,
"ripe" for an ontological verdict (he uses the German forensic
term "*Spruchreife*"). Thus the study of the special categories has
to wait for the progress of science as well as for the clarification
of the problems in general ontology, before the situation allows
ontological decisions.

The fact that ontology is Hartmann's central concern in philosophy may well suggest the idea that he and Heidegger were
basically working on the same problem, even though they did
not succeed in communicating about it. It is all the more important to point out that ontology, and particularly fundamental
ontology in Heidegger's sense, had a very different objective.
For Heidegger's ontology was based on the rigid distinction
between Being and things-in-being, and was meant to concentrate
on the problem of Being in contrast to the problem of the things-
in-being. To Heidegger the neglect of this distinction was the
original sin of all past metaphysics. In his eyes Hartmann, in
striving for an ontology which studied general structures and
fundamental categories of the things-in-being, was still guilty
of the same fundamental error. The fact that Hartmann refrained
from speculative metaphysics was relatively minor compared
with this basic fault – if it be one.

But there is perhaps an even deeper difference between
Hartmann's and Heidegger's ontological concerns. We saw that
for Heidegger the "wonder of all wonders" had been the experience of Being on the background of the Nothing as revealed
in anxiety, an experience which makes all differences among the

things-in-being appear as relatively minor. There is no evidence that Hartmann was similarly affected by this experience. If Hartmann has any comparable experience, it lies in a different direction: the experience of the irrational which surrounds the rational core of our knowledge.

What was the fundamental motivation for Hartmann's critical ontology? As far as Hartmann's writings reveal it, one can only describe it as the expression of a deep theoretical need, the ambition of the metaphysical mind to find unity and order in the world, a need, however, which was chastened by an uncommon self-discipline, as suggested by the defeat of the old speculative metaphysics, and stimulated by the opportunities which the widened scientific outlook had opened up. There is a temptation to seek in the author of the monumental *Ethik* a moralist interested primarily in reforming the world. Actually his temper was much more Hegelian, if not Aristotelian. This explains why he quietly went his way through the storms of the times without getting involved in them, though, especially in the Berlin of the thirties and forties, he lived close to the storm center. During the Nazi period he took no active part in the political struggle. Never did he take an open stand in the name of any ethical principles either for or against the new regime, which he survived unscathed. His concern even in ethics was contemplative. In the same spirit he continued his work on esthetics during the castastrophe of Nazi Germany and the siege and fall of Berlin. "In the midst of this collapse he wrote his pages, day by day," we are told by his wife, who edited this text.

This does not imply that Hartmann was the typical desk scholar, free from inner personal problems and tensions. Even his ontology reflects a peculiar balance between two seemingly opposite tendencies: an unusual passion for systematic order on the one hand and a remarkable self-restraint in claiming mastery of the problems on the other. Both tendencies seem to express a will to control, to sovereign power, in one case over his subject-matter in all its variety, in the other over his own systematizing inclinations. There was something of the sternness of the Baltic German about him. But he also showed a humility and humaneness in the breadth of his interests which make one think of another German Baltic philosopher, Kant.

Hartmann himself expressed this spirit best in the following passage:

The work of a person who wants to tackle the metaphysical problems in the critical manner demands ... the waiver of all hasty satisfactions by way of *Weltanschauung*, of grabbing for results; it demands the radical renunciation of any kind of premature construction of systems, the ruthless rejection of metaphysical needs ... Metaphysical research demands the long breath of being able to wait, the patient "aporetic" advance along the whole horizon of metaphysical problems, the inner detachment from types of world picture which tempt the longing eye. It is a philosophical ethos of toughness (*Härte*) and of intellectual self-discipline. Whoever cannot muster it relapses hopelessly into what is historically outdated and lost. He has not learned from the great failures of man's intellectual history. This is not the way to get beyond them. And no seeming "destruction" of tradition [an obvious allusion to Heidegger] can help him. – What is philosophically hardest is the most simple: the plain, sober exploration without pathos and sensationalism, the purity of the love of truth, the obedience to its law ... The seeker must not sell out for the sake of the more easily obtainable. He must not be discouraged if he, a mere link in a long historical chain, is denied the view of the fruits.[1]

His fundamental opposition to the spirit of existential philosophy is another consequence of this object-centered asceticism. One of its most characteristic expressions occurs in what is perhaps his most explicit attack on Heidegger and Kierkegaard with their emphasis on anxiety and death as privileged sources of ontological insight:

It is obvious that ... we have no foundation for deciding whether death is in any way particularly important for man. It is certainly not so as a mere ceasing of life – in fact, we do not know more about it. Of course it is bound to be terrifying for the one who leads his life exclusively in the interest of his own person and who understands the world as merely his own: the habitual perverseness of self-importance strikes back at the egocentric man. Death is relatively unimportant for the one who sees himself in genuine "ontic" attitude as an insignificant individual among individuals, as a drop in the total stream of world events, the historical as well as the even larger cosmic one, and knows how to resign himself in reverence before the great. This is the natural attitude of man, whose roots in life are still firmly established.[2]

Regardless of whether Hartmann misinterprets or exaggerates Heidegger's concern, this passage expresses better than many others his own ascetic suppression of the existential solicitude.

It was possibly the same metaphysical and existential asceti-

---

[1] *Systematische deutsche Philosophie nach ihren Gestaltern*, pp. 57–58.
[2] *Zur Grundlegung der Ontologie*, p. 197.

cism which was behind his theological agnosticism. It is an exaggeration to state Hartmann's theological position as a full-fledged postulatory atheism, based on the incompatibilities of theism with the demands of an autonomous ethics. Yet it is true that in his *Ethics* and particularly in its metaphysical parts Hartmann sees what are apparently insoluble antinomies between ethics and a supernatural theism, for instance between a theology of complete Divine providence and human responsibility, or between genuine ethical responsibility for one's own faults and salvation by passing on the guilt. Hartmann was ready to face the worst without any props of wishful thinking and believing. One of his last and proudest statements, from the unrevised part of his posthumous *Esthetics*, suggests that he succeeded in making not only a virtue but sense out of this assumed necessity:

The opposite of what the metaphysicians have always thought is true: precisely a meaningless world is the only meaningful world for a being like man: in a world full of meaning even without him, he with his gifts of bestowing meaning would be superfluous. (p. 408)

3. The Role of Phenomenology in Hartmann's Philosophical Development

The university of Marburg has played a momentous part in the fate of German phenomenology. In the late nineteenth century it had been one of the centers of Neo-Kantianism under Friedrich Albert Lange, the author of the celebrated *History of Materialism*. But its real importance as the citadel of logical Neo-Kantianism came in the days of Hermann Cohen and Paul Natorp. The sympathetic though reserved contacts between Natorp and Husserl during this period have been mentioned above. For reasons that need not concern us here the Marburg school began to change in character and interests during the second decade of the century. Cohen, especially after his retirement to Berlin in 1912, had turned his major attention to the philosophy of religion. Natorp had moved from his logical and methodological studies to problems of social education and even become interested in Dostoevski's religious mysticism. Ernst Cassirer, of the younger generation, gravitated increasingly toward the study of such cultural phenomena as the nature and role of symbolism.

It was in this atmosphere that the young student of medicine and classics from Riga, Nicolai Hartmann, began his philosophical studies in Marburg. He shared with the Marburg school the enthusiastic interest in ancient philosophy and particularly in Plato. Thus the voluminous thesis which he submitted for his habilitation in 1909 dealt with *Plato's Logic of Being*. The theme is as characteristic as the treatment, even in the light of Hartmann's later development. For it is not metaphysics proper that Hartmann seeks in Plato, but the logical aspects of the doctrine of Ideas, as had Natorp before him. But his interest is less in Plato's Ideas in general than in his Idea of Being. Yet this Being is not understood as opposed to the things-in-being, as Hartmann's rival Heidegger was to interpret Being fifteen years later.

However, the decisive period in Hartmann's development came in the second decade of the century when he turned to epistemology and began his "battle against the Marburg logical idealism." As an "essential influence" during this time he himself mentions the writings of Husserl and Scheler.[1] In 1921 the result of his successful emancipation appeared in the form of his momentous *"Outlines of a Metaphysics of Knowledge."* The title of this book announces programmatically the paradoxical and, to an orthodox Neo-Kantian, shocking thesis that epistemology itself implies metaphysics, although a metaphysics of a new type, i.e., critical ontology. This ontology itself was to be based primarily on phenomenology, but a phenomenology of Hartmann's own making. Nevertheless, Hartmann announced his new enterprise in terms so friendly to the Phenomenological Movement that he could easily pass for a full-fledged phenomenologist. Specifically, the book denounced the Neo-Kantian approach to knowledge for misinterpreting knowledge as a "positing," and at times even as a constructive and productive act. In opposition to this interpretation Hartmann attempted to show by means of his new phenomenology that knowledge was essentially an

---

[1] A particularly interesting document from this period is Hartmann's review of the contributions by Reinach, Scheler, Pfänder, and Geiger (in that order) to the first volume of Husserl's yearbook (Natorp had reported on Husserl's piece, the *Ideen*) for *Geisteswissenschaften* 1913/14 (republished in *Kleinere Schriften* III, 365–8). It leaves no doubt of the fact that even as an "outsider" Hartmann was deeply impressed by these demonstrations of phenomenology in action, even more than by Husserl's own more programmatic treatise, as a "sweeping (*grosszügig*) enlargement of the descriptive method" allowing the "immediate grasp of apriorities."

operation of grasping an independent object, in fact a thing-in-itself in the Kantian sense, a conception which he tried to rehabilitate. Phenomenology thus became the main tool for a new approach to knowledge which was to replace what Hartmann now characterized as its Neo-Kantian misinterpretation. – On the other hand, Hartmann took "the phenomenologists" to task for their insufficient epistemological neutrality, and for their commitment to a philosophy of immanence. For Hartmann identified phenomenology immediately with its idealistic version as it had become manifest in Husserl's *Ideen*. Instead, Hartmann at this stage wanted to keep his own phenomenology neutral to idealism and realism. And while he began his studies by a descriptive phenomenology of knowledge, he did not consider this a sufficient basis for the solution of the epistemological problem. It had to be followed by a different approach under the name of *"aporetics"* (i.e., literally, a study of impasses), which was to explore and make explicit the peculiar problems and difficulties in the interpretation of such knowledge. Only after the phenomena and problems of knowledge had been clarified would Hartmann consider solutions. They were to be supplied by critical ontology in the shape of "theory," a theory which, however, had to stay definitely free from "speculation."

In what sense, then, does Hartmann call his epistemology "metaphysics"? For one thing, he asserts that epistemology presupposes metaphysics, just as metaphysics presupposes epistemology. In contrast especially to speculative metaphysics, Hartmann speaks of a metaphysics of problems, designed to deal with problems of knowledge which contain an unsolved and in fact even an insoluble remnant, and are in this sense impenetrable and irrational. Here, then, the metaphysical is a horizon, as it were, to the soluble problems and as such a factum that can be explored by a descriptive phenomenology. It was the peculiar task of the *Metaphysics of Knowledge* to unfold this horizon in connection with our knowledge of real and ideal objects. At the end Hartmann gives a first application of this approach to the problems of value.

He returns to them in his *Ethik* (1925). The achievement of this work in richness of material and in clarity of organization is so impressive by itself that it is easy to overlook its significance

and its function in the framework of Hartmann's larger ontological enterprise. This oversight is aided by the fact that most
Anglo-American readers know only this one work, since thus
far only one shorter statement of the ontology is available in
translation. In fact, Hartmann himself does not dramatize his
ontological objective in the *Ethik* and almost seems to be torn
between this concern and his interest in ethics for its own sake.
Thus in the Introduction he disclaims any practical objectives
for ethics and wants the moral philosopher to refrain from taking
a stand on concrete issues. On the other hand his new ethics
is to represent a new ethos capable of supplying answers
for the spiritual need of the time and awakening a new
awareness of values. On such occasions one has the feeling
that Hartmann's subject-matter gets the better of his ontological detachment.

Of the three parts of this monumental work only the first,
dealing with the structure of the moral phenomena, bears the
title "Phenomenology" (of Morals) explicitly. However, even the
title of the second part, "Axiology" (of Morals), which presents
a detailed study of moral values, is apparently a synonym of
"phenomenology." Only the third part, the Metaphysics of
Morals, definitely transcends phenomenology by a comprehensive
discussion of the problem of free will. While thus the larger and
more impressive sections of the book are phenomenological,
giving concrete descriptions of values and virtues, Hartmann's
ultimate interest remains metaphysical. It should also be noticed
that all through this, his largest work Hartmann displays
intense interest in the ontological structures and laws of the
ethical phenomena, which he compares currently with those in
other fields. Thus ethics offers him a first occasion for describing
spheres and laws formerly neglected by ontology. It also gives
him a chance to formulate "categorial laws" such as the one
according to which the "lower" strata of being, exemplified by
the material world, are "stronger" than the "higher" ones, or
the one that the higher strata with their novel characteristics are
to a certain (but never defined) degree autonomous in relation
to the lower ones. The combination of these two laws allows
Hartmann to salvage enough freedom from determinism to make
room for a normative ethics. The *Ethics* illustrates also Hart-

mann's characteristic fondness for ferreting out aporetic difficulties and even insoluble antinomies. This almost self-torment-
ing tendency reaches its climax when Hartmann declares that
conflicts of duties cannot be resolved, yet that this does not acquit
their victims of guilt. On the contrary, it makes their guilt
necessary in a manner which reminds one of the doctrine of
original sin.

Hartmann freely states his indebtedness to Max Scheler's
Ethik, but without minimizing his dissents. These dissents in
objective, in approach, and in development deserve indeed
explicit acknowledgment. To begin with, Hartmann's ultimate
objective is the development of a critical ontology, Scheler's the
development of a philosophical anthropology as a new foundation
for modern civilization. Besides, Hartmann's ethics shows a
much more encyclopedic outlook than Scheler's. It tries to
embrace the whole historical range of values, i.e., not only the
ancient and Christian values but also those which Hartmann
recognizes in Nietzsche's "transvaluation of values." Compared
with Scheler's sweeping a priori claims, he also reveals a much
more tentative and flexible spirit. For Hartmann is keenly
aware that it is humanly impossible to embrace the whole range
of values. At least in this respect his approach is much more
empirical than Scheler's. Yet he is much more of a Platonist when
it comes to the structure of the values themselves. These are to
him ideal entities (*Wesenheiten*) with a peculiar type of ideal
being, which is one of the particular concerns of Hartmann's
ontology. While he disclaims a Platonic realism, he still assigns
to these entities the status of universals. Scheler's interpretation
is much less outspoken in this respect; to him values are neither
particular nor universal. Hartmann also rejects Scheler's favorite
theory of personalism, according to which persons are not only
of supreme value but can never become objects of knowledge.
Besides, there are characteristic differences between Hartmann's
and Scheler's tables of values. A good many of them are the
result of Hartmann's determined effort to keep the ethical
domain free from religious admixtures. Thus he omits what in
Scheler's case represents the highest value, that of holiness. Yet
he preserves some of its characteristics in such new values as
purity. On the whole Hartmann widens the range of Scheler's

non-formal values considerably, both as to the fundamental values and as to their embodiments in virtues.

The *Ethics* had given Hartmann a first chance to broaden his approach to a comprehensive critical ontology. His next book, "The Problem of Cultural Being" (*Das Problem des geistigen Seins*), contains another case study, starting from problems in the philosophy of history. The area which he tries to explore here covers what is in German called the *Geisteswissenschaften*, i.e., the social sciences and humanities, as opposed to the natural sciences. Here Hartmann wants to offer primarily an ontological study of the structure of the phenomena. Dilthey is his recognized but much too unsystematic predecessor, Hegel's "dangerous heritage" the challenge. In fact, Hegel, to whom Hartmann devoted a separate critical work, supplies the framework for the whole work by his distinction between three forms of the "spirit." Hartmann follows Hegel as far as the division of subjective (or personal) and objective (or social) spirit is concerned. However, for Hegel's "absolute spirit" Hartmann characteristically substitutes the "objectified spirit," i.e., the realm of human cultural creations, primarily in the field of art. Hartmann's objective was a phenomenology of the spirit, yet not one in the sense of Hegel's work by the same name, which had dealt with the forms of human consciousness, but in the sense of an ontological study of the phenomena which Hegel had taken up in his "Philosophy of the Spirit," i.e., in the third part of his *Encyclopedia of the Philosophical Sciences*. Nevertheless, Hartmann called the method of his book phenomenological, though not in Hegel's but in his own sense, namely as a description of phenomena.

Upon this widened foundation, Hartmann proceeded to present the systematic development of his critical ontology, on which he had been working since the time of the "breakthrough" of 1914. It appeared in four massive volumes, mainly during his years at the University of Berlin, where he had been called in 1931, after Heidegger had turned down the offer of that chair. Only the "Philosophy of Nature" was worked out during Hartmann's final period in Göttingen, his last academic station after his flight from Berlin in 1945. No brief summary can convey an adequate idea of the amount of material covered in this work, nor is this needed in the present context. Suffice it to point out that phenomenology is invoked as the starting point, but by no means the sufficient foundation, of ontology. It should also be mentioned that, in spite of the appearance of monumental rigidity, the new "system" is advanced in the spirit of tentativeness and readiness to revise. This applies particularly to the doctrine of the special categories in the last volume, the "Philosophy of Nature," which purports to be neither speculative nor completely fact-bound. Based upon the data, pre-scientific as well as scientific, it contains a systematization of the concepts in use in the natural sciences without accepting them uncritically. In particular, Hartmann keeps objecting to teleological thinking in the biological sciences in a way which has aroused vigorous protests on the part of the German neo-vitalists. The end of this philosophy of nature ties up with his earlier work on the problem of mental being.

Hartmann spent the balance of his amazing systematic energies on rounding out his philosophy by developing an esthetics and a logic. The "Ästhetik," of which one third had been completed in a final version, was published posthumously. In its concreteness and originality it is anything but a mere filler. Rather does it show the fruitfulness of Hartmann's ontology in its application to a new area. Phenomenology, particularly in Geiger's version, is credited with having paved the way for a new non-psychological esthetics. But only the new ontology in its orientation toward objects rather than toward acts is said to have the chance of attacking the whole range of esthetic phenomena.

Hartmann's achievement in developing his basic conception is unique in the German philosophy of the 20th century. He is even more unique among the philosophers connected with phenomenology, who have excelled more in changing their programs than in carrying them out. This makes it all the more important to determine whether Hartmann's phenomenology is sufficiently close to that of the phenomenologists to make him at least an associated thinker, separated from the Movement chiefly by personal circumstances, misunderstandings, and by a characteristic sense of independence which prevented him from identifying himself too closely with any other group.

What was this conception of phenomenology?

4. Nicolai Hartmann's Version of Phenomenology

Nicolai Hartmann makes use of phenomenology. But he does not want to be called a phenomenologist. This means not only that he objects to the phenomenology of the phenomenologists. It also means that he assigns limits to his own version of it, and seemingly rather narrow limits. For at first sight phenomenology is to him only the beginning of philosophy, the foundation over which he erects the real house of philosophy. How far is he right in this self-interpretation?

In order to appraise Hartmann's limited phenomenology we must first take account of his picture of the phenomenology of "the phenomenologists." This picture is, to say the least, a rather incomplete one. Except for his relatively late meetings with Heidegger in Marburg and Scheler in Cologne, Hartmann knew the Phenomenological Movement chiefly through its publications. Some of his estimates of "the phenomenologists" are so sweeping and plainly mistaken that one wonders whether his information about them was really adequate, or whether, after he had fought his way to philosophical independence, his desire not to be identified with any group did not get the better of him. The very label "the phenomenologists" makes it plain that Hartmann was not fully aware of the differences and cleavages within the Movement. Nor is his picture always the same and free from contradictions.[1]

---

[1] A few examples will illustrate this point:

1. For the Hartmann of the *Metaphysik der Erkenntnis* the phenomenology of "the phenomenologists" coincides with a philosophy of immanence. Hence their phenomenon is identified with an immanent object for a subject, and phenomenology made to coincide with the phenomenological idealism which was indeed Husserl's position after the *Ideen*. The fact that Husserl characterizes the intentional object as transcendent seems to be ignored; so is in general the very structure of the intentional act, which figures rarely if ever in Hartmann's account of Husserl.

2. "Phenomenology" is often characterized as an attempt to return to the "naive" or "natural" attitude. The fact that especially Husserl's phenomenological reduction was directed against the naive or natural attitude is not even mentioned.

3. "Phenomenology" is characterized as unscientific and, in the end, even anti-scientific. This strangely ignores Husserl's ideal of philosophy as a rigorous science, which at first implied that the exact sciences were a model to philosophy, and later that they needed and deserved philosophic buttressing, vulnerable as they were to intensifying "crises," by an even more rigorous super-science.

4. "Phenomenology" is represented as preoccupied with reflection upon acts but as neglecting more or less completely the study of contents. Here Hartmann seems to be overlooking strangely (a) the objective "pure logic" of the *Logische Untersuchungen;* (b) Husserl's later insistence on the strict parallelism between the noetic and the noematic and the consequent need of parallel studies of acts and contents; (c) the

However, in spite of these criticisms of "the phenomenologists," Hartmann never contrasted his own conception of phenomenology explicitly with that of "the phenomenologists." Only as he makes use of it does it become clear that this cannot possibly be the same kind of phenomenology as he has taken to task before. Apparently, in developing his own phenomenology Hartmann felt completely free to adapt the term to his own needs, regardless of "priorities."

Now Hartmann's own phenomenology, as he sees it, represents nothing but a phase, though the primary phase, of his philosophical method; as such, it is the necessary but not sufficient condition of genuine philosophic insight. It should also be realized that Hartmann's interest in problems of method is merely a secondary one. It was primary only as long as, during the period of the *Metaphysik der Erkenntnis*, he had first to remove the obstacles which previous epistemology, especially of the Marburg variety, had left in the way of his critical ontology. Once he had accomplished this to his own satisfaction, he composed his larger systematic works without the need of constant references to epistemology. Only in the last four chapters of the third volume of his ontological tetralogy does he return to a reflection on the method he had been using. This order is characteristic for Hartmann's entire approach. Method, for him, has to be developed in the actual task of handling the subject-matter and its problems. It is only after its test in action that reflection upon method makes sense.

The two most explicit statements about Hartmann's method in its developed form, both of which include characterizations of his phenomenology, are about twenty years apart. Hartmann himself does not imply that there has been any important change in his conception of phenomenology between these two statements. But there are nevertheless differences which should not remain unnoticed. They manifest themselves in the way in which phenomenology is matched with its non-phenomenological supplements. In the *Metaphysik der Erkenntnis* (1921) these are the concepts of "aporetics" and "theory"; in the *Aufbau der*

whole trend toward a phenomenology of the object (*Gegenstandsphänomenologie*) represented by phenomenologists like Moritz Geiger and Paul Linke, a trend which to the Göttingen and Munich Circles seemed to be the most important feature of phenomenology.

realen Welt (1940) phenomenology is followed by an "inferential" analysis, by a "dialectical method," and finally by a "synthetic" or "conspective" method. It would seem that the first statement is concerned more with stages in the exploration of a subject, the second more with the actual procedures used. In any case, these procedures are more differentiated in the later account.

In the earlier discussion, phenomenology is introduced as the mere description of the immediately given. It is to be followed by a systematic study of the difficulties, problems, and contradictions found in the given under the name of "aporetics." Only after this has been accomplished is Hartmann ready for a solution of these problems by what he calls "theory." Not all "apories" are soluble. If they are not, they are usually called "antinomies." In this case they are part of that remnant of unsolvable problems for which Hartmann reserved the name "metaphysical." As far as the third stage, "theory," is concerned, it should be noted that it signifies by no means merely hypothetical constructions without intuitive ingredients. For Hartmann rather thinks of it as a wider and more penetrating conspectus (*Zusammenschau*) which is intuitive in the sense of the Greek "*theoria.*" While Hartmann is not always too clear and explicit on this point, it seems safe to assert that even at this stage he is not so far away from the phenomenological approach as he himself seems to believe.

Besides, Hartmann realizes that phenomenology and aporetics actually have to be developed jointly or in immediate succession, as they are in the *Metaphysik der Erkenntnis*. It could also be pointed out that the phenomenology of "the phenomenologists" is by no means free from "aporetics." This applies particularly to Husserl, to whom phenomenology is certainly not a mere matter of description, but who is more than eager to dramatize the difficulties and problems raised by his findings. Nor can "theory" be considered inaccessible to phenomenology, provided it does not mean mere hypothetical construction. Phenomenology in Husserl's sense also implies the conspective evaluation of the claims to "rationality" ("*Vernunft*") to which our consciousness aspires.

Perhaps the most characteristic feature of Hartmann's phenomenology is the principle which he calls that of the *maxi-*

mum of givenness, and which has to be matched with the principle of the *minimum of metaphysics*. It states that "only the greatest possible maximum of givenness can satisfy a truly critical attitude." [1] It thus represents a challenge to the customary and supposedly scientific demand for a minimum of givenness known commonly as the principle of economy of thought and, outside Germany, as Occam's razor.

However, phenomenology does not end with such a jumbled collection of data. This is only its beginning. In order to orient ourselves in such a welter we need comparison and selection of the universal and essential. Hartmann thus subscribes to the familiar intuition of essences (*Wesensschau*) in the sense of the phenomenologists as an essential part of his own phenomenological method. [2] It is exemplified all through Hartmann's writings.

When Hartmann returns to the discussion of phenomenology in the *Aufbau der realen Welt* (1940), he is more interested in actual procedures of ontology than in the labelling of its stages. He begins with the descriptive-phenomenological phase as the starting point of what he calls analysis, which is to provide him with the main ontological categories – his major concern in the third part of his critical ontology. Actually, the discussion of this procedure is restricted to some five pages, and these are not very specific. They make it clear, however, that Hartmann assigns to his phenomenology the task of a non-selective description of the immediately given. He admits that it is a difficult and responsible task to determine in a concrete case what is "given." But there is also the problem that what is given depends to a large extent on the development of our scientific approach. In supposed contrast to "the phenomenologists," Hartmann considers it impossible to return from the scientific data to the naive ones. There is thus no alternative to starting from the changeable interpretations of the data embodied in our developing conceptions of the world. It is not easy to make out how many data this would include at our present stage. Of course

---

[1] *Metaphysik der Erkenntnis*, p. 42.

[2] This acceptance does not exclude misunderstandings of the procedure, such as Hartmann's identification of 'the essential intuition with the phenomenological reduction, the latter being interpreted as the omission of the accidental from the essential. (*Aufbau der realen Welt*, p. 47).

Hartmann's "givenness" goes far beyond mere sense data, and consists primarily of total objects (*Concreta*). One wonders whether it also includes cells, molecules, galaxies, and electromagnetic waves. However, the categories which are later extricated from the given, such as substance (interpreted as the continuum), process, and reality, are definitely part of Hartmann's immediately given.

The "descriptive-phenomenological" procedure is to be followed by the *analytical method*, which is to give us access to the categories within the full phenomenon or "concretum." For this analysis Hartmann also uses the expression "backward inference" (*Rückschluss*). However, closer inspection shows that it does not involve anything like a deductive reasoning. Its function is to make us find and see the abstract categories within the concrete phenomenon. It leads us to a secondary or mediated intuition. Thus the analytical method seems to be nothing but an isolating abstraction applied to the task of guiding us to those more formal characteristics which Hartmann calls "categories."

A third step in the development of critical ontology is what Hartmann calls the *dialectical method*. Its main function is to widen our perspective of the phenomena "horizontally," while the analytico-phenomenological approach had deepened it only vertically. There are, however, no speculative or constructive implications to this type of thinking. Nor is it meant to comply with a triadic scheme of thesis, antithesis, and synthesis. It simply moves from category to category, following the structural connections among the phenomena in which these categories present themselves. Hence all that seems to be involved in this step is a reaching out beyond the restricted field of first analysis toward an awareness of the wider context in which it stands. Its function is to prepare for an enlarged intuition.

The final step of Hartmann's ontological procedure is the *synthetic or conspective method* or stratified perspective (*Schichtenperspektive*). It is to provide a final unification of the categories throughout all the strata. This method is based on Hartmann's theory of strata of categories, which cannot and need not be discussed here. Even without this it is clear, however, that this final phase in the ontological method is nothing but a type of synthetic intuition. In view of this fact it would seem that Hartmann's additions to the phenomenological method are simply higher levels of intuition founded on more elementary intuitive acts. Phenomenology knows these under the name of supported acts (*fundierte Akte*).[1]

5. Illustrations of Hartmann's Phenomenology

It is not always easy to tell when Hartmann uses his phenomenological method, or even when he believes he is using it. For, especially in his ontological works, he rarely labels his procedure. In fact he mostly describes his results rather than tells us how he thinks he has come by them. The following selections cover only an insignificant part of what could figure as characteristic examples of his version of phenomenology, both in its strengths and its weaknesses.

The first example from his *Metaphysik der Erkenntnis* is explicitly called "phenomenology." No such label is attached to the section on the givenness of real being in the *Grundlegung der Ontologie*, which forms the foundation of Hartmann's realism, and which possibly comes even closer to the phenomenology of "the phenomenologists." Two typical but by no means central examples from the "phenomenological" part of Hartmann's *Ethik* will bring out some of his most original additions to phenomenological ethics. Even without specific documentation it should not go unmentioned that his posthumous esthetics contains some of his richest phenomenological findings. Here he develops Moritz Geiger's beginnings of a phenomenological esthetics in a manner comparable to the one in which he had systematized and redirected the much more ambitious – and loaded – ethics of Max Scheler.

a. 'METAPHYSICS' OF KNOWLEDGE – The first part of Hartmann's *Outlines of a Metaphysics of Knowledge* is devoted to the "Phenomenon and Problem of Knowledge," i.e., to the phenomenology and "aporetics" of knowledge. After a first section dealing with what is "unmetaphysical" in the problem of knowledge, namely its psychological and logical aspects, the

[1] See also Michael Landmann, "Das phänomenologische Moment bei Nicolai Hartmann" in *Erkenntnis und Erlebnis*. (Berlin, 1951, p. 64 ff.)

phenomenological section takes up the "metaphysical" problem, i.e., that of the relation between subject and object of knowledge, which logic has to leave aside.

It is on the basis of such a phenomenological analysis of the essential constituents of knowledge as such that Hartmann claims for it a number of characteristics of which I shall single out the following:

α. Knowledge involves the mutual basic separation (*gegenseitige Urgeschiedenheit*) of knower and known which he calls "transcendence" – obviously a new sense of the term.

β. Knowledge consists in a seizing or laying hold (*erfassen*) of an object, in pronounced contrast to an act of creating or producing it, as the Neo-Kantians had interpreted knowledge. This object must exist independently of our knowledge and precede it. Knowledge thus consists essentially in a "breakthrough" into the transcendent field. Otherwise it would not be knowledge. The assertion that such a seizing of the transcendent object itself is an essential feature of knowledge constitutes the initial and fundamental thesis of Hartmann's book. It represents Hartmann's bluntest challenge to Kant and the Neo-Kantians.

γ. The object of knowledge is more than an object for a subject. Being-an-object is only its secondary and incidental property, being-in-itself its primary nature. It becomes an object when it is "objected" (*objiziert*), exposed to a subject. Otherwise it is merely a potential object, capable of becoming an object (*objizierbar*) but otherwise "trans-objective" (*transobjektiv*). Thus the epistemological concept of object refers us back to the metaphysical concept of being-in-itself, and epistemology again presupposes metaphysics. Incidentally, not every being is capable of becoming object. Hartmann later introduces a range of irrational or "transintelligible" objects which he considers to be strictly unknowable. It would lead too far to include a discussion of these phenomena in the present account.

δ. The seizing operation of knowledge includes three phases, the subject's reaching out beyond himself into a transcendent and heterogeneous world, the laying hold of it, and the gathering into the subject (*einholen*) of the information about it.

Thus far Hartmann's account seems to reflect pretty much

the ordinary man's idea of what a cognitive enterprise should yield him. As such it suggests something like the catching of fish. Yet at this stage Hartmann seems to depart from such a rather common-sensic model and, what is more serious, from strict adherence to what is immediately given. Hartmann is of course well aware that the knower can never catch the object itself and haul it into himself, as it were. For the object known has to remain "untouched" (*unangetastet*) and can never become immanent. Hartmann's way out is to contend that what is actually brought back by our knowledge is an immanent double (*Wiederkehr*) of the object in the shape of a new creation (*Gebilde*), which he also calls the image (*Bild*) of the object.

What exactly is this immanent "image," and how do we know about it? Hartmann admits that it is not given directly like the object known. Only a reflective analysis can give us awareness of it. Such an analysis has to begin with cases of illusion (*Täuschung*). Here the image can be identified as such, once the illusion has been exposed. Now, starting from the realization that every supposed knowledge potentially harbors an illusion, Hartmann infers that all cognitive relations, even those which are not deceptive, contain a third element, often called "idea" (*Vorstellung*). This may not seem conclusive as a piece of argument. But even more important is the question whether he can produce phenomenological evidence for the assertion that all cases of would-be knowledge, including those that do not turn out to be deceptive, actually contain immanent "images." Hartmann, who had been challenged on this point by Paul Linke, thinks that once the possibility of illusion has been considered it becomes possible to see the image even in veridical knowledge in a manner comparable to our awareness of our own acts, i.e., as a result of subsequent reflection. The conjecture is not altogether unwarranted that Hartmann's image theory is the outcome not of direct phenomenology but of an attempt to reconcile his initial conception of what knowledge ought to be, namely a kind of catching operation, with the obvious fact that the victim of the catch remains at large and unaffected by our knowing.

Thus Hartmann's phenomenology of knowledge includes a curious mixture of courageous insistence on our unsophisticated view about the goal and nature of knowledge, namely as the seizure of independent objects, and of a more or less constructive reinterpretation of the phenomena by the introduction of such entities as "images," for which the evidence is certainly less direct and conclusive.

b. THE GIVENNESS OF REALITY – Ontology, as Hartmann conceives of it, is to start out in strict neutrality toward both idealism and realism. It describes the phenomena as phenomena. And Hartmann insists that we have no right to identify the phenomena of the things with the real things themselves, a confusion which he blames on "the phenomenologists."

However, a phenomenologically based ontology need not remain permanently neutral. Certain phenomena can give us access to the world of transcendent reality beyond. The key to reality lies in a group of acts which Hartmann calls "transcendent," obviously in a sense different from the one in which he had called the object of knowledge "transcendent." These acts "step beyond" themselves, as one literal meaning of the word suggests, and thus give us access to a sphere otherwise beyond the range of our consciousness. It is these acts in which reality itself, in contrast to mere phenomenality, is given.

There are, according to Hartmann, several such acts. Cognition is by no means the only and in fact not even the most telling one. Most important among these are the "emotionally transcendent acts," characterized by the ingredient of "activity, energy, struggle, involvement, risk, suffering, and being affected" (*Betroffensein*) (*Zur Grundlegung der Ontologie*, p. 177), in other words, by a real causal contact with the object before us. These emotionally transcendent acts Hartmann subdivides into active or spontaneous acts like willing, and receptive acts like rejoicing, which are Hartmann's chief concern. He also devotes attention to the prospective emotions, like expectation, preparedness, and presentiment, as well as to the acts of hope and fear, for which he makes no cognitive claims.

Within the objects approached by our knowledge Hartmann draws the familiar distinction between their whatness (*Sosein*) and their thatness (*Dasein*). Now theoretical cognition, as an act relatively detached from the fullness of real life, has no adequate hold on the thatness, according to Hartmann, but only on the whatness of these objects. It is the function of the non-theoretical transcendent or emotionally transcendent acts to establish valid contact with their thatness or reality. To be sure, Hartmann was not the first to claim for the "emotive" acts the function of revealing reality. Voluntaristic philosophers from Maine de Biran to Scheler had credited the spontaneous acts of will with the power to test reality and reveal it by the fact of resistance which they elicited from genuinely real objects. Hartmann's innovation consists in the assertion that it is the emotionally "receptive" experiences which provide even more valid evidence than the "spontaneous" ones.

What happens in these emotionally receptive acts, according to Hartmann, is that the knower is "hit" or struck (*betroffen*) by an "experience" in an emphatic sense of the word. To express it, German has an even more expressive word than *"Erfahrung"*: *"Widerfahrnis,"* i.e., an experience in which something "sails" into us, very much in the manner which is implied in the literal meaning of the English word "occurrence." *Erlebnis* in the sense of a living-through-an-experience and even of a suffering-through-it furnishes likewise forms of this emotional shock.

Now this reality-shock is certainly a thoroughly real event. As such it implies that we are affected by something obtrusive or offensive, the shocking or occurring object. Especially suffering tells us unmistakably about the reality of the source of this suffering. Hardness or roughness make us experience reality itself constantly and most adequately. Yet there are variations in the strikingness of this experience, depending on our involvement in it. Being shaken up, being gripped, being under the spell are all forms of this experience. But while the experiences and the corresponding forms of givenness vary, what is given through them, i.e., reality itself in its harshness, remains the same.

Compared with this form of givenness, the manifestation of reality by way of its resistance to our spontaneous acts of will appears to Hartmann as secondary. Much more telling is to him what the objects have to say to us of their own initiative. It is therefore mistaken to concentrate on the spontaneous acts exclusively. This becomes particularly misleading if, on this basis, one goes on with the voluntarist metaphysicians to interpret reality as the manifestation of a will.

This still leaves open the question whether this kind of givenness constitutes conclusive evidence of reality. It must be realized from the start that Hartmann never claims that the receptive emotional acts (anyway a dangerous misnomer, suggesting a pathetic fallacy) constitute valid evidence for the whatness of the phenomena. What is at stake is only their thatness. But even at that, Hartmann realizes that reality transcends the phenomenon. His assertion is merely that "in the mode of being affected and of its modifications the specific phenomenal content guides spontaneously and even imperatively (*gebieterisch*) and inevitably toward something which is not phenomenon but is something characteristically non-phenomenal or transphenomenal." [1] The difference between the theoretically cognitive acts and the emotional ones, as Hartmann sees it, lies in the fact that the latter are deeply imbedded in the reality of our full actual lives, while the former represent relatively exceptional, detached conditions.

Even the sceptic will hardly contest the obtrusiveness, harshness, and constraining power of the real, as revealed in the emotionally transcendent, and particularly in the emotionally receptive acts. But the greater impact of these experiences does not make them infallible. For even they can fool us, not only in dreams but, more seriously, in the case of compulsive ideas. Factors other than reality can account for the shock of the receptive acts. Hartmann has added an important chapter to the phenomenology of reality. But it would be an exaggeration to claim that on his own premises Hartmann has achieved an absolute breakthrough to reality itself.

c. THE DISCOVERY OF VALUE AND THE NARROWNESS OF THE VALUE CONSCIOUSNESS – The primary interest of the phenomenological part of Hartmann's *Ethik* lies in his systematic presentation of the values themselves. However, this does not mean that he can and does avoid all discussion of value consciousness and of its various forms. A case in point is his discussion of the way in which values are discovered.

Hartmann too is concerned about the fact that the ethical convictions and philosophies of individuals and civilizations

[1] *Zur Grundlegung der Ontologie*, p. 225.

differ and change. Yet he is firmly convinced that values are independent of our differing and changing valuations. Values are discovered as mankind develops and grows. It is in terms of such new discoveries in the realm of values that he explains the changes from the Greek to the Christian values, and again from the Christian values to the modern values of such a seeming revolutionary as Nietzsche. It is not the values that change, but the value consciousness in which values reveal themselves.

This however does not simply mean that we constantly add to the range of our values. For reasons not discussed, our human value consciousness is not capable of infinite expansion. It has a certain narrowness. Consequently, as we add newly discovered values at one end, we are apt to lose or to forget them at the other end. In other words, our value consciousness "migrates" across the field of values like a spot light. Thus changes in valuation are to be explained in terms of the different selections from the range of values. In spite of these limits, Hartmann admits expansive growth as well as contractive decrease of our range. But growth happens at the price of intensity and immediacy of the more limited experiences. Shifts in the movement of the value consciousness across the field of values occur at varying speeds, some so rapid as to amount to revolutions. To Hartmann an example of such a revolutionary shift was the discovery of the value of love-of-neighbor by Christianity.

The idea that values are the object of a process of discovery, while it has been implied by other phenomenologists, has never been stated as explicitly as by Hartmann. On the other hand, Hartmann does not describe the constitution of a genuine discovery in sufficient detail to distinguish it from pseudo-discoveries, where no "finding" of values takes place, but where simply our valuation changes under extraneous influences like fads and fashions.

d. ACTIVATED IDEALS (*Aktuales Seinsollen*) [1] – Hartmann's ethics does not simply take over Scheler's system of values. It modifies it in important places, and it adds to it in others. One seemingly minor but potentially very fruitful and characteristic

---

[1] Stanton Coit's translation (vol. I, p. 249) renders this term by "positive ought-to-be," a questionable equivalent.

addition, which incidentally Scheler himself seems to have welcomed, is exemplified in a type of oughtness which Hartmann inserts between the ideal ought-to-be and the ethical ought-to-do. It has its place whenever an ideal ought-to-be stands in conflict with the factual conditions. The result is a state of ideal tension between the two spheres. It is this tension which Hartmann designates by the term "actuality," implying that otherwise the ideal ought-to-be has merely potential status. There are degrees of this actuality, depending on the discrepancy between the two orders, but also upon the rank of the ideal ought-to-be. Devoting less than two pages to this phenomenon, Hartmann does little more than point to it. But they make it plain that the ideal tension so identified constitutes a phenomenon sui generis. More will have to be done to develop the full significance of this discovery.[1]

6. Toward an Appraisal of Hartmann's Phenomenology

Although Hartmann himself does not claim to be a phenomenologist, there is enough phenomenology in his critical ontology to call for its evaluation in the present context. Besides, as we have seen, there is much more phenomenology even in his "aporetics" and "theory" than he himself admits. For Hartmann certainly subscribed to the basic principle of phenomenology in the widest sense, the need of founding philosophy on the intuitive awareness of the phenomena, even though he states that thought has at times to transcend intuition (Anschauung). He also defends and practices all through his ontology the right of intuition of essences and of essential connections. And while it may be said that his primary interest centers on objects rather than on their way of givenness, he nevertheless devotes on occasion special attention to the problems of givenness (e.g., in his study of the transcendent acts); he does so perhaps even more in his esthetics, where the modes of appearance are of particular importance. It is true that Hartmann the realist does not practice Husserl's phenomenological reduction in an orthodox sense. Nevertheless it should be noted that he is anxious to begin his

---

[1] The writer has attempted this in an unpublished manuscript on the moral foundations of rights and duties, of which an installment appeared under the title "Zur Ontologie des idealen Sollens" in *Philosophisches Jahrbuch der Görresgesellschaft* LXVI (1958), 243–53.

ontology from a position neutral toward idealism as well as toward realism.

All this does not undo the fact that Hartmann never identified himself with the Phenomenological Movement as such. It would therefore be unfair to convert him posthumously into one of its members, be it only an honorary one. Let it simply be said that Hartmann's philosophy contains enough phenomenological ingredients to claim for him the status of an independent and highly unorthodox ally.

However, this fact alone does not yet imply a qualitative appraisal of his phenomenological achievement. In several respects this was an outstanding one. No other phenomenologist writes with the monumental simplicity and clarity which distinguishes his prose; hence none is equally translatable. At times this simplicity may be deceptive. For his clarity of expression does not always reflect an equal clarity of thought. But this does not diminish the merits of a style which is all too rare among German philosophers and hardly less so among the major phenomenologists.

Very much in contrast to Scheler, Hartmann is also unique in the clear and neat organization of his prolific production. Not all of it may be convincing. But he certainly does his utmost to save his reader from getting lost in the vast passages of his philosophical palace.

No other thinker connected with phenomenology has developed as comprehensive a system of philosophic thought as Nicolai Hartmann. This, at first sight, may be taken as dubious praise for a philosophy which has been suspicious of system building, at least in the speculative vein. It is therefore important to realize that Hartmann's type of systematic thinking is different, if not unique, inasmuch as it wants to present a system of problems, not of solutions. There is nothing ironclad and inflexible about his conclusions. He always leaves the doors ajar for more adequate solutions. And remarkably often Hartmann even has no door and leaves the problem completely open.

Such openness is certainly congenial to the spirit of phenomenological philosophizing, which does not and should not oppose the attempt at comprehensiveness, however far beyond our present reach. On the other hand, it would be inadvisable to recommend Hartmann's writing as a particularly good example of phenomenological method in operation. For what he presents is mostly the ready-made results, if not the frozen products, of his approach in a form which gives little insight into the way he has obtained them. In fact, the way in which Hartmann states his findings has often a crispness and finality which gives the appearance of dogmatic pronouncements. This often leaves to the more critical reader the unfortunate choice between having either to swallow or to reject wholesale.

In spite of Hartmann's anxiousness not to interfere with the given, one can also notice the shaping if not distorting influence of certain patterns of thought which may easily be left-overs from his Neo-Kantian past. There is in him a tendency to see the phenomena under the scheme of categories, even though the categories have lost much of their formalizing rigor. There is a fondness for stating general insights in the form of laws, which on closer inspection have little of the rigorousness of strict functional relationships, but are not much more than tendencies.

Finally, Hartmann almost seems to take pride in discovering irreconcilable antinomies and ultimate irrationalities. This inclination may have its uses in preventing glib harmonizations. But it can also lead – and it does at times in Hartmann – to a premature dropping of the problems, thus leaving us in an atmosphere of semi-mystery. Hartmann never freed himself completely from seeing the phenomena in the light of such defeatist schemes, in which one may well suspect remnants of Kantian and Hegelian dialectics. They do not block his access to the phenomena. But they interfere at times with their interpretation.

Hartmann's phenomenology may not be the purest form of phenomenology. But it contains some of its richest mines.

7. Hartmann's Following and Phenomenology

At this time it is difficult to form an estimate of how far Hartmann's philosophy has left a permanent mark on German philosophy. It is not even clear how far Hartmann has succeeded in attracting a more than temporary followership, ready to carry on his main ontological enterprise, as he always hoped and postulated. His academic influence was certainly slow in coming.

It was only during his Cologne years (1925–1931) that he seems to have had a larger and cooperative group of students. To these he gives conspicuous credit in the preface to *Das Problem des geistigen Seins*. There is less evidence that during the years of his climactic academic achievement, in Berlin and eventually in Göttingen, he attracted an equally responsive following. The memorial volume published by a group of his earlier and later students does not show how far the interest in his principal concerns is still alive. Possibly closest to it is now HERMANN WEIN in Göttingen. – But even more pertinent in the present context is the question of how far his followers have taken interest in his phenomenological studies. There is thus far no clear evidence of that.

SELECTIVE BIBLIOGRAPHY

Major works

Platos Logik des Seins (1909)
Grundzüge einer Metaphysik der Erkenntnis (1921)
   Translation: French (1947) by R. Vancourt
Ethik (1926)
   Translation: English (1932) by Stanton Coit – good, except for some technical terms.
Das Problem des geistigen Seins (1933)
Zur Grundlegung der Ontologie (1935)
Systematische Philosophie in eigener Darstellung (1935)
Möglichkeit und Wirklichkeit (1938)
Der Aufbau der realen Welt. Grundlegung der allgemeinen Kategorienlehre (1940)
Neue Wege der Ontologie (1949)
   Translation: English (1953) by R. C. Kuhn – good; some chapter titles oversimplified.
Philosophie der Natur. Abriss der speziellen Kategorienlehre (1950)
Article "Hartmann, Nicolai," in Ziegenfuss, Werner, *Philosophenlexikon* (1949)

Posthumously published

Teleologisches Denken (1951)
Ästhetik, edited by Frida Hartmann (1953)

Monographs in German

HEIMSOETH, HEINZ and HEISS, ROBERT, eds., *Nicolai Hartmann. Der Denker und sein Werk* (1952)

Studies in English

Mohanty, J. N., *Nicolai Hartmann and A. N. Whitehead. A Study in Recent Platonism*, Calcutta, 1957
Samuel, Otto, *A Foundation of Ontology. A Critical Analysis of Nicolai Hartmann* (1954)

Articles in English

Beck, Lewis W., "Nicolai Hartmann's Criticism of Kant's Theory of Knowledge," *PPR* II (1942), 472–500
Collins, James, "The Neo-Scholastic Critique of Nicolai Hartmann," *PPR* VI (1945), 109–32
Creegan, R. F., "Hartmann's Apriorism," *Philosophical Review L* (1941), 528–30
Eaton, Howard O., "The Unity of Axiological Ethics," *International Journal of Ethics* XLIII (1932), 23–36
Garnett, A. C., "Phenomenological Ethics and Self-realization," *Ethics* LIII (1943), 159–72
Gibson, W. R. Boyce, "The Ethics of Nicolai Hartmann," *The Australasian Journal of Psychology and Philosophy* XI (1933), 12–28; XII (1934), 33–61; XIII (1935), 1–23
Hazelton, R., "On Hartmann's Doctrine of Values as Essences," *Philosophical Review* XLVIII (1939), 621–32
Hook, Sidney, "A Critique of Ethical Realism," *International Journal of Ethics* XL (1929), 179–210
Jensen, O. C., Nicolai Hartmann's Theory of Virtue," *Ethics* LII (1942), 463–79
Landmann, Michael, "Professor Nicolai Hartmann and Phenomenology," *PPR* III (1944), 393–423
Oakeley, H. D., "Nicolai Hartmann's Concept of Objective Spirit," *Mind* XLIV (1931), 39–57
Ramsey, K. V., "Theism and the Ethics of Nicolai Hartmann," *Church Quarterly Review* CXIX (1935), 208–25
Schilpp, P. A, "Is Standpointless Ethics Possible?" *Philosophical Review* XLIV (1935), 227–32
Schlaretzki, W. E., "Ethics and Metaphysics in Hartmann," *Ethics* LIV (1943), 273–82
Smith, John E., "Hartmann's New Ontology," *Review of Metaphysics* VII (1952), 583–601
Walker, M. G., "Perry and Hartmann: Antithetical or Complementary?" *Ethics* XLIX (1938), 37–61

Ph. D. Theses

Hazelton, Roger, *The Relation between Value and Existence in the Philosophies of Nicolai Hartmann and A. N. Whitehead*, Yale University, 1937
Jino, David Norinoto, *Coherence in Hartmann's Ethik*. Boston University, 1941
Park, Dorothy G., *The Objectivity of Value: A Study of the Ethics of N. Hartmann*. University of Nebraska, 1957

SHEIN, LOUIS, *A Critique of N. Hartmann's Ethics*. University of Toronto, 1946

Most Comprehensive Recent Bibliography

BALLAUF, THEODOR, in Heimsoeth, H. and Heiss, R., eds., *Nicolai Hartmann*, pp. 286–308